THE ART OF LISTENING IN TH

The Art of Listening in the Early Church

CAROL HARRISON

OXFORD

UNIVERSITY PRESS

OXFORD
UNIVERSITY PRESS

Great Clarendon Street, Oxford, OX2 6DP,
United Kingdom

Oxford University Press is a department of the University of Oxford.
It furthers the University's objective of excellence in research, scholarship,
and education by publishing worldwide. Oxford is a registered trade mark of
Oxford University Press in the UK and in certain other countries

Published in the United States of America by Oxford University Press
198 Madison Avenue, New York, NY 10016, United States of America

British Library Cataloguing in Publication Data
Data available

Library of Congress Cataloging in Publication Data
Data available

ISBN 978-0-19-964143-7 (Hbk.)
ISBN 978-0-19-874495-5 (Pbk.)

for me marra
Martin Souter
great musician and oldest friend
with love

Contents

Preface

This book started life as one on music—on how people thought about music, and what evidence we have for its practice—in the early Church. It quickly became clear to me, however, that this particular subject would have to wait until the next book and that I first needed to examine the more basic question: how did people think about listening, and what evidence do we have of it in practice? The reader who might miss material on the liturgy, the psalms, early Christian hymns is to be reassured that it is to come. The reader who finds that there is just too much Augustine, however, must forgive me: having worked on him for so many years he does tend to take over, however hard one tries.

I was fortunate enough to be able to pursue some of the ideas for this book, and be inspired to follow others, through teaching an MA module on Transformative Listening in Durham. I'm very grateful to the students who have taken this module over the past few years for their valuable contributions. Some of my PhD students working on Music and Theology have also contributed more than they know to this book, especially Joshua Waggener, James Jirtle, and David Shirt. My wonderful colleague and friend in Durham's Music department, and collaborator for the Durham Network for Music Theology, Bennett Zon, is to be thanked for pursuing many of the ideas contained in this book with me, even if it was often in the agonizing context of making (unfruitful) grant applications. I have also greatly appreciated conversations with other colleagues in Durham: Lewis Ayres, Krastu Banev, and Robert Song deserve special mention (the latter, not least, for bringing my attention to McGilchrist). I am also very grateful to Andrew Louth for helping me to track down books, bibliography, and texts and for his work on the tacit (indeed, I am aware that this book probably tacitly owes a great deal to his thinking).

Beyond Durham I have greatly valued the encouragement, friendly interest, and scholarly advice of two colleagues, in particular: Gillian Clark, who has followed this book at every turn and become the best of friends; William Harmless for hugely enjoyable conversations on jazz, improvisation, and Augustine. The anonymous final reader for Oxford University Press is to be thanked for valuable suggestions on style (though I fear the sentences are still far too long) and substance.

Nearer home I must thank Isaac Harrison Louth for apposite quotations from Spenser to Emily Dickinson, for being an exemplary practitioner of the art of listening, and for offering the unsparing criticism which only a son dares give; Sasha Pokhilko for help with my Greek and for positively encouraging criticism.

A good deal of this book deals with the early Christians' ambivalence towards the senses and the body—they are at once too temporal, mutable, and distracting, and yet are a necessary constraint; indeed, they are the means to salvation, for fallen human beings. Towards the end of writing I have felt these tensions myself in ways I did not anticipate. My biggest debt of gratitude remains to the staff at University Hospital in Durham, the Freeman Hospital in Newcastle, and particularly Macmillan nurse Louise Hunter for keeping my mortal body and soul together for a while longer.

Introduction

VOICES OF THE PAGE

It would not be a wild overestimate to suggest that around two-thirds of the early Christian texts which we now read were originally spoken, rather than written, and were intended for hearers, rather than readers. They sounded, resonated, and impressed themselves upon the mind and memory through the ear rather than the eye. A significant part of this literature consists of sermons, which were often delivered *ex tempore* and recorded by a secretary, perhaps for later revision. Similarly, the records of ecclesiastical conferences, or public debates with heretics, are written transcriptions of originally spoken words. We also possess catechetical addresses, perhaps prepared by the bishop in advance, but almost certainly delivered directly to those who were being inducted into the faith prior to baptism. Other texts were perhaps originally written down, but even they are records of what was intended to be spoken aloud and heard by others: liturgical texts, creedal statements, prayers, poems, hymns, and, to an extent, letters.

Even theological treatises, and other works that were composed with readers in mind, are often written in a style which is virtually indistinguishable from those which were originally delivered orally. They are written as if they are directly addressing a hearer, rather than a reader, and use the 'voices' of rhetorical speech (direct address, question and answer, imaginary interlocutors) in order to engage the reader and to teach, move, or persuade them of what it is the author wishes to convey. As Longinus demonstrates quite clearly when he uses traditional rhetorical tropes to describe how a critic should go about analysing a text, it was simply a matter of accepted convention and style, unthinkingly adopted by the author (who had been trained in the liberal arts and rhetoric),[1] and expected and anticipated by the reader. There is barely a

---

[1] Kennedy (1980), 111, observes: 'Not only in Greece and Rome, but in medieval and renaissance Europe, rhetoric was studied at such an early age that like language itself, it tended to become an instinctive part of students' mental framework and to influence their formal expression in writing. In contrast, literary criticism was slow to develop in antiquity and was

text, then, which is not, in some manner, meant to be 'heard'; they are full of real and imaginary, heard and overheard 'voices'. If, as subsequent readers, we ignore this oral/auditory dimension, and block our ears to these voices, then I think we run the risk of being deaf to what they have to say.

Of course, it is one thing to analyse early Christian use of rhetorical language and techniques, but quite another to take account of the contribution of the (generally) silent hearer to what we read: to examine how they perhaps influenced what was said; to ask how, and to what effect, they heard and received the texts we now read. Who were these hearers? What presuppositions and prejudices, what education and expectations did they bring to what they heard? To what extent were they changed, or even transformed, by their listening? How, in short, did listening (as opposed to seeing or reading) work in a Christian context? These are the questions which I would like to try to raise, and hazard some preliminary answers to, in this book. We will therefore be examining not so much what early Christian authors said, but how what they said was influenced by their intended hearers, and how these hearers, in turn, heard, responded to, and were affected by, their words. One way of putting this is to suggest that in reading an early Christian text we are in fact eavesdropping on a conversation: we are overhearing words which are being spoken to someone else. What we are trying to establish, from what we *can* hear, is just what, precisely, is going on; who is saying what, to whom, and why? Above all, who is the silent interlocutor, how do they affect and influence the speaker, how do they hear and receive what is said, what is their response, how does it affect them? If we ignore the listener then we also close our ears to the real resonances of what is being said, for speech is an act which is always two-sided; it demands relation, participation, attentiveness, and response, and it is in this relationship between speaker and hearer that what is said becomes meaningful, and meaning is transferred and communicated.

We are not, however, generally accustomed to using hearing as our primary means of communication and learning in the twenty-first century; we live in a culture which is primarily visual rather than auditory, or, at least, in which the auditory is almost always subservient to the visual. Through printed books, newspapers, and magazines; email, Facebook, and Twitter; films, television, and DVDs; public art, galleries, and posters; PlayStations, satellite navigation, or GPS, communication takes place through seeing. What we see is, indeed, sometimes accompanied by an auditory component, but this is usually in the form of background commentary, mood music, electronic bleeps and blips to signify that something is happening, or recorded voices telling us we are on hold—rarely do we simply listen. Of course, listening has always—

never fully conceptualized . . . The use of topics, the structure of exordium, narration, demonstration, and conclusion, and the tropes and figures of speech are the clearest marks of rhetorical literature.'

usually—been a matter of watching a speaker, and, here, facial expression and gesture are important, but even when we do watch a speaker—for example, a newsreader on television or a teacher in a class—what they say, and even their facial expressions or physical gestures, are usually secondary nowadays to some sort of visual illustration: a chart, a film clip, a handout, a white board or PowerPoint presentation. When did you last simply listen? It seems that it is only when we listen to music in performance or on the radio, talk on the phone, or hold formal meetings for a particular purpose (counselling, law courts, political debates, sermons . . .) that we really practise the art of listening. This was also, of course, always the case; the differences I have mentioned between ourselves and antiquity are largely due to scientific, technological advances: the invention of the printing press, moving images on film, electronic imaging. Whatever the reasons, I do not think anyone would disagree that it is now harder for us to simply listen, and to begin to appreciate and understand a culture in which the art of speaking (rhetoric), and the discipline of hearing, were the determining factors in how people understood themselves, other people, and the world around them, and communicated with and influenced each other; a culture in which words had power—an almost magical power to expel evil, enchant, and cure[2]—and were not to be taken lightly.[3]

As well as scientific, technological changes, literacy is also a crucial factor in explaining why our culture is so oriented towards the visual rather than the auditory. We (at least, those of us who are privileged to live in the developed world) can read; information and learning comes to us from books, other printed media, and the Internet. In early Christianity this functional literacy was possessed by perhaps 10 per cent of the population.[4] It was the preserve of a very small group of male citizens who were literally and metaphorically free: free (rather than enslaved) citizens, who had been educated in the seven liberal

---

[2] This was a belief shared by Jews and Gentiles, pagans and Christians. Creation by God's word, Christ's miraculous healing by words (e.g. *ephatha*, be open), the power of words over demons, the use of exorcisms (see Chapter 4), incantations, amulets containing sacred texts, and divination from Scripture, all witness to this. Kalleres (2002); Lane Fox (1994); Gamble (1995), 238–40; Burton Christie (2001); Cox Miller (2001), 221–46; Kalleres (2002).

[3] Modern scholarship likewise tends to concentrate on the visual, rather than the auditory, in antiquity. A great deal of work has been devoted to early Christian art, sculpture, and architecture, and their impact on the viewer, but it is perhaps a symptom of our own cultural practices and presuppositions that almost no attention has been given to the impact of speaking on the hearer.

[4] Kaster (1988), 35–50, on literacy, illiteracy, and questions of definition. As Gamble (1995), 2, warns us, ' . . . we must be careful not to form too simple a conception of literacy and literary culture in early Christianity. They were not uniform over time, nor from place to place, or among individuals, and they do not lend themselves to easy generalization.' He cites Harris' (1991) work on literacy in the ancient world, in which Harris, using a broad definition of literacy as the ability to read or write at any level, estimates that, 'granting regional and temporal variations, throughout the entire period of classical Greek, Hellenistic and Roman imperial civilization, the extent of literacy was about 10 per cent and never exceeded 15–20 per cent of the population as a whole'. Cited in Gamble (1995), 4.

disciplines—those arts appropriate for free men (grammar, rhetoric, dialectic, arithmetic, music, geometry, astronomy). Having shared this homogenous education they were prepared for public service, and especially for those key jobs which required a facility in public speaking or rhetoric, and where the ability to teach, move, and persuade an audience of what they had to say was of the utmost importance: the law courts, the senate, the army, provincial administration. As we will see, this training meant that classical and early Christian culture was very much a rhetorical culture; one based on the practise and power of the spoken word. In this sense, we can speak not only of an oral culture, but of a much broader 'cultural' literacy, which those who possessed an ability to read and speak were instrumental in creating among a much larger, more diverse, less socially or gender exclusive group. The words of the formally educated—in teaching, law, politics, poetry, and (following the rise of Christianity) preaching and catechesis—were crucial in forming and perpetuating a shared world of memorial images, beliefs, expectations, and authorities, which together established what we have called a 'cultural literacy' or a facility for 'literate listening' among the illiterate majority in the ancient world.[5] The unlettered were able to 'read' and understand reality through the shared, often tacit, markers of complicit understanding, customary practice, and habitual ways of thinking created by speaking and hearing. It is this cultural literacy— the Christian culture which the writers and speakers we will be examining built up—rather than the formal literacy of the educated elite that will be our main focus of interest in examining how hearing formed, informed, and transformed the minds of early Christian listeners.

The primacy of the verbal over the written was generally taken for granted in ancient culture, even in contexts where written culture might reasonably be expected to take precedence over oral culture. For example, Plato's well-known account of the encounter between the Egyptian god Theuth and King Thamus, in the *Phaedrus*, simply reflects a long-standing judgement of the value of oral culture over written culture, as well as the tensions to which the growth of the latter could give rise.[6] Theuth, who had invented writing, tried to persuade Thamus to adopt it in order to 'make the Egyptians wiser and . . . improve their memories' (274E). Thamus disagrees: 'you who are the father of letters, have been led by your affection to ascribe to them a power the opposite of that which they really possess. For this invention will produce

---

[5] Trevett (2006), 17, describes this illiterate literacy well in relation to the first Christian churches: 'Becoming and being a Christian involved learning. Family and church alike were narrative institutions. People spoke and, since reading was synonymous with reading aloud, people listened.' She comments on the 'oral environment' (237) of the earliest Christians, who would have learned by listening to friends, resident elders, preachers, prophets, visiting ministers . . . , in synagogues, churches, families, households, and estates of slaves (17–18).

[6] See Notopoulos (1938), 476–9. For reflections on this tension in Christian monastic culture, see Burton Christie (2001).

forgetfulness in the minds of those who learn to use it, because they will not practise their memory' (274E–275A). He concludes that written words are only useful as a reminder of what we already know (275d–276a). Socrates concurs, describing writing as the illegitimate brother of speech, whereas speech itself is 'the word which is written with intelligence in the mind of the learner' (276A). He adds that, in contrast, writing is like a mute painting, which, if questioned, can only ever say one and the same thing; it has no way of explaining itself or of answering back if it is ill-treated (275D–E); better by far to have spoken words which can defend themselves and teach the truth effectively (276E). In this sense, Socrates observes that he prefers dialectic, the spontaneous improvisation of question and answer, in the attempt to discover truth (276E–277A). Words can speak and inscribe themselves on the mind of the listener; texts are mute and simply remind the reader of what they already know (through hearing). It is the job of the dialectician and rhetor (or, indeed, the Christian preacher, reader, or *psaltes*) to give texts a voice so that they can communicate and be heard.

As Gamble observes, it is in this sense that we should read Eusebius' famous account of Papias' words, not as a rejection of literacy but as a preference for the first-hand immediacy of the oral, which was shared by pagans and Christians alike in antiquity: 'But if anyone ever came who had followed the ancients, I inquired about the words of the ancients—what Andrew or Peter or Philip or Thomas or James or John or Matthew or any other of the Lord's disciples said, and what Ariston and the presbyter John, the Lord's disciples, were saying. For I did not suppose that things from books would benefit me so much as things from a living and abiding voice.'[7]

This emphasis on the oral rather than the written is no doubt also due to the fact that hearing had priority where one might least expect it. Even when someone could read, they would usually do so by reading aloud to themselves, enunciating what they read, so that reading effectively became a way of speaking the text, and speaking effectively became a way of reading and interpreting it.[8] This is a practice which might well be explained by the nature

[7] Eusebius, *Ecclesiastical History*, 3.39.3–4, cited by Gamble (1995), 30. Gamble observes that Papias' comment: 'is not peculiar to him but frequently appears in ancient literature and indeed constitutes a *topos* in certain contexts' (31).
[8] Perhaps the most famous example of this in antiquity is Augustine's description of his first encounter with Ambrose in his *Confessions* (6.3.3; Chadwick, 92). Augustine was struck by the fact that, although he did not restrict access to visitors, Ambrose was always to be found reading silently to himself, rather than aloud ('When he was reading, his eyes ran over the page and his heart perceived the sense, but his voice and tongue were silent'). This was obviously uncommon enough to strike Augustine as unusual, and needing explanation. He hazards a guess that Ambrose did not want to be disturbed by interested listeners who might be prompted to ask his advice or opinion about what they had heard if he was to read aloud—or perhaps, he suggests, he was simply saving his voice, which could easily become hoarse. One senses that Augustine, a bishop himself when he wrote the *Confessions*, is speaking from personal experience. Like

of the text itself: it more likely than not had no gaps between words; no capital letters or full stops; no commas, colons, or semi-colons; no paragraphs; indeed, no annotation or punctuation at all. It was simply a continuous block of words, or *scriptio continua*.[9] This solid block needed to be given form and shape. Its sense needed to be drawn out of it as a sculptor draws out a figure from a piece of marble. The most effective way to do this—and the one that was most commonly practisd in the classroom—was to read it aloud, to punctuate it through breathing, as it were; to pause at the end of each phrase, stop for breath at the end of each sentence, and even modulate the voice according to the sense.[10] In this way the words of the text were impressed upon the mind in precisely the same way as the words of a speaker: through aural images and physical punctuation. As Frances Young observes, 'a text was a form of recorded speech and it had to be realised to make sense, rather like playing a musical score'.[11] We have probably all shared this experience in singing, when our physical enunciation of the notes on the page enables us to identify their pattern, form, and shape, and gives them life and meaning, whilst simultaneously imprinting them on the mind by communicating them through the ears. We hear them first, by enunciating or singing them, and our hearing then enables us 'see' them, both on the page and in our understanding. In the same way, in reading, hearing came before seeing a word on the page. The physical act of speech or singing meant that body and soul were involved in the act of reading and understanding, and the simple act of enunciating a text somehow impressed it on the mind and soul more effectively. Gregory of Nyssa, in his *Treatise on the Inscriptions of the Psalms*,

---

Ambrose, he could get through more books if he read silently and wasn't disturbed. He, too, suffered from voice and chest problems. We might also reflect on the significance of Augustine's description of his reading of Paul at his conversion in the garden at Milan: 'I seized it, opened it and in silence read the first passage on which my eyes lit . . .' (8.12.29; Chadwick, 153). Balough (1927). See Gamble (1995), 203 n. 1, for further bibliography on reading in antiquity.

[9] Penny Small (1997), 9, refers to Morrison (1987) in this context: 'Ken Morrison makes the intriguing suggestion that to the Greeks and Romans their texts were never more than a "variant of oral utterance . . . due to the lack of procedures for transforming writing into text"', and adds that, 'only in the medieval period with the codex and its page format does "true" text appear'. Gamble (1995), 48, observes that *scriptio continua* was a Greek practice, but that 'The Romans, who were accustomed to dividing words in writing Latin, gave up that habit in literary texts in order to conform to the Greek custom. Punctuation marks, accents, and other lectional aids, when they did occur, are normally found only in texts used by scholars and students.' He observes that by the fourth century there was also a vogue for *colometric* presentation of texts, arranged in lines according to sense, rather than syllables (as in the *stichometric* presentation of *scriptio continua*), though still without any gaps between words, so that a good deal of the interpretation had already been done by the text, rather than being left to the reader. He assumes that manuscripts transcribed in this way must have been intended particularly for public reading (229–30).

[10] This was the practice of *lectio*, the first stage of reading a text, which was followed by *emendatio, ennaratio*, and then *iudicium*.

[11] Young (2007), 77.

therefore urges that, in order to make sense of a psalm, and relate its words to the thoughts it provokes, it should be read aloud.[12] Jean Leclerq appositely comments on the way in which monastic, meditative reading was a matter of both body and mind, observing that the monks 'read usually, not as today principally with the eyes, but with the lips, pronouncing what they saw, and with the ears, listening to the words pronounced, hearing what is called the "voices of the page"'.[13] It is perhaps for this reason that the monks in Pachomius' rule were required to learn to read and memorize the Scriptures, thereby more effectively impressing them upon the mind and heart.[14] The '*vox tenuis*' or low murmur which accompanied meditative reading is something that, Mary Carruthers observes, was also an aspect of composition. She notes that ancient writers frequently speak of the importance of listening to what they were composing.[15] Gamble, too, suggests that when an ancient author wrote out his own text, 'the words were spoken as they were being written, just as scribes in copying manuscripts practiced what is called self-dictation. In either case . . . the text was an inscription of the spoken word.'[16]

It was not only the nature of the written text which lent itself to reading aloud, but rather more ambiguous cultural concerns. Even when a Christian could read, he or she was more than likely put off by the rather crude, unsophisticated style of Scripture. It was not written by educated classical authors, but often by semi-literate peasants or fishermen. There was a yawning gap of cultural sensibility between the vulgarisms of the Old Latin translation of the LXX, or indeed the *koine* Greek of the authors of the New Testament, and the cultivated Latin or Greek of the classics to which any educated, literate person would be accustomed. There is quite a lot of evidence in the fathers' writing to suggest that they encountered problems in encouraging literate Christians to read, rather than just display their beautifully written codices in locked cabinets.[17] Moreover, those on the receiving end of their admonitions were likely to respond that they were not monks![18] As we will see, the fathers themselves evidently shared the cultured, literary scruples of the

---

[12] 2.196; Heine, 185.

[13] Leclerq (1977), 21.

[14] Gamble (1995), 170–1. Thus Robin Lane Fox (1994), 147–8, rather amusingly, but accurately, observes that, 'Thanks to Christian perfection, the map became dotted with something quite new: arsenals of sexually frustrated readers, stretching from Egypt to the coasts of Scotland.'

[15] Carruthers (1990), 198.

[16] Gamble (1995), 204.

[17] Chrysostom, *Homily on John* 32, in Gamble (1995), 233. Maxwell (2006), 98–103, confirms the suggestion that it was a reluctance, rather than an inability, to read among members of his congregation which underlies many of Chrysostom's admonitions. She identifies numerous references in Chrysostom's work which suggest both an access to the Scriptures and an ability to read across a broad social spectrum.

[18] Chrysostom, *Homily on Genesis* 21, in Gamble (1995), 232–3; Lane Fox (1994), 147.

educated, but overcame them by either treating Scripture itself as a work of literature capable of being read and interpreted in a manner similar to classical texts, by identifying and analysing rhetorical figures and tropes, or by adopting figurative methods of exegesis which enabled them to move beyond its crude surface to its inspired depths of meaning. We should note, however, that both of these strategies were effected largely through the vocalization and improvisations on Scripture made possible by speaking and listening to it aloud in sermons delivered to a congregation.

Practical concerns also lent themselves to reading texts aloud: the materials available for writing were both labour-intensive and cumbersome—papyrus or parchment rolls (scroll); wax tablets or papyrus sheets bound together (codex).[19] Each copy of a 'book' or text had to be manually transcribed; few people actually owned books or had access to them.[20] As a matter of practical necessity, therefore, texts tended to be read aloud to a group of listeners, rather than to oneself, privately, and their context was more often public and communal than private and individual. It might even be said that, to a large extent, the 'publication' of a text was an oral event, since it was more likely to become known through being read aloud than through its written text. As Gamble observes, 'In Greco-Roman society the illiterate had access to literacy in a variety of public settings.' Public readings of philosophy or poetry, in particular, are frequently referred to in classical literature, whether to a group of friends, in competitions, in the theatre, or as part of a spectacle.[21] In whatever form it was eventually received, the author of a text would, as we have just suggested, probably originally have had a listener in mind as they wrote. Not only would they have spoken what they were writing to themselves, or have anticipated an audience or hearer for what they were writing, and have composed in a spoken style, but more often than not they would have composed by means of dictation to a scribe (who might sometimes have also read back what had been dictated).[22] Goulven Madec conjures up a

[19] See Gamble (1995), ch. 2, for a careful treatment of the evidence. Penny Small (1997), 12, also mentions Etruscan linen books—folded lengths of linen in an accordion pattern. It is worth noting that although rolls were the most common form of 'book' in Greco-Roman and Jewish contexts, the Christians only ever really used the codex, which was not really regarded as a book at all, but more as a sort of temporary, private, utilitarian, erasable, and reusable notebook. There are many suggestions as to why this change came about (Gamble (1995), 49–66; Young (2007), 11–16) but no real answers.

[20] See Gamble (1995), ch. 3; Young (2007), 10–12.

[21] Penny Small (1997), 40, comments that 'publication throughout antiquity always had a large oral component', though she notes that public readings were not always very popular with, or well received by, audiences. In addition to these examples, Gamble (1995), 8, adds: '... street corner philosophical diatribes, commemorative inscriptions, the posting and reading of official decrees, the routine traffic of legal and commercial documents all brought the fruits of literacy before the general population, educating the public in its uses and popularizing its conventions'.

[22] This was common practice. Gamble (1995), 139, comments, 'For Augustine in particular, composing was always a matter of dictating (*dictare*), and once a fair copy was transcribed from

compelling picture of Augustine, the bishop and orator, dictating his works to a scribe, his hands uplifted in prayer.[23] This is far from our normal mental picture of someone bent over their desk with a stylus or quill in hand, or even typing on a computer keyboard, and cannot but affect the way in which we read their work. Even at the moment of composition, then, the author was addressing a listener (or hearing their own words read back to them), articulating his/her thoughts for both a real, as well as an imaginary audience, aware that what was said had to be capable of assimilation, memorization, and transcription, either by the scribe onto wax tablets, or by the ears and mind of the hearer onto the tablets of the soul.

In all of these respects, then, it is difficult to make strict distinctions between oral and literary culture in early Christianity. The evidence we have just considered suggests that, in almost every respect, they were closely interdependent. Even where books existed, the oral/aural was almost always given priority. The text was composed by speaking to oneself or by dictation to a scribe; it was written in a spoken, rhetorical form; 'published' by public reading; 'read' by being read aloud; taught by oral exegesis and discussion in the schoolroom,[24] or by *ex tempore* preaching and catechesis in the Church. Everywhere, the 'voices of the page' sounded in the ears of the early Christians, inscribing themselves on their minds and memories. As Gamble comments, 'Because authors wrote or dictated with an ear to the words and assumed that what they wrote would be audibly read, they wrote for the ear more than the eye. As a result, no ancient text is now read as it was intended to be unless it is also heard, that is, read aloud.'[25]

Georgia Frank's work on sight in early Christianity is, in many ways, a model for what can be done when we take the senses seriously in a theological context. Her observations on the need to distinguish between 'vision', or the physiology of sight, and 'visuality', or the cultural understanding of sight, are just as apposite to hearing (for 'vision' read 'hearing', and for 'visuality' read 'aurality'). She writes:

stenographic notes, of correcting (*emendare*). Once transcribed and corrected, texts were *emendatiora exemplaria* (corrected exemplars), and it was from these that copies were made.' See Houghton (2008), 22–43, for some fascinating insights on the use of stenographers and extemporary preaching.

[23] I often heard him make this point in his lectures on Augustine's *Confessions* at the Institut d'Études Augustiniennes, Paris. Jean Pépin, in his preface to Madec (1994), 5, alludes to this too.

[24] Young (2007), 76–7, who observes of the ancient classroom: 'the equivalent of our secondary literature was largely oral. Exegesis and commentary went on in class, as indeed to a fair extent it does still. The oral practice of exegesis was so much taken for granted that it is quite difficult to reconstruct how exegesis was done.' Gamble (1995), 31, likewise refers to 'the Hellenistic philosophical schools, where the transmission of tradition was thought to be ideally accomplished through personal tutelage and where books were often represented as written compendia of oral instruction best employed under the personal guidance of a teacher'.

[25] Gamble (1995), 204.

the quality of perceptions can differ according to the complex attitudes and beliefs assigned to sensory impressions. Thus it is helpful to distinguish between "vision"—the physiological and neurological processes involved in the act of seeing—and "visuality"—the meanings, properties, or values a given culture assigns to sight. "Vision" is explored through the study of optics, ophthalmology, neurology, and other disciplines concerned with the mechanics of sight. Understanding "visuality", however, is largely a reconstructive process, one that considers how language, symbols, myths, and values became attached to the act of seeing. Exploring visuality in a particular cultural context requires careful attention to the poetics and organization of visual experiences.[26]

This is something we will reflect on at greater length in Part One.

In our exploration of hearing, we should, therefore, first of all be alert to the fact that the way in which the ancients understood sense perception was rather different from our own, and that this influenced the way in which they both approached the act of hearing, and made sense of what they heard. As we shall see, hearing, along with the other senses, was primarily understood as the process by which images were impressed upon the mind. These images were then stored in the memory, to be recollected and represented to the mind on a future occasion. The fact that sense perception was able to directly impress and form the mind, like a seal upon wax, was obviously of the utmost significance: one had to be very careful what sort of perceptions one exposed oneself to, so that the mind was kept pure and untainted, rather than polluted and corrupted by dangerous and destructive sights and sounds. What one saw or heard had the potential to either form the mind to the true, good, and beautiful, or deform, deface, and destroy it by lies, untruth, and ugliness. The senses were, therefore, not something to be overlooked or neglected, but something to be watched over and controlled with the utmost vigilance.[27] The fathers, were, of course, notoriously suspicious of the senses (and the body), not least for this reason, preferring instead the direct, unmediated, immutable, and eternal knowledge of God which the mind possessed within, by divine illumination, rather than the indirect, mediated, mutable, and temporal revelation which was offered to the eyes or ears. The problem they had to face, however, was that sinful human beings had turned away from God's direct illumination of their minds in the Fall, and, having progressively darkened their minds and obscured the image of God by their sinfulness, they could now only be reached through His outward revelation and divinely inspired mediators. The incarnate divine Word, as well as Scripture and the words of the preacher, were part of this revelation, making speaking and hearing a difficult but unavoidable necessity. As we shall see, the fathers'

---

[26] Frank (2000), 103.

[27] This is especially seen in monastic literature and the Apophthegmata, Burton Christie (2001).

constant reflection on language and communication should therefore be seen in this theological context, as occasioned not only by their education in the liberal arts and rhetoric, but as the result of their reflection on the Fall and the way in which God now providentially intervenes to save fallen human beings through His Word. In their preaching and teaching they became part of this saving economy. Words not only possessed an almost magical power in ancient culture; as we shall see they could create a culture, and, in doing so, convert, reform, and save those who heard them.

Whilst paying attention to the way in which the physiological process of hearing was understood, then, we will also be attempting to engage in the 'reconstructive process' necessary to understand the significance of aurality in early Christianity. In Part One, we will begin by examining the ways in which the physical sense of hearing was described and evaluated in a Greco-Roman context, as well as in a specifically Christian context, in relation to the fathers' theological reflections on the necessary constraints of language and listening in the light of the Fall. We will then attempt to reconstruct the significance of aurality in early Christianity by first turning our attention to the primacy of listening in classical rhetorical culture, and then to philosophical and theological reflection on the nature and significance of the images created by sense perception—and especially hearing—upon the mind and memory, and their role not only in the formation, but the reformation and transformation, of early Christian identity and culture.

We have briefly examined the priority of the verbal over the written, and the magical power of the word in antiquity, but what we perhaps need to be aware of, before all else, is the *priority* of listening and the sheer power of the word in the formation of early Christian culture. In Part Two we will see that people first *heard* and only then believed; they converted to Christianity when it entered their minds and hearts through their ears and informed their faith. This is not to say that texts were not central to early Christianity (in many senses, of course, it was indeed a religion of the book: first of all the Hebrew Scriptures, and then the emerging collection of canonical literature). However, early Christians rarely *read* the word of God, they *heard* it sounded, and it was impressed upon their hearts and minds through the teaching of the Word of God incarnate, the *kerygma* of the early evangelists, catechetical instruction, the reading aloud of Scripture, preaching, prayer, and liturgy. In all these contexts it addressed them directly, with an inherent power, authority, and seductive grace, and they responded.[28]

[28] Kennedy (1980), 127, appositely observes: 'The word for "preach" in Mark 13:10 and commonly in the New Testament, is *kerusso*, which literally means "proclaim". It is what a herald (*keryx*) does with a message, a law, or a commandment. The message is a *kerygma*, or proclamation, and constitutes the gospel ("good news" *euangelion*). Christian preaching is thus not persuasion, but proclamation, and is based on authority and grace, not on proof... Its truth must be apprehended by the listener, not proved by the speaker. The reaction of a person in

Although the research of modern scholars can go a long way to establishing the original context of the early Christian texts we now read, it is, of course, almost impossible for us to retrieve the circumstances and manner of their original delivery. The facial expressions, bodily gestures, and tone of voice which communicate as much as what the speaker actually says; the sense of interpersonal resonance between the speaker and audience; the unified voices of the assembled faithful at worship, all, tantalizingly, elude us.[29] We catch only a distant echo of what makes spoken words so different from simply reading a text: the feeling of something immediate and unique, subject to emotions and hearer response; of something which is not fixed but has the potential for improvisation and play; of something which fixes the attention and fires the imagination; above all, of something which can achieve those moments of heart-stopping transcendence (for want of a better word) which only live performance seems able to inspire. It is this which we would like to try, in some measure, to recapture in the central chapters of this book, in relation to the practice of listening to early Christian catechesis, preaching, and prayer. As Corradi Fiumara has observed, 'No one would deny that talking necessarily implies listening, and yet no one bothers to point out, for example, that in our culture there has always been a vast profusion of scholarly works focussing on expressive activity, almost none in comparison, devoted to the study of listening.'[30]

We need to stop thinking about early Christianity in mute mode, allow it to sound and speak, and then listen to its echoes and resonances in those who heard it. Averil Cameron cogently highlighted this need when she wrote that, 'even when history itself has been feeling the effects of the heightened awareness of rhetoric...we might expect to see a greater stress on its [early Christianity's] rhetorical strategies and—in view of recent work on orality and the significance of writing—on the role of communication, written and oral, in its spread. It has barely been noticed as yet what an extraordinarily suitable field early Christianity provides for this kind of enquiry...it certainly does less than justice to the subject as a whole to concentrate on written texts, or on texts that would have been read only by an educated audience...But we can only dimly reconstitute the power of the spoken word, even when we know that it was great, and the critic must start somewhere.'[31] This book is an attempt to make a start, from the standpoint of the hearer.

the audience to the *kerygma* is like his reaction to a miracle, the direct embrace of authority: he believes it or he does not.'

[29] *Instructing Beginners in the Faith*, 15.23 (Canning, 113): 'you would learn more by watching and listening to us when we put our instructions into practice than by reading what we now dictate'.

[30] Corradi Fiumara (1990), 5–6.

[31] Cameron (1991), 3, 5.

In doing so, we should be aware that any attempt to examine the 'power of the spoken word' will not only have to face the problems of reconstructing the nature of what was heard, how it was heard, and what effect it had on the hearer, but will inevitably have to tackle some of the fundamental theological concerns which listening—and especially listening to God—raised for early Christian theologians. The fathers rarely talk about seeing God but they do talk about hearing God's Word at every turn. Of course, they were acutely aware that the eternal, transcendent God does not have lungs, a tongue, lips, or a voice in order to speak to our physical ears. Rather, they maintained that He communicates with fallen human beings indirectly; His Word resonates and echoes through created, temporal intermediaries and images. Listening to God is therefore never a straightforward matter. He cannot be grasped or captured directly, as He is, but His elusive voice must be patiently attended to, believed, and forever sought out. In Part Three of this book we will argue that, for the fathers, this is a process which has less to do with theology as a rational, systematic attempt to define and pin down explicit, verifiable facts about God, and more to do with theology as an art of listening to God. It was an art practised through the constant repetition of the faith—in teaching, preaching, prayer, and action—that thereby built up tacit, habitual modes of thinking and acting, which, in turn, could form the basis for creative representation or imaginative improvisations on the faith. Most importantly, it was an art which left open the potential for 'passing through' the created and temporal and reaching towards their transcendent source.

This book is, therefore, in many respects, an attempt to examine not only what and how early Christians heard, but how they practised the art of listening to a transcendent God, and the ways in which they were transformed by the process. Since, as we have already seen, the faith reached a largely illiterate majority through their ears, rather than through books or private study, the early Church perhaps more readily lends itself to this approach than other periods of Church history. From acquiring the 'grammar' or 'notation' of the faith through listening to careful catechesis in the rule or creeds of the faith, to hearing it played out in extemporary sermons of amazingly creative improvisations on the inspired text of Scripture, to conversing with God in prayer, the early Christian was initiated into the art of listening.

A consideration of early Christian reflection on prayer, or what conversing with God actually involved, will allow us to examine listening as both sense perception and spiritual perception: hearing with the ears and listening to God's presence in wordless silence with the heart and mind. The former is characterized by temporal succession; the latter by attentive stillness. The conviction of early Christian theologians that the latter was either inaccessible, or cannot be a permanent state for human beings, was based on their belief in human fallen-ness, on the one hand, and on God's infinite transcendence, on the other, which can never be fully grasped in words, images, or thought, but which necessitates a constant stretching out or passing through—something which, we will argue, is characteristic of the art of listening.

The question of how Christians listened to the faith and of how they could be said to hear God, was therefore one which prompted not only much of early Christian practice—in catechetical teaching in baptism, the exegesis of Scripture in preaching, or the practice of personal prayer and communal worship— but profound theological reflection on the nature of human fallen-ness and divine transcendence, the necessary constraints of divine–human communication and the transformative possibilities of the art of listening.

The following impromptu (like the two others which punctuate this book) is by no means a digression, but an attempt to clarify the nature of what we have called 'the art of listening' a little further, and to give voice to an idea which will hopefully re-echo and resonate for the reader throughout what follows.

First Impromptu

The Other Side of Language or 'listening to the voice of Being'

Listening is a matter for both the physical body and the mind. For the listener to be conscious of what they hear both sense perception and some sort of mental apprehension are required. The act of listening therefore involves two rather different modes of attention: one which is open to the sheer 'is-ness' of a thing in all its manifold, fleeting, embodied diversity; another, which fixes what comes to the physical ears so that it can be captured, laid out, and presented to the mind for inspection. The fragile butterfly of sound needs to be captured and pinned down, as it were, for its details to be analysed. Both modes of attention—the embodied and the cognitive—are necessary for sound to be heard. The question is, how can the distinctive characteristics of embodied sound be carried over/preserved in its cognitive recording?

In Part One, which follows, we will try to locate hearing in its embodied context by considering how the ancients understood sense perception and how the wider social, cultural, and theological contexts in which sense perception took place, and was assimilated by the mind, had a crucial role to play in how it was apprehended. In other words, we will be attempting, as much as possible, to allow for the fact that the subject of this book is one that takes place in a context quite other than the one in which we now find ourselves constrained to consider it: listening is first and foremost a physical, temporal, and mutable matter; it is personal, relational, and open to endless resonances. When we attempt to reflect on it and try to articulate something about it, however, we do so with the mind, and in order to do that we inevitably tend to capture it in disembodied words, images, or concepts, which are fixed, and which, to a large extent, separate out, and bring into focus what was originally a live, integrated whole. It seems that, in the process of recording what we hear, so that we can grasp and comprehend it for ourselves, as well as communicate it to others, we simultaneously lose what really characterizes it. Like the recording of a piece of music, what was originally a unique event, subject to the elusive relation between performer and audience, and open to the endless possibilities of live performance, becomes, through the process of recording, fixed, repeatable, impersonal, and—not quite dead, but lacking spontaneity and the thrill of what might happen next. The constraints of the recording process are inevitable if we want to 'hear' and reflect upon the performance beyond its immediate context, but it is therefore doubly important that we remain aware that there is something missing: that we continue to remember that what we now hear is simply a fixed, albeit accurate, record. In reality, anything can happen, and the actual performance is not as repeatable, or as easy to analyse, as the recording might lead us to suppose.

In a recent book, entitled *The Master and his Emissary*,[1] Iain McGilchrist, a practising clinical psychiatrist, as well as a distinguished professor of English literature, has offered a magisterial account (which he is perhaps alone uniquely qualified to give), of the division between the left and right hemispheres of the brain, in terms of both cognitive science and the history of Western culture. The title, taken from a fable by Nietzsche, expresses his conviction that, instead of remaining attentive to the right hemisphere of the brain (the master), the left, dependent hemisphere (the emissary) has increasingly taken over the dominant role for itself, to such an extent that the right hemisphere—the side which connects us to the world—has been progressively lost.[2] Anyone who has read his work will be aware that what we have described as the gap between listening and the cognitive recording of what is heard, is indebted to McGilchrist's reflections, for it would seem that the characteristic features of listening are also those of the right hemisphere of the brain, which deals with the complex world of embodied experience, in contrast to the left hemisphere, which deals with the ordered world of disembodied, intellectual understanding. McGilchrist argues that what is *present* (or *presenced*) to the right hemisphere in the broad, general context of experience and sense perception is then *re-presented* in the left hemisphere in the narrow, decontextualized world of words and categories.[3] Thus, whereas the right hemisphere is always aware of what lies *beyond* what is actually perceived—of what McGilchrist calls 'the Other'—and of the shifting, tacit, unexplored depths and intrinsic openness of what is perceived in personal encounter, the left hemisphere is aware simply of what is set out before it—of the static, familiar, represented world of facts which are known with complete certainty.[4] Thus, whereas the right hemisphere deals with the wider picture, the left deals with specific details: the right intuits meaning in context, from gesture and tone of voice, the left deducts meaning from disembodied facts;[5] the right is sensitive to metaphor, irony, and humour, the left takes things literally;[6] the right has a memory for people and faces, the left has a memory for facts;[7] the right is open

[1] McGilchrist (2010).   [2] McGilchrist (2010), 204.
[3] McGilchrist (2010), 31, 38, 178–9.   [4] McGilchrist (2010), 80.
[5] McGilchrist (2010), 61.   [6] McGilchrist (2010), 71, 82.
[7] McGilchrist (2010), 54, 95.

to the 'new' and explores and reaches out after meaning, the left deals with what is routine and familiar, grasping it and using it mechanically.[8]

McGilchrist is insistent that the differences he describes between the two hemispheres do not lie in *what* the brain does, for both right and left hemisphere are involved in the same activities, but rather in *how* it operates, and, specifically, in the different kinds of attention the two different hemispheres give to the world.[9] This distinction is crucial, he argues, for *how* we attend to something in turn determines both the nature of what we attend to, and who we are that attend to it;[10] attention is a moral act.[11] As McGilchrist observes, 'One way of putting this is to say that we neither discover an objective reality nor invent a subjective reality, but that there is a process of responsive evocation [or what we have called "transformative echoes"]; the world "calling forth" something in me that in turn "calls forth" something in the world.'[12] The question is, do we attend to the world in a manner characteristic of the left hemisphere or the right hemisphere? Do we attend to it as a thing or as a person?[13] As something to be grasped and used or something we empathize with?[14] As something that is fixed and certain, or as something open which invites exploration?[15]

In reminding us of the distinctive characteristics of right-hemisphere attention, and the importance of returning to them, rather than handing ourselves over to the ever increasing grasp of the left hemisphere in our history and culture, McGilchrist is, I would suggest, also arguing a case for the importance of the type of attention which is characteristic of listening, as opposed to that found in cognitive recording. We will be pursuing these insights in Part Three, using what we have discovered of how early Christians actually thought about and exploited the process of listening in their catechesis, preaching, and practices of prayer. In this introductory impromptu, however, I would like to pursue a little further McGilchrist's insights on how we might return from a predominantly left-hemisphere attention to things, to what was originally, and should ultimately be, a right-hemisphere attention, since in doing so we will effectively also be mapping out the course of this book.

All understanding, he argues, originates first of all with the right hemisphere—with sense perception, experience, and affective intuition of the shifting, ambiguous world that presents itself to the attention.[16] It is then subject to the detailed dissection of the left hemisphere with its logical,

---

[8] McGilchrist (2010), 44, 94, 127, 171.   [9] McGilchrist (2010), 3.
[10] McGilchrist (2010), 28, 167.   [11] McGilchrist (2010), 133.
[12] McGilchrist (2010), 133.   [13] McGilchrist (2010), 170.
[14] McGilchrist (2010), 28.
[15] McGilchrist (2010), 170–1—in other words, from a scientific perspective or from the perspective of belief.
[16] McGilchrist (2010), 179, 184–91.

analytical, abstract categorizations. As McGilchrist puts it, in relation to the operation of the left hemisphere,

> we are no longer patient recipients but powerful operators . . . The values of clarity and fixity are added . . . which makes it possible for us to control, manipulate or use the world. For this, attention is directed and focussed; the wholeness is broken into parts; the implicit is unpacked; language becomes the instrument of serial analysis; things are categorised and become familiar. Affect is set aside, and superseded by cognitive abstraction; the conscious mind is brought to bear on the situation; thoughts are sent to the left hemisphere for expression in words and the metaphors are temporally lost or suspended; the world is re-presented in a now static and hierarchically organized form.[17]

We should note that words and language only appear when the thoughts of the right hemisphere are sent to the left to be expressed in a logical and linear manner. This might well prompt us to reflect that the innate intuitions of the right hemisphere are perhaps similar to the direct and intuitive knowledge of God which some early Christian writers held that human beings enjoyed before the Fall, and before the indirect, conscious categories of language were needed in order to convey what they had lost[18]—for language, like all left-hemisphere activity, makes explicit what was hitherto implicitly understood, and, in doing so, effectively fragments what was tacitly intuited as a whole into discrete/separate parts. McGilchrist gives the example of a musician, who, when practising a piece, consciously dissects it in order to concentrate on particularly difficult bits, on phrasing or intonation, but who then returns to an almost unconscious, intuitive sense of the whole when performing it.[19] The musician's practice is, so to speak, like the translation of direct, right-hemisphere intuition into words. As we will see in the first part of this book, the translation of right-hemisphere intuition into words might also be likened to the revelation of God in human history, the incarnation, or the Scriptures: it is what we have referred to as a 'necessary constraint' or 'necessary limitation', given to fallen human beings by God in order to remind them of what they have lost and to lead them back to Himself. Chapter 4, on Christian catechesis and the development of explicit, highly organized 'rules of faith' or creeds, which set forth God's revelation in a systematic, memorable way, are another example of our attention being focused, particularized, and made specific—or, in McGilchrist's terms, made part of the left hemisphere—so that it can once again be returned to the direct intuition of the right hemisphere.

---

[17] McGilchrist (2010), 195.

[18] Indeed, McGilchrist convincingly argues for the priority of music—an intuitive awareness of intonation, phrasing, rhythm, and harmony—over language in human communication. McGilchrist (2010), 100–2.

[19] McGilchrist (2010), 195.

So, the logical categorizations of the left hemisphere have a role in bringing to conscious reflection what is intuitively known by the right, so that what is implicit might be identified and named,[20] and so that the truths of human existence (or, in a Christian context, the object of faith) might be set forth, either for those who are unaware of them or those who have lost sight of them, so that they can once again become the focus of their attention. This is necessary and possible because only the left hemisphere possesses language, in other words, a voice. The right hemisphere's intuitive, empathetic know-ledge is, by nature, silent; it lies, like listening, on the other side of language.[21] Whereas the left can build up elaborate systems, bit by bit, into permanent and solid structures, the right deals only with what is new, unfamiliar, and therefore, by definition, ambiguous and elusive. We will be examining these two types of attention in what follows. Chapter 4 will examine the work of the early Christian catechist, who attempted to put into words an intuitive faith, brought about by God's temporal revelation, in the form of rules of faith or creeds, in order that their catechumens might, through memorizing and reciting them, be enabled to articulate, voice, and communicate their faith. Chapter 5 will examine the words of the early Christian preacher, who, through a sort of free extemporization on the inspired text of Scripture, attempted to catch the echoes and resonances of this systematic teaching, so that their listeners might be moved not only to believe, but once again to respond to the transcendent God, and relate to Him in their lives and actions. Chapter 6 will examine this attentive, transformative hearing, or response to God, in the practice of prayer.

But there is a problem: McGilchrist constantly reminds the reader that we can be deafened by listening to the words of the left hemisphere, and by left-hemisphere categorizations, so that we no longer 'hear', or attend to, the silent, intuitive communication of the right.[22] He writes, 'Today all the available sources of intuitive life—cultural tradition, the natural world, the body, religion and art—have been so conceptualised, devitalised and "deconstructed" (ironized) by the world of words, mechanistic systems and theories constituted by the left hemisphere that their power to help us see beyond the hermetic world that it has set up has been largely drained from them.'[23] It is as if we fail to look beyond the recording of a piece of music to remember the fact that it is, in fact, simply a representation of a unique, live performance; or as if the musician fails to look beyond the dissected phrases they have rehearsed while practising, to the piece of music as a whole; or as if the listener fails to move beyond the formulaic recitation of the creed, or the words or the preacher, to

---

[20] McGilchrist (2010), 195.
[21] McGilchrist (2010), 73, 228–9.
[22] McGilchrist (2010), 73: 'Perhaps it is not, after all, so wide of the mark to call the right hemisphere the "silent" hemisphere: its utterances are implicit.'
[23] McGilchrist (2010), 224.

hear and respond to the God whom they reveal and recount. Instead, we must recognize words for what they are: a re-presentation of a reality which lies beyond them. As McGilchrist writes,

> representations [of experience in the left hemisphere] build on what is known with something that is known. These could be words or mental images . . . Thus it is that we have the illusion of something being brought into being by being put together. All language is inevitably like this: it substitutes for the experienced ambiguity and uncertainty of the original encounter with . . . a sequence of apparently fixed, certain pieces of information.[24]

The right hemisphere's knowledge is, by nature, silent, because it works tacitly and intuitively: the more it is expressed in words, the more difficult it is to retrieve; indeed, the more it is expressed in words, the more it is lost and deadened. McGilchrist identifies such things as the performance of music and dance; courtship, love and sex; humour; artistic creation; religious devotion; recognizing another person . . . all of which depend on the tacit and intuitive in order to exist at all.[25] If we try to explain them in words—to dissect, capture, or pin them down—then we effectively kill them.

What we are left with, then, are words—necessary words if we are to express our intuitions—but which, if they are not used in full awareness of the fact that they are a very blunt instrument, of limited use and effectiveness, can all too easily kill exactly what it is that they attempt to convey. It is this dilemma which Patricia Cox Miller, reflecting on Origen's hermeneutics, aptly describes as the 'abysmal paradox' of using words to say that we cannot use words. She cites J. Hillis Miller: 'without the production of some schema, some icon, there can be no glimpse of the abyss, no vertigo of the underlying nothingness. Any such schema, however, both opens the chasm, creates it or reveals it, and at the same time fills it up, covers it over by naming it, gives the groundless a ground, the bottomless a bottom.'[26]

So how should we use words? How can they be listened to so that they can be effectively heard? How can we move back from left-hemisphere attention to retrieve right-hemisphere attention; back from the explicit to the tacit, from words to their referent and meaning, from the bottom to the bottomless? This will, in effect, be the subject of this book, but it would be useful to reflect on these questions in a general way here, before we move even further, as it were, into left-hemisphere territory ourselves.

McGilchrist makes the case that although the work of the philosopher naturally tends to fall within the realm of the left hemisphere,[27] some notable figures, such as Husserl,[28] Merleau-Ponty,[29] and Heidegger,[30] have betrayed

---

[24] McGilchrist (2010), 231.   [25] McGilchrist (2010), 127, 180.
[26] Cox Miller (2001), 216, citing Miller (1976), 11.   [27] McGilchrist (2010), 89.
[28] McGilchrist (2010), 144.   [29] McGilchrist (2010), 148.
[30] McGilchrist (2010), 149ff.

an awareness of precisely the constraints noted above, and have felt compelled to give an account of the right hemisphere's reality.[31] Theologians, of course, tend to be acutely conscious of these 'necessary constraints', since their subject is a transcendent, ineffable one, which lies, by definition, firmly within the right-hemisphere realm of tacit, intuitive knowledge of what defies linguistic expression. An awareness of what McGilchrist calls 'the Other', or of what lies beyond language, whilst taken as read by the artist, musician, or lover, and, to a large extent, the poet,[32] is also, then, acutely felt by philosophers and theologians alike. The problem is that, unlike the artist, musician, or lover, the only medium of expression open to the philosopher or theologian is words.

McGilchrist's solution is a thoroughly theological one (though he is careful to avoid theological concepts or terminology): he suggests that we need to let our attention rest not just *on* the word, or object, but to *pass through* it.[33] In other words, we must treat all linguistic expression as metaphorical:[34] not as an end in itself, but as a means to an end; as a sign which communicates something beyond itself.[35] In theological terms: we must treat words as revelatory or as sacramental; as communicating something of divine truth in embodied form. In this way the object or words cease to be merely a fixed or static thing but become something living, they embody the reality that lies both within and beyond them, and demand a response. Early Christian interpretation of Scripture is a good example of this process: rarely does it remain at the level of the literal meaning, rather, we find early Christian exegetes and preachers attempting to plumb its fathomless depths through such methods as allegorical, figurative interpretation, all the while acutely conscious of its transcendent, immutable, divine subject and inspiration, and of their inability to ever fully comprehend or grasp it in words.[36] McGilchrist writes similarly of music ' . . . it does not so much use the physical to transcend physicality, or use particularity to transcend the particular, as bring out the spirituality latent in what we conceive as physical existence, and uncover the universality that is, as Goethe spent a lifetime trying to express, always latent

---

[31] McGilchrist (2010), 177, 135.

[32] vl84.

[33] McGilchrist (2010), 182.

[34] McGilchrist comments on the root of the word in Greek, which is 'to carry across'—*meta* (across) *pherein* (carry). McGilchrist (2010), 116, 179.

[35] McGilchrist (2010), 116. It is a use of language in which, as he puts it, 'words are used so as to activate a broad net of connotations, which though present to us, remains implicit, so that the meanings are appreciated as a whole, at once, to the whole of our being, conscious and unconscious, rather than being subject to the isolating effects of sequential, narrow beam attention' (116). We will see just this process at work in the fathers' exegesis of Scripture in their sermons.

[36] As Cox Miller (2001), 178, puts it, 'their interpretive structures were ghosted by an ironic "so to speak" . . . viewing language as evocative rather than as prescriptive . . . writers . . . developed a hermeneutic that might best be characterized as a poetics of reading . . . theologians used language to produce intimations of divinity rather than systematic definitions'.

in the particular. It is also a feature of music in every known culture that it is used to communicate with the supernatural, with whatever is by definition above, beyond, "Other than" our selves.'[37] In a more general context, he observes, 'I believe that the essential difference between the right hemisphere and the left hemisphere is that the right hemisphere pays attention to the Other, whatever it is that exists apart from ourselves, with which it sees itself in profound relation. It is deeply attracted to, and given life by, the relationship, the betweeness, that exists with this Other. By contrast the left hemisphere pays attention to the virtual world that it has created, which is self-consistent, self-contained, ultimately disconnected from the Other, making it powerful, but ultimately only able to operate on and know itself.'[38] We must realize that we cannot simply appropriate or grasp what we attend to, be it words or any other reality; rather we must relate to it and reach out (*ad-tend*)[39] towards it. Interestingly, McGilchrist expresses these insights in auditory terms, quoting George Steiner's comments on Heidegger. Steiner observes, 'For Heidegger . . . man is only a privileged listener and respondent to existence. The vital relation to otherness is not, as for Cartesian and positivist rationalism, one of "grasping" and pragmatic use. It is a relation of audition. We are trying to "listen to the voice of Being".'[40]

It is precisely this 'listening to the voice of Being', this silent, intuitive reaching out towards the Other, which this book will attempt to trace. It involves a movement from the early Christian's right-hemisphere-type attention—their open, patient, intuitive 'listening' to God's inward illumination and His temporal, embodied revelation, to their left-hemisphere-type attempts to articulate this revelation in words, and to systematize and categorize it so that it could be identified and communicated to others.[41] Then, most importantly, it will trace the movement back to their right-hemisphere-type attempts to unfold, pass through, and reach beyond these words and categories, through preaching and prayer, improvisation and allegory, imagination and mimesis, to hear and attend to the echoes of their eternal, incorporeal, immutable source.

---

[37] McGilchrist (2010), 77.

[38] McGilchrist (2010), 93.

[39] McGilchrist (2010), 169: 'to attend means, precisely, to reach out a hand towards: we reach out—"ad-tend"—in order to give, as well as to take'.

[40] McGilchrist (2010), 152.

[41] As McGilchrist puts it, 'Within the realm of the left hemisphere . . . there is also the possibility of an "unfolding" of what is implicit, which, if returned to the right hemisphere, will lead to something greater and better coming forward . . . If we subject a work of art, say, or even the human body, to detached, analytic attention, we lose the sense of the thing itself, and its being in all its wholeness and otherness recedes. But the result of such attention, provided it is then relinquished, so that we stand in a state of openness and receptivity before the thing once again, may be a deeper and richer "presencing".' McGilchrist (2010), 232.

Part One

An Auditory Culture

Nature has given to each of us two ears and one tongue, because we ought to do less talking than listening.

Plutarch, *On Listening to Lectures*, 3

When Plato describes the way in which the gods 'speak' through the poets he suggests that divine inspiration can work with the most unpromising material—indeed, that the god chooses the *least* promising in order to better demonstrate his presence. The worst poet can therefore become the most seductive and compelling, their divine inspiration or possession making what they say not a matter of art (*techne*), but of divine power (*Theia dunamei*); they become like a magnetic field attracting whoever hears them to the source of their words.[1] Plato observes that, 'There is good evidence for this in Tynnichus of Chalcis, who never composed a poem worth remembering except the paean which everybody sings, perhaps the most beautiful of all lyrics, a real "windfall of the Muses" as he says himself. Herein god seems to me to have shown, to prevent us being in any doubt, that these beautiful poems are not human and of men, but divine and of the gods, poets being merely *interpreters* of the gods, each possessed by his own peculiar god. To demonstrate this, the god deliberately sang the most beautiful song through the mouth of the worst poet.'

The Christian God seems to have worked in the same way, choosing an odd assortment of human intermediaries—an unmarried mother,[2] shepherds, uneducated fishermen, a carpenter's son—and embarrassingly second- rate literature, in order to communicate his divine Word to the ears of human beings. Why use such rough and ready, earthy material?

---

[1] Plato, *Ion*, 533–4 (Winterbottom, 4–5). Even statues of gods could therefore act as their interpreters, or 'voice', and there are many accounts of statues speaking or weeping: Lane Fox (1986), 102–67; Francis (2003); Cox Miller (2009), 137–9.

[2] Jütte (2005), 92, notes that Our Lady herself is sometimes depicted as conceiving the Word of God through her ears: the altar of the Passion at the former Cistercian convent church in Marienthal zu Netze shows the child Jesus and the Holy Spirit, in the shape of a dove, emerging from God's mouth on a sheaf of rays that glides towards Mary's ear.

Following Plato, we will argue that the answer lies precisely in the disjunction between message and medium. The fact that the eternal, immutable, incorporeal God speaks to us in and through temporal, mutable, corporeal sense perception means that the messenger and their words can never be taken as an end in themselves but always draw their listeners beyond themselves, as inexorably as a magnetic field, to their source and inspiration. It is as if, in communicating God's truth, the human voice is speaking a rather puzzling foreign language, at once alien and compellingly beautiful, which must be interpreted, and its meaning sought out, in order to be heard and understood. This disconcerting process of interpretation—of hearing divine truth in and through its earthly echoes—of discovering *res* (reality/truth) through *signa* (signs/words/images), is precisely the challenge which early Christian listeners faced.

1

Listening in Cultural Context

> I sense that these pinnae that I turn and turn back in me like antennae are to
> a large extent determined, in their internal movements, by a whole body of
> laws . . . I inherit them, I receive them, I borrow them without even having
> chosen them. This ear that I lend is certainly above all lent to me.[1]

In the Introduction we observed that the uneducated, illiterate early Christian
(and they were the vast majority) depended primarily on words, communicated to their ears through the physical sense of hearing, as the medium
through which they received God's message, rather than, say, reading a written
text with their eyes. In reflecting on the significance of this fact we must
remember that the ancients—just as much as modern anthropologists—were
well aware that, in theory and in practice, sense perception is far from a neutral
or objective business: the role of the different senses is determined (and, in its
turn, determines) the wide range of customary practices, tacit assumptions,
and agreed conventions that identify and constitute a culture.

As we will see below, different cultures have evaluated and hierarchized the
senses in different ways, some emphasizing sight, others hearing (and yet
others taste, touch, or smell). What anthropologists refer to as the 'ratio' or
'balance' of the senses in a particular culture inevitably affects every aspect of
it—from how its members relate to the world and to each other, to its
language, symbols, and rituals. Constance Classen, for example, has shown
how, at least in the West, the senses have been used to define and promote
gender differences: men, who engage with the public realm, have been associated with the 'higher', rational senses of sight and hearing, while women, who
are primarily identified with the domestic sphere, have been associated with
the 'lower', more corporeal senses of taste, touch, and smell.[2] She comments
that, 'The symbolic division of perception into masculine and feminine terri-
tories carried immense weight. Men were believed to be empowered by
God and nature to see and oversee the world. Women were required by the

---

[1] Szendy (2008), 13.   [2] Classen (1998), in Howes (2003), 55.

same forces to stay at home, stitching the clothes, stirring the stew, and rocking the cradle.'[3]

If we are to get a sense of the role of listening in early Christianity, we must therefore examine not only theories of sense perception (though. as we shall see, these are important and revealing in themselves) but the practice and effect of listening in the wider context of early Christian society and culture. The work of the cultural historian Alain Corbin on village bells in nineteenth-century France has been one of the most influential examples of scholarship in this respect.[4] In his work *Village Bells: Sound and Meaning in the 19th-Century French Countryside*, the sound of the bell is shown to be a marker of temporal, physical, personal, and spiritual space, measuring out the daily events, geographical boundaries, individual lives, and devotional practices of the village, through its diverse ears. He thereby demonstrates that the resonating echoes of bells effectively shaped social, cultural, and religious order and harmonized time, space, people, and the divine. As Smith observes, Corbin argues that 'we must understand the actual ways in which people understood the senses, their relation, and their social meaning, and to do so demands that we listen to multiple voices from multiple contexts and discourses'.[5]

There is, of course, always a risk of failing to hear the 'multiple contexts and discourses' and of being deafened by the educated elite, not least because, through their articulate speech and their ability to write, they alone actually achieved a voice which we can still hear. Their listeners remain mute for us, unless we are prepared to pay attention to 'the other side' of speaking: to the reception of their words; the echoes and resonances of their voices, and to their effect—and they did indeed have a dramatic effect—in shaping the lives, words, and actions of their listeners, their social and cultural practices, their religious devotion and rituals. Similarly, we must not ignore their role in hallowing out sacred spaces, bringing sacred literature to life, giving meaning to sacred history, and allowing the images and figures of the faith, in their turn, to speak and resonate in the hearts of minds of those who perceived them. These resonances and echoes are sometimes difficult to hear when all we now possess is a written text, but if we are not attentive to them, we will fail to appreciate what early Christian culture meant for those who belonged to it.

SEEING AND HEARING: THE RATIO OF THE SENSES

Homo sapiens means a 'knowing' or 'tasting' man; *sapientia*, or wisdom comes from the verb *sapere*, to taste. Classen has interestingly observed that the

[3] Classen (1995), 70.   [4] Corbin (1998).   [5] Smith (2007), 15.

words we use to refer to thinking and understanding rely heavily on both visual terminology (we talk about a 'point a view', an 'overview', or an 'observation'; we 'enlighten' and 'focus'; we say 'I see' in order to communicate that we have understood), and on tactile or kinaesthetic terms (such as apprehend, brood, cogitate, comprehend, conceive, grasp, mull, perceive, ponder, ruminate). But she notes that, 'significantly, auditory terms rarely serve as metaphors for thought or intelligence in English'. She suggests that 'this is perhaps because hearing is conceived as a passive sense, receiving information but not probing it. Therefore, rather than being associated with intelligence, hearing is associated with obedience (*obaudire/audire*: Greek), so if to hear is to obey, to obey is to hear.'[6] Whatever the reason, and we will discuss it further in Chapter 6, what such terminology suggests, even when we simply take examples drawn from the English language, is that, as Classen concludes, 'we think through our senses'; that the way we understand the senses influences not only the way we express ourselves, but how we think about ourselves, our association to the world, and how we act in relation to it. In short, as philosophers such as Merleau-Ponty, Polanyi, and Ricoeur confirm,[7] perception is not just a physical act but a personal and cultural act.[8] What Classen refers to as 'the cultural construction of perception'[9] becomes much more obvious when we look beyond Western, visually based culture, to other, very different cultures, in which other senses predominate (her own special study was of the Suya of the Brazilian Mato Grosso, who associate hearing with understanding, rather than sight: 'The Suya term "to hear" (*kumba*) also means to understand, while the expression "it is in my ear" is used by the Suya to indicate they have learned something, even something visual such as a weaving pattern. Sight, in fact, is considered by the Suya to be an anti-social sense, cultivated by witches').[10]

What then, of Western culture, or indeed, of classical and late antique culture? It is obvious that a predominantly visual culture tends to emerge the more we concentrate on written texts, whilst a more auditory culture comes to the fore the more we concentrate on the illiterate hearers of texts. The former tends be characterized by the intellectual concerns of 'high' culture, the latter by the more everyday concerns of 'low' culture. This is, of course, a rather obvious generalization, but what has been written by scholars across the disciplines in relation to the history of Western culture lends it some weight, not least because such terms as 'visual' or 'auditory' have become a sort of 'rule of thumb' to sum up a whole range of diverse characteristics

---

[6] Classen (1993), 58–9. We see the same in the German *horen* (to hear) and *gehorchen* (to obey).
[7] Merleau-Ponty (1945); Polanyi (1958); Ricoeur (1990).
[8] Classen (1993), 1.
[9] Classen (1993), 9.
[10] Classen (1993), 9.

within a culture under a single heading. However, we will argue that such labels are more often than not misleading, and that the high and low, visual and auditory, are always inseparably linked; that although the ratio or balance of a particular sense might vary, this more often depends on the context in which it is examined, rather than holding true of a culture as a whole.

The work of Marshall McLuhan and Walter Ong in the second half of the last century has perhaps been the most influential in attempting to articulate the way in which the division between auditory and visual culture has influenced Western thinking, even though there are few who would entirely agree with all their findings today. For McLuhan and Ong the division amounts to a 'great divide',[11] one that separates primitive, oral cultures from more developed, Western, visual cultures.[12] They contend that the chasm which separates these two cultures opened up in the shift between orality and literacy, which came about as a result of the printing revolution, when words no longer sounded and resonated as voices but became objects to be seen and contemplated on the page. Both lament the modern 'diminution of hearing' which came about through the 'technologizing of culture'. For Ong, it has been observed, 'the ear . . . stands as the other to modernity's fractioning eye, the embodiment of the bardic and the inspired, and the now muted vehicle of both community and God's revelation'.[13] This divide was finally set in stone by the Enlightenment: as Schmidt puts it, 'With its clear-eyed pursuit of detached observation, imperial sweep, and visual instrumentation, the Enlightenment was the keystone in the eye's ascendency.'[14] As we will see, while the invention of the printing press, and the ascendency of reason in the Enlightenment, did indeed work to emphasize what has been called the 'ocularcentrism'[15] of modern culture, an auditory culture has never quite been eclipsed in the way that scholars like McLuhan and Ong would have us believe,[16] nor is the priority of the visual something new: it was just as characteristic of classical and late antique culture (as well as of Byzantine and medieval culture) as it is of our own. The reasons for vision's pre-eminence have much deeper roots than either the 'technologizing of culture'[17] or the Enlightenment pursuit of reason.

---

[11] E.g. McLuhan (1964); Ong (1982).

[12] Schmidt (2003), 46, comments that: 'with an unreflective colonialist lens, McLuhan made Africa his imaginary . . . "The African" lived in "the magical world of the ear", while modern Western "typographic man" lived in the "neutral visual world" of the eye. The one was a world of vision, objectification, and progress; the other a world of sound, magic and timelessness.'

[13] Schmidt (2003), 45.

[14] Schmidt (2003), 42.

[15] Schmidt (2003), 44.

[16] Schmidt (2003) and (2000) does a good job in presenting evidence for the continuance of auditory culture in modernity and, as a result, achieves a more balanced picture.

[17] McLuhan (1969); Ong (1982).

Let us return to antiquity. Classical philosophy understood vision and hearing in very different, contrasting ways, which inevitably had far-reaching repercussions on how they were ordered or hierarchized, and on the way in which they influenced cultural conventions, and ways of thinking and behaving. Vision was generally thought to be effected by a continuous stream of rays which were emitted by the 'lamp' of the eye. These rays reached out and touched the object of perception so that it was immediately and simultaneously imaged in the mirror of the eye.[18] There were no gaps in vision—either spatial, temporal, or perceptual—rather, the eye was present to its object immediately, continuously, without any intervening distance or lapse of time. Hearing was a very different matter: it was generally thought to be effected by a blow between solid objects, which struck the air, and which then travelled, as single mass of air, the distance between the initial impact and the ear. It then stuck a surface in the ear, making it resound or resonate, so that the sound could be registered by the brain.[19] Theophrastus describes this resonating echo: 'Hearing is by means of the ears . . . because within them is an empty space, and this empty space resounds. A kind of noise is produced by the cavity and the internal air re-echoes this sound.'[20] The process of hearing was therefore full of gaps—between the sounding object and the air, the blow to the air and the blow to the ear, the ear and the perception of the brain. It was external, sequential, discontinuous, and mediated, contingent upon acts and events occurring outside of the perceiving subject. Whereas the object to be seen was always there, irrespective of the viewer, what was heard was always dependent upon the hearer's active participation and response to capture it as it happened, in time and space. Whereas sight was a matter of direct contemplation, hearing was a matter of indirect echoes and resonances. The hierarchy of sight and hearing was therefore effectively written into their working: in the contrast between immutability and mutability; permanence and change; presence and distance; proximate and mediated; simultaneity and sequence; continuity and discontinuity; internal and external; contemplation and action;

---

[18] Chidester (1992), 2–5, for references; Beare (1906); Sorabji (1977); Jütte (2005), 31–53. This is a synthesis of the basic features of ancient theories. There are, of course, variations: Plato taught that the visual rays from the eye are unified with reflections from the object and external sources of light (such as the sun) to form what Chidester describes as 'a unified, continuous and immediate connection between the seer and seen in the process of vision' (Chidester (1992), 4); Aristotle, on the other hand, rejected the ray theory in favour of a transparent, potential medium of vision which became light when acutalized; the Stoics explained vision by means of a visual cone consisting of spirit, air, and light which enabled direct contact to be made between the eye at the apex of the cone and the object of vision at the base (Chidester (1992), 4–5). Whatever their differences, in all these theories, vision was immediate and continuous.

[19] Chidester (1992), 6–8, who cites Aristotle, *De Anima*, II.8; Plato, *Timaeus*, 67 A–C.

[20] *De Sensibus*—quoted by Jütte (1995), 32; Or as Aristotle (*De Anima*, II.8) puts it, 'the sound we hear is always the sounding of something else, not of the organ itself. That is why we say that we hear with what is empty and echoes, viz. because what we hear with is a chamber which contains a bounded mass of air.'

freedom and necessity,[21] all the values which classical philosophy valued were clearly embodied in sight, whilst everything it sought to resist was embodied by hearing.

Early Christianity therefore emerged within a culture where the ratio of the senses was weighted firmly towards the visual; one that valued sight, the process of sight, and the characteristics of sight as those which best lent themselves to philosophy—to love of wisdom or love of God. Of course, this was a matter of balance: the other senses were not thereby rejected (how could they be?) but they were most definitely demoted, or even held in suspicion, as too corporeal, too tied up with time and change, too likely to lend themselves to excess, and, above all, too prone to distract the intellect from its pursuit of the true, the good, and beautiful. Even sight was not immune from this suspicion, but when knowledge of God, the ultimate goal of the Christian life, was described, it was almost always expressed in visual terms—as vision of God, contemplation of God.

A HIERARCHY OF PERCEPTION: INTELLECT AND SENSE PERCEPTION

In theory

That seeing God was a matter of intellectual 'vision' rather than physical vision is beyond question: it was universally held that God was better known by the mind than the senses—at least in theory, and at least before the Fall. As we shall see, these two reservations—in theory, and before the Fall—will prove to be highly significant ones, not least in reconfiguring the balance or ratio of the senses in early Christianity. If we remain within the pre-fallen realm of theory for just a moment, however, we can observe that a suspicion of the senses and an exaltation of the intellect was as paradigmatic for early Christianity as it had been for Greek philosophy. It is difficult to think of a specific example to illustrate this point as it is simply all-pervading and informs everything that the fathers thought or wrote. Gregory of Nyssa's *On the Inscriptions of the Psalms* is as good an instance as any. Like the classical philosophers he opens his treatise with a discussion of how we achieve blessedness or happiness (*eudaemonia*), and, like them, he concludes that it has two faces: separation from evil and the attainment of virtue (1.1.8). Whereas evil delights sense perception, virtue brings joy to the soul (1.2.11). He therefore urges that we

---

[21] Chidester (1992), ch. 1, draws out these differences in relation to classical philosophy and contemporary work in the phenomenology of perception (Merleau-Ponty (1945); Jonas (1966)).

must turn away from involvement in the senses; in material, physical reality and towards contemplation of the good, which forms us in virtue. The good which must be sought out and imitated is, of course, God, and the divine nature is not such as can be known by sense perception but only by the intellect. Commenting on Psalm 4:7, 'The light of your face has been imprinted on us, Lord', Gregory clearly has in mind the classical understanding of sight as the emission of a ray which touches its object so that it can be mirrored in the eye: he observes that 'sense perception is not of the nature to touch that light which radiates from the face of God . . . For the prophet does not seem to me to understand the face of God which is contemplated in certain imprints as anything other than the virtues, for the divine form is imprinted in these' (1.4.30). God is therefore known, not by the images created by sense perception but by the imprint of the virtues on the soul. Gregory also follows the philosophers in teaching that everything is to be judged on the basis of one's ultimate goal or end—and for the Christian that is nothing other than God. In this life the Christian therefore lives in hope, looking towards God with the 'eye of his soul' and passing over everything that appears to the senses (1.6.45). Towards the end of his treatise Gregory succinctly sums up the early Christian attitude to the senses thus:

> Two (principles) are understood in human nature, the one is the life of the flesh which operates by means of perceptible things, and the other is the spiritual and immaterial life which is accomplished in the intellectual and incorporeal life of the soul. For it is not possible to participate in the two at the same time, for zeal for the one produces the negation of the other. Therefore, if we are about to make the soul a dwelling place of God, we must depart from the tabernacle of the flesh. (2.6.64)

What Gregory has to say about the role of the senses in pursuit of blessedness is entirely characteristic of both classical and early Christian thought, and reveals the deep roots which the latter had in the former. He demonstrates how classical theories of sense perception, such as the ray theory of vision, were simply 'taken as read' and then applied in a Christian context to talk about how we contemplate (or, more precisely, fail to contemplate) God. Classical culture and learning were drawn upon to promote a way of life—virtuous action and hope and longing for vision of God—which effectively 'writes off' life in the body and the activity of sense perception as the location of evildoing; as merely a temporal distraction from contemplation of the eternal God, who is known not through the corporeal senses but by means of incorporeal virtues.

These insights were confirmed and compounded by the Christian doctrine of creation from nothing. The fathers all maintained that human beings are creatures—temporal, mutable, corporeal beings who are drawn from nothing and who will tend back to nothing without their Creator. The doctrine of creation from nothing (*creatio ex nihilo*) was unique to Christianity, and the ontological divide it posited between created beings and the transcendent Creator seemed to inevitably give rise to a negative attitude to the senses. In theory, as we have just seen in Gregory of Nyssa, it was held that the yawning chasm between created human beings and the transcendent divine Creator could be bridged only by our becoming more like Him; by imitating Him and by seeking to attain what it is that we lack and He possesses—virtue, truth, goodness, beauty (which are all, by definition, eternal, immutable, and incorporeal). What holds us back is precisely that which links us to the world, in other words, our bodily senses. The fathers therefore counselled an order of virtue—one in which the senses were relegated to strict subservience and obedience to reason, or were interiorized and spiritualized, so that, as we shall see later in this chapter, they were no longer physical senses but ways of describing how the soul 'senses' God.

In theory, then, classical eudaemonism was compounded with a Christian theory of creation from nothing to render sense perception either obsolete, wholly subject to the intellect, or spiritualized beyond recognition. At least, this is the theory which we find being rehearsed at every turn by the fathers. In practice, however, it is something that they all, in different ways, find themselves forced to acknowledge is unrealizable by human beings in this life. Their reasons are ones we will be examining at more length at various points in this book, but at this point we will briefly summarize them before reflecting on the crucial role which the senses—and especially the practice of listening—came to play in Christian culture as a result.

In practice

The senses did not go away. They proved to be far less tractable to incorporeal virtue, and much more difficult to subject, or spiritualize out of corporeal existence, than the classical philosophers or Christian teachers might have hoped. The very existence of Christianity, its doctrine of creation, its Scriptures, its long history across the centuries, its faith in the incarnate God, its preachers and teachers, its liturgy and sacraments, all gave the lie to a theory of intellectual contemplation of the divine which, in practice, had evidently proved unrealizable in this life. The reasons were twofold: human corporeality and human fallen-ness. The fact that human beings had been created by God with bodies that relied on sense perception, as well as souls, was one which could not be ignored; moreover, in falling away from God, through sin, they had obscured or lost whatever direct, intellectual, spiritual perception of God they had enjoyed before their Fall and were now reduced to perceiving whatever they could of Him indirectly, through their physical senses. God's revelation of Himself in His creation, in sacred history, in His inspiration of the prophets, preachers, and teachers, His becoming man, His offering of

Himself in the physical elements of bread and wine, were all indications of the way in which He had graciously and providentially sought to address the consequences of human fallen-ness and to allow human beings to encounter Him precisely where they had fallen—in the created, temporal, mutable, corporeal realm of sense perception.

After the Fall

We will examine the effects of the Fall, with particular reference to listening, in more detail in Chapter 3, but we should note here that it was the determining feature of early Christian attitudes to sense perception, and effectively shifted the balance of the senses away from a privileging of vision towards the need for the other senses, and especially hearing. It is not an exaggeration to say that the Fall effected a revolution in the way in which the senses functioned in Christian life and culture: they became the means through which God revealed Himself, communicated with, indeed, reformed and transformed fallen human beings. They could not simply be left behind or vilified. The mystery of the incarnation was the mystery of God taking a human body in order to communicate with human beings in and through the body—through sight, hearing, taste, touch, and smell.

A 'CORPOREAL TURN'?

'What time th'eternall Lord in fleshly slime/Enwombèd was'[22]

It is therefore somewhat odd to find patristic scholars referring to a 'material turn' or a 'corporeal turn' in Christian culture in the fourth century, after the conversion of the Emperor Constantine to Christianity in 312, as if this was something radically new, and as if Christianity not always been a religion of embodiment: of incarnation, and faith in a God who saves human beings through the body. Had Christianity not always been a society shaped by persecution: by the offering of one's body for the sake of one's faith; by martyrdom, physical suffering, and the celebration of the martyrs' lives, words, and actions? Was it not a tradition rooted in the creating, inspiring, prophetic Word of God, which had sounded and resonated in the Old Testament and took corporeal form in the New Testament? Was it not characterized by a culture which had always been acutely conscious of being

---

[22] Spenser, *Faerie Queene*, II.x.50.2–3.

in the world, even while it longed to escape it? What might a 'material' or a 'corporeal turn' mean in such a context?

For most scholars it represents the changed status of the Church in the years following Constantine's conversion. After the edict of toleration in 313, the Church was no longer a target for persecution, pushed to the margins, denied any public presence or official acknowledgement, its members made to feel like 'resident aliens'. Rather, it was granted a real presence—in Church buildings, ornate liturgies, religious houses, art and literature, public officials, canons and councils, holy places, and a sacred geography. In short, it became very much at home in the world, with a material culture to rival that of the Greeks or Romans.[23] For some recent scholars this 'material turn' is also evidenced in an emphasis on the body and bodily experience in a manner which had simply not been possible before Constantine. After his conversion, the bodies of saints, relics, icons, and other sacred images could be venerated as places of divine presence.[24] Previously austere Christian art, ritual, and devotional piety could become 'a feast for the physical senses'.[25] As Susan Ashbrook Harvey puts it, 'At every turn, Christianity engaged a tangible, palpable piety physically experienced and expressed.'[26] It is therefore argued that a new 'visceral' piety, which engaged the body as never before, emerged as a result of Christianity's new-found status.

A 'material turn' is certainly beyond question. Christianity enjoyed a physical presence, and a freedom for liturgical, devotional expression, which was impossible before its legalization. A 'corporeal turn', however, if such there was, is, I think, rather less dramatic than it has been presented. It is hard to think of early Christianity, with its unique doctrine of creation from nothing; its painful awareness of human fallen-ness and sinful flesh; its acute sense of divine presence and revelation in theophanies and salvation history; its sensitivity to the inspired words of prophets, evangelists, and preachers; its veneration of the martyrs, saints, and holy men and women, in Gospels, Acts, Lives, and imaginative apocryphal works; its faith in the incarnation of God Himself; its commemoration of Christ's bodily passion and death; its partaking of Christ's flesh and blood in the Mass; its understanding of the Church as the body of Christ, taking any more of a 'corporeal turn' than it already had! Certainly, the average pagan thinker would be hard pushed to say how it could differ more dramatically than it already did in this respect from Greco-Roman religion and culture. Its corporeal imagination was already in such robust health it was difficult to see that it required any further inspiration.[27]

---

[23] E.g. Ashbrook Harvey (2006), 46.   [24] E.g. Cox Miller (2009), 3–4.
[25] Ashbrook Harvey (1993), 57.   [26] Ashbrook Harvey (1993), 58.
[27] Though we should note Susan Ashbrook Harvey's ((2006), 110–33) interesting observations on the way which fourth/fifth century theologians such as Lactantius, Gregory of Nyssa, Theodoret of Cyrus, and Nemesius of Emesa, 'drew on the science of the human body as it was presented in the academies of their day to demonstrate the intrinsic goodness, beauty, and

My point here is not to criticize the work of other scholars (the work that has been done on the role of relics, icons, and sacred images is immensely valuable, whether it represents a 'corporeal turn' or not) but to underline the important fact that there had always been an ambivalence and tension with regards to the physical senses—between theory and practice; pre-Fall and post-Fall; in relation to the world and in relation to God—which was rooted precisely in the inherent corporeality of the Christian faith from the very beginning. From the moment Adam and Eve were placed in the Garden of Eden the senses had played a crucial role, not only in precipitating the Fall, but in mediating between human beings and God, and in enabling human beings to return to their Creator and be reformed and transformed in His image.

In reflecting further on this point, it might help, I think, if we return for a moment to the distinction between sight and hearing. With the exception of Susan Ashbrook Harvey's wonderful work on the role of smell, or the olfactory imagination, most of the work that has been done on the 'corporeal turn' concentrates almost exclusively on sight—on texts, relics, icons, or sacred images and the visual images they created in the minds and imaginations of their readers.[28] For example, most of the textual examples which Patricia Cox Miller cites in her work, *The Corporeal Imagination*, are drawn from rhetorical exercises which attempt, through the creation of vivid word-pictures, to involve the reader in what is being described by making it as corporeal—or as lifelike and realistic[29]—as possible. In other words, they are drawn from the well-established classical genre of *ekphrasis*.[30] Cox Miller is obviously well aware that such rhetorical descriptions had been standard practice from classical antiquity onwards, but she seems to overlook the significance of this for a theory which locates the 'corporeal turn' in the fourth century. What is also overlooked is the important fact that the so-called 'visceral seeing' which such exercises evoked in the minds of their recipients was more often created, not by the act of seeing or reading, but, for the illiterate majority, by speaking and hearing. *Ekphrases*, or any other verbal descriptions which enabled the hearer to 'see' what was being described and to feel as if they were in its presence, more often than not entered the mind through the ears rather than the eyes.[31]

As we have already indicated, it was not just vivid accounts of saints' bodies, relics, and icons, that disclosed divine presence and inspired the 'sensory' or 'corporeal imaginations' of early Christians (though these are undeniably

foresight of God's work as Creator' (110). Their positive attitude to the created body was no doubt firmly rooted Christianity's long-standing emphasis on the corporeal as God's creation and as revealing divine action and will.

[28] E.g. Cox Miller (2009), 7–8, 14–15.
[29] *Enargeia*—Webb (1999), 64.
[30] Cox Miller (2009), 9.
[31] Webb (1991, 1999).

important), but every aspect of God's temporal, corporeal revelation which they encountered through their own bodies—their physical senses, and especially their ears—which imprinted itself as images upon their minds and thereby formed their faith and transformed their Christian identity. From the moment of creation, and especially after the Fall, Christianity understood God to be present in His material creation, and in the body and the senses of His mediators. He was believed to speak and act in and through them to impress corporeal images on the minds and hearts of those who thereby perceived Him, in order to reform and transform them in His image.

In the following two sections I would like to examine two contexts in which the process of hearing was thought to inform or transform the mind of the hearer, and examine the way in which early Christian thought and practice was influenced by them. The first is the classical practice of rhetoric; the second is the understanding of sense perception as the impression of a mental image. Both will subsequently have a bearing on our consideration of the practice of early Christian teaching and preaching in relation to the hearer.

2

Rhetoric and the Art of Listening

'Soulbending sovereign of all things.'[1]

That hearing could be just as 'visceral' as seeing is suggested by the following quotations concerning the power of rhetoric:

> And when he let the great voice go from his chest, and the words came drifting down like the winter snows, then no other mortal man beside could stand up against Odysseus.

Homer, Iliad[2]

> The crash of his thunder, the brilliance of his lightning, make all other orators, of all ages, insignificant. It would be easier to open your eyes to an approaching thunderbolt than to face up to his unremitting emotional blows.

Longinus, On Sublimity, 34.4 (Winterbottom, 177)

> He whose eloquence is like to some great torrent, that rolls down rocks and 'disdains the bridge' and carves out its own banks for itself, will sweep the judge from his feet, struggle as he may, and force him to go wither he bears him. This is the orator that will call the dead to life ... it is in his pages that his native land will cry aloud.

Quintilian, Institutio Oratoria, 12.10.61 (Loeb, 314–15)

It could be argued that classical culture was wholly directed towards the hearer, in that its educational system, its legal and political practice, its ceremonies, literature, and art, were all founded upon the art and practice of rhetoric; the art of speaking in such a way that the hearer's mind and emotions should be impressed and moved by what they heard, so that they assented to, and acted upon it. We can learn a great deal about the silent hearer, the privileged recipient of some of the highest and best of classical learning, simply

---

[1] Cicero, *De Oratore*, 2.44.187 (Loeb, 332–3) quoting the poet Pacuvius, cited in Vickers (1988), 76.

[2] 3.216–23, tr. Richmond Lattimore (Chicago, 1951), quoted by Vickers (1989), 4.

by bearing in mind that what is said, and how it is said, in so many different contexts, is shaped by their presence, and by a desire to inform, move, and persuade them by what they heard.

Classical culture and the culture of the early Christian centuries (contrary to the theories of McLuhan and Ong) was not, of course, primarily an oral culture, but a written one. It was a culture of the book, and especially of the literature of classical paganism, but it depended on educated, literate, articulate individuals to continue and communicate it to an illiterate majority.[3] In the Introduction we noted that an education, in any form, was available only to a very small minority in antiquity. The vast majority therefore depended upon the educated few to 'hear' written texts, and, more importantly, to mould and shape a culture in which what they heard could be received in an informed way. It was the educated few, adept in the art of rhetoric, who effectively constituted and shaped a common culture, since it was they who had the position and power to influence law and politics; access history, tradition, and philosophy in classical literature; and the means and expertise to communicate and inculcate it by their rhetorical speech. They were educated and trained to speak, and they spoke in order to be heard. In doing so, they created what we have called an 'auditory' culture; a culture based on speaking and hearing, shared by literate and illiterate alike.

The art of speaking did, however, have its roots in an oral history which stretched back well before the beginnings of writing. As Vickers points out, the *Iliad* and the *Odyssey*, which record the oral epic tradition that developed between 1250 BC and around 750 BC, are structured around speeches given by the main characters in relation to the different situations they found themselves in. The immense importance and power of the speech in these works to determine people's thinking and behaviour, the course of events, an individual's fortunes, simply cannot be overlooked, and was tremendously influential as a model in classical rhetorical theory. The fact that classical education from Isocrates (436–388 BC) onwards,[4] had as its goal the formation of someone who could deploy the techniques of rhetoric (so-called 'technical rhetoric') and convince an audience by their words was, of course, determined primarily by practical concerns. It was intended to produce future lawyers, judges, governors, senators, and military commanders—men in whose hands the security, peace, democracy, and general order and well-being of the Empire could

---

[3] For reflection on these observations in relation to New Testament studies, see Horsley (2003); Niditch (2003), 43, who writes, 'Within a "great divide" conceptual framework, Biblical studies tended to suggest that early, simple oral works gave way to sophisticated written works produced by a literate elite. Scholars are now beginning to see that orality and literacy exist on a continuum and that there is an interplay between the two modalities, a feedback loop of sorts.'

[4] The most influential works on rhetoric were by Plato (who was notoriously critical of it, in the *Phaedrus*; *Gorgias*); Aristotle (*Rhetoric*); Cicero (*De Oratore*; *De Inuentione* (c.87 BC)); Quintilian (*Institutio Oratoria* (92–4 BC); the anonymous *Rhetorica ad Herennium* (c.84 BC).

confidently be placed. At first sight, the system of education itself does not appear very practical in this regard: it consisted of a study of the seven liberal disciplines, literary and mathematical arts which would enable the student to read, analyse, and critically judge a text, and, most importantly, be able to address an audience so as to teach and persuade them of its truth.[5] Moving from elementary study with a grammaticus to more advanced study with a rhetor, it could take over eight years, and had almost nothing to do with the actual practices of government, the legal system, military operations, nor with an overall grasp of history, philosophy, or language,[6] but rather had everything to do with the rules and techniques needed to establish the student's social standing and enable them to communicate effectively, so that they were able to secure positions of influence, and the agreement of those over whom they were placed. The art of speaking, or the art of being heard effectively, was clearly valued above all else, and everything else was presumed to follow from it. As Peter Brown eloquently observes, 'In late antique culture, *logoi*, dignified words carefully composed and delivered, were expected to work their way into the heart like bars of ancient, reverential music, an intimate Orpheus killing the beasts whose disruptive power lay so close to the surface of late Roman life.'[7]

The educational curriculum we have just described was one which was adopted without any real variation throughout the Empire, east and west. As a result, it produced a group of citizens who shared a common formation, culture, or *paideia*, and who could communicate with each other in the confidence that they would be recognized as fellow members of a prestigious and privileged elite.[8] They had read the same texts, their minds had been shaped by the same influences, they could make allusions without having to explain themselves, and their shared background brought with it a mutual understanding, respect, and ease of relation. Nothing had to be proved; everything was a matter of tacit recognition and understanding. When they did have to convince and persuade each other of something, they knew the rules and played the same game: they spoke the same 'language', as it were, adopted the same strategies, respected the same authorities, and were able to recognize each other's skill and success.

What this meant for the hearer should not be overlooked: an homogenous culture, shared by all those best placed to communicate, shape, and inform it, was an important factor in ensuring ease of understanding on the part of the hearer, confidence of expectation, and the ability to 'hear' allusions and tacit

---

[5] Marrou (1948), part 1; Kaster (1988); Young (2007), 76–80, on Quintilian's description of how grammarians taught their pupils to establish, construe, interpret, and explain a text.

[6] Kaster (1988), 12: 'Merely pedantic (it is said) where not superficial, it first choked the spirit of literature with its rules, then hid the body under a rigid formalism.'

[7] Brown (1992), 50.

[8] Kaster (1988), 14.

references without needing to have them explained. The hearer was therefore predisposed by this common culture to listen to a speaker effectively, to be susceptible to their strategies, and amenable to being taught, delighted, and persuaded by them. In a real sense, the illiterate majority were able to share and benefit from the universal system of education which pertained throughout the Empire, and effectively participate in it through hearing its literate practitioners.

So how was rhetoric understood by its proponents and what was this common 'auditory' culture—shared by the literate and illiterate alike—of speaking and listening? Quintilian (*c.* AD 40–95), one of the most influential writers on rhetoric in antiquity, offers a classic definition of rhetoric which sums up its characteristic features: it is the art of speaking well: 'bene dicendi scientia'. As Quintilian's careful description of the stages in the formation of the rhetor makes clear, the art or knowledge of rhetoric was one that was acquired through years of study. There were many textbooks on rhetoric, but they were essentially manuals of practical advice: rhetoric was always more than theory, and what was described in textbooks was meant for guidance in practising the art. Rather like a book on playing the 'cello, in which music theory and notation need to be explained; bowing and fingering techniques might be described; positions enumerated . . . without the actual practice of playing the instrument; without performance, the book would be of little interest or use. It was the same with works on rhetoric: techniques, methods, and examples were described; types of oratory,[9] stages of composition,[10] parts of speech,[11] enumerated and elucidated; bodily positions and gestures recommended; models offered for emulation; different modes of speech assessed[12] . . . but they were written not just to be read and studied, but to be put into practice in speech and, above all, to be heard. Rhetoric is the art of speaking *well* (*bene*) in both senses of the word: both effectively, in relation to one's hearer, and to promote the good. Rhetoric, unlike all the disciplines which led up to, and prepared for it, was therefore a practical, performance art/discipline, not just a rational, theoretical one.[13] Whereas students might be urged to study the disciplines in order to move 'from the corporeal to the incorporeal',[14] rhetoric, even though it was generally regarded as their culmination and goal, was firmly rooted in the everyday, the temporal and

---

[9] E.g. forensic, deliberative, epideictic.

[10] Invention/*inuentio*; arrangement/*dispositio*: style/*elocutio*; memory/*memoria*; delivery/*pronunciatio*.

[11] Introduction (*exordium*); narration (*narratio*); division (*partitio*); proof (*confirmatio*); refutation (*refutatio*); conclusion (*conclusio*).

[12] Plain/subdued, middle/temperate, grand/vigorous.

[13] Even music was categorized as one of the mathematical disciplines, and studied in terms of numerical proportions.

[14] Nichomachus of Gerasa, *Introductio Arithmetica*.

corporeal; it never lost sight of the other side of speaking, that is, of the art or sense of listening. It is therefore clear that rhetoric had always effected what has elsewhere been referred to as a 'material' or 'corporeal turn' in classical and late antique culture.

In much the same way as the senses and sense perception, the practice of rhetoric was to be the cause of much tension and dispute concerning its relative merits, and use, in comparison to the more theoretical arts, and especially philosophy, which communicated knowledge directly to the intellect. Rhetoric could easily tend to look more like a skill (*techne*) rather than an art (*artes*). This impression was reinforced by the goal of rhetoric. Cicero famously described the three aims or goals of rhetoric as 'to teach, to delight, and to move [or persuade]' (docere/probare, delectare/conciliare, mouere/flectere),[15] and related them to the three modes or styles of rhetorical speech, the plain, the middle and the grand.[16] Classical culture tended to view this list as an ascending scale: the primary aim of rhetoric was not only to teach, or even to delight and please an audience, but, above all, to move and persuade them so that they were brought to accept and to act upon what they heard. The practice of rhetoric, whether in the law court (forensic rhetoric),[17] the forum (political/deliberative rhetoric), or on public, ceremonial occasions (epideictic)[18] was therefore primarily aimed at moving or persuading the hearer, by impressing the words which were spoken upon their hearts, minds, and souls.

HEARER RESPONSE THEORY

If we are to appreciate what this meant for the hearer in classical and early Christian culture, we need techniques and tools rather different from those of reader–response theorists, and must consider what an analysis guided by audience/hearer response might look like. This is not as difficult as it might, at first, seem, however, for we are immeasurably assisted by the classical rhetorical textbooks themselves, which invariably analyse the various techniques and figures of rhetoric in direct relation to their intended effect upon their hearers. From what we have already established, we should not be

---

[15] *De Oratore*, 27.115 (Loeb, 280–1). Kennedy (1980), 35 n. 40, describes this triad as 'the central concept of Cicero's rhetorical theory'. Cf. *Brutus*, 49.185 (Loeb, 156–9).

[16] Quintilian, *Institutio Oratoria*, 12.10. 58–9 (Loeb, 312–13).

[17] As described in Aristotle's *Rhetoric* and Cicero's *De Inuentione* and the *Rhetorica ad Herennium*.

[18] For the three forms, see Aristotle, *Rhetoric*, 1358b 1–13 (Loeb, 32–5). *Epideictic*—a rhetoric of praise or blame—was often used in panegyrical orations to extol a particular person and to move the audience (and speaker) to admire and emulate them.

surprised to find that this is most often done, not in terms of how to teach a particular fact or truth, but how to present it so that it arouses the emotions and passions of the hearer and thereby moves or persuades them to act upon it.

It was rhetorical figures which formed the backbone of the study and practice of the art of rhetoric, and it is these which we find enumerated, illustrated (often by examples from previous great speeches), and discussed, in almost all the rhetorical textbooks. The descriptions are often highly involved and technical, but their aim was practical: to enable the speaker to sound as natural and uncontrived as possible; to convey emotions so vividly and directly, with so much lifelikeness and force, that they thereby inspired and effected the same emotions in their audience. They therefore give us an invaluable insight into the 'hearer response' theories that made speaking effective. Their goal, as Longinus, in his treatise *On Sublimity* puts it,[19] was to enable the speaker 'to run away with his audience' (16.2), to stir them to compassionate, empathetic identification with the emotion he conveyed, so that they shared it, were moved by it, and were irresistibly overcome by it, unaware that it had been effected by rhetorical artifice (17.1–2). Like Longinus, who acknowledges that the task of enumerating all the rhetorical figures would be 'a vast, or rather infinite labour' (16.1) we might simply take a few examples as illustrations.

Rhetorical questions and answers, or *anthypophora*, are a straightforward example. Longinus cites a passage from Demosthenes (*Philippics*, 1.4; 4.4), in which urgent questions are piled up one after the other concerning Philip of Macedon's conquest of Greece: 'Or—tell me—do you want to go round asking one another "Is there any news?"? What could be hotter news than that a Macedonian is conquering Greece? "Is Philip dead?" "No, but he's ill." What difference does it make to you? If anything happens to him, you will soon create another Philip . . .', on which he comments:

> Put in the straightforward form, this would have been quite insignificant; as it is, the impassioned rapidity of the question and answer and the device of self-objection have made the remark, in virtue of its figurative form, not only more sublime but also more credible. For emotion carries us away more easily when it seems to be generated by the occasion rather than deliberately assumed by the speaker, and the self-directed question and its answer represent precisely this momentary quality of emotion. Just as people who are unexpectedly plied with questions become annoyed and reply to the point with vigour and exact truth, so the figure of question and answer arrests the hearer and cheats him into believing that all the points were raised and are being put into words on the spur of the moment. (18. 1–2)

---

[19] Russell and Winterbottom (1972), 143–87.

Longinus also offers the example of *asyndeton* (the absence of connectives) where 'words tumble out without connection, in a kind of stream, almost getting ahead of the speaker'; of *anaphora* (initial repetition), *ekphrasis* (vivid description), and *epanaphora* (intensive repetition). By combining them together in a legal defence, the orator deploying these figures seems to be doing exactly what a bully does in subduing his victim—'hitting the jury in the mind with blow after blow. Then he comes down with a fresh onslaught, like a sudden squall' (19.1–20.3). *Polysyndeton* (the addition of conjunctions), on the other hand, has the opposite effect: 'the urgent and harsh character of emotion loses its sting and becomes a spent fire as you level it down to smoothness by the conjunctions . . . it loses the free abandon of its movement and the sense of being, as it were, catapulted out' (21.1).

Developing the idea that rhetoric succeeds best when it seems most lifelike and natural—when, as he puts it, 'art . . . looks like nature' (22.1)—Longinus gives the example of *hyperbaton*, where words or thoughts are arranged by the speaker in a sequence which seems disordered and disarranged, in order to convey emotional disturbance, a sense of immediacy, or force of circumstance. He observes that

> People who in real life feel anger, fear, or indignation, or are distracted by jealousy or some other emotion (it is impossible to say how many emotions there are; they are without number), often put one thing forward and then rush off to another, irrationally inserting some remark, and then hark back again to their first point. They seem to be blown this way and that by their excitement, as if by a veering wind. They inflict innumerable variations on the expression, the thought and the natural sequence. (22.1)

Hyperbata (like the playing of a consummate jazz player) also give a sense of immediacy in their transpositions, improvisations, and extemporizations. Reflecting on Demosthenes' use of this figure, Longinus observes,

> His transpositions produce not only a great sense of urgency but the appearance of extemporization, as he drags his hearers with him into the hazards of his long hyperbata. He often holds in suspense the meaning which he set out to convey and, introducing one extraneous item after another in an alien and unusual place before getting to the main point, throws the hearer into a panic lest the sentence collapse altogether, and forces him in his excitement to share the speaker's peril, before, at long last and beyond all expectation, appositely paying off at the end the long due conclusion; the very audacity and hazardousness of the hyperbata add to the astounding effect. (22.3–4)

Simpler techniques which Longinus considers include changing the case, tense, person, number, or gender of a word. For example, using the present tense gives a great sense of immediacy (25.1); using the plural might emphasize the gravity or grandeur of something (23.1–4); an imaginary second person serves to invite the hearer to imagine themselves in the midst of whatever is being described (26.1); words directed to an individual (26.3), or direct speech, make the hearer more involved, attentive, and excited (27.1).

Finally, Longinus observes that *periphrasis*, or, as he puts it, 'the lyricising of bare prose' can be highly effective in engaging the hearer (if used in moderation!): 'as in music the melody is made sweeter by what is called the accompaniment, so periphrasis is often heard in concert with the plain words and enhances them with a new resonance' (28.1). Most important, however, is the choice of the *right* words: 'correct and magnificent words'. 'This is something,' Longinus observes, 'which all orators and other writers cultivate intensely. It makes grandeur, beauty, old world charm, weight, force, strength, and a kind of lustre bloom upon our words as upon beautiful statues; it gives things life and makes them speak... beautiful words are the light that illuminates thought' (30.1).[20] It clearly requires a rhetor to write about rhetoric!![21]

The outward sign of the inward effect which the speaker had upon the emotions and feelings of the hearer is, of course, the effecting of a response. Rhetoric depended on an audience, and speaking and hearing were mutually interdependent. The accomplished rhetor was the one who could see and hear the success of his speaking in the audience's reaction. We are not accustomed to the sort of audience interaction which Cicero describes in the following description of a model speaker, but it was clearly the norm in antiquity: 'When the speaker rises the whole throng will give a sign for silence, then expressions of assent, frequent applause; laughter when he wills or, if he wills, tears; so that a mere passer-by observing from a distance, though quite ignorant of the case in question, will recognize that he is succeeding and that a Roscius is on the stage.'[22] The audience could, as the saying goes, 'become like putty in the hands' of a trained rhetor.

Despite the fact that the art of speaking was so central a feature of classical culture it was not without its critics. What we have just seen of its emphasis on delight (*delectare*) and persuasion (*mouere*) rather than teaching (*docere*); on the affective rather than the rational; the aesthetic rather than the moral, did little to recommend it to those who devoted their lives to the search for wisdom, or *philosophia*, and who believed that reason and ethics should determine human conduct, not an appeal to the senses or emotional states and feelings. Cicero might well have been right when he refers to how the hearer is 'affected by something resembling a mental impulse or emotion, rather than by judgement or deliberation. For men decide far more problems

---

[20] In addition to the figures mentioned by Longinus, we might add: *aposiopesis*—breaking off in mid-sentence; *apostrophe*—exclamation or appeal to others; *hyperbole*—overstatement.

[21] We will leave what Longinus has to say about genius (or natural, rather than artistic or contrived, eloquence) until Chapter 7.

[22] Cicero, *Brutus*, 84.290 (Loeb, 252–3), cited by Vickers (1989), 37.

by hate, or love, or lust, or rage, or sorrow, or joy, or hope, or fear, or illusion, or some other inward emotion, than by reality, or authority, or any legal standard, or judicial precedent or statute',[23] but this would do little to recommend rhetoric to those who valued reason, authority, and law over against impulse, irrational feeling, and illusion. It could appear that the art of rhetoric was ethically neutral and wholly arbitrary; that the rhetor could sway his audience to whatever course of action he desired, simply by verbal artifice and emotional display; that rhetoric was essentially art for art's sake; a pleasing performance that could all too easily tend to superficiality, excess, and pride. The power of rhetoric to pierce the soul, imprint itself upon the mind and move the heart, was undisputed, but it might just as easily wound, disfigure, and mislead the soul, as heal, inform, and inspire it to virtue. The tension between philosophy and rhetoric, and the long history of debates concerning their relation and relative merits, was an inevitable one, and forms the background for a great deal of the literature we now have on rhetorical theory and practice. Such debates are clearly part of the wider debate, which we will examine in the final chapter of this book, on the role of the intellect or the bodily senses in apprehending truth.

One of ways in which this tension was often expressed was in terms of the common rhetorical distinction between *res* (reality or truth) and *uerba* (words or signs):[24] critics observed that whilst rhetors concerned themselves with mere words and signs (*uerba*; *signa*), the philosopher was concerned with the reality and truth (*res*) to which words, at best, merely pointed; that whilst the rhetor was preoccupied with the tongue (*lingua*), the philosopher spoke to the brain (*cor*); that whilst the rhetor's concern was finding the means to convey the truth (*modus proferendi*), the philosopher's was the manner of discovering it (*modus inueniendi*). Philosophy had to do with knowledge (*episteme*) of eternal, immutable realities; rhetoric had to do with opinion (*doxa*) expressed in temporal, mutable words which came and went like the wind.[25]

This is not, of course, to say that the philosophers did not use rhetoric to undermine, refute, and reject it, or that rhetors were not often also philosophers, who were trained in the liberal arts and who deployed them in the service of their speech! The generalizations we have just made have a degree of truth, but they are in fact just as partial, arbitrary, and ambivalent as most of

---

[23] Cicero, *De Oratore*, 2.42.178 (Loeb, 324–5). Vickers (1989), 77, also cites Quintilian, who likewise emphasized the primacy of appeal to the emotions in rhetoric: 'it is in its power over the emotions that the life and soul of oratory is to be found' (*Institutio Oratoria*, 6.2.7 (Loeb, 48–9)).

[24] Quintilian, *Instituto Oratoria*, 3.5.1 (Loeb, 36–7).

[25] These comments are based on Vickers (1989), ch. 3. Matters were made worse by what has been labelled the 'Second Sophistic'—a flowery, overblown style of rhetoric in which substance was very much subsumed by style, content by form, practical utility by performance, so that the art of rhetoric became very much a matter of 'art for the sake of art'. See Dunn (2004), 27, for reflections on its appearance.

the criticisms which were levelled at rhetoric. The truth is to be found, as usual, in a more moderate middle ground, and especially among those who, like Cicero, sought to defend the use and practice of rhetoric and to find common ground between the arts of rhetoric and philosophy, just as we have seen Christianity finding a role for sense perception in relation to the pursuit of eternal, immutable, truth. It is to their arguments that we should turn.

A DEFENCE OF SPEAKING AND HEARING

As we have seen, the study and practice of rhetoric had emerged, evolved, and found its raison d'être, from the fifth century BC onwards, in preparing individuals for public service. As the most influential works on rhetoric make manifestly clear, it was, by definition, involved in the active life, and was often defended as being a civilizing force, one which effectively established and defended peace, order, and justice throughout the Empire, allowed human beings to realize their true humanity, and which was devoted to the 'common good'.[26]

Far from being ignorant, the rhetor was popularly perceived as the acme of the learned and cultured man, trained in the disciplines,[27] assiduously practising and refining his art,[28] able to discover and present the truth through the art of speech.[29] In short, the rhetor was far from being just a performer: he was a consummate statesman, with a duty to society; a philosopher, who could not only establish the truth (*res*) but communicate it in speech (*uerba*); a physician who could treat the soul with the healing salve of words.[30]

Against the charge that rhetoric was merely contrived and could be deployed in the service of promoting and persuading of good and evil alike, it was frequently argued that eloquent speech was not so much an acquired art as a natural accompaniment of wisdom; that it arose naturally and instinctively in the person who was speaking the truth; that it had its own force, independent of rules or techniques, and was at its best an inspiration which came to its human speakers, rather than one they invented themselves.[31] And

---

[26] Vickers (1989), 8–12, 156–9, 171. For a traditional defence of rhetoric, see Tacitus, *Dialogue on Orators*, 5 (Russell and Winterbottom, 113).

[27] Tacitus, *Dialogue on Orators*, 31–2 (Russell and Winterbottom, 133) laments the demise of orators of old, who were accomplished in all the disciplines.

[28] Quintilian, *Instituto Oratoria*, on the formation and training of the rhetor and the need for constant practice.

[29] Isocrates, *Antidosis*, 253–7, in Vickers (1989), 156: 'none of the things which are done with intelligence take place without the help of speech'.

[30] On classical, philosophical 'psychagogic' rhetoric, see Walker (2000); Maxwell (2006), 13–30; Kolbet (2010), 19–61. This is considered further in Chapter 5.

[31] E.g. Tacitus, *Dialogue on Orators*, 8 (Russell and Winterbottom, 115).

against the common charge that rhetoric was simply preoccupied with aesthetics—with contrived artistry in order to entertain, delight, please, and flatter an audience—the crucial role of delight (*delectare*), as the second element of Cicero's three aims of rhetoric, needs to be remembered. As O'Donnell puts it: 'Between *probare* (the establishment of a fact) and *flectere* (stirring the audience to act), *delectare* is the crucial moment of motivation.'[32] Delight could have a key role to play in motivating an audience to accept, and to act upon, the true and the good.

It seems that the key factor was not the nature of rhetoric itself; both its proponents and its detractors acknowledged its enormous power upon its hearers. The real question was how, and to what ends, this power should be used in relation to the hearer. This is the question which was to so exercise the fathers of the Church.

CHRISTIAN SPEAKING AND HEARING

That we can now read the work of individual early Christian writers is testimony to the fact that these authors were educated; they belonged to that small, elite minority who, as we noted above, had enjoyed the privilege of a Greco-Roman training in the liberal arts, and, in most cases, to the even smaller minority who had advanced to the stage at which they were proficient in the art of rhetoric and were able to utilize it before an audience of present listeners, or absent, attentive readers. Cyprian, Arnobius, Lactantius, Augustine, Chrysostom, Basil of Caesarea, Gregory of Nyssa . . . were all, formerly, rhetors or teachers of rhetoric; Tertullian was a professional lawyer; Ambrose a provincial governor, before they became Christians.

There were no Christian schools to rival, or even offer an alternative to, secular, pagan education. This means that all the Christian authors we are now able to read were obliged, without exception, to assimilate and articulate their Christian faith from within a very particular context: they necessarily lived out their Christian lives as privileged, educated members of the Greco-Roman aristocracy, whether they liked it or not. Their minds, habits, attitudes, and instinctive ways of thinking and speaking had been shaped by their educational formation, and this was not something they could simply slough off like a snake's skin. As we shall see, these dual cultures—Greco-Roman and Christian—were not always easy to harmonize, and each Christian writer had to make his own attempt to resolve the potential dissonances. What their hearers and readers therefore heard were a multitude of variations on the common theme of

---

[32] O'Donnell (1992), II, 131.

Christianity and Greco-Roman culture. Some speakers achieved a wonderfully balanced two-part fugue, in which the individual voices of the two cultures remained quite distinct within a complex, exquisitely balanced counterpoint. Others attempted to wholly excise what they regarded as a dissonant and discordant voice, and to achieve a purely Christian solo line. Still others harmonized the two voices with such care and expertise that they were able to sound as one, the two supporting and enhancing each other so that they became virtually indistinguishable. Whatever the final sound, the materials which had been used to create it were always the same: Christian faith, tradition, and culture and Greco-Roman education, tradition, and culture. These provided, as it were, the notation, the key signatures, and models for composition. They were what the audience anticipated and expected, and allowed for informed and fruitful—or what we have called, literate—listening.

If we do not pay attention to the rhetorical culture we have outlined above, we will fail to appreciate why the fathers wrote and spoke in the way did; why their style is so distinctive and yet so easily identifiable as that of an educated person of their day; what their hearers expected of them; how their hearers were able to hear them effectively. Their modes of address, their methods of exegesis, their techniques for teaching, engaging, and moving their hearers, the sheer audience-orientated, and, above all, hearer-orientated nature of their work, are all rooted in this common culture. By writing and speaking in this way they met with listeners already attuned to hear and receive what they had to say, even if the content was radically new. Their manner of address was largely a matter of what we have referred to as a shared 'auditory culture'; of tacit, taken-for-granted conventions and practices of speaking and hearing, which then facilitated the communication, and, above all, as we shall see in the following chapters, the reception, of Christian teaching and faith. Even those fathers who sought to eradicate any taint of Greco-Roman culture—of pagan culture and superstition, as they saw it—from Christianity, did so by instinctively, and presumably unselfconsciously, drawing upon it. We frequently find them rhetorically undermining and attacking rhetoric.[33]

In his work on early Christian texts, Gamble contrasts 'literary criticism' and 'rhetorical criticism' in patristic scholarship. Though similar to literary criticism, Gamble observes that rhetorical criticism 'is distinguished by its interest in both the modes of persuasive argumentation and the functions of rhetoric under social circumstances'. It 'aims to identify the units, techniques, style, and structures of large blocks of argumentative discourse, and indeed of entire documents, and to comprehend the presuppositions and functions of their use in the specific historical and social contexts in which they

---

[33] See discussion in Oberhelman (1991), 121–6.

were deployed'.[34] I would suggest that for 'rhetorical criticism' we could equally well read 'auditory criticism' in this context, thereby emphasizing the often overlooked role of the hearer in rhetorical practice. Auditory criticism shares with rhetorical criticism the attempt to analyse how a text is arranged and presented in order to communicate with a hearer, to facilitate their understanding and effect their response in particular circumstances. Indeed, the oral/auditory element is perhaps the biggest single difference which sets rhetorical criticism apart from traditional literary criticism: the one is concerned with appreciating how a text was composed and structured in order to be heard; the other with analysing a piece of literature in its own terms, independent of a hypothetical reader or listener. Rhetorical (or auditory) criticism can only be understood in terms of its relation to another; literary criticism can stand alone. The fact that almost all classical literature, including patristic literature, is also rhetorical, in the sense that it was probably composed by dictation to a scribe, intended for oral delivery, read by reading it aloud, and intended for a listener, means that 'rhetorical' or 'auditory' criticism is indeed the most appropriate way for the scholar to engage with these texts. Responsible literary criticism in antiquity became, as we saw in the case of Longinus earlier in this chapter, essentially an exercise in rhetorical/auditory criticism.

Besides this, we have seen that in antiquity 'rhetorical' or 'auditory criticism' was nothing new. It is not a construct of modern scholars, foisted on ancient texts in order to accommodate them to whatever critical approach is currently in vogue, but was a well-developed art in which all the fathers had been trained, and which they practised in their writing and speaking in an (almost) unselfconscious way. The attempt of modern scholarship to engage in this sort of criticism—one so foreign to it in many ways—is therefore really no more than an attempt to read the fathers in their own terms.

THE EARLY CHRISTIAN SPEAKER

The effect of the fathers' words on their audiences was significantly helped by the status which they had acquired, and the respect, authority, and power they commanded, in their changed social and historical context. Most obviously, they were literate, and, as Gamble has observed, 'in a community in which texts had a constitutive importance and only a few persons were literate, it was inevitable that those who were able to explicate texts would acquire authority for that reason alone'.[35] But this was not the only reason for their authority: as

[34] Gamble (1995), 35, and see footnote 28 for examples of this sort of criticism in NT scholarship.
[35] Gamble (1995), 9–10.

we have seen, literacy usually accompanied social standing; it was the elite who were educated for public service, and Christian bishops, a good number of whom had been former rhetors, lawyers, or governors, became, as it were, the new educated aristocracy. As Peter Brown comments, 'Having made the passage, the Christianised aristocracy brought the literary culture with it as naturally as it brought the traditional values and perquisites of family and class.'[36] Christian bishops found themselves, like the philosophers, rhetors, judges, and politicians they had been, the holders of tremendous prestige, status, and power. They had intellectual and social standing, powers of legal arbitration, influence (albeit limited) in Roman government, and their voices—articulate, learned, cultivated, and persuasive—could not be ignored. In fact, they stood in a uniquely powerful position: one foot firmly rooted in the past, in classical culture, education, and the social prestige and status it endowed; the other foot placed firmly in the new Christian present, in Christian culture, tradition, and the social prestige and status it increasingly lent to its members now that the emperor himself was Christian. They spoke with confidence (*parrhesia*), in a manner that was expected of those who imparted ultimate insights into wisdom, or who held positions of authority. They therefore commanded their audiences' attention and respect, even though what they had to say was entirely new and revolutionary. The presuppositions and attuned ears of the fathers' audiences, the fathers' own accomplished speech, and the authority which their particular social and historical context lent their words, combined to create a potent and persuasive force before which their hearers, like those swept off their feet by the rolling torrents of Demosthenes' rhetoric, would find it difficult not to yield.[37]

All the fathers, insofar as they were educated and could write, were trained in the art of addressing what they had to say to an audience of listeners. Earlier on in this chapter we caught a glimpse of how ambivalent this cultural heritage could be, in the tensions which arose between the rhetor and the philosopher: between the person actively involved in public service, speaking to inform, delight, and persuade his listeners of whatever case he had to promote—or worse—merely to entertain and flatter them—and the contemplative, withdrawn from the world, seeking truth and wisdom by intellectual and moral purification, suspicious of the arbitrary, potentially immoral pleasures of mere words. The fathers whom we now read found themselves on both sides of this divide, and were forced to reconcile within their own lives, actions, and words the antitheses and ambivalences which this dual identity necessarily incurred. They were increasingly involved in the life of the Empire as prominent local figures, legal arbitrators, and representatives of the Church to the Roman authorities. As bishops they played a highly public role in administration of

---

[36] Brown (1992), 177.
[37] Brown (1992) on the role of bishops in the Christian Empire.

the money and property which the Church could now legally own, its charitable institutions and care for the poor and needy, its daily services, and, above all, in preaching, teaching, baptizing, ordaining, and protecting its life and faith from heretical or schismatic threats. Indeed, it is difficult to imagine a more onerous or demanding job, or one more involved with worldly business and distractions, than that of a bishop in the fourth/fifth centuries. In the midst of all these demands the bishop also sought (or more accurately, fought) to find time to withdraw, to pray, to contemplate, to reflect upon the truths of the faith, to read and write. In doing so, the fathers seem to have done what few classical philosophers or rhetors had done before them, to bring together the two vocations within their own person: they not only sought to discover, and to live according to, the truth, but sought to communicate it to others and to present it to them in such a way that they were moved and persuaded to understand, believe, and act upon it. Indeed, they were living embodiments of the generally accepted truth that rhetoric could only truly be effective in informing and persuading a listener if it was spoken by someone who himself embodied what he taught,[38] and whose words were rooted in the true, the good, and the beautiful, rather than arbitrary persuasion and flattery. If there was a tension between the two vocations of the philosopher and the rhetor— the man of the intellect and the man of the senses—in Christianity it was more often than not a tension which arose within one individual, rather than between two different people or roles. How difficult this attempt to hold together the intellect and the senses, the sacred and secular, the holy and the profane, devotion and distraction, could prove to be is seen quite clearly in the conflicted career of someone such as Gregory Nazianzen.[39] To what extent it was actually possible can be seen in the delicate balancing act achieved by the likes of Chrysostom or Augustine. As we shall see, what is clear is that the corporeal, temporal, and mutable context of human life in the world, and of human communication through the senses, following the Fall, was not simply avoided and shunned, but accepted and exploited as the unavoidable context in and through which human beings must communicate with each other and with God—especially through speaking and listening. The monk-bishop was a figure which first emerged during this period, and the distinctive social and historical circumstances in which this was possible provide the context in which we must attempt to discover what they thought about their own use of rhetoric in addressing their various audiences, and how their words were heard and received by those to whom they ministered.

The precarious balance between these two worlds and modes of living is one that preoccupied all the fathers. The sort of questions which exercised them

---

[38] A commonplace in classical rhetorical works and frequently echoed by the fathers, e.g. Augustine, *On Christian Doctrine*, 4.27.59; 29.61 (Robertson, 164, 166).
[39] Radcliffe Reuther (1969).

were along the lines of: How was the truth first to be discovered, and then how could and should it be communicated? How did Christian culture relate to pagan, secular culture? To what extent was it acceptable and appropriate to use the methods, techniques, and practices of the philosopher, the grammarian, and the rhetor? These are, of course, precisely the questions which we see being addressed by Augustine of Hippo in his work devoted to the subject of Christian teaching and learning: *On Christian Doctrine.*

Modus inveniendi: training literate listeners

In the prologue with which he felt it necessary to preface *On Christian Doctrine* Augustine is at pains to make clear that all teaching and learning is due to God's gift. It is something that we receive from God and then share with others, rather than something which comes from ourselves. Works such as his own, which aim to advise on how to discover the truth in Scripture, and then how to communicate it, are nevertheless necessary, he argues, even though some have had the truth directly revealed to them. Indeed, it is precisely because of this that it was written: the truth must be taught, communicated, and shared by those who have received it, rather than simply proudly possessed: 'For charity itself, which holds men together in a knot of unity, would not have a means of infusing and almost mixing them together if men could teach nothing to men.'[40] The life of the philosopher, as it were, is therefore not a solitary quest, but a social one: he is compelled to become a grammarian and rhetor, enabling others to discover, understand, and act upon the truth. As Augustine puts it in relation to reading and listening: 'He who reads to others pronounces the words he recognizes; he who teaches reading does so that others may also read; but both make known what they received. In the same way, he who explains to listeners what he understands in the Scriptures is like a reader who pronounces the words he knows, but he who teaches how the Scriptures are to be understood is like a teacher who advises how the words are to be read. Just as a man who knows how to read will not need another reader from whom he may hear what is written when he finds a book, he who receives the precepts we wish to teach will not need another to reveal those things which need explaining when he finds any obscurity in books, since he has certain rules like those used in reading in his understanding.'[41] What Augustine is therefore aiming at is to train Christians to become literate listeners; able to hear and 'read' the faith as instinctively as someone who has been taught how to read a book they have taken up. In this way, they will be able to take up the Scriptures, or hear them, and 'by following certain traces . . . may come to

[40] Prologue 6 (Robertson, 6).   [41] Prologue 9 (Robertson, 7).

the hidden sense without any error'.[42] What understanding he had received from God he imparts to his readers and hearers so that they too might be in a position to discover it and share it with him—to become, like him, a literate listener. He is thus not telling them what to understand, but how to come to understanding themselves; the understanding is not something he gives and his hearers receive, but something that is given by God which they both share: they are fellow listeners. 'For no one should consider anything his own, except perhaps a lie, since all truth is from Him who said, "I am the truth". For what have we which we have not received? And if we have received, why do we glory as if we had not received it.'[43]

What are the 'certain rules' which make this common listening—the *modus inveniendi*—[44] possible?

In book one Augustine proceeds in exactly the same way as Gregory of Nyssa in *On the Inscriptions of the Psalms*—by raising the question of ultimate ends, or happiness. He establishes that nothing is to be ultimately enjoyed or taken as an end in itself but God; that everything created, corporeal, temporal, and mutable is but a sign or pointer to its eternal, immutable Creator, the Trinity. The classical rhetorical distinction which we have already considered, between *signa* and *res*, serves Augustine well in this context: Scripture is a sign (*signum*) whose meaning, end, and truth (*res*) can be found only in God. The 'rule' Augustine identifies in order to summarize this conviction is the double commandment of love of God and love and neighbour: any meaning that we find in Scripture which agrees with this commandment is a legitimate one; any meaning that diverges from it is unacceptable and untrue. In a sense, he is summarizing the faith, finding a 'rule of thumb' which allows the reader or hearer to be a literate listener: to judge intuitively, implicitly, and without any hesitation whether a particular reading is acceptable or not. This is the general key signature, as it were, for the text of Scripture, which ensures that it remains harmonious, and which allows all its readers and hearers, however educated and accomplished, or illiterate and uninformed, to hear its true meaning.

But what of the details? How should Christian exegetes go about interpreting the 'signs' of Scripture—the corporeal medium which communicates God's inspired message or 'truth'—and how far is it legitimate for them to use the tools ready to hand—the practices, techniques, and disciplines which were second nature for anyone educated in the liberal arts? Augustine's rule of thumb is that anything that is helpful in interpreting the Scriptures might legitimately be taken over from pagan culture and practice for Christian use—

---

[42] Prologue 9 (Robertson, 7).

[43] Prologue 8 (Robertson, 6–7), quoting John 14:6 and 1 Cor. 4:7.

[44] Augustine clearly has the two stages of classical reading in mind at the very beginning of the work when he observes: 'There are two things necessary to the treatment of the Scriptures: a way of discovering those things which are to be understood, and a way of teaching what we have learned. We shall speak first of discovery and second of teaching' (1.1.1) (Robertson, 7).

just as the Israelites, in plundering the Egyptians, were simply taking back what was rightfully theirs.[45] This is why Scripture becomes the paradigm or rule of what is acceptable and useful in pagan culture, and what is to be rejected as hostile or useless. For, unlike pagan tradition or superstition, Scripture is not based on human invention or institution, but is *given* by God. It therefore embodies/incarnates divine truth; it contains the *res* or truths of the faith, not just *signa*. Like the words of Plato's pagan poet, it is the inspired word of God.

But although Scripture is inspired and embodies divine truth it is still difficult to interpret. In book 3 Augustine continues to deal with what he describes as 'difficult or ambiguous' signs. At the beginning of this chapter we asked why God would use such rough and ready material to communicate his truth, and suggested that the answer lies in the disjunction between medium and message: the fact that the truth is communicated through signs, through human language, stories, figures, and images, which are the product of social and cultural convention, means that it is rarely on or near the surface, but must be sought out in and through them. Scripture's signs must be appreciated for what they are—inconclusive, open-ended, opaque, elusive, and all too human, but also authoritative, definitive, and unique, containing within themselves divine truth. It is the task of the exegete, and, most especially, of the preacher, to elucidate these signs and communicate their truth to their listeners. Contrary to theories of a fourth-century 'corporeal turn', the truth had always been communicated to the senses through corporeal images and signs which conveyed divine presence.

Modus proferendi: speaking for Christian listeners

The central and determinative role of reading, hearing, and listening to Scripture in the formation of Christian identity, culture, and practice cannot, therefore, be overestimated. This is presumably why *De Doctrina Christiana* does not end with book three and its consideration of how to go about interpreting the difficult or ambiguous signs of Scripture (*modus inueniendi*), but continues with a further book, which attempts to deal with how the exegete should go about communicating their truth, in teaching and preaching, to a listening audience (*modus proferendi*). It was in this context that all the fathers began to feel most acutely the ambiguity of their classical education, and the rules, conventions, habits, and practices it had instilled within them, and which they applied unselfconsciously in other contexts. When they

---

[45] 2.40.60–1 (Robertson, 75–6). Origen, *Letter to Gregory*, 1–2 (Trigg, 210–11); Gregory of Nyssa, *Life of Moses*, 2.115–116 (CWS, 81). Augustine cites the examples of Cyprian, Lactantius, Victorinus, Optatus, and Hilary, in the West, who have all done this (2.40.61) (Robertson, 76).

turned to reading Scripture, and especially when they attempted to preach on Scripture, things became rather more difficult. There were two main reasons: first of all, Scripture was most definitely not a classical text: it lacked the polish, the observance of rules of style, the studied rhetorical artifice, the sheer persuasive elegance and refinement to which they had become accustomed in their study of the Greek or Latin classics. For the Latin fathers especially, who had to rely on rather uneven, not to say rough and ready, translations, it came as a rude shock to realize that the inspired, authoritative word of God, the truths of their faith, were communicated in such crude, vulgar, second-rate prose; that it was the work of fishermen not scholars; that it offended against almost every rule of accepted style and expression. It failed miserably to even attempt to do what was expected of an author in teaching or expressing any truth: to delight and persuade the hearer and reader so that they might welcome, and more readily accept and act upon it. The attempt to make Scripture palatable for their listeners, who were habituated to classical rhetoric, was as much a case of personal concern and scruple for the fathers faced with this task, as it was of addressing others.[46]

The fathers inevitably reacted to this stumbling block—this radical disjunction between medium and message—in different ways. How could they re-educate their own cultured sensibilities, their own finely attuned ears, so that they were not offended when Scripture was heard and read aloud? How could they effect this re-education for their hearers? The first step was to be aware of the problem and of the 'clash of sensibilities' which Scripture provoked. The jarring vulgarity of Scripture, when heard by classically trained ears—or simply by those attuned and habituated to hearing classically trained speakers—could not simply be ignored. Was Scripture thereby undermined and diminished? Were the expectations and practices of classical culture to be questioned and re-evaluated? Were they inappropriate for Scripture? If so, why and how? If not, could Scripture somehow be retrieved and shown to measure up to its standards? These were critical questions for both the teacher and his listeners, and touched on the very nature of the culture that they tacitly shared and which made effective communication possible.

We see Augustine uneasily, and rather self-consciously, attempting to come to terms with some of these questions and dilemmas in book four of *De Doctrina Christiana*.[47] He treads a precarious tightrope, aware that he cannot avoid the issue, but conscious that there are no easy or straightforward answers. We therefore find him offering a number of different, sometimes rather contradictory, observations or arguments. Some are tentative, others are more assured and authoritative. They all, in one way or another, concern

---

[46] For differences in attitude to classical culture in East and West, see Kaster (1988), 74–6; Harrison (2004), 53–4.

[47] Harrison (2000).

the relation between classical rhetorical theory and practice, the text of Scripture, the task of the preacher, and the role of the listener. The generally accepted status of classical theory is, significantly, taken as a given: Augustine rehearses the familiar Ciceronian description of the three styles of rhetoric—the subdued, the moderate, and the grand—and the three aims of the speaker—to teach, to delight, and to persuade/move. He refers to particular rhetorical techniques, to stylistic commonplaces, to the way in which they are anticipated by the hearer or reader, affect them, and thereby effect the speaker's goal. At each stage he reconsiders, re-evaluates, and reorders classical theory and practice in relation to the Christian Scriptures and preaching upon them, according to his unquestioned conviction that Scripture contains the truths (*res*) of the faith, and is the authoritative word of God. He makes careful concessions, rehearses rather forced arguments, but his belief in Scripture's authority never wavers. In the process, the norms, habits, and conventions of classical culture undergo a profound re-evaluation, and Scripture emerges not as a work hostile or alien to it, but as a paradigm for clear, cogent, honest, and wise communication of the truth. Its eloquence is not overlooked, but rather artificially (somewhat farcically) demonstrated in relation to passages from Paul and Amos. Indeed, these passages read more like the former rhetor's somewhat embarrassed attempt to reconcile himself (and other educated minds) to Scripture, by demonstrating its rhetorical pedigree, than a convincing proof.[48]

What is more important is Augustine's characteristically Christian insistence that rhetorical speech does not require the contrivance of rhetorical rules, but naturally, spontaneously, and in a totally unselfconscious manner, accompanies wisdom (4.6.10; 4.7.21; 4.20.42); that it is acquired in a similarly uncontrived and disingenuous manner through hearing, writing, dictating, and reading Christian literature (4.5.7).[49] These comments endorse our earlier observations on the way in which Christian culture was formed, and the way the illiterate majority of Christians were initiated into, and imbibed, it, through hearing—through dictation, voiced reading, singing, and preaching upon the Scriptures. Augustine seems to want to argue here that Christian eloquence is therefore a matter of natural acquisition, through exposure to, and participation in, the oral communication of its truth, rather than a matter of rules. It is analogous to the way in which a child learns to speak—not by learning rules but by hearing and practice (and to speak correctly, by growing up among people who speak grammatically) (4.3.5). In a similar vein, he

[48] Though other fathers, too, attempted to defend Scripture as a work of literature, comparable to the classics. Fredouille (1985), 32, refers to Ambrose *ep.* 8.1—'Ambroise...note que la beauté litteraire de la Bible est une beauté inspireé: mieux encore, l'art des écrivains bibliques est, à ses yeux, la source et le fondement de toute écriture artistique.'

[49] See Graumann (1997) for similar ideas in Ambrose, who talks about the inherent *gratia* or grace and beauty of Scripture and Christian preaching on it, which derives from its inspiration, rather than the application of any rhetorical rules.

insists that clarity and a simple, subdued style are generally to be preferred to the excesses of the temperate or grand style;[50] that teaching is given priority over delight or persuasion; that truth or the meaning (*res*) of what is said matters more than the words (*uerba*) in which it is expressed. Augustine therefore observes of the Christian preacher: 'In his speech itself he should prefer to please more with the things said than with the words used to speak them; nor should he think that anything may be said better than that which is said truthfully; nor should the teacher serve the words, but the words the teacher' (4.28.61). In short, just as book 2 surveyed the whole of classical culture in relation to Christian culture based upon Scripture, so in book 4 the aims and values of classical rhetoric are judged against the aims and values of Christian preaching based upon Scripture, and are evaluated as useful or dangerous, and taken over or repudiated, accordingly. What is notable is that while Augustine, along with all of the fathers, understandably stresses the importance of clarity and simplicity in expressing the truth, and gives priority to the aim of teaching, he still allows a significant role for delight, the second aim of Cicero's rhetor and the goal of the moderate or temperate style of rhetoric, and also for persuasion, the third aim of rhetoric and the goal of the grand style. But, for Augustine, the preacher should adopt the techniques of these styles only as a means to an end – to inspire delight in, love of, and obedience to, the truth—rather than for the simple end of delight or pleasure in the words alone: 'That which the moderate style urges, that is, that the eloquence itself be pleasing, is not to be taken up for its own sake, but in order that things which may be usefully and virtuously spoken, if they require neither a teaching nor a moving eloquence, may have a knowing and sympathetic audience which sometimes may assent more readily or adhere more tenaciously to that which is said because of the delight aroused by that eloquence . . . Thus we use the ornaments of the moderate style not ostentatiously but prudently, not content with its end that the audience be pleased, but rather using them in such a way that they assist that good which we wish to convey by persuasion.'[51] He therefore effectively rethinks Cicero's definitions, urging that in everything he says, the preacher should aim to inculcate understanding (Cicero's teaching), willingness (Cicero's delight), and obedience (Cicero's persuasion), and to use whatever style, or combination of styles, is necessary to effect these responses in the listener—simple, moderate, or grand. Augustine characteristically adds that often the simple style—with a few natural and unostentatious rhythmic closings (of course)—can delight and excite the listener even more effectively than the other styles: 'it does not come

[50] Though he does allow for the use of the other two styles where appropriate: the temperate to praise the truths of the faith and the grand style to instil their acceptance and action upon them (4.20.39–21.50) (Robertson, 146–58).
[51] 4.25.55 (Robertson, 162). Cf. 26.57 (Robertson, 163–4).

forth armed or adorned but, as it were, nude, and in this way crushes the sinews and muscles of its adversary and overcomes and destroys resisting falsehood with its most powerful members' (4.26.56). In fact, he is aware that the styles and their goals are inseparably interrelated; that in order to achieve delight or persuasion the hearer must first be taught; in order to achieve willingness or obedience, the hearer must first be instructed. Likewise, there can be no persuasion without delight, or obedience without willingness.[52] The styles and techniques of classical rhetoric are there to be deployed by the Christian preacher, but their ends are subtly refocused in terms of inculcating understanding, willingness, and obedience to the truth in the listener. In the end, Augustine wants to conclude that it is the substance of what he says, not his style, that matters; it is *what* is said that pleases, not *how* it is said, for truth has its own beauty and force; it is *res* that matter, not *uerba*: 'In his speech itself he should prefer to please more with the things said than with the words used to speak them; nor should he think that anything may be said better than that which is said truthfully; nor should the teacher serve the words, but the words the teacher.' That this appears as a sort of afterthought, following a whole book devoted to rhetoric, suggests that the latter was not something that could be simply left behind—at least by Augustine.[53] Rather, he seems to be concluding that rhetoric need not be rejected by the Christian preacher, but should always be subservient to the expression of truth rather than an end in itself. In this sense *De Doctrina Christiana* has gone full circle, and the careful distinctions between *res* and *signa*, and use (*uti*) and enjoyment (*frui*) in book one have been applied to exegesis and preaching in a manner which reinforces the conclusion Augustine made there: that what matters—the truth, *res*, or substance of what is said—is God the Trinity, and, above all, love of God and love of neighbour, and any interpretation of Scripture, or any use of rhetorical style in teaching and expounding it, should always have this as its meaning, substance, end, and goal.[54]

Unsurprisingly, Augustine's uncomfortable ambiguity concerning the role and use of classical rhetoric by the Christian preacher was evidently shared by most of the fathers. Like them, his dilemma was not *whether* it should be used—he assumes that and takes it as a given—but *how* it should be adopted in a Christian context. His subsequent confused and embarrassed assessment of the Scriptures according to its standards, his highly self-conscious assessment of its uses and abuses, his careful reassessment of it in relation to the Christian preacher and his listeners, their understanding, wills, and actions, are all characteristic features of the fathers' approach.

---

[52] 4.26.57–58 (Robertson, 163–4).

[53] Or any of the other fathers, who make very much the same observations, whilst continuing to use and value rhetoric themselves. Ellspermann (1949).

[54] Sutherland (1990), 152: 'Words become for him a means instead of an end, the end unattainable without the means, the means empty without the end. And this unity of ends and means is part of that greater unity which is love.'

The same uneasy self-consciousness (and, one senses, mistrust of himself) is found on many occasions in Gregory Nazianzen's sermons. Significantly, he is also aware that his listeners share his unease about too blatantly adopting a rhetorical style, and this acts as a moderating influence on any temptation he might have to excess, or to play to the gallery: he will not only be aware of his own failings, but those in the gallery will be aware of them too! Gregory's sensitivity to his hearer's response is a clear measure of how deep-seated and all-pervasive Christian unease about rhetoric was. It was shared not only by its educated practitioners but by their illiterate and uneducated listeners too. Thus, Gregory frequently—rhetorically—insists that his main concern is not rhetoric but truth, clarity, and simplicity in order encourage virtuous action. In his funeral oration for his sister, Gorgonia, for example, he asserts: 'No place will be given here simply to what delights the ear, even if we should wish to do so; for the listener stands here, like a skilled umpire, between my speech and the truth, giving no praise to words that are undeserved, but demanding what is deserved—and that is only just. So we shall take the truth as our norm, and look to it alone, not regarding any other considerations that might sound attractive to the lowly crowd' (1)... 'We will spurn all attempt to make our language elegant and graceful, since the one we are praising also went un-adorned, and her very lack of ornament was her beauty; we will fulfil our duty of paying her memorial honours, as the most pressing of debts, and at the same time we will try to educate the public to imitate her virtue eagerly, since our most serious concern is to use each of our words and actions to form those entrusted to our care' (2). It is clear that when, elsewhere, Gregory describes for Nectarius the ideal form of letter writing, he has in mind all forms of Christian communication: it should speak to the simple and the educated, being natural, direct, and conversational for the former, but rising above the general level for the latter; it should not wholly reject stylistic features but make as modest and restrained a use of them as a weaver does of purple wool (unless, of course, it wants to highlight them by sending them up in a joke); it should contrive (unselfconsciously) to be as natural and unforced as possible![55]

This humble superiority, unconscious contrivance, deliberated naturalness, and rhetorical rejection of style makes the fathers unsettling reading, but it is the uneasy sense of uncomfortable compromise, of their embarrassed reluc-tance to appear in anything but an educated and learned dress, that gives us an insight into the real ambivalence which both speakers and hearers felt in attending to Christian truth. Despite all of Gregory's protestations, his work (in this case his encomium on Basil) has been described by a recent scholar as, 'probably the masterpiece of sophistic Christian oratory, an extraordinary tour

[55] *Letter* 51 To Nicoboulos (Daley, 177–8).

de force, replete with subtle variations on familiar topics, figures of speech, rhetorical comparisons, reminiscences of Plato, Greek history, and mythology, and an emotional peroration'.[56] No wonder Gregory was self-conscious in this respect, but he was by no means alone. Almost all the fathers rhetorically admonish against excessive use of rhetorical, stylistic features; they emphasize the need for clarity, simplicity, truth, and their desire to instruct their hearers and encourage them to virtue, in preference to overblown, flowery, theatrical language which merely flatters or entertains the listener. Yet they almost all acknowledge—sometimes in theory, and invariably in practice—that, in fact, rhetoric cannot be entirely abandoned in the pursuit of these objectives: that a carefully chosen word, a particular stylistic idiom, a certain rhetorical technique, a pleasing and delightful manner of speech, and apposite allusions, are not without their uses. Indeed, Gregory's poetry, and his considered defence of it in precisely these terms,[57] are a good example of this. In short, the fathers were all aware that although rhetoric most definitely had its uses, they had to self-consciously moderate and reform the habits of their upbringing and culture, the theories and practices of their education, their customary ways of thinking, speaking, and hearing, in order to conform themselves and their hearers to Christian faith, thought, and practice.[58]

It should not, of course, surprise us to find that it was the business of communication—of speaking and listening—that lay at the heart of the transition from paganism to Christianity, for language, more than perhaps any other feature of a culture, is a matter of convention, of general consensus and agreement, and of tacit, habitual practice. It embodies, expresses, and furthers a common understanding and tradition—in the context of both high, intellectual culture, and common, everyday interchanges between human beings. Conversion meant a self-conscious rethinking of the culture to which one belonged, and of its relation to Christian faith, truth, and practice. But just as Christianity did not completely overturn, transform, or replace Greco-Roman society, but rather emerged from within it, and was inevitably shaped by it, in a slow, faltering, but gradual process of mutual accommodation and transformation, so too, its ways of speaking and listening did not abandon Greco-Roman rhetorical culture, but achieved distinctiveness only in close but uneasy relationship to it. It is this process of transformative listening, this attentiveness to the ultimate truth or message of Christianity, mediated to human beings within the medium of the language and signs of Scripture, and Christian teaching and preaching, so as to create truly literate Christian listeners, which we will be tracing in Part Two.

---

[56] Kennedy (1980), 143–4.
[57] *Carmina* II.1, 39, *On His Own Verses* (Daley, 163–5).
[58] This is a vast topic and we have only given a few examples. See Ellspermann (1949); Harrison (2000), ch. 2, for further examples and discussion.

3

Images and Echoes

The memory of Him who became visible in the flesh is burned upon my soul.

John Damascene, *On the Divine Images*, 1.22[1]

Come then, your ways and airs and looks, locks, maiden gear,
gallantry and gaiety and grace,
Winning ways, airs innocent, maiden manners, sweet looks,
loose locks, long locks lovelocks, gaygear, going gallant,
girlgrace—
Resign them, sign them, seal them, send them, motion them with breath,
And with sighs soaring, soaring sighs deliver
Them; beauty-in-the-ghost, deliver it, early now, long before death
Give beauty back, beauty, beauty, beauty, back to God, beauty's
self and beauty's giver.

Gerard Manley Hopkins, *The Leaden Echo*
and the Golden Echo (1930), 55

And what if sound echoed off the prison wall opposite them? When any of the passers-by spoke, don't you think they'd be bound to assume that the sound came from a passing shadow?

Plato, *Republic*, 515c (Waterfield, 241)

One of the most ancient and long-lasting classical ideas,[2] which the fathers unquestioningly shared, was that sense perception—listening, as well as seeing, smelling, touching, and tasting—was to be understood as the act of inscribing or engraving an image upon the mind and memory.

---

[1] Cited by Frank (2000), 178 (Louth, 36).

[2] Carruthers (1990), 16, writes, 'The metaphor of memory as a written surface is so ancient and so persistent in all Western cultures that it must, I think, be seen as a governing model or "cognitive archetype".' She later notes (p. 21) that when Plato uses it in the *Theaetetus* he says that he is developing a metaphor already implicit in Homer, and Socrates stresses that the image is not new, but a very old one.

The idea that images were imprinted upon the mind or memory as mental pictures (Greek: *phantasmata, eikon*; Latin: *imago, simulacrum*), in the same way as a seal makes an impression upon wax, was the most common means of describing the way in which the mind either learnt something new or became aware of, and stored within itself, any sensation brought to it by the five senses of the body. So, in the *Theaetetus*, Plato uses the analogy in relation to both the images created by internal, discursive reflection, and to those created by sense perception. In both cases it is a matter of memory and learning. He comments, 'Imagine that our minds contain a block of wax . . . whenever we wish to remember something or see or hear or conceive in our own minds, we hold this wax under the perceptions or ideas and imprint them on it as we might stamp the impression of a seal ring. Whatever is so imprinted we remember and know so long as the image remains; whatever is rubbed out or has not succeeded in leaving an impression we have forgotten and do not know.'[3]

In the Introduction we noted that in antiquity authors 'wrote' by dictating to a scribe; readers read a text by voicing it aloud; works were 'published' primarily through public performance. Thus, whatever text we now read, the author was probably composing more for the ear than for the eye, with a concern for how what they had to say would be heard, received, remembered, and recollected by the listener rather than the reader. As we have just seen in relation to the practice of rhetoric, this could not but affect the manner in which the speaker or author expressed themselves, the techniques they used, and the goals they had in mind. Given that the process of speaking and listening was commonly understood as the creation of a mental image, inscribed upon the memory, they presumably wished to speak or write in order to literally make an impression upon the mind of their listeners by what they had to say; to engrave vivid, lifelike, easily recollected images upon their memories—images which were familiar enough to find a place in its existing storerooms, but unfamiliar and challenging enough to prompt independent appropriation, reflection, and perhaps action.

This book will argue that the oral delivery and aural reception of the Christian message was instrumental in building up an inner world of images, constructed by the memory, which effectively created literate early Christian listeners: in the next chapter we will examine how these images were initially impressed, organized, and stored, ready for retrieval, by examining the various modes of Christian catechesis. In Chapter 4, with reference to early Christian preaching on Scripture, we will examine the way in which this retrieval took place through creative improvisations on the text of Scripture. In the final chapter we will see that the process by which the images created by listening

---

[3] 191D-E quoted by Carruthers (1990), 21.

were impressed, stored, and then re-presented was one which, on the basis of certain fixed and necessary beliefs, involved a great deal of freedom for imaginative reappropriation, open-ended investigation, creative allusion, and daring, extemporary variations on the central themes of Christianity. Thus, a rich, complex, and multifaceted grasp of the faith was built up, which both created 'literate listeners', and, most importantly, left (perhaps even leaves) open the potential which only live performance possesses for reaching out towards, and even touching, the 'transcendent'. First of all, however, we must examine in more detail the understanding of sense perception as the impression of an image, and then the nature of the images themselves.

SENSE PERCEPTION AND THE CREATION OF IMAGES

There has been a notable emphasis on images across the disciplines, leading one author to coin the idea of a 'pictorial turn'[4] in recent scholarship, but, as this expression suggests, the emphasis has, significantly, been almost entirely upon the role of the visual. The period we are examining is no exception to this, with important works on the role of images and the visual/visuality appearing in the field of late antique art history, history, theology, and sociology.[5] But that the basic image-making capacity which human beings possess is in fact sense perception, and the fact that images can be created and represented through speaking and listening (or even touching, smelling, and tasting) as well as through the eyes, seems to have been generally overlooked.[6]

When the ancients turned to consider the nature of sense perception the crucial question was the perennial one of the relation between the soul and the body. This was especially the case because it was universally held that the soul could not, itself, be affected by the body; the higher could not be affected by the lower. What came to the mind through sense perception could not, therefore, be thought of in terms of the body affecting the soul, mind, or memory, but had to be formulated rather more subtly in terms of the soul's impassible awareness of the body's *passio* or experience. In this way, sense perception could be understood as a matter of the soul's perception by means of the body; in other words, the soul, or higher part of the human being, is conscious of the perceptions of the body, or lower part, and simply uses it as an instrument in order to be aware of what comes to it from outside. The fathers use expressions

---

[4] Mitchell (1995) coined the term 'pictorial turn'.
[5] Francis (2003), 576 n. 2, for references, including Averil Cameron (1991); Elsner (1995); Bulloch et al. (1993); Vasaly (1993); Goldhill and Osborne (1994); Georgia Frank (2000).
[6] With the notable exception of Ashbrook Harvey's (2006) work on smell.

such as the *attentio* or *intentio* of the soul—its vital attention or concentration—in order to describe the manner in which the soul is present to, and
aware of, what the body suffers or perceives, without itself being affected by it.[7]
The soul therefore receives perceptions by its own activity, or act of will, rather
than by any passive impression or influence from the body.[8] As a result of its
attention, the soul creates images in the mind or memory of what it has
become aware of by its concentration upon the body's activities and perception. This accounts for the psychology of perception; the other side is the
actual physiology of perception. This was explained in terms which we have
already encountered, and which are perhaps familiar to us from the medieval
idea of the humours of the body: the soul was thought to send out messengers
(or pipelines, passages, roads, streets,[9] or rays[10]) to the sense organs, which in
turn moved the relevant receptors in those organs to enable them to receive, or
be impressed by, the activity which came to them from outside.[11] The soul was
therefore present throughout the body and moved something luminous in the
eyes, airy in the ears, moist in the mouth, dark in the nostrils, earthy and
muddy in touch . . . which enabled it to register the body's perceptions and
create images of them in the mind or memory, so that they could be immediately recorded, stored, and be ready for retrieval.[12] What was a matter of
corporeal sensation therefore immediately became a matter of spiritual sensation; perception by the body became something that the soul could 'perceive'
and reflect upon inwardly; perception (*sentientis*) became conception (*cogi-
tantis*).[13] Sense perception, then, is in fact the perception of *images* of corporeal, external things, created by the soul in the mind. As Augustine puts it,
' . . . it is not the body that makes its own image in the spirit, but the spirit itself

---

[7] As Augustine puts it, 'I think that sensation is "a bodily experience of which the soul is not
unaware"' (*On the Greatness of the Soul*, 23. 41 (ACW 4, 104). Cited by O'Daly (1987), 86, to
whom I am indebted for the following section.

[8] Relevant texts include Augustine, *On the Greatness of the Soul*, 23.41 (ACW 4, 104–5) on
the body's *passio*; *Letter* 166.2.4 (WSA II/3 80–81) on the 'vital attention' (or *intentio*) of the soul.
One wonders how much the fathers drew on existing arguments to preserve the superiority of the
soul in relation to the body when they attempted to tackle the question of how Christ, the Logos,
could be said to suffer human sensations, emotions, and pain. The language of impassible
awareness, such as Cyril of Alexandria uses, was, one might presume, already available in this
context.

[9] *Literal Commentary on Genesis*, 7.13.20 (WSA I.13 332–3); 12.20.42 9 (WSA I.13 486–7).
As O'Daly (1987), 81, observes, Augustine was clearly able to take over the discovery of the
nervous system and its functions which had been elaborated by the Alexandrian physicians
Herophilus and Erasistratus, and then by Galen.

[10] *The Trinity*, 9.1.3 (WSA I.5 272–73); *s.* 277.10 (WSA III.8 38–9).

[11] 'The soul therefore receives from these quasi-messengers information about any bodily
things that are not hidden from it' *Literal Commentary on Genesis*, 7.14.20 (WSA I.13 333).

[12] *On Music*, 6.5.10 (FC 4 336).

[13] *The Trinity*, 11.1.5 (WSA I.5 306–7). Again, one might look at Augustine for a clear
statement of these ideas as he considers them directly in *Literal Commentary on Genesis* book 7
and book 12; *The Trinity*, 11; *On Music*, 6.

which makes it in itself with a wonderful swiftness that is infinitely removed from the sluggishness of the body; so no sooner is the body seen by the eyes than its image is formed without the slightest interval of time in the spirit of the person seeing.[14] It is not the body, you see, that senses, but the soul through the body, using it as a kind of messenger in order to form in itself the message being brought in from outside. And so no bodily vision can occur unless spiritual vision also occurs simultaneously; but they are not told apart except when the sense is withdrawn from the bodily object, and what was being seen through the body is now still to be found in the spirit.'[15]

The exact relation between the external, corporeal object sensed, the form in which it is sensed, and the spiritual image of it seen and known in the mind is rather ambiguous. Augustine tries to minimize the difference when he writes, 'We do not distinguish . . . the form of the body we see, from the form which is produced by it in the sense of him who sees; since the union of the two is so close that there is no room for distinguishing them.'[16] Rather, he observes, it is like the imprint of a ring on wax while the ring is still present in the wax.[17] The joining of the two is made possible by the soul's attention or intention, which records the impression as an image in the mind or memory. But what exactly was the nature of these images?

THE OTHER SIDE OF LANGUAGE

In order to begin to answer this question, it is necessary, first of all, to examine the role played by images in a theological and philosophical context, and, most especially, to examine those images which were thought to be innate to the mind—the unmediated images which it was believed it contained within itself, which had not come to it from outside, but that constituted both its ontological identity and epistemological certainty, for it is in relation to these primordial images, as it were, that the images created by sense perception must be evaluated.

There was general agreement in antiquity that the human mind contained certain innate truths or laws by which it could judge whatever came to it from the senses. These rules were variously referred to, but were more often than not associated with the seven liberal arts, which were, as we have seen, those disciplines in which every educated person was informed. The rules or laws of grammar, dialectic, mathematics, geometry, rhetoric, music, philosophy, and astrology, were thought to be expressions of the eternal, immutable, innate

---

[14] *Literal Commentary on Genesis*, 12.16.33 (WSA I.13 481–2).
[15] *Literal Commentary on Genesis*, 12.24.51 (WSA I.13 492–3).
[16] *The Trinity*, 11.1.2–3 (WSA I.5 304–5).
[17] *The Trinity*, 11.1.2–3 (WSA I.5 304–5).

truths which every human being possessed in a direct and intuitive manner within their own minds. They were the means by which their temporal expression in mutable, physical reality, or in the practice of the disciplines, could be judged, thus facilitating a movement from the mutable to the immutable. A person could therefore judge that a circle was perfectly round because they possessed the rule or law of roundness in their minds. Alternatively, they could judge that a building was perfectly symmetrical because they possessed the rule of symmetry; or that a piece of music was harmonious because they possessed the rule of harmony. Most importantly, they could identify the true, the good, and the beautiful because they already knew what they were in their eternal, immutable form. Thus, in his famous investigation of the memory in *Confessions*, Book 10, Augustine discusses not only what comes to the memory from outside, through sense perception, but also the ideas (*rationes*) that the memory possesses in an unmediated, direct, and intuitive way within itself, but which he realizes could lie dormant, and one could remain unaware of, unless they were recalled from their storage places by questions and thought. These are the disciplines of the liberal arts; 'notions where we do not draw images through our senses, but discern them inwardly not through images, but as they really are and through the concepts themselves'.[18] In a manner that recalls Plato's *Meno* he reflects,

> For when I learnt them, I did not believe what someone else was telling me, but within myself I recognised them and assented to their truth. I entrusted them to my mind as if storing them up to be produced when required. So they were there even before I had learnt them, but were not in my memory. Accordingly, when they were formulated, how and why did I recognise them and say, 'Yes, that is true'? The answer must be that they were already in my memory, but so remote and pushed into the background, as if in most secret caverns, that unless they were dug out by someone drawing attention to them, perhaps I could not have thought of them.[19]

THE IMAGE IN PHILOSOPHICAL CONTEXT

For Plato, if we might hazard a generalization, the ideas or forms are those eternal, immutable,[20] 'essential Forms'[21] which are known directly by reason, without the aid of the senses.[22] In contrast to sense perception, and to the

---

[18] *Confessions*, 10.11.18.   [19] *Confessions*, 10.10.17.
[20] It is important for Plato that the forms are unchangeable, in contrast to the phenomenal world, *Phaedo*, 78c–80b (Gallop, 29–32).
[21] *Euthyphro*, 6d9 (Loeb, 20–3).
[22] *Phaedo*, 65d–66a (Gallop, 11–12).

images impressed upon the mind by the senses (which are merely the subject of opinion, formed by 'lovers of seeming') they are the object of knowledge, known directly by philosophers, or 'lovers of wisdom'.[23] Plato not only thinks in terms of the rules or laws of the disciplines, such as mathematics, but in terms of ethics and the ideal forms or ideas of the virtues.[24] The virtues, like the disciplines, are first of all known directly by the mind, or reason, and then, in turn, inform our engagement with the temporal, mutable world of the senses. Whereas the disciplines allow us to identify and judge images of the truth, the virtues allow us to live and act in accordance with them. However, we must not ignore the fact that the phenomenal world, for Plato, has its existence only by participation in the forms.[25] This is clearly set forth in relation to the idea of beauty, most famously in the *Symposium*, but in a succinct manner in the following observation by Socrates in the *Phaedo*: 'It seems to me that if anything else is beautiful besides the beautiful itself it is beautiful for no reason at all other than that it participates in that beautiful . . . nothing else makes it beautiful except that beautiful itself, whether by its presence or communion or whatever the manner and nature of the relation may be.'[26] Whatever the manner, there is a real sense in which, by participating in and imitating the forms, the phenomenal world might reveal something of them, remind human beings of their existence,[27] or, at least, point or admonish towards them. As Plato observes in the *Republic*, 'We must be able to discern the presence of these Forms [temperance, courage, liberality, high-mindedness, and all other kindred qualities] themselves and also of their images in anything that contains them, realizing that, to recognize either, the same skill and practice are required, and that the most insignificant instance is not beneath our notice.'[28] In this crucial sense, images are not just secondary, derivative, temporal, and mutable copies, but are treated positively as both participating in the forms and facilitating the ascent towards them.

The myth of the cave in *Republic* (514a–518b) sets out the role of images in this ascent most clearly: from the images of images ('artefacts, human statuettes, and animal models carved in stone and wood and all kinds of materials stick out over the wall' (515a)) to the images themselves (the 'artefacts'), to the objects themselves, to the idea of the good itself (and the allegory of the sun).

---

[23] *Republic*, 479e, 480a (Waterfield, 201–2).

[24] *Euthyphro*, 6d (Loeb, 20–3).

[25] *Phaedo*, 100b–e (Gallop, 56–7).

[26] 100b–d (Gallop, 56–7), quoted by Raven (1965), 90.

[27] Plato thinks that we knew the forms before birth and now need to be reminded of them through sense perception: *Phaedo*, 72e–76c (Gallop, 21–6).

[28] *Republic*, 402c, in Raven's translation, Raven (1965), 124—although the exact interpretation of this passage, and whether Plato is in fact referring to the Socratic universals rather than the ideas, is disputed. See Raven (1965), 124–6.

As well as speaking of recollection, Plato most commonly describes this ascent as a process of education: as the gradual habituation of the soul to the light which is always present and innate to it, but which it is not yet able to look upon. Immediately after the myth of the cave he insists that education is not so much a matter of putting sight into blind eyes, or teaching someone what they do not yet know, rather, he observes, 'An implication of what we are saying . . . is that the capacity for knowledge is present in everyone's mind. If you can imagine an eye that can turn from darkness to brightness only if the body as a whole turns, then our organ of understanding is like that. Its orientation has to be accompanied by turning the mind as a whole away from the world of becoming, until it becomes capable of bearing the sight of real being and reality at its most bright, which we're saying is goodness.'[29] The real question is how this conversion is effected. For Plato it is most definitely a pursuit of wisdom, the work of the philosopher, who, in the *Republic*, must first of all undergo ten years of propaedeutic studies in arithmetic, geometry, stereometry,[30] astronomy, and harmonics. Like the liberal arts, these disciplines serve to lead the soul away from their mutable traces in temporal reality to their eternal, immutable truth. Five years studying dialectic then follow, but whereas the propaedeutic disciplines appear to be wholly concerned with reason, the discipline of dialectic is based more on question and answer—on conversation. Like Augustine's reflections on how he becomes aware of the presence of the truths of the disciplines which were innate in his memory, dialectic enables the soul to discover the truth within itself by prompting it to respond to an appropriate question—in other words, a question which sends it in the right direction to discover the answer it already possesses.

Raven notes, however, that although Plato is positive about the role of the disciplines in training and converting the soul, he is much more ambivalent about other images through which the forms are expressed, and particularly what we might now call the 'fine arts', in contrast to the rational disciplines of the liberal arts: the former were regarded merely as technical arts (*artes/technai*), as more 'hands on', in the sense of crafts such as weaving or woodwork, but also included what we would now classify as the fine arts or performance arts, such as painting, sculpture, dance, and acting, in contrast to the liberal arts (*artes liberales*). The former tend to be treated negatively, as images of images; copies or imitations of objects which are themselves only images, and therefore twice removed from the idea or form they express. As Raven puts it, 'Any particular bed can only be a very imperfect embodiment of the Idea of Bed, and any painting of that particular bed, however lifelike, can only be a copy of a copy.'[31] We should note, however, the significant role given to dialectic, and therefore to dialogue, conversation, question and answer, in

---

[29] *Republic*, 518c (Waterfield, 245). Quoted by Raven (1965), 176.
[30] The science of measuring solid objects.   [31] Raven (1965), 185–6.

the conversion of the soul towards wisdom and contemplation of the forms. Although language is itself an image, which might well be regarded like those of the 'fine arts', as a copy of a copy (a word is an image of a particular reality which is itself an image of the forms), it is given a much more positive role by Plato in the context of the liberal art of dialectic, in that it enables the mind to remember what it already contains, to recollect and gather together the truth it already knows, and to turn itself towards the contemplation of this truth. The sense of hearing, and the images it creates, therefore has a crucial role to play. Conversion is not just a matter of seeing, but of speaking and hearing, leading to mental reflection, recollection, and appropriation. The people trapped in the cave not only saw the shadows of images of images, but heard echoes of voices.[32] What were the voices echoing, and what resonances did they prompt in the minds of those who heard them?

THE IMAGE IN THEOLOGICAL CONTEXT

The role of the image in a theological context, whether created by sense perception, or innate to the mind, is just as complex and ambivalent, but just as central, as in Platonism. More fundamental than the innate presence of the truths of the disciplines, for Christian theologians, was the ontological contingency of the human being as the image of God, for, prompted by Genesis, they concluded that the human person is created in God's image, and that this describes their relation to, and most especially, their contingency and dependence upon, God. In this context, 'image' was understood not merely as a copy or imitation, but (as we have already seen in some aspects of Plato's thought), as participating in, and deriving its existence from, the reality which it reflects.

As James Francis notes in a fascinating article on verbal and visual representation from the second to the fourth centuries, the question of how sacred images participated in and communicated the divine was one which exercised much ancient philosophy. The presence of the truths of the disciplines (harmony, symmetry, order) in mutable reality was one way of approaching the question of how the eternal and immutable could be said to be present in the temporal and mutable, and was often used by theologians to explain how we are able to apprehend the Creator through His creation. The fact that things exist because of their participation in, and relation to the forms, was another way of addressing this question, and it is in this context that humankind's creation in the image of God was articulated. Clearly, the relation between

---

[32] 515b (Waterfield, 241).

creation and Creator, by which human beings could be said to be in God's image, was understood more as a response of the mind, will, or reason, than of ontological identity, and it was upon the mind's relation to, and participation in, its Creator, that a human being's continued existence was believed to depend. The creature, created from nothing, must convert, or turn towards its Creator in order, literally, to exist, or stand out from nothingness; if it falls away from its Creator it will fall back into nothingness or non-being, and gradually cease to exist. This movement was understood by the fathers as an intellectual and moral one, a movement of the reason and the will (or love), in a manner similar to the Platonists' ascent to the forms (or the Neoplatonists' ascent to the One) through reason and the virtues. Human beings were therefore understood to be in the image of God in their mind or reason, which set them apart from the beasts, and to retain this image required a continual movement of the will towards Him. If this faltered then the image would become obscured and dulled, and it would lose the innate, direct, intuitive knowledge of its Creator which it had enjoyed when it reflected Him directly and clearly.

This understanding of the image of God in humankind is a central feature of patristic theology. In a homily on the Beatitudes, commenting on 'Blessed are the pure in heart, for they shall see God',[33] Gregory of Nyssa summarizes the understandings of the image we have outlined above, in the course of considering the ethical implications of being 'in the image' for his congregation. Of course, Gregory comments, no one can 'see' God, in the sense of apprehending the divine nature, since He is 'by nature above every other nature ... beyond the senses and beyond the mind'.[34] Gregory therefore suggests other ways in which God might be known. It is possible, he observes, 'by means of the wisdom that can be seen in all things to have some sort of perception of him who made all things in wisdom', but he adds that in this case we simply perceive the work of art, rather than the artist; God's artistry, rather than his actual nature. Similarly, just as the order of creation might tell us something of God's wisdom, our own existence might tell us something of God's goodness, and anything that makes the mind aware of the virtues brings God before our eyes, but in none of these cases do we actually 'see' God's nature or essence, rather, he observes, each 'imprints upon our souls the image of a divine and noble idea'. We 'see' God in the images imprinted by his works, actions, and words upon the soul, rather than God Himself. Gregory puts it thus, 'For God who is by nature beyond our sight is visible in his activities (*energeiai*), being perceived in the characteristics (*idiomata*) that surround him.'[35] Gregory insists that what is important in understanding what 'seeing God' is, is not so

---

[33] *Homily* 6 On the Beatitudes.
[34] *Homily* 6 On the Beatitudes (Meredith, 94).
[35] *Homily* 6 On the Beatitudes (Meredith, 95).

much the rational aspect of knowing or understanding something about God, as the sense of actually 'having God within'. What Gregory has in mind here, is, I think, rooted in the Platonic idea of the participation of the image in the archetype, which we suggested was articulated in a Christian context in terms of the image of God in humankind. This is precisely the illustration Gregory proceeds to give.

In a manner that directly echoes the way in which sense perception (including hearing) was thought to create mental images in the mind of the one who sensed, Gregory observes that 'When you were first created God imprinted upon you reflections of his own nature not unlike someone impressing the form of a seal upon wax.'[36] These impressions Gregory describes as the soul's 'Godlike beauty', its 'likeness to the archetype',[37] in other words, its capacity to reflect the divine nature, and thereby 'have God' within itself. In order to preserve the image and enable it to continue to reflect the divine— in order to participate in God, in other words—human beings, Gregory urges, must keep the image pure, clean, and untainted by vice or sin. This is, for him, the meaning of the Beatitude, 'Blessed are the pure in heart, for they shall see God.' He observes, 'the pure of heart becomes blessed, for by contemplating his own purity he sees the archetype in the image'. Echoing the image of the cave in Plato's *Republic*, and making clear the relation of the image of God in human beings to God Himself, Gregory adds, 'In a similar way, those who contemplate the sun in a mirror, even though they do not look straight at the sun, see the sun no less in the ray in the mirror than do those who look directly at the circle of the sun. So too you, even though you be inadequate for the contemplation of the unapproachable light, if you return to the grace of the image which was planted in you at the beginning, you will find what you look for within you.'[38]

This is all well and good, but, as Gregory immediately acknowledges, the problem is that human beings have fallen from their initial creation in the image of God, and the purity, holiness, and simplicity required to image God, or to directly reflect the sun, have been misted over, defiled, and obscured by sin.[39] It is in this context that the incarnate Christ's words and teaching—in other words, God's bodily, external communication to the senses, through speaking and listening—like Plato's dialectic—become crucial, for only so, Gregory concludes his sermon, can human beings be enabled to regain or restore the purity of heart which allows them to reflect, and have God, the archetype, within.[40]

---

[36] *Homily* 6 On the Beatitudes (Meredith, 96).
[37] *Homily* 6 On the Beatitudes (Meredith, 96).
[38] *Homily* 6 On the Beatitudes (Meredith, 96).
[39] *Homily* 6 On the Beatitudes (Meredith, 97). What Gregory describes here of the effect of sin upon the will is very close indeed to the Western idea of original sin.
[40] *Homily* 6 On the Beatitudes (Meredith, 98).

It is this need for external communication to the senses which Augustine describes in *On Genesis against the Manichees*, where he identifies the inward truth, which those who convert towards their Creator possess, as an inner spring which wells up within to water their soul. When they turn away from the Creator, however, this spring dries up, and they are subsequently dependent on the rain which falls from the dark clouds of human preaching and teaching, or from the cloud of Christ's flesh,[41] which 'poured out most generously the rain of the holy gospel'.[42] Chrysostom makes a very similar observation, in much the same words, in relation to the apostles who received the Holy Spirit at Pentecost: '. . . they had the fount of teaching welling up in their mind . . . For that reason there was no need for instruction or catechesis.'[43] The contrast is therefore between the interior image, created and maintained by the response of faith (purity of heart) to God's direct, inward address to the soul or mind, and the need for mediated, outward preaching and teaching. The latter is crucial for those who have obscured and defaced the inward image, in order to inspire and inform their faith anew, to cleanse and purify the image within them, and thereby reform and restore it, so that it can reflect and 'have' God once again within.

INNER WORD

Another notable way in which early Christian thinkers describe the contrast between innate images and those impressed by sense perception, in relation to the exercise of listening, is their use of the idea of an 'inner word' or 'inner thought' to refer to words and thoughts which are heard and understood without language,[44] and which precede linguistic expression or formulation. The inner word is 'couched in the heart, nude to the thinker, till it is clothed by the utterance of the speaker so that it may proceed forth'.[45] The idea of an inner word is therefore used to describe the way in which God is heard by the mind without audible words or sounds;[46] the teaching of Christ,

---

[41] *On Genesis against the Manichees*, 2.5.6 (WSA I.13 74–5).
[42] *On Genesis against the Manichees*, 2.5.6 (WSA I.13 74–5).
[43] Chrysostom, *On Eleazer and the Seven Boys*, 10, 12 (Mayer and Neil, 128–9).
[44] Rist (1994), 38, refers to *On the Trinity*, 15.3.19 (WSA I.5 409): 'It is the thought formed from the thing we know that is the word which we utter in the heart, a word that is neither Greek nor Latin nor any other language; but when it is necessary to convey the knowledge in the language of those we are speaking to, some sign is adopted to signify this word.'
[45] *Sermon*, 187.3.3 (WSA III.6 28–9) quoted by Matthews (1972), 176–90.
[46] *Tractates on John's Gospel*, 54.8 (FC 88, 308): 'The Truth . . . speaks within, it instructs without sound, it floods with intelligible light.'

the inner teacher (*magister interior*), who communicates directly to the mind;[47] the thoughts of the mind before they are articulated and put forth in words.[48] The fact that the inner word is referred to as a 'word', then, is clearly metaphorical, but nevertheless tells us something about how it was understood—as containing an idea to be communicated; as the meaning which language is ultimately used to express (or, at least, to attempt to express); as the medium by which God informs, and Christ addresses, the mind. It is linguistic in its function, but non- or pre-linguistic in nature. In fact, the idea of an inner word allows us to understand something of the entire anthropology of the inner man and the inner, 'spiritual' senses, which early Christian thinkers constructed in order to talk about the feelings, thoughts, movements, and life of the soul or mind, in contrast to the body.[49] Bodily, sensual—and auditory—analogies clearly proved to be the most effective means of doing this. Thus, early Christian writers commonly use such expressions as the 'voice of the heart', the 'eyes of the mind', or the 'ears of the soul'. In the light of what we have already seen of their use of the language of image for both the image of God in man, and the images created by sense perception, we should not underestimate these analogies. They are analogies, just as the image is an analogy, but they are not *just* analogies: they are verbal images or signs which not only refer to, but express and, as it were, 'embody' or even 'incarnate' a reality—God's presence to the soul and the way in which the soul senses, and relates to, this presence—or, in Gregory's words, 'has' God within it.[50] How do these inward images relate to the images impressed upon the mind by the temporal, mutable, sense perceptions of the body?[51]

[47] *The Teacher*, 9.38 (LCC 6, 95).

[48] *The Trinity*, 15.3. 17–20 (WSA I.5 407–11).

[49] On the spiritual senses, see M. Canévet, *Dictionnaire de Spiritualité* 14, 598–617; Rahner (1932); Wolfson (1935); Dillon (1986).

[50] Hauck (1988) notes Origen's use of the idea of a 'divine sense' (Prov. 2:5)—a superior, incorporeal sense, possessed by those 'divine and inspired men' such as the prophets and apostles, which perceives divine things and has spiritual insight and communion with God, against Celsus' criticism that Christians simply rely on sense perception—and refers to *Contra Celsum*, I.48. Cf. Ambrose, *Explanatio psalmorum*, XII (XLVII 1–4), referred to by Sears (1991), 36. On the spiritual senses, see Rahner (1932); Harl (1975).

[51] The fact that we often use inner speech in order to think and articulate ideas to ourselves, or can listen to things inwardly, without sounding them, is often overlooked, but perhaps deserves more attention. As Ihde (2003), 64, observes, 'Although there has been a vast amount of work done on philosophical problems of language, little has been done concerning the examination of concrete forms of thinking as inner speech considered as a type of auditory imagination . . . As an *accompaniment* to the rest of experience it is a most "inward" continuity of self presence and the hidden presence of an experiential polyphony.' Cf. Davies (2006).

THE FALL (AGAIN)

As will now be clear, it is to the Fall, and its effect on the image of God, that we must turn for an answer to this question. We have seen that the result of humankind's self-referential pride was that human beings turned away from God, the source of their existence and illumination. Their sin obscured their capacity to reflect God, and to know or 'have' God within, by clouding over, or obscuring, the image of God which they once possessed. Human beings are now no longer able to image their eternal, immutable archetype, but are conformed to the temporal, mutable, created world and have themselves become part of it; glued to it, as it were, or fragmented and dissipated by their attachment to its temporal mutability. In order to restore and reform the image, early Christian theologians taught that God acted to address human beings in the realm into which they had fallen—the temporal, mutable realm of the senses; that the images impressed upon the soul by His temporal revelation—the teaching and preaching of His Word, His apostles and preachers; the prayers, psalms, and sacraments of His Church—could, in their turn, serve to impress, inform, and reform the image of God, which had become obscured in the soul. Whereas God had once been heard directly, silently, and without words or particular languages by the soul, He is now heard in the languages created by human convention, echoing and resonating in the sounding voices of His created intermediaries, to the bodily ears.

We see these two types of divine address set forth quite clearly in Augustine's reflections on Paradise. He seems to maintain that speaking and hearing were not necessary before the Fall. Although Adam and Eve were created with ears, and Genesis tells us that God spoke to them in the Garden, Augustine still insists that language was simply a possibility, rather than an actuality or necessity, before the Fall. It only becomes necessary for God to communicate with them in spoken words, or for Adam and Eve to communicate with each other, *after* the Fall. Before the Fall they could have done so internally, directly, and intuitively; after it they must do so externally, indirectly, and with great effort. Language is, then, very much a consequence of the Fall: a necessity, a penalty, and a labour, which arises when interior, direct communication is no longer possible because human beings have turned away, and shut their ears and eyes to it. Augustine frequently reflects on the way in which spoken language can serve just as easily to veil and hide one's thoughts as to reveal and communicate them; how it can lie, misrepresent, be misunderstood or misinterpreted;[52] how difficult he finds it to submit to the tedious, haphazard, and exhausting process of trying to find the right words to express something

---

[52] *On Order*, 2.51 (FC 5, 328–9); *Enarrations on the Psalms*, 54.11 (WSA III.17 64–5).

which he understands perfectly well in his own thoughts.[53] Moreover, the diversity of languages which was visited upon those who attempted to build the tower of Babel, in order to undermine their united pride by making it difficult for them to communicate with, or understand, each other's intentions, is a clear illustration of the way in which language, and speaking and hearing, is characteristic of human division, fragmentation, and pride rather than consensus, unity, and humility.[54] But this is, of course, only one side of the picture.

The other side is that language becomes, as we have seen, the means by which God now addresses his fallen creatures, and the means by which they can hear him, albeit through echoes and resonances, in the temporal, mutable realm of their Fall. So, how does language, or external communication through the sense of hearing, work? We have already examined the notion of an inner thought or 'word', which takes the form of no particular language until it is articulated or communicated in speech, so that it might be conveyed to the mind of another person, in order that they too might have and understand it. Language, then—or at least, one particular language—is not so much how we think, as how we communicate. As we will see, images in the mind are not necessarily visual or verbal (or, for that matter, tactile, olfactory, or gustatory) but in a manner we have already touched on in relation to the 'inner man' and will need to consider later in this chapter, somehow precede these sensory forms, and assume them only to communicate themselves to the mind of someone else. An inward, silent, naked thought, or 'word', therefore assumes language as a sort of clothing, in order to appear outwardly, so that it might be seen or heard by the senses of another person, and then make an image in their mind, so that they, too, might be able to 'see' or 'hear' it. In short, language is an outward vehicle which is used to convey a thought or idea from one mind to another; the inner 'word' or thought which it conveys remains in the mind of the speaker, and then, having been impressed by the sense of hearing, dwells in the mind of the hearer, but whereas the thought remains, the language is temporal and mutable.[55] In theory, therefore, language is simply an external mediator, which serves its purposes and then passes away; it is not the reality or thought itself. In practice, as we shall see, it is rarely the case that one can so

[53] *Instructing Beginners in the Faith*, 2.3 (Canning, 55–6): 'It is the same with me too: I am nearly always dissatisfied with the address that I give. For the address I am so eager to offer is the superior one which I enjoy again and again in my inner being before I begin to formulate it in spoken words. And when I find that my actual address fails to express what I have before my mind, I am depressed by the fact that my tongue has been unable to keep up with my intellect.'

[54] *Enarrations on the Psalms*, 54.11 (WSA III.17 64–5); cf. *Sermon*, 266.2 (WSA III.7 267–8) on Pentecost.

[55] This was variously expressed: in rhetorical terms, such as *res* and *signa*; in philosophical terms, such as the Stoic *logos endiathetos* and *logos prophorikos*; in theological terms, such as the consubstantial logos and the incarnate logos.

easily separate out a word from what it signifies. External images and signs were regarded as in some sense holy or sacred, and, as we have seen in Chapter 2, a Christian theology of the incarnation led to a more positive evaluation of the role of the temporal, sensible, and mutable in communicating the divine, not just in the Son, but in the other aspects of God's temporal revelation, and most especially in Scripture, preaching, teaching, and sacraments. As we shall see below, this had as much to do with the nature of God as of fallen human beings or the nature of language itself.

IMAGES AS A NECESSARY CONSTRAINT

It is clear that however provisional, transient, and frustrating language and communication through the sense of hearing was thought to be, it became, for early Christian theologians, what we might call a necessary constraint or limitation. We will encounter this idea again, in Chapter 4, as we proceed to consider the ways in which Christian teaching and preaching established rules, summaries, and statements of faith which served to impress upon the minds of listeners the parameters, or necessary constraints, within which the faith might most effectively be heard, stored, and subsequently reflected upon. Here, we might consider it in a more general way, both in relation to language itself and in relation to that which it communicates in Christian teaching. Just as Clement of Alexandria describes Christ's incarnation as a *perigraphe*—a necessary limitation or delimitation of the divine nature, so that it might be known and grasped by human nature,[56] so God's use of language—of spoken or written words which are received by the physical senses, might be regarded as a necessary constraint or limitation of divine meaning to human understanding and powers of perception. This was necessary, not just because human beings had lost the inward, direct knowledge of Him which they enjoyed as His image, before the Fall, but, as many of the fathers point out, because of the divine nature itself, which will always transcend human knowing or comprehending. Just as even Adam and Eve could not see or hear God directly before the Fall, but could only contemplate Him indirectly, reflected in His image, so we, having obscured that image by our Fall, can only apprehend something of the divine nature indirectly and allusively, through verbal images; through language used analogically, metaphorically, and figuratively. This is a point made most forcibly by Gregory Nazianzen, in his *Theological Orations* and by Gregory of Nyssa in *Against Eunomius* book two, and is one which we will follow up in much more detail in Chapter 7, but here we might

---

[56] Clement of Alexandria Fragment 36 (GCS Clement Alexandrinus III, 219) Irenaeus against Heresies, 4.4.2 (ANCL 5, 384–5).

note that it is tacitly acknowledged in everything that early Christian theologians speak or write. Language is deployed in this way to convey precisely what it is not. It cannot be taken as an end in itself, or idolized, but points beyond itself to—perhaps—communicate something of its infinite, transcendent subject. It simultaneously veils God, and enables Him in some way to be revealed. It demands both faith in what cannot be seen, and a capacity for openness, imagination, and playful improvisation, in the attempt to articulate and receive it, on the part of both speaker and the listener.[57] The statements of apophatic theology, which convey, through the language of negation, what God is not, are an extreme example of these functions of language and of the necessity of constraints.

Although all early Christian writers are acutely aware of the difficulties and necessary constraint of finding words to express their inward understanding and thoughts, they are clearly also conscious of the fact that this is precisely what God, in His grace, has done in order to address fallen humanity. Their descent, as teachers and preachers, is simply a following of the descent, or 'delimitation', of the Word of God to assume flesh and speak to us in a manner we can hear and understand. We will examine the relation between the incarnation, the preacher, and transformative listening at more length in Chapter 5 as it is perhaps the definitive example of language, or external communication to the sense of hearing, being used in a positive context in order to form, reform, and transform the listener.

IMAGES (AGAIN)

What then was the nature of the images (*typos*; *figura*) themselves, which the soul creates in the mind or memory through sense perception? The image of a seal upon wax, as Carruthers emphasizes, is primarily a visual one, concerned with expressing how the mind 'sees' what it perceives through the images created by sense perception.[58] But we should be aware that the image of the

---

[57] Young (1980) talks of the ability of such language to 'explode literalism' and refers to the work of scholars such as Sallie McFague and Janet Soskice who discuss the 'generative' character of metaphorical expression (which is another, very suggestive, way of putting what I have just tried to express). This is a point to which McGilchrist (2010) (see First Impromptu) also gives great emphasis.

[58] Carruthers (1990), 27, is, in fact, insistent on the primacy of the visual in speaking of mental images. She makes the point that such images were understood as in some sense spatial, and that this is why 'the ancients persistently thought of *memoria* as a kind of eye-dependent reading, a visual process. There is no classical or Hebrew or medieval tradition regarding an "ear of the mind" equivalent to the "eye of the mind".' What we have seen of the fathers' reflections on the 'inner man', however, rather belies this observation.

seal on wax is, itself, simply an image—an analogy or metaphor—and that although the analogy of writing upon the memory, and of seeing the images inscribed upon it, is commonly used, we should not therefore conclude that the images created by the senses are, in fact, perceived by the mind or memory simply in a manner resembling bodily sight. They are also perceived in a manner resembling bodily hearing, touch, taste, and smell. Augustine hints at what sort of image and perception this might be—albeit in a rather vague way—in relation to hearing, when he attempts to describe the contrast be-tween the permanent presence of the internal 'images' of the disciplines of the liberal arts and impressions or 'traces/vestiges (*uestigio*)' made by sounds upon the mind or memory. He writes in *Confessions*, 10, 'It [the disciplines of the liberal arts] is not a sound which has passed away, like a voice which makes its impression through the ears and leaves behind a trace (*uestigio*) allowing it to be recalled, as if it were sounding though in fact it is no longer sounding.'[59] As we saw above, the fathers often refer to the different 'senses' of the inner man, who not only sees, but hears, smells, tastes, and touches when he recalls, reflects upon, and represents the inner, spiritual images which the mind or memory contains—whether these are innate images, or ones that have come to him from the soul's sense perception through the body. What is certainly the case is that when the fathers describe the activities of recollection, reflection, and representation, it is more often in the language of sensation—of seeing, but also of hearing, feeling, tasting, and even smelling—than that of rational, intellectual knowledge. The inner man 'knows' by seeing, hearing, tasting, smelling, and touching, rather than intellectual exercise. What he possesses is more a matter of intuition than of rational insight. The fact that, as a fallen creature, he is now dependent on the images that come to him from the senses, rather than inward illumination, goes part of the way to explaining this emphasis on the inward senses, but, as we have suggested, it is also at least partly due to the nature of the transcendent, immutable truths which cannot be grasped directly by the reason or intellect, but only conveyed allusively, through images, metaphors, and figures, which are better apprehended by the senses and by the imagination, than by rational enquiry. Perhaps even more importantly, in this context, however, we should remind ourselves that the images which are created by the soul in the memory, on the basis of sense perception, are more often than not 'synaesthetic' images—images created by a combination of senses. We rarely simply see something, or remember what we have seen, without also being aware of what we also heard, felt (and perhaps even smelled and tasted) at the same time. The memorial image that is created as a result of, say, attending a church service, would no doubt be a combination of images in which what was heard was remembered and

---

[59] *Confessions*, 10.9.16.

impressed along with what was seen, smelled, touched, and tasted at the same time—the preacher's resonant voice, the ornate Church architecture, fragrant incense, a cold marble pillar, the bread of the Eucharist. The image would combine the sensory impressions to impress a multifaceted mental image of a particular moment or event, person, or place.[60] We should also not forget that, in addition to sense perceptions, the mind could also store feelings and emotions connected with the image.[61] No doubt such synaesthetic images were more forceful and evocative, insofar as they were more detailed and specific, with no particular omitted. One sense could predominate, but once recalled it would bring with it all the others that contributed to the particular recollection.[62] What we can certainly conclude is that memorial images were rarely—despite what Carruthers, and the many other scholars who simply concentrate upon the visual, wish to suggest—purely, or even primarily, visual.

In order to illustrate this we might think of the images impressed upon the mind or memory when we listen to a piece of music. We do not 'see' them, but they enable us to recall the piece of music, to reflect upon it, to repeat and perform it again. What sort of images are they? They are certainly not verbal or visual, in the sense of a written inscription or impression which the mind can see and 'read' (unless, of course, we also have access to a written score or notation). Augustine, we have just seen, calls the images or impressions made by sound 'traces' (*uestigio*), which remain in the mind when something has been heard. The mind is clearly able to perceive these images or 'traces/ vestiges' in some way other than 'seeing'. Of course, even the mind's 'sight' is simply a metaphor for its being aware of something (and often of its understanding something) since the mind does not actually possess physical eyes to see, just as it does not possess ears to hear, or a nose to smell. Again, we must take seriously the fact that the inward perception of memorial images

---

[60] For the example of the Church of Hagia Sophia in Constantinople, see Cherry (2005).

[61] *Confessions*, 10.14.21. (The fact that we can recall what we felt on a particular occasion but no longer experience the emotion itself leads Augustine to examine the relation between mind and memory: 'We call memory itself the mind. Since that is the case, what is going on when, in gladly remembering past sadness, my mind is glad and memory sad? My mind is glad for the fact that gladness is in it, but memory is not saddened by the fact that regret is in it. Surely this does not mean that memory is independent of the mind. Who could say that? No doubt, then, memory is, as it were, the stomach of the mind, whereas gladness and sadness are like sweet and bitter food. When they are entrusted to the memory, they are as if transferred to the stomach and can there be stored; but they cannot be tasted.' In fact, what he says elsewhere about the power of the memory and its images to affect present emotions and feelings might lead us to question these observations.)

[62] There is a striking scene in one of the films contained in the movie, *Paris, Je t'Aime* (Victoire International and Pirol Production, produced by Claude Ossard and Emmanuel Benbihy, 2006) in which a young blind man receives a phone call from his girlfriend, and can immediately visualize her and being with her. In fact, this is the case for most of us: we hear the voice of someone we know well and we can 'see' them, conjure up their presence and all the intangible aspects of what it feels like to be with them. One sense activates, or conjures up, the others.

(whether visual, auditory, or related to any of the other senses, or a combination of the senses), although originally made possible by the formation of images impressed by the soul in sense perception, is not, strictly, a matter of the senses but of some sort of awareness of the mind, memory, or soul, which often happens to be expressed in metaphors derived from sense perception. Just as this awareness is not strictly verbal or visual, nor is it strictly sensory; these are simply convenient metaphors and analogies to express how memorial images are formed, recalled, and used inwardly. Even the language of 'image' is, itself, metaphorical, and is used to express the objects of the mind's perception. It is in this sense, I think, that we can speak of a sort of inward, as it were, 'cognitive', literacy, before we can speak of a visual, functional, or even verbal literacy. Individuals can receive, reflect upon, and represent information before they can articulate it in either words or in writing. We saw this when we discussed the other side of language: the 'inner word', or the pre-verbal intuition which the mind possesses before it attempts to articulate it in language (or music), but it is also the case for much of what the mind receives and contains. The process of speaking, and also the process of hearing, is, in fact, something secondary; as we have seen, it is a necessary constraint in order to form and inform the mind of another; to convey what is in the mind of one person to the mind of another; to teach, move, and persuade another person; to unify speaker and listener and to create a common, shared understanding.

So we have arrived at a position where we can clearly state what images are not, but it is extremely difficult to say what they in fact are. The only thing we can say with certainty is that they *are* copies, imitations, and representations, either of eternal, immutable ideas, or copies, imitations, and representations of things perceived by the senses. In neither case are they the thing itself. What we need to take seriously in what follows, therefore, is that in the case of listening, as in the case of all the senses, what is actually recorded in the mind when we listen is not the actual sound, but some sort of image of the sound— an encoded sound (to use a modern analogy)—which the mind is able to store and retrieve. We are dealing not with the object itself, or with some literal, fixed, definitive representation of it, but with an analogy, an approximation, or parallel. The image created by hearing, or indeed any of the senses, is but a secondary impression, an allusive sketch, which suggests the thing itself, but which can certainly not be taken for it. This, as we shall see, is both its strength and its weakness. Like language, it is a sign and symbol of something other than itself. As we shall see more clearly in Chapter 7, it is more a matter of personal, subjective apprehension, determined by culture, habit, and convention, rather than reason or rules. And like language, it is always more than simply an image or sign, but can 'embody' reality itself.

MEMORY

In order to understand just what this 'encoding' involves, and therefore, perhaps, something more of the mental or cognitive images created in the mind by listening, we will conclude this chapter with an investigation of the nature and role of memory, since it was here that both innate images, as well as those brought to the mind by sense perception, were thought in some sense to dwell.

The memory was, in fact, thought of as a sort of giant storehouse—a library or treasury in which images were deposited by being sorted and allocated to various designated places, so that they could be recalled and recollected whenever they were appropriate or needed. In the *Rhetorica ad Herennium* Cicero calls these places *loci*, or 'backgrounds': 'those who have learned mnemonics can set in backgrounds what they have heard, and from these backgrounds deliver it by memory. For these backgrounds are very much like wax tablets or papyrus, the images like the letters, the arrangement and disposition of the images like the script, and the delivery is like the reading.'[63] In short, the memory was thought of rather like those huge, old, leather-bound, loose-leaf catalogues that one used to find in the Bodleian Library, in Oxford, until the mid-1980s, in which each new entry was individually inserted by being first impressed on a piece of paper by a typewriter and then pasted alphabetically into the relevant section of the appropriate subject catalogue, where it joined other similar works for future perusal by the interested researcher. The difference is that the initial impression was created not by the force of a typewriter key upon a ribbon but by sensation, or a combination of sensations, upon the surface of the mind.[64] Augustine vividly describes this process in *Confessions*, 10: 'Memory preserves in distinct particulars and general categories all the perceptions which have penetrated, each by its own route of entry. Thus light and all colours and bodily shapes enter by the eyes; by the ears all kinds of sounds; all odours by the entrance of the nostrils; all tastes by the door of the mouth. The power of sensation in the entire body distinguishes what is hard or soft, hot or cold, smooth or rough, heavy or light, whether external or internal to the body. Memory's huge cavern, with its mysterious, secret, and indescribable nooks and crannies, receives all these perceptions, to be recalled when needed and reconsidered. Every one of them enters into memory, each by its own gate, and is put on

---

[63] *Ad Herennium*, 111.17, cited by Carruthers (1990), 28.
[64] Plato, *Theaetetus*, 191 D–E, cited above; cf. Aristotle, *De memoria et reminiscentia*, 450a25: 'The change that occurs marks [the body] in a sort of imprint (*eikon*/copy), as it were, of the sense-image, as people do who seal things with signet rings' (cited by Carruthers (1990), 16).

deposit there. The objects themselves do not enter, but the images of the perceived objects are available to the thought recalling them.'[65]

We have noted that the power of words, and the force of listening, to form and reform the mind was something of which the ancients were acutely conscious. What one listened to mattered; how one listened was crucial, since what one heard could purify the soul or pollute it. So powerful were these images that the fathers constantly warn their congregations to be on their guard as to what experiences they expose their senses to. Chrysostom warns his listeners that when they go to the theatre and watch a prostitute speaking and behaving disgracefully, they take this into their minds: 'when the theatre is finished and she has gone,' he observes, 'the image of her is stored up in your soul—her words, her appearance, her glances, her walk, her rhythm, her enunciation, her lewd tunes, and you go away taking with you countless wounds'.[66] Memorial images were not just images, but inherently powerful agents of formation and transformation in the mind.

The fact that human beings were understood to be dependent on the external communication of the truth; on the revelation of God through words, people, or events, rather than through an inward, direct, and intuitive awareness of His truth such as they enjoyed before the Fall, meant that the classical understanding of sense impressions forming mental images took on an even greater significance for the fathers. Hearing became the means by which God was understood to communicate with human beings; the means by which we receive, respond to, and come to perceive His truth. What was needed, therefore, was a means of ensuring that what came to the soul through sense perception made positive impressions upon the mind or memory, and created images which would help reform the primordial and enduring image of God which had become obscured though sin, rather than wound and deform it.

The memory, we have noted, was understood as a vast storehouse, with designated places where the images created by sense perception were organized, sorted, and stored for future retrieval and recollection. Early Christian writers realized that was needed was a system, or means of classification, whereby this process could take place in a way that built up the faith of the individual Christian hearer and enabled them to make sense of what they heard in the many different contexts in which the Christian message came to them and imprinted itself, through hearing, upon their minds and memories. We therefore find that they tended not only to emphasize the need for faith in what was now mediated to human beings through the senses, and in images, rather than directly and intuitively, but to emphasize the need for summaries of the faith, in order that each person might have, as it were, a set of

---

[65] *Confessions*, 10.8.13.
[66] *New Homily* 7 Against the Games and Theatres, 267.2–6 (Mayer and Allen, 122).

overarching images—key, paradigmatic images—which provided a sort of filing system into which the multitude of diverse images brought to their minds by the senses might be placed, stored, and be ready for informed retrieval, reflection, and representation when the need arose. Such summaries, as we know, took the form of rules of faith, followed later by creedal statements. These, in turn, conformed with Scripture and the way in which it was interpreted and taught within the tradition of the Church. Above all, these summaries took the form of overarching 'rules', such as the double commandment of love of God and love of neighbour, which embodied an understanding of the entire Christian revelation in all its parts, and in relation to which nothing could ever be discordant. With these structures firmly in place the Christian believer had a ready-made storage system embedded in their memories, ready to assimilate whatever they heard in a constructive way, which would help form and build up their faith rather than deform or undermine it. It is this process which we will be examining in Chapter 4.

Part Two

Theme and Variations

4

Catechesis: Sounding the Theme

> What is all that time for, during which they hold the status and title of catechumen, if it is not for them to hear what a Christian should believe and what kind of life a Christian should lead?
>
> Augustine, *On Faith and Works*, 6.9 (WSA I.8, 232)

> For, 'everyone who calls upon the name of the Lord will be saved'. But how are men to call upon him in whom they have not believed? And how are they to believe in him of whom they have never heard? And how are they to hear without a preacher? And how can men preach unless they are sent?
>
> Rom. 10:13–15

In Chapter 3 we examined how listening was understood as the inscription of images upon the memory, which were not only stored there but retrieved and represented so as to form (and reform) the mind of the hearer. We see this process at work in a Christian context, beginning with the initiation of early Christians into the faith and body of the Church through the rite of baptism. Those who were being prepared for this solemn rite were officially inscribed as 'hearers' (*auditores*; *audientes* in the West)[1] or catechumens, who would then undergo a period of intense instruction, or catechesis, in the faith they were to embrace—usually through an extended series of addresses or sermons given by their local bishop.

The root of the word 'catechesis' lies in the word for an echo, and this encapsulates well the idea that a catechumen was one in whom the faith was made to resonate in their reception of it through their ears. It is clearly in Chrysostom's mind when he refers to his baptismal instructions as setting up echoes in the minds of his hearers so that they can remember, retrieve, and, above all, act upon them, when he is no longer with them. He opens his *Twelfth Instruction* with the comment, 'First I have come to ask your loving assembly for the fruits of my recent discourse. For I do not speak only that you

---

[1] They are otherwise referred to in the West as *competentes* (petitioners) or *electi* (elect, chosen ones), and in the East as *photizomenoi* (those being illuminated).

may hear, but that you may remember what I said and give me proof of it by your deeds; rather, you must give proof to God, who knows your secret thoughts. This is why my discourse is called a catechesis, so that even when I am not here my words may echo in your minds.'[2]

HEARING AND BELIEVING

All the fathers, without exception, were agreed that the catechumen—the one who was preparing for baptism—did not actually become one of the faithful (Latin *fideles*; Greek *pistoi*[3]) until he or she was baptized. In other words, the process of baptismal catechesis or instruction (accompanied, as we shall see below, by various ascetic exercises, exorcisms, and anointings) was thought of as a process of *formation*, in which the faith was gradually inscribed upon the minds and wills of those who received instruction in it, so that they came to truly possess it; to 'know' and understand it or, as it was commonly put in the East, to be 'enlightened' by it. Only then, having first heard, and then believed, was the Holy Spirit, and the ability to pray and act as a believer, given in baptism. These three stages: first hearing, then believing, then baptism/enlightened prayer and action, enumerated by Paul in the quotation from Romans 10:13–15 cited at the head of this chapter, structured early Christian identity and understanding of initiation.

These three stages clearly structure the account of the first Christian mission in Acts. The whole book resonates with the urgent proclamation of the *kerygma* to Jews and Gentiles—a message which is lost on those whose ears are 'heavy of hearing',[4] but which inspired belief in the ears of those 'who have ears to hear' (Matt. 11:15), and those like Lydia, the seller of purple goods, whose ears have been opened by God (Acts 16:14), so that they become believers, are baptized, and begin to pray and do God's work. The words which were heard when Peter 'opened his mouth' and spoke at Joppa, in Acts 10:34–43, are as good a summary as any of what moved the minds and hearts of his hearers to believe, and then to receive the Holy Spirit and speak in tongues:

---

[2] *Baptismal Instruction*, 12.1 (ACW 31, 173). Latantius, *On the Workmanship of God*, 8 (FC 54, 26) makes the point that the ears are designed in such a way that they capture sound so that it resonates within them, rather than allowing it simply to fly past them, and adds, 'These ears, then, might get their name (*aures*) from the drinking in (*hauriendis*) of voices.'

[3] E.g. Cyril of Jerusalem, *Catecheses*, 5.1 (Yarnold, 112); Ambrose, *On the Sacraments*, 1.1 (Yarnold (1994), 99); Augustine, *Sermon*, 132.1 (WSA III.4, 325); Chrysostom, *Baptismal Instruction*, 11.11 (ACW 31, 164).

[4] Acts 28:27, quoting Isaiah 6:9–10.

Truly, I perceive that God shows no partiality, but in every nation anyone who fears him and does what is right is acceptable to him. You know the word which he sent to Israel, preaching good news of peace by Jesus Christ (he is Lord of all), the word which was proclaimed throughout all Judea, beginning from Galilee after the baptism which John preached: how God anointed Jesus of Nazareth with the Holy Spirit and with power; how he went about doing good and healing all who were oppressed by the devil, for God was with him. And we are witnesses to all that he did both in the country of the Jews and in Jerusalem. They put him to death by hanging him on a tree; but God raised him on the third day and made him manifest; not to all the people but to us who were chosen by God as witnesses, who ate and drank with him after he rose from the dead. And he commanded us to preach to the people, and to testify that he is the one ordained by God to be judge of the living and the dead. To him all the prophets bear witness that everyone who believes in him receives forgiveness of sins through his name.

This urgent first Christian preaching already reverberates with a polyphony of other voices: God's word to Israel; Christ's good news; John the Baptist's preaching; the witness and testimony of the Apostles. But Peter states the substance of the good news with a spare and direct simplicity: Christ's Lordship; his baptism; his healing ministry; his death on a cross; his resurrection on the third day; the Last Judgement; his fulfilment of prophecy; his forgiveness of sins. Peter's powerfully concise message is far removed from the frequently long, discursive homilies of the fathers, but what it states encapsulates precisely what it was they were seeking to communicate and to set echoing in the minds of their hearers. His words are like the clear, note by note statement of a theme, which then becomes the subject of elaborate variations. The fathers' teaching never loses sight of the theme—it is explicitly present in their rules of faith, their summaries of the apostolic teaching, their creation of the creeds, their emphasis upon the Lord's Prayer, their rules of thumb (such as the double commandment) for exegesis—and everything they say is a tacit exposition, variation, or recapitulation of it. It is with the manner in which this theme was first sounded, and then made to echo in the minds of its hearers, that we will be preoccupied in this chapter; in Chapter 5 we will examine the variations and recapitulations.

From what we have just seen, the act of hearing, or at least of effective hearing, was clearly understood in direct relation to faith in the early Church. Hearing was somehow regarded as the necessary prior essential in order to inspire or faith. How did this work, and why was hearing, in particular, so crucial?

It appears, first of all, that for the fathers, there is a right sort of hearing which enables the listener to believe, and there is also a wrong sort of hearing which can cut the listener off from faith. The Jews, for example, are generally characterized as listening but not actually hearing, in that they read or hear their

Scriptures, but do not believe; hence they do not actually 'hear' them at all. As Cyril of Jerusalem observes to his catechumens when commenting on arguments from prophecy, 'The Jews read these words, but do not hear them; for they have stopped the ears of their heart in order not to hear.'[5] Effective hearing therefore seems to lie, not so much in the acquisition of knowledge as in a right orientation of the will; in opening the 'ears of the heart'; in a willingness to receive what is heard and to allow it to impress itself upon the mind in such a way that it forms or transforms it—a process which could equally well describe how we come to believe.

The evidence of the effect of right hearing upon the mind and will is therefore seen, first, in the faith of the hearer and then in their words and actions: addressing the object of their faith in prayer, seeking Him in hope and love, and acting in accordance with His will. These effects are more often than not attributed to the action of God, in His Word and Holy Spirit, rather than to anything done by the hearer, but still, it is primarily through hearing that early Christian writers describe both the formation of faith, and the actions and prayers inspired by it. Augustine summarizes this threefold process when he paraphrases the verses of Romans 10.13–15 we have already noted: 'So preachers were sent, they preached Christ. By their preaching the peoples heard, by hearing they came to believe, by believing they called upon God's name.'[6] He elaborates on these stages further when he uses them to structure his *Enchiridion*, a sort of handbook of Christian doctrine. Like faith, doctrine is here understood not so much as a matter of right knowledge, but of a right attitude of the will, or right worship, expressed in faith, hope, and love. The work falls into three parts: the first considers the objects of faith through an exposition of the Apostles' Creed; the second considers the objects of hope through an exposition of the petitions of the Lord's Prayer; the third considers the objects of love through an exposition of the Gospel. Christian doctrine, or orthodoxy, is therefore set forth to Augustine's correspondent Laurentius as primarily a matter of the right operation of the will in faith, hope, and love towards God—in other words, of right praise or worship (*doxa*) rather than a matter of right thinking or opinion. Hearing the Creed, the Lord's Prayer, or the Gospels, therefore, impresses not so much a knowledge of particular articles of the faith upon the mind as a right orientation upon the will, moving it to call upon God in faith, hope, and love for what cannot, as yet, be known or seen in its fullness.

---

[5] *Catecheses*, 12.13 (Yarnold, 145); cf. 13.25: 'The Jews are hard of hearing . . .'; 13.31 where Cyril has Christ say to the thief who was crucified with him, '"Amen, I say to you, today you will be with me in Paradise" for today you have heard my voice and not hardened your heart.' One thinks of the hardening of Pharaoh's heart in this context (Yarnold (2000), 156, 158).
[6] *Sermon*, 57.1 (WSA III.3, 109).

The three stages of hearing, believing, and then praying also naturally structure Augustine's approach to baptismal catechesis. As we shall see in more detail later in this chapter, two of the most significant landmarks in the catechumenate were the *traditio symboli*: the handing over and learning of the Creed, so that it could be publically recited, or handed back (*redditio symboli*), and the *traditio orationis*: the handing over and learning of the Lord's Prayer. The Creed was learnt first, Augustine states, so that having received and retained how they are to believe in God the candidates could then learn how to call upon God, their Father, in the Lord's Prayer, for, as he invariably observes, following Paul, 'How shall they call upon one in whom they have not believed?' (Rom 10:14).[7] Hearing the Creed, and being informed by the faith, they are thus led to turn their minds and will to God in prayer.

That faith, hope, and love, or the process of hearing, believing, and praying, informed and inspired by the Creed, the Lord's Prayer, and the Gospel, was not one that ended in baptism, but was a matter of lifelong formation, is evident in the fact that the process was repeated every time a liturgy was celebrated, and in the father's clear teaching that human beings needed to continually repeat the Creed and the petitions of the Lord's Prayer in order to form and reform their faith, hope, and love until the life to come. Augustine therefore presents his teaching, and the readings and hymns heard in church, as a sort of daily bread, sustaining Christian pilgrims until they reach their goal. In *Sermon*, 57, on the Lord's Prayer, he comments,

> the fact that I am dealing with this subject for you, and that you hear readings in the Church every day, is daily bread; and that you hear and sing hymns is daily bread. These are the things we need on our pilgrimage. But when we finally get there, do you imagine we shall be listening to a book? We shall be seeing the Word itself, listening to the Word itself, eating it, drinking it, as the angels do now. Do the angels need books, or lectures, or readers? Of course not. They read by seeing, since they see Truth itself . . . So much, then, for our daily bread, to show that this petition is necessary for us in this life.[8]

The contrast between the body's present need, indeed hunger, for sense perception—and especially for hearing the Word—stands in sharp contrast to the way in which all its senses—hearing, sight, taste, touch, and smell—will possess and be possessed; consume and be consumed, by the Word in the life to come. The angels are simply left to permanently practise the goal of the process which human beings must continually repeat; having drunk their fill of the Word, Augustine comments that 'they burst out into praise, and are never wanting for praises to sing. "For blessed are those" says the psalm, "who dwell in your house; for ever and ever shall they praise you" (Psalm 84:4).'[9]

---

[7] *Sermon*, 56.1 (WSA III.3, 95).   [8] *Sermon*, 57.7 (WSA III.3, 112).
[9] *Sermon*, 58.6 (WSA III.3, 120–1).

Of course, the constant repetition of readings from Scripture, the recitation of the creeds, and the hymns and prayers heard in church, would contribute not only to the formation of the faith, hope, and love of the individual Christian but to the formation of Christian doctrine as it is normally understood. As the repeated hearing of these expressions of the faith made them more and more ingrained in Christian language, thought, and practice, they inevitably also informed reflection on the difficult questions of Christology, pneumatology, Trinitarian theology, ecclesiology, and sacramental practice, which heresy, schism, and the attempt to defend the faith and the body of Christ were to constantly pose. A tacit, almost intuitive response had been engraved upon the minds of those who had heard, believed, and prayed the faith from the catechumenate onwards, which could not but inform any attempt to explicitly formulate and defend the faith when occasion arose. It has been observed that someone like Cyril of Jerusalem is much more conscious of this in his catechetical homilies than Augustine, who was more preoccupied with orthodoxy as the formation of a correct attitude of mind than correct doctrines.[10] Whatever the emphasis in baptismal instruction—on orthodox faith understood as a matter of either true worship or true thinking—its inherently formative, provisional, temporal nature was acknowledged by all: it was, above all else, a matter of hearing and receiving the faith, and faith, by definition, is faith in what is, as yet, unseen and beyond human knowing in this life. We have already examined Augustine's vision of the eschatological transformation of hearing into the full possession of the Word with all the senses in the life to come. Other fathers stress the eschatological acquisition of full knowledge or understanding. The fact that there is a sort of proleptic knowledge, as it were, which is communicated by hearing and believing, just as for Augustine there is a sort of proleptic worship, is an indication that the faith, which hearing God's Word impresses, plays an important role: it gradually forms and orientates the mind and will towards its unknowable and ungraspable object so that it can be fully known and grasped in the life to come. As Chrysostom comments to the baptized, 'I promised to tell you why we are called the faithful. Why then, are we called this? We faithful have believed in things which our bodily eyes cannot see. These things are great and frightening and go beyond our nature. Neither reflection nor human reason will be able to discover and explain things; only the teaching of faith understands them well. Therefore God has made for us two kinds of eyes: those of the flesh and those of faith.'[11] This is the case

---

[10] As Kreider (1941), 47, observes, 'Cyril's priorities were clear. He was concerned about purity of belief, to which he devoted at least twenty times the attention he gave to changed behaviour. His teaching against "the brood of heretics" was vastly more practical, more "how-to-do-it", than his much briefer teachings on behaviour could be. For Cyril, conversion meant, above all, believing the right things.'

[11] *Baptismal Instruction*, 11.11 (ACW 31).

because faith is not something we acquire but is something which is *given* to us: what is heard and believed is God's Word; His divinely inspired Scriptures; the divinely inspired words of His preachers and teachers; psalms, hymns, and prayers. These are all the work of His Word, and it is this Word which the catechumen hears, at first outwardly with their ears, then inwardly, as it impresses itself upon their mind and will, so that they might embrace it in its fullness in the life to come. Hearing thus enables us to grasp, in faith, what otherwise goes beyond what bodily eyes can see or human reason can discover and explain.

The crucial movement from outward to inward hearing; from baptismal instruction to becoming one of the 'faithful', in whom the faith was impressed as a seal upon the mind and heart, is a movement effected by the gift of the Holy Spirit in baptism. Cyril of Jerusalem reflects on the transformation which baptism effects thus:

> Up till now you have been called a catechumen, one who hears from the outside. You heard hope, but you didn't know it. You heard mysteries, but you didn't understand them. You heard the Scriptures, but you didn't understand their depth. But now you are not hearing a sound outside you but one within, for now the Spirit lives in you and makes your mind God's home. When you hear what is written about the mysteries, then you will understand things which you didn't know.[12]

It is clear that what Cyril is referring to as 'inward hearing' is primarily the ability to hear and understand what is said when the mysteries of the faith, which have been prepared for in catechetical instruction, impressed through teaching and preaching, sealed by the Holy Spirit in the rite of baptism, and participated in for the first time in the candidate's reception of the Eucharist, are finally explained, and their significance made clear. There is now, in a sense, both an outward and inward hearing, since what is heard by the ears can be received, interpreted, and understood by what has already been imprinted upon the mind and heart by the gift of God's word in instruction, preaching, baptism, and the Eucharist. It is as if the themes (the creeds, summaries, and statements) stated so carefully during catechetical instruction, which have been inscribed upon the mind of the catechumen in order to prepare and inform it for baptism, and which have been sealed by the gift of the Holy Spirit in baptism and the Eucharist, are now able to echo and find a resonance with the explanation of the mysteries which are imparted to the newly baptized member of the Church, thus making them truly one of the faithful—a literate listener.

We saw Chrysostom distinguishing between two types of seeing earlier in this chapter: with the eyes of the flesh and the eyes of faith. Cyril of Jerusalem's

---

[12] *Procatechesis*, 6 (Yarnold, 81).

parallel distinction between two types of faith is a convenient summary of the outward and inward hearing we have just attempted to describe: the first type of faith, he states, is our listening to, and assent to, doctrines; which he presumably understands as the process whereby the soul willingly listens to God's words, imprinting them upon the mind or memory (what we described as right hearing earlier in this chapter, as opposed to the Jew's hardness of hearing and unwillingness to 'hear' Christ in the Scriptures); the second is the faith given by Christ as a grace, through the Holy Spirit, which 'doesn't only concern doctrines, but can produce effects which transcend human powers'.[13] Cyril does not expand on what he means by this rather enigmatic statement, but, given that it appears in the context of a baptismal homily on faith, we might hazard a guess that he is referring to the gift of the Holy Spirit in baptism to the one who has heard the faith aright, and is able to profess it at baptism, so that their sins are forgiven and they are initiated as one of the faithful. Thus, outward hearing becomes inward hearing through God's gracious gift of the Holy Spirit in baptism.

The presence of an inner teacher, speaking to the inner ears, is a commonplace in patristic teaching, whether this teacher is identified as the Holy Spirit or Christ. As we have already noted, this is an idea which is used figuratively, to refer to the soul's attentiveness to God's words and its willingness to be formed by them, but it is also used literally, to refer to the presence of God's grace, of His Word and Holy Spirit, within the soul, impressing and forming it in His image. But we must not forget, however, that, as we saw Chapter 3, in sinful, temporal human beings, inward hearing of the inner teacher depends, first and foremost, upon the teaching which has already informed the mind and will by means of *outward*, preparatory, formative hearing or catechesis. It is this which enables it to be attentive to, and to receive the grace of God's gift of inner teaching and formation which begins in baptism; the theme cannot create echoes or resonances until it has already been stated and heard. The fathers therefore often refer to their catechetical instruction as something which, as it were, prepares the ground of the soul for planting;[14] or makes ready the jar of the soul to receive God's grace. As Chrysostom comments in reference to adoption by the Spirit in baptism, 'so get your soul ready like a jar, to become a son of God, "God's heir" and "Christ's fellow-heir" (Rom. 8:17)— provided you get yourself ready to receive, provided you approach in faith, so as to become one of the Faithful; provided you lay aside the old man in earnest'.[15]

The anointings, exorcisms, scrutinies, and spiritual/ascetic exercises which were an intrinsic feature of the catechumenate were also interpreted in this

---

[13] Cyril of Jerusalem, *Catecheses*, 5.10–11 (Yarnold, 112–13).
[14] Chrysostom, *Baptismal Instruction*, 1.47 (ACW 31, 41–2).
[15] Cyril of Jerusalem, *Catecheses*, 3.15 (Yarnold, 95).

same context, as cleansing the soul, ridding it of evil, preparing it for the reception of the Holy Spirit and the forgiveness of sins in baptism. For example, the anointing of the ears, in particular, was understood as God opening, or wakening, the ears so that they might be able to hear.[16] Chrysostom therefore likens the catechumen preparing their soul for baptism, by getting rid of all evil habits, to a painter preparing his canvas for colours that cannot be erased, by first of all cleansing it of all dirt.[17]

The regular reading of Scripture during the formation of the catechumenate was also understood as fashioning the soul according to the Word, and, above all, since we cannot hear or see God Himself, as enabling it to listen to His incarnate Word, and to be moulded and conformed to Him. As Irenaeus forcefully puts it,

> For in no other way could we have learned the things of God, unless our Master, existing as the Word, had become man. For no other being had the power of revealing to us the things of the Father, except His own proper Word . . . Again, we could have learned in no other way than by seeing our Teacher, and hearing his voice with our own ears, that, having become imitators of his works as well as doers of His words, we may have communion with Him.[18]

The hearing, learning, and recitation of the Creed and the Lord's Prayer during the catechumenate was also primarily understood as preparing and forming the mind and will of the hearer in order to receive the grace of faith in baptism and become one of the faithful.[19] That it is primarily hearing which is needed in order to prepare the mind and will, rather than seeing, or any of the other senses, is made clear in the fathers' understanding of the 'catechumen' as one who hears, in whom what is heard sets up echoes so that it is remembered and informs the mind and will. Every aspect of the catechumenate, then— from the fathers' regular instructions and sermons, Scriptural readings, the hearing, learning, and recitation of the Creed and the Lord's Prayer, daily prayers, the powerful words of the exorcist, the anointing of the ears—seems to have been directed at preparing and forming the mind and will through the ears, so that it is ready to receive (or resonate with) the gift of the Holy Spirit.

Finally, faith had always been understood by the fathers as a 'necessary preconception' for understanding. The idea of *aesthesis katalepsis* is a philosophical one, used notably by Clement of Alexandria in the second century, but it expresses well what we have called the proleptic, preparatory, formative

---

[16] Cyril of Jerusalem, *Mystagogic Catecheses*, 3. 4 (Yarnold, 177) comments, 'First you are anointed on the forehead . . . Next you are anointed on the ears, so as to be given the ears spoken of by Isaiah (50:4 (LXX)): "And the Lord has given me an hear to hear" and by the Lord in the Gospels: "He that has ears to hear, let him hear" (Mt 11:15).'

[17] *Baptismal Instruction*, 12.23 (ACW 31, 179–80).

[18] *Against Heresies*, 5.1.1 (ANCL 9, 55).

[19] E.g. Ambrose, *On the Sacraments*, 3.12–15 (Yarnold (1972), 126–7).

nature of the hearing of the faith during the catechumenate. Most of the fathers stress that the catechumen only becomes one of the faithful at baptism, for only then, having received the grace of the Holy Spirit in the forgiveness of sins, are they able to begin to understand the instruction they have received and the mysteries of baptism and the Eucharist.[20] Some fathers, such as Chrysostom and Augustine, give this instruction immediately beforehand; others, such as Ambrose, Cyril of Jerusalem, and Theodore of Mopsuestia give it immediately afterwards. All would agree that understanding only follows faith, and that the faith formed by hearing during catechesis, and sealed by the Holy Spirit in baptism, enabled understanding of the instruction in its mysteries (by which they generally mean its sacraments), which was given either immediately before, or in the week after, baptism.[21] But we also saw that even this 'understanding' is itself partial and provisional, and will only be complete when the faith, hope, and love formed in the soul by hearing gives way to possession of their object in the life to come, so that all that is left is endless praise; the theme of the faith must continually echo and resonate in this life, until it is resolved in a final coda.

THE RULE OF FAITH

What was this 'theme'? For various reasons, and in different contexts, the fathers attempted to state the faith as simply and concisely as possible; to summarize it, and to communicate it in such a way that it could be readily memorized and was rendered uncompromisingly clear in the minds of the faithful. 'Rules of faith',[22] such as we identified in Peter's speech in Acts 10, were a feature of Christian teaching, self-understanding, and initiation, from the very beginning. They reappear at every turn: in discussions about what should be included in the canon of Scripture; in Scripture itself; in the heroic confessions or witnesses to the faith made by the martyrs against their persecutors; in reasoned apologies or defences of faith against heretics; in the fathers' preaching and teaching; the prayers and hymns of the faithful; Eucharistic prayers; the threefold interrogation and statement of faith in the

---

[20] E.g. Ambrose, *On the Sacraments*, 1.1 (Yarnold (1972), 99) Addressing the newly baptized Ambrose comments, 'I shall begin now to speak of the sacraments which you have received. It was not proper for me to do so before this, because, for the Christian, the faith must come first. That is why, at Rome, the baptized are called the faithful; and our father Abraham was made just not by his works but by faith.'

[21] E.g. Chrysostom, *Baptismal Instruction*, 11.16 (ACW 31, 165).

[22] *Regula* (*kanon* in Greek—a measuring rod or yardstick used to test for straightness). Summaries of the faith were early referred to as 'rule of faith', 'rule of truth', or simply as 'the tradition'.

Trinity, Father, Son, and Holy Spirit, in baptism; the words of exorcism; the later, formal creeds of the Church, drafted by councils and recited in the liturgy. They varied from short, ejaculatory confessions or prayers, such as 'Jesus is Lord', to summaries of key beliefs set out in an extemporary fashion as occasion and context demanded, to the lengthy, formal creeds of the great Churches which needed to be handed over, expounded, memorized, and recited aloud.[23] In almost all cases (with the exception, perhaps, of certain anti-heretical texts) they were originally spoken, or intended for oral delivery; to be received by the ears, and impressed upon the minds of both the speaker and the hearer through listening. Their particular form and purpose, combined with their delivery, give us a direct insight not only into what early Christian teachers understood the elements of the faith to be, but precisely what it was they wanted to impress upon the minds of their hearers. Despite their varied forms—indeed, perhaps because of the variations—they also offer us a unique opportunity to begin to hear the harmonies and resonances within the polyphony of voices which is early Christian literature: we also, as it were, become initiates, and are made aware of the grammar that structures early Christian writing and which allows us to interpret it.

The most important features of the rule of faith for the fathers were its unity, continuity, and universality: it always and everywhere communicated the same basic message, and was publically proclaimed to everyone who was able and willing to hear it. These key features were believed to reside in its origin: it derived from Christ's teaching to the apostles; the apostles' proclamation to the Churches; the Churches' faithful teaching in the present. As Irenaeus famously put it, 'This, beloved, is the preaching of the truth, and this is the manner of our redemption, and this is the way of life, which the prophets proclaimed, and Christ established, and the Apostles delivered, and the Church in all the world hands on to her children.'[24] Elsewhere he makes clear the crucial role of the Church in the present: 'the Church . . . though disseminated throughout the whole world, carefully guards this preaching and this faith which she has received, as if she dwelt in one house. She likewise believes these things as if she had but one soul and one and the same heart; she preaches, teaches and hands them down harmoniously, as if she possessed but one mouth.'[25] The rule of faith therefore had an authority which was both historical and publically verified: it had been said or done by Christ, witnessed first-hand by the apostles, and passed on in the teaching of the Church by bishops duly ordained in apostolic sees, and in direct succession from them.[26]

---

[23] See Cullmann (1949); Hall in Hazlett (1991a), 101–12, for references.

[24] *Demonstration of the Apostolic Preaching*, 98 (MacKenzie, 28).

[25] *Against Heresies*, 1.10.1 (ACW 55, 49).

[26] Irenaeus, *Against Heresies*, 3.3.2–3 (ACW 64, 32–3) refers to 'the faith proclaimed to men, which has come down even to us through the successions of the bishops . . .' By this order and

These are elements which are most notable in early writers such as Irenaeus, Tertullian, or Origen, for whom they were crucial aspects of the Christian faith in defending it against the heretical Gnostic schools, but they subsequently became defining features for all the fathers who wanted to emphasize the authority of the Christian faith—or tradition (as it increasingly came to be called, drawing upon its nature as a teaching handed down (*tradere*) by the faithful)—in the various contexts we indicated above. Irenaeus provides us with a wonderful glimpse of this tradition at work when he reflects on his encounters with Bishop Polycarp of Smyrna, who had himself conversed with John and other apostles, and who handed on their words and what he had heard to him. In a letter to the Roman priest, Florinus, Irenaeus observes, 'To these things I listened eagerly at that time, by the mercy of God shown to me, not committing them to writing, but learning them by heart. By God's grace, I constantly and conscientiously ruminate on them . . .'[27] Hearing, mental inscription, and graced reflection are all, as we are now well aware, character-istics of faithful, right, and, we might now add, 'traditioned' hearing. It is this sort of hearing which Irenaeus describes in the Churches where the apostles did not leave writings, but simply an oral tradition, and most especially among the barbarians, who could not read Greek, but heard, believed, and then passed on the faith by word of mouth: 'Those who, in the absence of written documents, have believed this faith, are barbarians, so far as regards our language; but as regards doctrine, manners and conversation, they are, because of faith, very wise indeed.'[28] In other words, they, too, have become literate listeners.

The master key, as it were, to the rules of faith in their various forms, and their effective tradition, was, of course, the Word of God: Creator; inspirer of the prophets; incarnate; enScriptured; preached; confessed. It was the Word who acted, who was enunciated, and who was heard as they were passed on; who echoed and resonated throughout Christian tradition and gave it its unity, continuity, and universality. The danger of distortion, which inevitably occurs in any oral tradition, was circumvented by the fact that it is the *same* Word which acts and speaks in each instance: the Word of God the Father, the Creator, Redeemer, and Trinity. What was important, therefore, was to remain faithful to this Word, and to its tradition, as it was handed on in Scripture, preaching, and worship.

When Irenaeus set out to write what he entitled a *Demonstration* (*epideixis*) *of the Apostolic Preaching* it was precisely this presence of the Word that he was setting out to 'demonstrate' or prove, as we noted briefly in the quotation

---

succession, the tradition that is in the Church from the apostles and the preaching of the truth have come down to us.'

[27] Irenaeus, *Letter to Florinus*, in Eusebius, *A History of the Church*, 5.20 (Williamson, 169).
[28] Irenaeus, *Against Heresies*, 3.4.2 (ANCL 5, 265).

from *Against Heresies*. Origen does the same when he begins his magisterial work *On First Principles*.[29] He makes clear at the very beginning of the Prologue that the whole faith rests on Christ, his words, and teaching: that, 'All who believe and are convinced that grace and truth came by Jesus Christ and that Christ is the truth derive the knowledge which calls men to lead a good and blessed life from no other source but the very words and teaching of Christ' (1). But he insists that this is not just Christ's teaching in the flesh, but that of the Word in the Old Testament, through the prophets, and of the same Word in the New Testament, through his apostles. This Word is not, however, unambiguous, and Origen is aware that even the opinions of those who believe in Christ often conflict concerning the nature of God, Christ, the Holy Spirit, or the heavenly powers. He therefore insists that 'it seems necessary to lay down a definite line and unmistakable rule in regard to each of these, and to postpone the inquiry into other matters' (about which, it becomes clear, he means doctrines which are less plain) until afterwards. What is plain, and what we can know with certainly concerning God, the Trinity, Origen tells us, can be found in 'the teaching of the church, handed down in unbroken succession from the apostles' and that 'that only is to be believed as the truth which in no way conflicts with the tradition of the church and the apostles' (2). Such doctrines he summarizes in creedal fashion, beginning with the doctrine of God as Creator, the God of the Old Testament and the patriarchs and prophets, the Father of Jesus Christ, the God of the New Testament and the apostles; the doctrine of Christ, his incarnation, virgin birth, death, passion, resurrection, and ascension; the doctrine of the Holy Spirit (4); the doctrine of the soul, its reward or punishment depending on the exercise of its free will, and its bodily resurrection (5); the doctrine of the inspiration of the Scriptures (8). Doctrines such as the origin of the Holy Spirit (whether he is begotten or unbegotten), the origin of the soul, the nature of the devil and his angels, of the angelic powers, and of what existed before or after the world, on the other hand, are all doctrines which are somewhat less definite and remain to be clarified through 'clear and cogent arguments' and Scripture, but Origen is confident that once this is done he will be able to produce a 'single, connected body of doctrine' (9). Thus, whilst he is quite clear that there is a plain, definite set of doctrines which have been imparted to us by apostolic tradition, handed down in unbroken succession by the Church, and based upon the revelation of the Word in the Old and New Testaments, he also identifies the important role of Scripture in clarifying those doctrines which are less plain and clear in the tradition.

The interdependence of Scripture and tradition was one which all the fathers assumed in their attempts to faithfully establish and expound both of

---

[29] References are from Butterworth (1936).

them. Both, as we have seen, were known largely through being heard in a multitude of different contexts, which would lead to their being remembered, believed, and practised. In this way Scripture and the apostolic tradition presumably impressed not only their own set of mental images, but would inevitably resonate with, and thereby inform, illuminate, and reform existing images of each other (just as we noted doctrinal reflection being gradually informed by early Christian listening earlier in this chapter). Thus, as much as by Origen's 'clear and cogent arguments', uncertain doctrines were clarified by the more certain (a practice which we often see at work in patristic sermons in relation to particular Scriptural texts), and a single body of faith would emerge. It was also the case that one confirmed and lent coherence and authority to the other: resonance with the rules of faith was a measure for judging whether or not a work should be included in the emerging canon of Scripture and was a key to its subsequent interpretation; resonance with Scripture, in turn, lent ultimate authority to the rules of faith,[30] especially as they gradually took fixed creedal forms which were understood (as we shall see in more detail later in this chapter) as nothing more than short summaries of Scripture which were indispensable in allowing the faithful to begin to be initiated into its mysteries.[31] This was the case because both were thought to be inspired by the Holy Spirit and to communicate Christ, the Word of God. As Cyril of Jerusalem puts it in relation to Scripture, 'Everything about Christ is included in Scripture; nothing is unclear or unattested. Everything is inscribed, not on tablets of stone, but on the prophetic monuments, written unmistakably by the Holy Spirit.'[32] One could therefore be used to interpret the other, and both together represented the essential form in which the Word of God shaped early Christian hearing, belief, and action, and, in turn, early Christian identity and self-understanding.

Scholars such as Frances Young have referred to the rules of faith we have just outlined as those statements which 'articulated the essential hermeneutical key without which texts and community would disintegrate in incoherence',[33] in other words, they provided a sort of 'authoritative reception'; an oral, remembered understanding by which the 'intuitive intent' or 'mind (*dianoia*)' of Scripture could be both heard and understood by the Christian community, and thereby also inform it.[34] In *On First Principles*, Origen, like Irenaeus, emphasizes the unity, continuity, and universality of the apostolic rule of faith; both point to the need for coherence within the rule based upon a single,

---

[30] E.g. Cyril of Jerusalem, *Catechesis*, 4.17: 'For this is the guarantee of our Creed, not clever argument, but proof based on Scripture' (Yarnold, 103).

[31] E.g. Augustine, *On Faith and the Creed*, 1.1 (WSA 1.8, 155–6); Cyril of Jerusalem, *Catechesis*, 5.12 (Yarnold, 113).

[32] Cyril of Jerusalem, *Catechesis*, 13.8 (Yarnold, 153).

[33] Young (2007), 21.

[34] Young (2007), 28.

unifying factor. We have seen that, for both of them, the rule of faith—the 'hermeneutical key'; the 'mind' or 'hypothesis' of Scripture[35]—was found in Christ, the Word of God, and it is this which one commentator on Irenaeus' *Demonstration* aptly describes as 'the one "scope", that is (in the sense of *skopos*) the centre and horizon, the substance and the goal, of both Scripture and tradition, for what it is in itself alone without any other consideration, and clearing the ground so that it can be perceived and allowed to speak for itself on its own terms'.[36] Christ, the Word, is therefore the determinative theme which resonates in the hearer's mind as it is initially impressed, and then developed, recapitulated, and played in infinite variations in early Christian rules, tradition, and Scripture. It is Christ, the Word, who provides the essential harmony, unity, and continuity to the many different contexts and forms in which He appears:[37] He is both word and meaning;[38] *signa* and *res*; and the former, wherever it sounds, is true, because the latter is the truth itself.

It was the common confession of Christ, then, from the earliest catch-phrases, slogans, and confessions of the apostolic Church, through to the various rules of faith and the developed creeds, which almost certainly allowed, indeed inspired, the sort of variations that we have mentioned earlier in this chapter. They were possible because whatever form they took they had the same object and thus always resonated with the truth which he is. What they communicated, therefore, was not so much particular doctrines or ideas as the Word of God Himself, who, once heard, inspired belief, followed by prayer/action. It was a long while before any of the rules or summaries of tradition became fixed and uniform, and when it did happen it was necessitated by particular historical circumstances rather than desired for its own sake. Until the mid-fourth century the Church seems to have been content with the glorious polyphony of the Word of God sounding, echoing, and resonating in many forms and contexts. Following the conversion of Constantine it sought a single note line at the same time as it was seeking a single, united Empire under a single rule or monarchy and (if some theologians and legislation had their way) under a single faith in the One God. As we shall see in Chapters 5 and 6, the ad hoc, extempory variations, and improvisations remained in sermons, hymns, and prayers, but the fluidity and flexibility

---

[35] Both terms used by Young (1990), ch. 3.

[36] MacKenzie (2002), 35, observes that this foreshadows Athanasius' emphasis on Christ as the '*skopos* of the Scriptures and the faith, which point to him as their centre, content and horizon' and refers to *Contra Arianos*, 3.29.

[37] This is something which Cullmann (1949), 57, endorses in his survey of what he calls 'early Christian confessions'. He writes, 'We can conclude that the divine Sonship of Jesus Christ and his elevation to the dignity of *Kyrios*, as consequence of His death and resurrection, are the two essential elements in the majority of the confessions of the first century.'

[38] Young (2007), 35, refers to Quintilian's distinction between *ho lektikos topos* (the verbal dress) and *ho pragmatikos topos* (the subject matter) (*Institutio Oratoria*, 10. 1 and 2).

which had been found in rules of faith and variations in creedal statements, in the hands of different authors, in different contexts and regions, gave way to universally fixed formulae. What had been more in the nature of a 'key signature', which allowed for many different compositions as long as they harmonized and were in the same key, now became a definitive theme to be repeated by all.

THE NARRATIVE OF THE FAITH

Although Christ is the key to the rule of faith, the theme it played out usually took the form of a historical, chronological story of God's interaction with humanity, beginning with creation, proceeding through the patriarchs and prophets of the Old Testament, to His incarnation, passion and resurrection in the New Testament, and the preaching, teaching and sacraments of the Church into the present. This story was one which every catechist sought to inscribe upon the minds of their hearers. It represented the relation between God and His creation in a form which resembled less a list of doctrines or ideas, and more a story, or a performance, in which the faith came memorably and engagingly to life through particular characters, events, and speeches which all harmonized with the Word of God.

When the presbyter Deogratias wrote to his bishop, Augustine of Hippo, for advice on how to go about instructing his catechumens for baptism, he received, in response, a treatise which we now know as *Teaching Beginners in the Faith*. As we shall see in more detail in the Second Impromptu, Augustine's primary concern is to ensure that the speaker is sensitive to the needs and limitations of his hearers so that the faith could be effectively communicated. But he also gives an example of catechetical instruction, both to show how his advice can be put into practice, and to give an idea of what it should contain. The contents take the form of a narrative of the faith— a rhetorical *narratio* or connected story—recounting the history of God's saving actions, such as we have seen outlined above, dwelling on the more exciting episodes and the most colourful characters so that they might be considered and admired,[39] retain the attention of the hearer, and thereby be inscribed upon their mind and taken to heart—in other words, believed and acted upon.

Augustine, in his turn, was no doubt inspired by his African predecessor, Cyprian, whose *To Quirinum* was perhaps also a response to a request concerning catechesis. It takes the form of three books, which echo the process

---

[39] *Instructing Beginners in the Faith*, 3.5 (Canning, 64–5).

of hearing, believing, prayer/action which we already have identified as characteristic of early Christian catechesis. The first book sets forth the Christian *narratio* by giving a detailed account of salvation history through a string of biblical quotations; the second concerns Christology (or the *skopos* of Scripture and salvation history); the third contains Christ's precepts and teaching, which emphasize belief, and, above all, action.

In the East, Irenaeus similarly sets forth the idea of a divine *oikonomia* (dispensation or economy), in the history of God's providential salvation through His Holy Spirit. It is a story held together by the Spirit's inspiration and action, both in the past and in the Church in the present, giving not just a sense of identity, but of real belonging and unity, 'For where the Church is, there is the Spirit of God; and where the Spirit of God is, there is the church, and every kind of grace.'[40]

Apprehending the Christian faith as a story was, of course, inherent in its understanding of itself as a religion of fulfilment; as already possessing deep roots and a long history in Judaism, in God's relationship with Israel, and the teaching of the prophets. From the very beginning Christ had been understood as the Messiah, the promised deliverer, and the language, imagery, and Scriptures of the faith had been moulded by the profound resonances which at least Jewish Christian writers heard with their past when the *kerygma* of Christ's life and teaching were proclaimed (the case of Gentile Christians, was of course, rather different, as we see in Acts). Their sense of community and identity, and their imaginative thought world, had been moulded by a history which they understood to be continuing in the present. The early Christians therefore heard and understood themselves to be placed in the context of an ongoing story in which they now had a central role to play.

Like most stories in the ancient world, this was one which was handed on by word of mouth; it was part of a tradition, recounted by a speaker and received by attentive listeners. The framework of the story, its 'hermeneutical key', or 'skopos' was, as we saw above, the history of a person, the Word of God, and of his interaction with the world. Telling and hearing the story, handing it on, as it were, became a way of participating in it, and moving it forward, as it continued from the Old Testament to the New; from the apostles to the Church, for it was still unfinished and unresolved, and its conclusion lay in the future, with the Last Judgement and the life to come. Speaking and hearing therefore had a crucial role to play in both its continuation and its fulfilment,

---

[40] *Against Heresies*, 3.24.1 (ANCL 5, 370). An insight echoed throughout Western ecclesiology, in Cyprian and Augustine, for whom the grace of God can only be mediated in the true Church—in other words, the Church where his Spirit is present. Irenaeus' words sound very like Cyprian's: 'He cannot have God as a father who does not have the Church as a mother' in *On the Unity of the Catholic Church*, 6 (FC 36, 100).

and it is this which all Christian teachers had in mind as they recounted it, over and over again, in many different contexts.[41]

Augustine's sample catechesis in *Instructing Beginners in the Faith* is not, therefore, at all unusual, but simply a very good, extended example of the way in which all Christian teachers sought to communicate the faith. The *narratio* of the faith was no more, and no less, than an extended exposition of the rule of faith, and fulfilled the same purpose in perhaps a more effective way because the story form made it more engaging, the characters more vivid, the episodes more compelling, and the overall sense of involvement more immediate and inspiring. Narratives were therefore related to rules of faith rather as a piece of music is to its key signature; a set of variations to a theme, or an opera to a leitmotiv: they were the rules of faith in performance, played out for entertainment and instruction. The difference was that, whereas pieces of music usually reach a coda, and plays reach a final act, the Christian narration was still in progress, caught up between creation and the end of the age, and was therefore all the more engaging, in that the audience had a role in its actual completion. They too became actors and had parts to play: hearing the faith, as we have seen throughout this chapter, meant not only hearing and believing but also prayer and action, in hope and love, for what cannot yet be known or grasped. Narratives of faith, like the rule or Creed, therefore constituted less an objective, definitive, fixed statement as what Andrew Love has described as a 'resting place'; they were, as he puts it, articulations of 'Christian understanding, prepared by culture and re-received and re-interpreted in every generation'. In other words, they were part of an ongoing process of reception and interpretation which kept them alive and open to new contexts, receptions, and performances.[42]

Indeed, rather unsurprisingly, it appears that the pattern of early catechetical instruction resembles nothing more than the traditional stages of a rhetorical speech: *narratio*—the setting forth of the details of a case or history (in a Christian context, the rule of faith and the history of salvation); *explicatio*—careful explanation of their significance; *demonstratio*—proof of their veracity and authority (in a Christian context, for example, demonstrating agreement with Scripture or fulfilment of prophecy); *exhortatio*—exhortations to act upon what had been set forth, explained, and proved to be true, by believing it and allowing it to inform one's actions and (in a Christian context) prayers.

---

[41] See Young (1990), ch. 4, on typological exegesis in relating Old Testament and New Testament and the idea of salvation history or tradition as a performance.

[42] Love (2008), 62. Cf. Ayres (2005), 33, who observes that the *regula fidei* shows 'significant modifications in sense and usage as the social, cultural and polemical context of the Church changed' and that 'developing engagements with rhetorical, moral and educational theory provided opportunities for the *regula fidei* to acquire new significations'.

'HENCEFORTH, LET OUR LIFE BE STRANGE AND DIFFERENT'[43]

It was not only the narrative of the faith, set forth in catechetical instruction, which involved the hearer in its ongoing performance; the whole of the catechumenate, and especially the rite of baptism itself, developed as a highly dramatic piece of theatre in which the story of the faith—the Fall and redemption, conversion and confession of faith, death to sin and resurrection to new life, movement from darkness to light—was not only recounted, but actually re-enacted through gestures, ritual actions, words, and symbols.

The catechumenate itself was a matter of the utmost secrecy, in order to guard the mysteries of the faith from the uncomprehending ears and eyes of the uninitiated. Those who were about to be initiated found themselves caught up in it in such a way that their minds and hearts were prepared to receive and understand these mysteries through bodily actions (anointing, exorcisms, ascetic exercises such as fasting, abstinence from sex, ritual washing) and through the bodily senses. As we have seen, the primary sense that was engaged during catechesis was hearing, but later, in the baptismal rite itself, seeing, tasting, touching, and smelling were also important as the candidate passed from the darkness of the night to the light of the dawn; was touched upon the eyes and ears; faced West to renounce Satan and East to confess Christ; was anointed with chrism; stripped naked and immersed three times in an octagonal, tomb-shaped font; clothed in white garments; processed from the dark of the baptistery to the light of the church carrying a lighted taper; tasted the body and blood of Christ (and perhaps also milk and honey). The secrecy, accompanied by dramatic actions which engaged all the senses, was specifically designed to inspire awe and to be literally impressive and memorable; to engrave the event upon the memories of those who performed and heard it, so that their minds and hearts were prepared for the gift of the seal of the Holy Spirit in baptism itself.[44]

As William Harmless has observed,[45] symbol, bodily gesture, biblical story, and spoken words often interpreted each other in the catechumenate. So, for example, the symbol of the West, facing to the West, the Exodus story, and the formula of renunciation would mutually inform and illuminate each other. What the candidate heard, in the many different forms and contexts we are examining in this chapter, was therefore reinforced, and its mental impression made more effectively, by being caught up in the complex drama of the re-enactment of the story of the faith which baptism represented. A synaesthetic

---

[43] Chrysostom, *Baptismal Instruction*, 4.26 (ACW 31, 76).

[44] Hence the title which Yarnold (1994) gave to a book containing his translation of Ambrose's *On the Sacraments* and *On the Mysteries—The Awe-Inspiring Rites of Initiation*.

[45] Harmless (1995), 72.

combination of the senses, which we have noted is characteristic of the way in which the images of sense perception are generally impressed and remembered, was therefore especially evident in the context of the catechumenate and baptism.

Indeed, it is clear that the dramatic involvement of the other senses, along with hearing, made what the candidate heard more effective, and inculcated an attitude of 'right' hearing, or a right orientation of the will, to hear and then believe and act. This was not least because, first of all, the aim of most of the actions performed (anointing, exorcisms, ascetic exercises . . .)[46] was precisely to bring about moral conversion, repentance, and a purification and reorientation of the sinful will towards God. Being a catechumen was a demanding task, likened to participating in an athletic competition or engaging in military conflict; bad habits and the temptations of Satan were overcome by strict ascetic practice, head-on conflict, and constant vigilance.[47] Secondly, the retelling and re-enactment of the narrative of salvation set up a multitude of resonances and echoes with past listening and existing mental images.[48]

The movement of the candidate from the darkness of sin to the light of faith, following the movement of the drama of salvation history, and the movement from what we have called outward to inward hearing, were all understood to be effected by the work of the Holy Spirit. It was the Holy Spirit who inspired the prophets, the apostles, Scripture, the Church's preaching and teaching, the rules of faith, and the Creed, who thereby impresses the images of the faith upon the heart, and who ultimately inscribes the seal of faith in baptism, so that the initiate is enlightened. What was this 'seal' (*signaculum* (Lt); *sphragis* (Gk))?

When Augustine argues against the Donatists' practice of rebaptism he gives the example of the seal (*signaculum*),[49] which authenticated a soldier when he was conscripted into the army, and which could not be removed; he remained forever a member of the military and could be identified as such. Similarly, Augustine argues that the seal of ordination and the seal of baptism permanently mark the priest and the Christian with God's grace and cannot be repeated.[50]

---

[46] As Harmless (1995), 251, identifies them—the *competentes* fasted each day until the ninth hour (3 p.m.); abstained from meat and wine and kept their diet simple; if married, abstained from sex; distributed alms; sometimes spent the night in prayer; refrained from bathing until Holy Thursday.

[47] Harmless (1995), 253, for references.

[48] Melito of Sardis' *On Pascha* is an excellent example of these multiple echoes and resonances at work in a homily probably intended for the Easter vigil.

[49] Generally thought to be a sort of tag, in a pouch which he wore around his neck, and which bore his personal details and an authenticating seal or *signaculum*. Cf. Ambrose, *On Virgins*, 3.4.20 (Ramsay, 111) where the creed/symbol is compared to the military oath (*militiae sacramento*) and described as 'the seal of our heart' (*nostri signaculum cordis*).

[50] Augustine, *On Baptism against the Donatists*, 1.4 (NPNF 4, 414).

The fathers similarly refer to the 'seal' or sign of the cross, which was placed on the forehead when a candidate enrolled as a catechumen,[51] as 'a holy, indelible seal';[52] 'the indelible seal of the Holy Spirit'; the 'seal' of baptism.[53] 'Seal' therefore seems to refer both to the way in which God's grace is impressed or 'sealed' upon the heart of the believer,[54] as a document is sealed in order to validate its contents, and to its sacramental indissolubility. Unlike other impressions made upon the mind by the senses, it is an impression made directly by God's grace and cannot be removed, dissolved, or repeated.

It was this which the catechumen received at baptism, as he or she was initiated into the body of the Church as one of the faithful; one in whom the faith had been sealed or inscribed upon their heart by the Holy Spirit. The whole process of outward instruction and hearing, which impressed itself upon the mind and will of the hearer during the catechumenate, was therefore a preparation for this inward hearing and reception of the seal of God's Spirit.

HANDING OVER AND HANDING BACK

Foremost among the impressions received by outward hearing during the catechumenate was, of course, the Creed (*symbolum*), which Ambrose describes to the newly baptized as 'a spiritual seal . . . our heart's meditation and as it were an ever present guard'.[55] This was the first of the mysteries preserved by the discipline of secrecy, or the *disciplina arcani*, to be revealed to the candidates. The formal process of *traditio* or 'handing over' the Creed (the *traditio symboli*) was undertaken by the bishop, at a fixed point during Lent.[56]

---

[51] Cyril of Jerusalem, *Catecheses*, 4.14 (Yarnold, 102).

[52] Cyril of Jerusalem, *Procatechesis*, 16 (Yarnold, 85).

[53] Cyril of Jerusalem, *Procatechesis*, 17 (Yarnold, 85).

[54] S. of S. 8:6: 'Pone me ut signaculum super cor tuum.'

[55] Ambrose, *Explanation of the Creed*, 1 (Connolly, 19).

[56] Usually at the end of the fourth week of Lent, two weeks before Easter, and a week before it was handed back and the Lord's Prayer was learned. This is a practice which had become common in the West by the fourth century. Carpenter (1993), 376–7, questions just how far back this practice can be traced before the fourth century and concludes that the evidence is ambiguous since 'symbolum', in early texts, may not mean a declaratory creed but rather refer to the baptismal act as a whole, including the interrogations, responses, and triple immersion. In reference to Lietzmann's work, he summarizes the history of interrogatory and declaratory creeds thus: 'Lietzmann finds the second century prolific in summaries of the faith, some Christological, some based on the threefold Name, and some having yet other structural forms. Within the similar forms the details and emphasis varied. No writer down to and including Tertullian can be quoted as showing exclusive attachment to one structural form of summary, much less to one exact formula. Gradually, however, certain forms and finally a certain formula attained exclusive predominance locally. To this general picture drawn by Lietzmann we can now add the point that the local victory of the particular formula was completed and rendered permanent by the establishment at the same time in the third century

He would recite it and then deliver a series of sermons which attempted to expound its meaning and to suggest techniques for remembering it, so that it could be handed back, or publically recited by the catechumen in a liturgical context, a week later (the *redditio symboli*).[57] In the intervening week, and with the help of his or her sponsors, the candidate would be expected to learn the Creed by heart, and to engrave it upon their memory, in order to hand it back faithfully at the appointed liturgy. In this way they were marked out as members of the fellowship of the Church, as if by a password.[58] Perhaps the most famous example of such an occasion, which gives us valuable details as to how it was organized, and a wonderful insight into the importance of the public, spoken delivery of the Creed, and the effects which hearing it had on both the speaker and hearer, is that of the well-known, former pagan rhetor, Victorinus, which Augustine recounts in his *Confessions*.[59] It is worth quoting at length:

> Eventually the time came for him to make his profession of faith. Custom decrees that those who are approaching your grace in baptism make their profession in the presence of the baptised community of Rome, standing on a raised platform and using a set form of words which has been entrusted to them and committed to memory. Simplicianus told me that Victorinus had been offered by the priests the option of making his statement more privately, for it was customary to offer this concession to people who were likely to lose their nerve through shyness, but that he had chosen rather to proclaim his salvation before the holy company. What he taught in rhetoric was not salvation, he said, yet he had professed that publicly enough. If he was not afraid to address crowds of crazy people in his own words, how much less ought he to fear your peaceable flock as he uttered your word? As he climbed up to repeat the Creed they all shouted his name to one another in a clamorous outburst of thanksgiving—everyone who knew him, that is; and was there anyone present who did not? Then in more subdued tones the word passed from joyful mouth to joyful mouth among them all: 'Victorinus! Victorinus!' Spontaneous was their shout of delight as they saw him, and spontaneous their attentive silence to hear him. With magnificent confidence he proclaimed the true faith, and all the people longed to clasp him tenderly to their hearts. And so they did, by loving him and rejoicing with him, for those affections were like clasping hands.

---

of the practice of the traditio and redditio symboli; first, perhaps, in Rome, then in other Western churches and in the East.'

[57] The evidence suggests it was handed back either as part of the baptismal liturgy on Easter Eve, or on Palm Sunday. Kelly (1972), 33–4; Hart (2000), 647.

[58] Augustine, *Sermon*, 214.12 (FC 38, 142): 'For this reason the creed is called the *symbolum* because in it the approved belief of our fellowship is contained and but its profession, as by a password, the faithful Christian is recognised.'

[59] *Confessions*, 8.2.5 (Chadwick, 136–7).

The brief period of time between the *redditio* and baptism itself was spent in learning and receiving instruction on the other mystery of the faith to be imparted before baptism, the Lord's Prayer (*traditio orationis*), which we will examine in more detail in Chapter 6.[60] In other words, as Augustine often puts it, having learnt what faith in God is, the candidate would then learn how to call upon Him.[61] Thus, the soul was effectively inscribed with the images of faith through hearing, receiving, and delivering the Creed and the Lord's Prayer, so that they could be finally and definitively sealed by the Holy Spirit in baptism. In other words, the Christian identity which the candidate had professed could be verified and indelibly authenticated.

An examination of how the fathers viewed the role of the Creed, and the process by which it was handed over, learned, and recited, gives us a good insight into their understanding of the art of listening. The Creed was no more, and no less, than a rule of faith, received and handed down by the Apostles,[62] which had achieved a degree of fixity and consensus by being adopted by a local church, or later, agreed upon by an ecumenical council. Like the rules of faith, it shared the essential quality of being a summary of the main elements of the faith that could be easily remembered and recalled to mind,[63] which provided a place within which everything else that was heard could be placed and with which it could resonate,[64] as well as providing a defence against heresy entering the mind and corrupting it.[65] As Augustine puts it, 'The Creed builds up in you what you ought to believe and confess in order to be saved. Indeed, these truths, which you are about to receive and which should be entrusted to memory and professed in your speech, are neither new

---

[60] See, e.g., Augustine, *Sermons*, 56–9 (WSA III.3, 95–131). Like the Creed it was read aloud, explained line by line in a series of sermons, and handed back on Holy Saturday.

[61] *Sermon*, 56.1 (WSA III.3, 95).

[62] Ambrose, *Explanation of the Creed*, 10 (Connolly, 24–5): '. . . in the case of the Symbol which we have received, handed down from the Apostles and composed by them, we are bound to remove nothing and to add nothing'.

[63] Ambrose, *Explanation of the Creed*, 3 (Connolly, 20): 'Well then, the holy Apostles being met together made a brief summary of the faith, so that we might have the whole purport of our faith comprised in short. Brevity is needful, that it may be always remembered and recalled to mind.'

[64] As Augustine puts it in *On Faith the Creed*, 1.1 (WSA I.8, 155): 'This is the Catholic faith known as the creed and committed to memory by believers, a vast subject contained in such few words. It is for the benefit of beginners and those still on milk food; reborn in Christ, they have yet to be strengthened by a detailed spiritual study and knowledge of the divine scriptures and so are presented with the essentials of faith in a few sentences. However, for those who have advanced further and who, imbued with true humility and genuine charity, aspire to the divine teaching, the creed would of necessity have to be explained in much greater detail.'

[65] Chrysostom, *Baptismal Instruction*, 1.22 (ACW 31, 31): 'You must have these articles of faith accurately fixed in your minds, that you may not be easily overwhelmed by the deceits of the devil. But if the Arians wish to trip you up, you should know for sure that you must block up your ears to what they say.' Cf. Ambrose, *Explanation of the Creed*, 3 (Connolly, 20). The *ears* therefore become a place where orthodoxy and heresy do battle to fix themselves in the mind. Cf. Cyril of Jerusalem, *Catechesis*, 4.2 (Yarnold, 98).

nor unfamiliar to you, for you are accustomed to hear them set forth in various ways in the holy Scriptures and in sermons delivered in the Church. But now they are to be handed over to you gathered together, arranged in a fixed order, and condensed so that your faith may be well grounded and preparation made for your manifestation of that faith without taxing your memory. These are the truths which you are going to hold in mind assiduously and recite from memory.'[66]

We observed a move to increasing fixity after Constantine's conversion to Christianity, when it seems that the large influx of pagan converts, and the attempt to define orthodox faith in a public, conciliar, oecumenical context, against heretical threats such as Arianism, eventually led to the promulgation of a fixed, universal Creed at Constantinople. Early, so-called 'interrogatory' Creeds,[67] which were commonly used during the triple immersion in water at the moment of baptism, and took the form of a threefold questioning on the candidate's faith in the Father, Son, and Holy Spirit, and a threefold affirmation or response, were later accompanied by longer, fixed, 'declaratory' creeds, from the third century onwards.[68] Whatever form they took, and however flexible or fixed, local or oecumenical, written or oral the creeds were, they were all intended to be delivered: in the teaching and preaching by which they were handed over, and in the response, confession, or public recitation by which they were affirmed and handed back. In both cases they were spoken and heard, so that the handing back effectively became an echo or mirror of the handing over. As Cyril of Jerusalem puts it, hearing the Creed recited will 'rekindle the memory of what [has] already [been] learned',[69] or, as Augustine puts it, 'treat your creed as your own personal mirror. Observe yourself there, if you believe all the things you confess to believing, and rejoice every day in your faith.'[70] In the resonances and the reflections which it thus created in the minds of the speaker and hearer the Creed worked as all catechetical instruction was intended to work: it was not only heard but effectively impressed itself upon the mind so that it could be remembered, reflected upon, and allowed to inform the soul by setting up echoes within it.

The importance of 'engraving' the Creed on the memory, and writing it upon the heart, by reciting and memorizing it, rather than writing it down on paper, was therefore stressed by a number of early Christian writers, not just to preserve the *disciplina arcani* (though this was an important feature of oral/

---

[66] Augustine, *Sermon*, 214.1 (FC 38, 130).

[67] Kelly (1972), 90; Hippolytus, *Apostolic Tradition*, 21, 22 (*c*.200 ad); Whitaker in Ferguson (1993), 379–90. It continued to be part of the rite of baptism even when the more formal, fixed Creed was also used.

[68] Hart (2000), 636–59, for texts and bibliography.

[69] Cyril of Jerusalem, *Catechesis*, 4.3 (Yarnold, 98).

[70] *Sermon*, 58.13 (WSA III.3, 124), referred to by Harmless (1995), 283.

aural delivery and learning),[71] or in fulfilment of Jeremiah's prediction of the new covenant which God would write in the mind and heart (Jer. 31:33),[72] but to ensure that it had the desired effect upon the mind and heart of the hearer. As Cyril of Jerusalem urges, 'I want you to memorize it word for word, and to recite it very carefully among yourselves. Do not write it down on paper, but inscribe it in your memories and in your hearts . . . listen to the Creed and memorize it . . . "hold fast to the traditions" (2 Thess. 2:15) which will now be entrusted to you; and engrave them "on the tablet of your heart"(Prov. 7:3)'.[73] Augustine similarly recommends that his catechumens frequently repeat to themselves what they have heard so that, as he puts it, 'You will believe what you hear yourself saying, and your lips will repeat what they believe.'[74] In this context Augustine spells out the process we have traced in this chapter by emphasizing first listening, then believing, then action in order to be formed and transformed in the faith: 'The creed is learnt by listening; it is written, not on tablets nor on any material, but on the heart. He who has called you to his Kingdom and glory will grant that, when you have been reborn by his grace and by the Holy Spirit, it will be written in your hearts, so that you may love what you believe and that, through love, faith may work in you and that you— no longer fearing punishment like slaves, but loving justice like the freeborn— may become pleasing to the Lord God, the giver of all good things.'[75]

The emphasis upon memorization also led the fathers to recommend techniques to assist this: Ambrose draws attention to the fact that the twelve phrases of the Creed can be related to the twelve apostles and that these twelve phrases can be divided into three groups.[76] Cyril of Jerusalem recommends listening to the Creed as well as frequent repetition of it (whilst ensuring it is not overheard by the uninitiated).[77] Augustine urges his hearers to 'say it on your couches, think it over in the streets, be mindful of it when eating, and, even when your body sleeps, guard it in your hearts'.[78] Repeated recitation and listening to the Creed, which was, of course, a key characteristic of the Creed as it was used in the liturgy, is therefore also recommended for personal use, not just to make sure that it is known precisely, but, as it were, to form one's

---

[71] Ambrose, *Explanation of the Creed*, 12 (Connolly, 26–7).

[72] Augustine, *Sermon*, 212.2 (FC 38. 120–1).

[73] Cyril of Jerusalem, *Catecheses*, 5.12 (Yarnold, 113–14). Cf. Ambrose, *Explanation of the Creed*, 12 (Connolly, 26): 'It can be remembered all the better if not written down . . . For what you write, feeling safe as being likely to read it again, you are unlikely to say over in daily meditations; but what you do not write you are afraid you may forget, and so you are likely to say it over every day.'

[74] Augustine, *Sermon*, 398; *On the Creed, to Catechumens*, 1.1.l (WSA III.10, 445), quoted by Harmless (1995), 276.

[75] Augustine, *Sermon*, 212.2 (quoted by Harmless (1995), 275–6) (FC 38, 120–1).

[76] *Explanation of the Creed*, 11 (quoted by Harmless (1995), 97) (Connolly, 25–6).

[77] Cyril of Jerusalem, *Catechesis*, 5.12 (Yarnold, 113–14).

[78] Augustine, *Sermon*, 215.1 (FC 38, 142–3).

identity: daily repetition ensures that, like putting on clothes, it dresses the soul, and provides a mirror so that one never forgets one's identity as a Christian.[79]

The fact that the Creed provided a concise summary of the whole of Scripture, which could easily be held in mind, was, of course, the main reason why it was able to have the effects we have mentioned. When Irenaeus describes his *Demonstration of the Apostolic Preaching* as a 'manual of essentials, that by little you may attain to much, learning in short space all the members of the body of the truth, and receiving in brief the demonstration of the things of God',[80] he clearly understands the rule of faith as fulfilling the same function. Like the later creeds, it made the formidable edifice of the Scriptures accessible to the simple by laying, as Cyril of Jerusalem appositely puts it, clear and firm foundation stones, which allowed the hearer to hold the basic pattern of the faith in their minds and hearts. Thus, whatever they subsequently heard could be built upon these foundations, buttressing and strengthening them, so that the individual stones could gradually, one by one, and step by step, be carefully and harmoniously incorporated into a connected whole.[81] Cyril similarly likens the learning of the Creed to the sowing of a mustard seed; small in itself, but containing the spreading branches of the fully grown plant.[82] The building blocks or seeds which constituted the Creed were therefore very much like the formulas, word groups, and fixed patterns that oral poets memorized by constant repetition and which they then used in order to construct and compose their poems orally or spontaneously.[83] It is this process of construction and growth which we will be examining in Chapter 5, in relation to preaching in the early Church.

Little is said about the role of the catechumen's sponsor in baptism, apart from passing references to his or her role in helping them learn and memorize the Creed, but this itself is a good example of the need for spoken words rather than a written text. Presumably the sponsor would hear the candidate practise aloud, repeatedly, until they were able to inscribe it sufficiently upon their memories to repeat it unfalteringly. Thus, the sponsor's hearing, as it were, assisted the candidate's mental inscription of the Creed they were attempting to learn by encouraging them to speak it aloud and hear it themselves. As we saw Augustine observe above: 'You will believe what you hear yourself saying, and your lips will repeat what they believe.'[84] Similarly, the loving and rejoicing response of those who listened silently to Victorinus' confident profession

---

[79] Augustine, *Sermon*, 58.13 (WSA III.3, 124).

[80] *Demonstration of the Apostolic Preaching*, 1 (MacKenzie, 1).

[81] Cyril of Jerusalem, *Procatechesis*, 11 (Yarnold, 83); Augustine, *On Faith and the Creed*, 1.1 (WSA I. 8, 155).

[82] Cyril of Jerusalem, *Catechesis*, 5.12 (Yarnold, 113–14).

[83] Notopoulos (1938), 465–73; Jousse (1925), 191.

[84] *On the Creed, to Catechumens*, 1.1 (WSA III.10, 445).

of the Creed presumably assisted his entry into the faith, since they thereby effectively embraced him into the body of the Church. Speaking and hearing, as we have so often had occasion to notice, are therefore inseparably linked with inscription and initiation: there is no speaking without hearing, and hearing always has an effect upon the heart of both speaker and hearer.

THE POWER OF WORDS

The real force of even everyday words to mould the soul, for good or ill, which we observed in Part One, is therefore frequently emphasized by the fathers in their attempts to purify and prepare the hearts and minds of their listeners for baptism. As Chrysostom—who seems to have been particularly preoccupied with identifying and dealing with sins of speech—observes, 'The devil tries to hurt us in every way, but especially through our tongues and mouths. He finds no instrument so suitable for deceiving and destroying us as an undisciplined tongue and a mouth that is never closed.'[85] Thus, we find him repeatedly warning his listeners against the effects which idle chatter or overhearing could have upon their souls and admonishing them: to 'keep your tongue employed exclusively in hymns and praise, in reading of the divine word, and in spiritual conversation';[86] to pray,[87] or simply to curb their tongues, refrain from bad company,[88] and stay silent.[89] As well as idle distraction, such talking and hearing could, of course, damage the soul by what was actually said; the tongue must be kept clean 'of all disgraceful and outrageous words, blasphemy, perjury and all other sins of this sort' he admonishes. Cyril of Jerusalem also urges women to remain silent, and to do what must have seemed totally counter-intuitive in antiquity—to 'sing', say their prayers, and read Scripture *silently* (perhaps mouthing the words, but certainly not by making any sound, which might, presumably distract overhearing males).[90]

In particular, Chrysostom seems to be acutely concerned that the purity of heart which the catechumens are about to acquire at baptism should not be sullied immediately after by their ingrained habits of speech, and to ensure that they do not, as he cogently puts it, 'take the tongue which serves such awesome mysteries, which has become purpled with a blood so precious, and which has become a sword of gold, and to change its course to abuse, indolence and ribald jests'. Instead, he urges, 'Have reverence for the honour

---

[85] Chrysostom, *Baptismal Instruction*, 4.30 (ACW 31, 78).
[86] Chrysostom, *Baptismal Instruction*, 4.25 (ACW 31, 75–6).
[87] Chrysostom, *Baptismal Instruction*, 8.17 (ACW 31, 126–7).
[88] Chrysostom, *Baptismal Instruction*, 4.25 (ACW 31, 75–6).
[89] Chrysostom, *Baptismal* Instruction, 12.37 (ACW 31, 184).
[90] Cyril of Jerusalem, *Procatechesis*, 6.14 (Yarnold, 84).

God has bestowed on it, and do not lead it down to the vileness of sin.'[91]
Foremost among the ingrained habits of speech which Chrysostom attempted
to counter was that of oath-taking, an activity to which his congregation were
clearly unconsciously (and therefore all the more dangerously) addicted and
which was a part of their everyday lives, both in business transactions and
personal relations. Their bishop seems to have been similarly addicted to condemning the practice and devotes large sections of his baptismal instruction to
stressing the gravity of an oath: it is not just a form of words but it puts the life
of the soul at risk.[92] Having offered the salient and sobering example of
Herod's oath to Herodias, he draws the moral that taking an oath is always
a no-win act: if we swear to do an unlawful deed we are condemned for doing
it; if we do not do it we are condemned for not keeping our oath: 'On either
side is a precipitous cliff, on each side is inevitable death both for those who
keep the commandment and for those who fail.'[93] Having heard his injunctions and warnings against taking oaths he is aware that his congregation are
now in even more peril, for with hearing comes responsibility: the catechumens can no longer blame ignorance or unthinking habit; they have heard
their bishop's words, bear them in their hearts, and to disobey him therefore
carries an even graver penalty than before he spoke. Chrysostom thus leaves
them on the eve of baptism, about to jump from the 'precipitous cliff' sided by
death on every side, into the life-giving waters of the font, with Christ's words
ringing in their ears: 'If I had not come and spoken to them, they would have
no sin. But now they have no excuse for their sins (John 12:22).'[94]

As we saw in Chapter 1, words (and the hearing of them) were thought to
possess an inherent power for the ancients. This was dramatically demonstrated at a number of points during the catechumenate, not least in the
expulsion of evil by the words of the exorcist, the binding contract entered
into with God in the words of renunciation and the profession of faith, and the
communication of God's grace in the invocation of the Holy Spirit.[95] In all of
these instances it was words—solemnly enunciated, faithfully professed, confidently prayed—that effected a dramatic transformation. What we must
remember is that the one affected by such words was not just the speaker
but, perhaps first and foremost, the hearer—both in the sense of the hearing of
words one has oneself spoken and in the sense of the hearing of the person to
whom they are addressed. As we shall see in more detail in Chapter 6, when we
look more closely at the practice of prayer, it can be a complicated business
determining who is the intended hearer and quite what effect is intended, but

[91] Chrysostom, *Baptismal Instruction*, 12.17 (ACW 31, 178).
[92] E.g. Chrysostom, *Baptismal Instruction*, 9.36–47 (ACW 31, 143–6).
[93] Chrysostom, *Baptismal Instruction*, 10.20 (ACW 31, 156).
[94] Chrysostom, *Baptismal Instruction*, 10.29 (ACW 31, 159).
[95] Or in some baptismal liturgies, in the candidate's threefold profession of faith during the
triple immersion (Hippolytus, *Apostolic Tradition*).

at least in the case of exorcism things are rather more clear cut: the intended recipient of the exorcist's words was most definitely the catechumen and the evil which had taken possession of his or her soul (in the sense of the sins which rendered them under the power of the devil); their intended effect was the expulsion of sin so that the catechumen could be freed from slavery to Satan and made ready to receive God's grace. That the 'frightening and horrible'[96] words of the exorcist, which were usually taken from Scripture, did indeed have such an effect, was a clear demonstration of their inherent power; they not only put sin and the devil (the harmful wild beasts inhabiting the soul)[97] to flight but, as it were, furnished the hitherto empty and desolate room of the soul so that it became a royal palace, fit for God.[98] Exorcisms—or the speaking of a power-filled word—however unfamiliar to us, were, of course, practised by Jesus in the New Testament, were one of the earliest attested features of baptismal preparation,[99] and remained an intrinsic part of the catechumenate throughout the patristic period. Their disappearance in our own day is no doubt a marker of the parallel disappearance of faith in the transformative power of what Chrysostom describes as 'those awesome words'.[100]

The power of sin and its possession of the catechumen was also formally renounced in a ceremony which took place at the very beginning of the baptismal liturgy, in which the candidate turned to the West and uttered a formula of renunciation (usually, 'I renounce thee, Satan, your pomps, your service and all your works') and then turned to the East to profess their faith in Christ. These words were clearly regarded as just as binding and effective as those of the exorcist. Chrysostom likens them to a binding contract, which was written not on paper with ink, but made by the tongue, heard and witnessed by the angels, registered in heaven, and written indelibly in God by the Holy Spirit. When the candidate uttered the formula of renunciation and professed their faith, therefore, their words were heard and inscribed not just upon their own hearts, but in God, so that a sort of eternal, unbreakable, contract of faith was entered into with Him. As he puts it, 'since all of us have made our agreement with Him, writing is not in ink but in the spirit, not with the pen but with our tongue. For the tongue is the pen with which we write our contracts with God . . . We confessed His sovereignty; we rejected the domination of the devil. This was the signature, this the agreement, this the

---

[96] Chrysostom, *Baptismal Instruction*, 10.16 (ACW 31, 154–5). Kalleres (2002).
[97] Chrysostom, *Baptismal Instruction*, 10.17 (ACW 31, 155).
[98] Chrysostom, *Baptismal Instruction*, 10.16–17 (ACW 31, 154–5); cf. 2.12 (ACW 31, 47–8).
[99] E.g. *Didache* and the *Epistle of Barnabas*, where catechesis is presented in the context of the doctrine of two ways: that of Christ and that of Satan. *Apostolic Constitutions*, 7.41.
[100] Chrysostom, *Baptismal Instruction*, 2.12 (ACW 31, 47–8). See ACW 31, 219 n. 29, for examples of the words of exorcism.

contract.'[101] This idea of writing in God, or, as he puts it elsewhere, writing in the 'books of heaven'[102] is an unusual one but it indicates the power of words to impress themselves upon the hearer, to make an indelible mark, and to create a bond between speaker and listener in a manner which we will consider in more detail in the Second Impromptu.

---

[101] Chrysostom, *Baptismal Instruction*, 3.20; cf. Chrysostom, *Baptismal Instruction*, 4.31 (ACW 31, 62–3, 78).

[102] Chrysostom, *Baptismal Instruction*, 2.17 (ACW 31, 49–50).

Second Impromptu

Playing Ball: The Art of Reception

In our attempts to examine the way in which early Christians were initiated into the faith we have aligned ourselves with them, as hearers, in order to listen to the lectures, sermons, and instructions, the creed, hymns, and prayers, which would have resonated and echoed in their ears and minds during the catechumenate. In this way we have overheard what the fathers wanted their audiences to hear and how they thought their instruction should work, and have established something of their aims and methods, either by inference, or by listening to what they actually have to say, in theory, when they consciously reflect on them. We have therefore heard and learned a lot about speaking, and the art of delivery of the Christian message, with the hearer in view, but now we must pause to reflect on the art of hearing, the art of receiving of the Christian message, with the speaker in view. The obvious reason this is all too often overlooked is that the hearer is (usually) mute, and we can only imaginatively enter with them into their reception of what is heard. The less obvious, but more telling reason, is that this is how the subject of listening, or reception, was generally approached in antiquity: from the viewpoint of the speaker, and, as we have seen in Chapter 2, through the highly developed rules and methods of the art of rhetoric, which does indeed have a lot to say, directly and indirectly, about the intended effect of what is said on the hearer. But hardly anywhere do we find someone reflecting directly on the art of hearing, the art of reception, and what it might involve for the silent listener. There is, as far as I am aware, one exception: Plutarch's short treatise, in his *Moralia*, on *The Art of Listening to Lectures* (*De recta ratione audiendi*).[1] In this work we are given a rare and fascinating glimpse of the other side of the picture: his intended reader is that rare thing, not a budding rhetor, being instructed how to prepare and deliver a speech, but a pupil, a listener, being instructed how to listen to what they

[1] Henceforth: *On Listening. Plutarch's Moralia*, vol. 1, tr. Frank Cole Babbitt, Loeb Classical Library, 197 (London, 1969), 201–62; Brian P. Hillyard, *Plutarch, De Audiendo: Text and Commentary* (Salem, NH, 1988).

are taught so that they attain the truth. It therefore provides an invaluable, albeit pagan, counterpart to what we have so far examined in relation to Christian catechesis.

The fact that the work comes from a pagan author, and is intended for those who are being initiated, not into the Christian mysteries, but into philosophy, is not the stumbling block it might at first seem: anyone familiar with early Christianity will know that it was commonly regarded, by Christians as well as pagans, as a philosophy—a love of wisdom. The real difference was that Christians believed that they possessed ultimate wisdom; not just *a* philosophy, but the true philosophy, which had been fully and finally revealed in the incarnate Christ, and this meant that Christianity now superseded all the other philosophical schools. Plutarch, on the other hand, merely talks about 'philosophy', rather than any particular school, and his concern is that his reader should be aware of what is necessary to advance towards it by rightly receiving instruction in it through his or her ears, and not cut themselves off from it through their own failings, foibles, and bad habits.

The similarities between Plutarch's work, and a work such as Augustine's *Instructing Beginners in the Faith*,[2] which we have already encountered above, are therefore striking and profound. The latter is, of course, yet another Christian work on how to teach, how to address an audience, how to communicate God's Word, and to ensure that it is effectively remembered, engraved upon the mind, and allowed to echo and resonate within it in such a way that it informs the hearer's words and actions. However, the reason why this particular work has so much in common with Plutarch's is that in it Augustine seems to make every effort to tacitly discount rhetoric, to have nothing to do with it, and to concentrate instead on the message rather than the medium; the motivation rather the method; the goal rather than the way to it: in short, he concentrates first, second, and last upon love, and the giving and receiving of love as the message, motivation, and goal of the speaker, rather than on the speaking and hearing of rhetoric. The result is that the traditional concentration on the calculated use of rhetorical strategies to communicate what one wanted to say with the greatest force, in order to have the desired effect upon the hearer (to teach, to move, and to persuade) is replaced by love, which is shown to have its own power to communicate, to inspire, and to motivate, quite independently of the power of rhetorical speech. Above all, love is shown to require a far more reciprocal and participatory approach to communication than the standard model of a speaker and a mute hearer.

---

[2] *De Catechizandis Rudibus* (*Corpus Christianorum Latinorum*, 46), written around AD 400. I have used Raymond Canning's translation (*Instructing Beginners in the Faith*), which appears in John E. Rotelle (ed.), *The Works of Saint Augustine: A Translation for the 21st Century* (Hyde Park, NY 2006), and all the citations below are taken from this.

How much this approach was influenced by the embarrassment Augustine shared with other, educated early Christian thinkers concerning the very simple, somewhat vulgar and crude language of Scripture as the bearer of truth, rather than the eloquent works of classical literature and rhetoric, is, of course, a matter for debate. What is clear is that he emphasizes both the inherent eloquence of wisdom and love, irrespective of the outward form and style, or 'carnal wrappings', in which they are presented, and therefore also the inherent eloquence of Scripture, which is inspired by, and communicates, God's wisdom and love. This is most especially the case when Scripture is interpreted allegorically and its inner, spiritual meaning and beauty is discovered beneath what might appear a rather unpromising and off-putting body. He reflects that, 'It is indeed most useful for these people to know that, just as the soul is valued more highly than the body, so too are the meanings of words to be valued more highly than the words themselves.'[3] This movement from the letter to the spirit, from words to ideas, is thus one from outward appearances and style to substance and truth—whether the outward appearance is attractive and pleasing or modest and plain is not, or should not, be of real importance. The hearer, for his part, must therefore, 'listen to the words of the instruction for their truth rather than for the eloquence with which they are spoken, just as they should give preference to having sensible friends rather than good-looking ones'.[4]

What is of utmost importance is not, Augustine stresses, eloquent, beautiful speech, but rather the intention or motivation of the speaker—his 'affection', or desire and love for God—and it is this which the hearer must attend to, respond to, and value. As he puts it, 'Let them also recognize that the only utterance to reach the ears of God is the devotion of the heart.'[5] The challenge for such a hearer in antiquity, in which the educated person would unthinkingly and intuitively respond to measured, elegant prose, is one which we cannot underestimate. If, Augustine comments—and he seems to think this likely—'they happen to notice some bishops and ministers of the Church lapse into barbarisms and grammatical mistakes when calling upon God, or fail to understand the words that they recite, and punctuate them incorrectly' they should not be disconcerted, but should realize that, whereas 'while to be well-spoken in the law courts is a question of oratorical style, in the Church it is a question of prayer'.[6] This was a tall order, but the emphasis on love and desire, rather than eloquent speech, significantly shifted the dynamics of speaker and listener: what was required of the speaker was a genuine motivation; what was required of the hearer was to divest themselves of centuries of tradition,

---

[3] *Instructing Beginners in the Faith*, 9.13.
[4] *Instructing Beginners in the Faith*, 9.13.
[5] *Instructing Beginners in the Faith*, 9.13.
[6] *Instructing Beginners in the Faith*, 9.13.

culture, and habit; to divest speech of its cadences, rhythms, and imagery, and to attend, like God, only to its naked affection or desire.

Plutarch, too, is keen to radically shift the balance between speaker and hearer: to set traditional rhetoric, or what he calls 'the art of delivery' in its place, and instead to concentrate on what we have described as the 'art of reception', or the art of hearing. His reasons are those which the philosophers traditionally rehearsed against the rhetors or sophists, and which the fathers also shared: the accomplished rhetor is a dangerous man in that he can use his art, which rests more on appearances and style than substance or truth, to make truth and falsehood equally attractive and pleasing.[7] He possesses the power to deceive, to dissimulate, and to conceal his thoughts, whilst so sweetening his 'voice by certain harmonious modulations and softenings and rhythmic cadences, as to ravish away and transport [his] hearers'.[8] He is, above all, an entertainer, who uses his performance to attain the momentary adulation and praise of his audience, rather than to secure their lasting moral good.[9] The young hearer, for his part, therefore needs to be constantly on his guard, like a 'keen and heartless critic', to ensure that he is not swayed or 'swept away' by external appearances: 'his grey hair, his formality, his serious brow, his self assertion; or the reaction of other listeners: 'the clamour and the shouting of the audience as he brings them to their feet';[10] but always seek, as Plutarch puts it, to 'strip off the superfluity and inanity from the style[11] . . . and to use all diligence to sound the deep meaning of the words and the intention of the speaker, drawing from it what is useful and profitable, and remembering that he has not come to a theatre or music hall, but to a school and classroom with the purpose of amending his life by what is there said'.[12] In other words, he must keep in view what will cleanse and profit his mind and soul and inspire enthusiasm for virtue and goodness; he should pursue 'the life, the actions, and the public conduct of a man who follows philosophy'.[13] It therefore appears that, in the delivery and reception of rhetorical speech (and all public address was rhetorical in antiquity), there is a real conflict in purpose between speaker and hearer—at least for one who wants to pursue the philosophic life—which means that the hearer can never simply lapse into the role of passive recipient, but must exercise constant vigilance, judgement, and care in separating out the subject matter from the style, and the meaning from mellifluous but potentially misleading words.

For Plutarch, therefore, philosophy, or love of wisdom, has the same role as love of God for Augustine: it effectively replaces the 'art of delivery' or effective speaking, with the 'art of reception' or effective hearing. And, as we shall see

[7] *On Listening*, 7 (Loeb, 220–5).   [8] *On Listening*, 7 (Loeb, 225).
[9] *On Listening*, 7 (Loeb, 225).   [10] *On Listening*, 7 (Loeb, 220–5).
[11] *On Listening*, 8 (Loeb, 225).   [12] *On Listening*, 8 (Loeb, 226–7).
[13] *On Listening*, 9 (Loeb, 228–9).

later in this impromptu, the 'art of reception' involves much the same synergy, or reciprocal give and take of speaker and hearer, and their mutual participation in the act of communication and reception, as the rhetorical 'art of delivery'. The crucial difference is that, whereas it appears to be inherent in the nature of wisdom and love that they both inspire and demand to be communicated and responded to in wisdom and love,[14] the same cannot be said of the nature of rhetoric, which is by nature indeterminate and can equally promote good or evil, virtue or vice, in its hearers. The initiate therefore needs to learn how to acquire the 'art of reception' or the 'art of hearing', by which Augustine means attending to love of God, and Plutarch means, above all, attending to love of wisdom or philosophy.

We observed that the avowed intention of both treatises was initiation: for Plutarch it is an initiation into philosophy for the young man who has completed his education, is leaving behind his guardians, and needs to be instructed in 'how rightly to listen to the voice of persuasion' so that he attains a virtuous life controlled, no longer by his guardians, but wisdom or reason.[15] For Augustine, it is initiation into the Christian faith at baptism; the treatise is a response to the priest, Deogratias, who had requested guidance on how to go about imparting the faith to those, known as the *accedentes*, who were drawn to it and who were considering enrolling as catechumens. Both Plutarch's young man, and Deogratias' interested enquirer needed to be given an overall view of what it was they were to be initiated into—love of wisdom and love of God—so that they could subsequently receive whatever they heard with true discrimination.

'NEITHER A BATH NOR A DISCOURSE IS OF ANY USE UNLESS IT REMOVES IMPURITY'[16]

Plutarch, like Augustine and his fellow Christian thinkers, regards the instruction that accompanies initiation into philosophy as primarily a process of formation of character, rather than the acquiring of knowledge. It was intended less to impart information or facts and more to enable the true discrimination characteristic of the art of hearing, by purifying and cleansing the mind and will, and enabling the initiate to acquire habits of thought and action, so that on encountering wisdom (or love) they might be properly prepared to recognize it, receive it, be informed by it, and act upon it. Hence, both Plutarch and Augustine emphasize the need for moral and

[14] *On Christian Doctrine*, 4.6.10 (Robertson, 124).
[15] *On Listening*, 1 (Loeb, 204–5).
[16] *On Listening*, 8 (Loeb, 226–7).

spiritual reformation and healing, and seem to prefer the medical analogy of necessary suffering under the treatment of a doctor in order to regain health, rather than the analogy of a teacher and pupil. As Plutarch puts it to the one unwilling to accept rebuke or correction, 'Just as one who runs away from the physician after an operation, and will not submit to be bandaged, sustains all the pain of the treatment, but waits not for its benefits: so when the word has cut and wounded a man's foolishness, if he give it no chance to heal and quiet the wound, he comes away from philosophy with a smart and pain but with no benefit.'[17] He therefore advises that, 'as though at some solemn rite of novitiate which consecrates him to philosophy, he should submit to the initial purifications and commotions, in the expectation that something delectable and splendid will follow upon his present distress and peturbation'.[18] Augustine, similarly, likens the preacher to a physician who administers different remedies appropriate for the different needs of his congregation,[19] and mentions the service temptations are in training the faithful.[20] Interestingly, he also reflects on the manner in which the preacher's own sufferings and endurance, in attempting to communicate his meaning to recalcitrant hearers, can make his work ultimately more rewarding and enjoyable, and how his grief can fuel his words to make them more glowing and impassioned.[21] For both writers, the will is formed and reformed through suffering temptations and overcoming difficulties in the exercise of love or wisdom, rather than through the pleasant distractions of rhetorical entertainment and flattery.

It is in this context that Plutarch likens initiation into philosophy to learning to read or write, or play a musical instrument: they are at first challenging and difficult; one makes mistakes; they take time and patience; but if one learns the rules, is not put off by unfamiliar terms and knotty problems, and persists until the subject becomes familiar and hence, more pleasurable, it will then bring illumination and 'inspire . . . a passionate love of virtue'.[22] Plutarch might well be describing the ascetic exercises, instruction, and means of learning of the faith (such as the *narratio*, the *traditio*, and *redditio symboli* and the *traditio orationis*) in preparation for baptism which we have outlined above. The learning and practice of rules so that they resonate and echo in the mind, bring illumination, and inspire prayer and virtuous action is a familiar one and one which we find Augustine clearly rehearsing in the second part of *Instructing Beginners in the Faith*, where he gives both a long and a short example of a Christian *narratio* (or account of God's action in history), from Genesis to the Church in the present, so that

[17] *On Listening*, 16 (Loeb, 250–1).
[18] *On Listening*, 16 (Loeb, 250–1).
[19] *Instructing Beginners in the Faith*, 15.23.
[20] *Instructing Beginners in the Faith*, 7.11.
[21] *Instructing Beginners in the Faith*, 14.21.
[22] *On Listening*, 17 (Loeb, 250–3).

Deogratias might get some idea of what such an account should contain and how to structure and order it so that everything becomes, for the hearer, a lesson in love: 'Certainly, it is not enough to fix our own gaze on *the object of the commandment*, which is *love from a pure heart and a good conscience and unfeigned faith* (1 Tm 1: 5), and to make all that we say accord with this standard; toward it we should also purposefully turn the glance of the person for whose instruction we are speaking.'[23] Like Plutarch addressing his novice, every piece of advice Augustine gives Deogratias, or any other catechist, always has in view the mind of the hearer and what is needed to form and inform it in love of God and neighbour.

'RIGHT LISTENING IS THE BEGINNING OF RIGHT LIVING'[24]

In antiquity it was generally held that words had an inherent, almost magical power. One aspect of this was their power to inform and shape the mind of the hearer by impressing images which were stored in the memory, hence the importance which was placed on right listening, so as to form the mind, and the avoidance of the wrong listening, so as not to deform it. It is this concern to inculcate right listening which lies behind both Plutarch's and Augustine's emphasis on substance over style, and on love of wisdom/God as informing right listening and therefore right action, or virtue. Indeed, Plutarch observes at the very beginning of his treatise that listening is the only one of the senses through which virtue can get a hold in the young, if—as he puts it, 'they be uncontaminated and kept from the outset unspoiled by flattery and untouched by vile words'. He adds that, 'For this reason Xenocrates advised putting ear-protectors on children rather than athletes, on the ground that the latter have only their ears disfigured by the blows they receive, while the former have their characters disfigured by the words they hear.'[25] Early instruction in philosophy is therefore essential in growth towards virtue, and the acquisition of what Plutarch calls a 'habit of listening'[26] crucial in acquiring it. Indeed, this habit must precede all attempts to speak, for, as he puts it, 'in the use of discourse its proper reception comes before its delivery, just as conception and pregnancy come before parturition'; we must therefore have our minds informed by wisdom through listening before we can deliver it in speaking. Thus, Plutarch observes that, just as horses are trained to develop a mouth for the bit, so

---

[23] *Instructing Beginners in the Faith*, 3.6. Cf. 6.10.
[24] *On Listening*, 18 (Loeb, 258–9).
[25] *On Listening*, 2 (Loeb, 206–9).
[26] *On Listening*, 3 (Loeb, 210–1).

teachers should seek to develop in their pupils a 'good ear for speech, by teaching them to hear much and speak little'.[27] The importance of developing a habit, or 'ear', for listening, is, he adds, the reason for the common saying: 'nature has given to each of us two ears and one tongue, because we ought to do less talking than listening'.[28]

A PSYCHOLOGY OF LISTENING

Rhetoric, or the art of delivery, was primarily intended to instruct, move, and persuade the hearer of whatever it was the speaker wanted to communicate. It therefore relied, to a large degree, on techniques which were based on a careful analysis of human psychology—of how the mind and will worked in receiving, accepting, and acting upon what came to them through the ears. It is therefore no surprise to discover that when Plutarch turns to consider the art of reception, with the aim of developing habits of hearing by which wisdom can be retrieved from the finely woven web of psychological games and manipulation in which rhetorical speech caught its victims, he too works at a highly developed level of psychological insight and subtlety. The same is also very much the case for Augustine, in his attempts to ensure that the preacher bypass the labyrinthine passages of classical rhetoric and instead focus his listeners' attention simply and wholly upon the innate eloquence of God's communication to human beings.

It is clear that both authors are acutely aware that, although their message is actually very simple, and their single focus is love of wisdom/God, it is human beings whom they are attempting to instruct in how best to communicate and receive it, and they must therefore contend with the multitude of distractions, temptations, and competing goals which assail the human will, as well as with human self-interest, pride, or sheer laziness. What is striking, therefore, is that neither treatise actually has much to say directly about love of wisdom/God, but both are largely taken up with a consideration of the obstacles which stand in the way of effective speaking and hearing, together with advice on how best to overcome them. This does not mean that our two authors do not, therefore, have much to say implicitly about the nature of love of wisdom/God in the course of their analysis of the human failings and foibles which stand in the way of communicating and receiving it, since the latter are, of course, the obverse of it, and the manner in which they are overcome, very much a demonstration of love of wisdom/God in action.

---

[27] *On Listening*, 3 (Loeb, 212–13).   [28] *On Listening*, 3 (Loeb, 212–13).

Whilst Plutarch writes primarily with the hearer in view, and Augustine writes primarily for the speaker, both, as we have seen, share the same goal: right hearing or reception of love of wisdom/God. Placing the two treatises alongside each other therefore gives us a fascinating glimpse into both sides of the equation, of speaker and hearer united by a common goal: the speaker must speak so as best to enable his hearer to grasp love of wisdom/God; the hearer must listen so as best to grasp the love of wisdom/God in what the speaker says. Both, however, as we shall see, suffer much the same obstacles and failings in their task, and the remedies for both are, perhaps not surprisingly, very similar.

First of all, there are the practical difficulties which affect both the speaker and his hearers, which must be taken account of, and attended to, before effective communication can take place: social and educational background;[29] gender and age; health or illness; attention span . . . all needed to be taken into account—perhaps more so in antiquity, when only a very small minority of the population were literate, educated, free citizens; women were free only to marry and have children and had no education or role in public affairs; the hearer was accustomed to having their attention held by rhetorical speech. Plutarch, as we have seen, was writing for the very specific ears of young men finishing their studies, but Augustine, who almost always has in mind a very mixed congregation, betrays his long experience and real sensitivity as a teacher in enumerating such factors and how one might deal with them: for example, he is (no doubt from personal experience) well aware that someone educated in the liberal arts needs to be treated in a rather different manner from the labourer who has come in from the field;[30] that the custom by which a speaker sat but hearers stood could lead to gaping yawns, restless shifting, and distracted looks signifying a desire to depart (he devotes a large section to discussing this custom and when it might be appropriate to offer the listener a chair, make one's speech more exciting, or simply promise an early conclusion).[31] He is acutely aware of the challenges of different audiences and the context in which the speaker is heard: whether it is in private, to an individual; or in public, to a mixed crowd; to few or many; whether the audience is sympathetic or hostile; learned or unlearned, or both; city bred or rustic, or both; whether it is to a class of pupils or a congregation of believers; whether it

---

[29] *Instructing Beginners in the Faith*, 15.23.
[30] *Instructing Beginners in the Faith*, 8.12; 9.13
[31] *Instructing Beginners in the Faith*, 13.19. Cf. Plutarch's attempt to address these outward demonstrations of disaffection in the hearer when he writes that 'the following matters, even with speakers who make a complete failure, are, as it were, general and common requirements at every lecture: to sit upright without any lounging or sprawling, to look directly at the speaker, to maintain a pose of active attention, and a sedateness of countenance free from any expression, not merely of arrogance or displeasure, but even of other thoughts and preoccupations', *On Listening*, 13 (Loeb, 242–3).

is a discussion in which all take part, or a speech to which all listen. He is also aware that the feelings of the speaker cannot but affect those of the hearer, and vice versa, and that hearers also affect each other.[32] He concludes that whatever the speaker's circumstances, audience, or personal feelings, what he says and how he says it should be dictated by love: 'Although we owe the same love to all, we should not treat all with the same remedy. And so, for its part, this very love is in pain giving birth to some, makes itself weak with others; devotes itself to edifying some, greatly fears giving offense to others; bends down to some, raises itself up before others. To some it is gentle, to others stern, to no one hostile, to everyone a mother.'[33] The speaker's behaviour and character therefore becomes a highly effective demonstration of his message (as classical rhetoric had always emphasized).

But, of course, whatever the practical circumstances, the right motivation and behaviour does not always occur for either the speaker or hearer, and it is with identifying and addressing their inevitable failings, as we noted, that Plutarch and Augustine are first of all preoccupied. As one might expect, for both of them, it is the characteristic human failings of envy and pride, self-conceit, or misguided admiration that hinder the speaker from communicating, and the listener from attaining, love of wisdom/God. By distracting, confusing and closing the mind in on itself, these failings all, effectively, make communication impossible, cutting the speaker off from the hearer and vice versa, thus severing themselves (and others, if they show off by asking too many questions)[34] from what would be to their good.[35] For example, Plutarch describes the conceited listener with truly Evagrian psychological insight and subtlety: 'An offensive and tiresome listener is the man who is not to be touched or moved by anything that is said, full of festering presumption and ingrained self-assertion, as though convinced that they could say something better than what is being said, who neither moves his brow nor utters a single word to bear witness that he is glad to listen, but by means of silence and an affected gravity and pose, seeks to gain a reputation for poise and profundity; as though commendation were money, he feels that he is robbing himself of every bit that he bestows on another.'[36] As a speaker, Augustine is evidently well acquainted with the type of hearer Plutarch describes; certain people 'blinded by senseless spite, are glad that we have

---

[32] *Instructing Beginners in the Faith*, 15.23. Plutarch also discusses the effect which hearers can have on each other: *On Listening*, 13 (Loeb, 238–9); *On Listening*, 18 (Loeb, 256–7), for example, by distracting others with their demonstrations of enthusiasm or holding each other back with incessant (inane and superfluous) questions; the desire to show off.

[33] *Instructing Beginners in the Faith*, 15.23.

[34] *On Listening*, 18 (Loeb, 256–7).

[35] *On Listening*, 5, 7, 13, 17, 18 (Loeb, 5, 7, 13, 17, 18, 214–17, 220–5, 250–5, 254–9). *Instructing Beginners in the Faith*, 4.8, 8.12, 11.16, 13.18.

[36] *On Listening*, 13 (Loeb, 236–7).

blundered—rumour-mongers, slanderers, detestable creatures in the eyes of God (Rom 1: 29–30)—we should let them provide us with an opportunity to exercise forbearance and compassion . . . '[37]

But Augustine is also well aware that such failings can equally be those of the speaker, who would prefer to remain with his own thoughts, occupy himself with more erudite reading, or simply not be drawn away from something more interesting, than to have to descend to try to articulate what he understands perfectly clearly in his own mind to an uncertain audience. He observes with some feeling, and evident conviction, 'the fact that what we perceive silently with our minds brings us greater delight and holds us more tightly, and . . . we still prefer to hear or read something which has been better expressed and which can be delivered without effort'.[38] The preacher's frustration at having to repeat familiar things in childish terms; his weary experience of not being able to find the right expressions for what he understands intuitively in his own mind; his uncomfortable sense of simply not knowing how what he says is being received, of risking misunderstanding or causing offence; the sheer labour involved in patient explanation in simple and plain language, combined with the sort of recalcitrant, obstinate, or impassive hearer we have just encountered, were certain to make him a reluctant, dejected, and therefore almost certainly an ineffective—speaker. Evidently drawing on his own extensive experience in these matters, Augustine outlines these difficulties for Deogratias, in *On Teaching the Unin-structed*,[39] and then elaborates on them in some detail,[40] as six factors which might hinder the preacher in his attempts to articulate the message of love of God for his hearers.

But having described the manifold difficulties encountered by both speakers and hearers in their attempts to deliver and to receive love of wisdom/God, neither Plutarch or Augustine stop there; the primary aim of their respective treatises is to advise on how these difficulties might be overcome. As we noted above, their answer appears to lie in the motivation or intention of the speaker and hearer: for wisdom and love have their own innate eloquence and power to teach, to move, and to persuade the hearer to embrace them and to act upon them, and this natural eloquence and power lends itself to the inadequate efforts of speaker and hearer, to make what they say and hear effective and self-fulfilling. The most important thing for both authors is therefore not so much *what* is said and heard, in terms of subject matter, facts, or information, but rather *how* it is said and heard—in other words, with love of wisdom/ God—by which it becomes clear that, in practice, they mean with the virtues

---

[37] *Instructing Beginners in the Faith*, 11.16.
[38] *Instructing Beginners in the Faith*, 10.14.
[39] *Instructing Beginners in the Faith*, 10.14.
[40] *Instructing Beginners in the Faith*, 10.14–14.20.

or attitudes of mind characteristic of love of wisdom/God: with restraint, without envy, with patient attention, humility, goodwill, delight, cheerfulness, generosity, and empathy. Anyone who speaks in such a manner will be heard in such a manner, and anyone who listens in such a manner will receive what they hear in such a manner. The message and the medium, the motivation and the effect are therefore all the same: love of wisdom/God.

It is striking that, in setting out the ways in which the difficulties encountered by both speaker and hearer are overcome, Augustine and Plutarch largely coincide in their description of the virtues or attitudes of mind required. The list, as we have set it out, reminds one of Paul's encomium on love in 1 Cor. 13. What is notable is that all the virtues or attitudes are rooted in the interaction of speaker and hearer; in their mutual participation in the task of communication; the necessary reciprocity of giving and receiving; the synergy required for effective hearing to take place. What Augustine says about teaching, Plutarch echoes in relation to hearing.

Plutarch, in particular, seems to demonstrate exceptional insight into the ways in which hearers might, as it were, 'work with' a speaker to enable them to perform their task effectively: they should listen silently, attentively, with restraint and respect, and refrain from interrupting them or disputing what they say; even if they are clearly wrong, they should give them time and space to get themselves out of the pit they have dug for themselves rather than being forward or contentious;[41] they should try not to ask too many questions, either to show off or from sheer exuberance.[42] When they do ask questions, it should be ones calculated to play to the speaker's perceived strengths rather than their obvious weaknesses;[43] in other words, the hearer should try not to be too critical, to judge the speaker fairly, do them justice, and enable them to show themselves to their best advantage. Rather than criticize, the hearer should apply the standard they have applied to the speaker to themselves and learn from their weaknesses as well as their strengths.[44] In short, the speaker should acquire what Plutarch calls 'a habit of patient attention'.[45]

It is clear that Plutarch's hearer would require a real humility to attain this habit (for example, in learning from a speaker's faults rather than in criticizing them; in allowing them to play to their strengths rather than their weaknesses; in refraining from showing off with difficult questions). Augustine attempts to inculcate the same attitude in the preacher who might be reluctant to leave behind his own thoughts to face the disconcerting challenge of instructing the simple, uneducated, positively dull members of his congregation: he should

---

[41] *On Listening*, 4 (Loeb, 212–15).
[42] *On Listening*, 4, 12 (Loeb, 212–15, 232–7).
[43] *On Listening*, 11 (Loeb, 232–3).
[44] *On Listening*, 6 (Loeb, 218–19).
[45] *On Listening*, 12 (Loeb 236–7).

take the occasion to practise humility; to imitate Christ's descent, in love, to take flesh, become a child, and, like a nurse, speak in the 'shortened and broken words' of children—to make himself 'weak to the weak, in order that He might gain the weak'.[46] The patient humility of the hearer should therefore be met by the patient humility of the speaker, so that the one can effectively learn and the other effectively teach.

The same holds true of the other virtues both authors recommend: they are reciprocal, and are required by both speaker and hearer for effective communication to take place. A good will, or what both authors also describe as friendliness and cheerfulness, generosity and graciousness, is an obvious example. We have already seen Plutarch urging restraint in the one who might be disposed to criticize and find fault with a lecture, so that they rather seek to learn from its faults and find what is best in it: he must listen 'cheerfully and affably as though he were a guest at some dinner or ceremonial banquet, commending the speaker's ability in those parts wherein he achieves a success'.[47] As Plutarch observes, the one who attends lectures is not like a judge in a court, who must receive what is heard with justice rather than goodwill, but can afford to find some good even in a speaker who offends against most of the rules of delivery, so that he still benefits in some way from hearing him. He comments, 'the ancients gave Hermes a place beside the Graces from a feeling that discourse demands, above all, graciousness and friendliness. For it is not possible for a speaker to be a failure so abject and complete that he does not afford something meriting commendation, an original thought, a reminiscence from others, the very subject and purpose of his discourse, or at least the style and arrangement of his remarks.'[48] Just as bodily gesture and facial expressions were regarded as an intrinsic part of the way in which a speaker communicated their message, so Plutarch urges that the hearer should also ensure that they encourage the speaker by making their friendly disposition evident to them in, for example, 'a gentleness of glance, a serenity of countenance, and a disposition kindly and free from annoyance'.[49]

Augustine gives exactly the same advice to the speaker who must try to overcome any reticence, fear, or exhaustion they sense in their hearers by what he describes as 'the force of kindly exhortation . . . by bringing before him the consideration of our brotherly affinity', by conciliating him with the friendliness of what is said and reviving him with the demonstration of honest cheerfulness.[50] He also betrays the same benevolent attitude to any signs of failure in his hearers—whether they be attributable to educational level, mental

---

[46] 1 Cor. 9:22, in *Instructing Beginners in the Faith*, 10.15.
[47] *On Listening*, 6 (Loeb, 216–19).
[48] *On Listening*, 13 (Loeb, 238–41).
[49] *On Listening*, 13 (Loeb, 242–3).
[50] *Instructing Beginners in the Faith*, 13.18–19.

and physical endurance, weakness, sheer laziness, or simply an inexplicable disinclination to attend and learn. His ideal speaker should respond to such failings with intuitive sympathy, human empathy, and seek to find ways to address them and help the hearer to overcome them: the speaker should establish the capacity of the hearer and then accommodate themselves to their level;[51] they should learn as much as they can about their current state of mind and adjust their discourse to it;[52] be sensitive to signs of mental and physical exhaustion and try to revive the hearer's attention with an unexpected remark or a gripping, extraordinary story; alternatively, they should simply offer them a seat.[53] If the hearer remains sluggish and senseless they should simply pray for them.[54]

THE KINDLING OF LOVE

Plutarch's hypothetical teachers were evidently less engaging than Augustine's ideal preacher; indeed, Plutarch emphasizes the need for the hearer to simply put up with, and make the best of, indifferent speech, to such an extent that he rarely mentions an element which is central to Augustine's advice to the speaker: the need for delight in effective communication. To take delight in what one is saying, to be able to communicate that delight so that the reader is drawn to participate in it and share it, is, for Augustine, the spark which ignites the fuse of effective communication between speaker and hearer: the delight of one kindles that of the other, engages the attention, motivates the will, and inspires action. Of course, the speaker must ensure that it is good delight, leading to virtuous action, rather than delight in what is evil, sinful, and destructive. Plutarch does touch on this when he observes that discourse works best when it is treated not as an end, but as a germ and seed which must be held in the memory and then developed and expanded by the listener: the mind does not, he observes, with another metaphor, 'require filling like a bottle, but rather, like wood, it only requires kindling to create in it an impulse to think independently and an ardent desire for the truth'.[55] Augustine uses the same image of the kindling of desire to describe the way in which the speaker responds to the hearer's desire to learn: 'How much more then should we be pleased when people now come to us to acquire knowledge of God himself, for to acquire knowledge of God is the object of all our learning. How much more too ought we to find refreshment in their fresh approach, so that,

---

[51] *Instructing Beginners in the Faith*, 13.18, 15.23.
[52] *Instructing Beginners in the Faith*, 5.9.
[53] *Instructing Beginners in the Faith*, 3.5, 13.19.
[54] *Instructing Beginners in the Faith*, 13.18.
[55] *On Listening*, 18 (Loeb, 256–9).

if our preaching customarily lacks warmth, it may catch fire from the unaccus-
tomed attention with which they listen.'[56]

The motivation and end of right delight for Augustine is love (*caritas*, or
love of God and love of neighbour), and it is this which prompts him to return
to it at every turn in *On Teaching the Uninstructed*. More often than not, love
simply becomes synonymous with right delight, in his descriptions of how,
and to what end, the speaker should frame his discourse: 'Certainly, it is not
enough to fix our own gaze on *the object of the commandment*, which is *love
from a pure heart and a good conscience and unfeigned faith* (1 Tm 1: 5), and to
make all that we say accord with this standard; toward it we should also
purposefully turn the glance of the person for whose instruction we are
speaking.'[57] This is achieved, above all, by drawing the listener's attention to
Christ's demonstration of God's love in condescending to take flesh and to die
for us, as it is this unmerited love of someone higher than itself which
unfailingly kindles the soul to an answering love: 'the dull heart is aroused
when it feels itself loved, and the already passionate heart is stirred up still
more when it realizes that its love is reciprocated'.[58]

Right listening or right reception, is thus the beginning of right speaking
or right delivery. Both what is heard and what is spoken is right love—of
wisdom/God, and it is this which kindles the spark between the two, and
ignites the desire of the hearer to patiently and attentively listen and receive,
and the desire of the teacher to patiently and attentively speak and to
deliver. For both, love of wisdom/God has its own innate eloquence and
power to inspire, kindle, and ignite its effective reception and delivery. In
other words, love of wisdom/God is the necessary constraint which moves
the hearer to hear and the speaker to speak.[59]

[56] *Instructing Beginners in the Faith*, 12.17. Cf. *ep.* 55.11.21: 'I think that, as long as it is still
involved in the things of the earth, the feeling of the soul is set afire rather slowly, but if it is
confronted with bodily likenesses and brought from there to spiritual realities that are symbol-
ized by those likenesses, it is strengthened by this passage, and is set aflame like the fire in a coal
when stirred up, and is carried with a more ardent love toward rest.'

[57] *Instructing Beginners in the Faith*, 3.6. Cf. 4.8, 6.10.

[58] *Instructing Beginners in the Faith*, 4.7. Cf. 10.14, 12.17.

[59] *Instructing Beginners in the Faith*, 1.1–2, Augustine says to Deogratias, 'the demands of the
situation have impelled you to urge me, in the name of the love that I owe you, not to refuse, in
the midst of my other responsibilities, to write something for you on this subject. For my part,
I have a debt of love and service not only to you personally but also to mother Church as a
whole.' *On Listening*, 1 (Loeb, 204–5) similarly represents reason (*ton logon*) or philosophy/love
of wisdom as the controlling agent of the young man who is leaving behind the guardians who
have hitherto been paid to exercise this control: '. . . you have often heard that to follow God and
to obey reason are the same thing, and so I ask you to believe that in persons of good sense the
passing from childhood to manhood is not a casting off of control, but a recasting of the
controlling agent, since instead of some hired person or slave purchased with money they now
take as the divine guide of their life reason . . .'

What role, then, do the hearer or speaker themselves play? They must not only learn how best to receive but how to respond: to the controlling power of reason/wisdom; to the constraint of God's love. The fact that both love of wisdom and love of God are received and delivered *through* words means that hearer and speaker must both demonstrate the sort of benevolent goodwill we have described above. Plutarch likens this to playing throw and catch: 'just as in playing ball it is necessary for the catcher to adapt his movements to those of the thrower and to be actively in accord with him, so with discourses, there is a certain accord between the speaker and the hearer, if each is heedful of his obligation'.[60] This means that the hearer must make allowances for the speaker, find the best in them, and be prepared to catch whatever is thrown at them, however unwelcome or uncomfortable it might be; to be prepared to suffer (and perhaps be reformed by) what they receive from controlling reason/wisdom.[61]

For Augustine, communicating the love of God is a matter of first listening and only then of speaking. First, the preacher must listen to God's inspiration or revelation; inwardly, through the Holy Spirit and through prayer,[62] and outwardly, through the incarnation of His Son, the Scriptures, or the voice of His preachers. Only then can he become a speaker, constrained by the love of God to communicate to his hearers, to let them hear God speak through him, and to allow them to become listeners as he has listened, so that they can, together, hear His Word. As we have seen, to do so the preacher must follow God's loving descent to communicate with fallen humanity, to accommodate himself to them, sympathize with them, use words to speak to them in a manner they will understand—and, like Plutarch's listener, this is something which he might well prefer to avoid, but is constrained to suffer through love of God and neighbour (*flectamur facile, ne frangamur*).[63] Both hearer and speaker are therefore active participants in the process of communication; they must both play ball, be sensitive to the other, constrained by love of wisdom and love of God. It is this reciprocity which we will see being played out in Chapter 5, on preaching in the early Church.

---

[60] *On Listening*, 14 (Loeb, 244–5).
[61] *On Listening*, 16–18 (Loeb, 246–59).
[62] *Instructing Beginners in the Faith*, 7.11: 'when he who is listening to us—or, more precisely, listening to God through our agency . . .'; 11.16: 'if we cheerfully allow Him to speak through us in accordance with our capacities'; 14.22: 'For it not so much I who say these words to you as it is love itself that says them to us all, the love *that has been poured out in our hearts by the Holy Spirit who has been given to us* (Rom 5: 5).'
[63] *Instructing Beginners in the Faith*, 14.20.

5

Preaching: Variations on the Theme

Farewell, lovers of language: the bustle, the crowds, scribes seen and unseen, this barrier straining under the pressure of those crowding close around the word![1]

The age of interminable speeches seems to have been blessed with a gift of interminable listening.[2]

There is evidently a strong element of necessity and constraint in what the fathers write about the different types of summaries of the faith we encountered in Chapter 4. The teachings they summarize, and the doctrines they impart and inscribe, are not a matter of random selection, but of divine, Scriptural, apostolic, and traditional authority; they are not words of human choosing or invention but the words of God. As Augustine puts it in relation to his own catechetical teaching, 'For it is not so much I who say these words to you as it is love itself that says them to us all, the love 'that has been poured out in our hearts by the Holy Spirit who has been given to us (Rom. 5:5).'[3] They are therefore fixed, unchangeable rules which, once heard, are engraved upon the mind and heart in order to provide the pigeonholes, as it were, in which the various elements of the faith can be stored and retrieved in the believer.[4]

Thus far, I have no doubt given the impression that, when duly inscribed by summaries of faith, the mind of the early Christian resembled nothing more than a very rigid, highly organized, filing system, in which everything was effectively stored according to clear, universally recognized formats, was duly labelled, annotated, and ready for efficient reference and retrieval. In fact, by the end of this chapter on early Christian preaching, I hope we will see that, in reality, just the opposite was the case, and that, whilst rules, summaries, and statements were indispensable in informing the faith of believers, and constituted the

---

[1] Gregory Nazianzen, *Oration* 42.26 (Daley, 154).
[2] Van der Meer (1961), 176.
[3] Augustine, *Instructing Beginners in the Faith*, 14.22 (Canning, 108).
[4] E.g. Cyril of Jerusalem, *Catechesis*, 5.12 (Yarnold, 113): 'For the articles of the Creed were not put together according to human choice; the most important doctrines were collected from the whole of Scripture to make up a single exposition of the faith.'

necessary safeguards against misunderstanding or heresy, in reality they functioned as grammar and punctuation do in a piece of writing, or music theory and notation in a piece of music. In other words, they constituted the formulas and fixed patterns, the necessary constraints and structures, which served to then open up a freedom for creative re-presentation, imaginative reappropriation, and extemporary reflection on the faith as it was found in Scripture and tradition.[5] Thus, they both provided a basic theme for the infinite improvisations which we hear in early Christian preaching on Scripture and, at the same time, structured the internal, architectural acoustic, as it were, of the minds of those who heard them so that, once heard, Scripture could reverberate and resonate with infinite echoes.

PREACHER AND AUDIENCE

Having undergone the rigorous and highly dramatic process of catechesis, baptism, and first communion, the new initiates would emerge into the 'theatre of the Church'. Here they would find themselves key players in the regular re-enactment of the narrative of the faith in the liturgy, caught up in the regular cycle of Scriptural readings; performers in the singing of the psalms; a live, responsive audience for the preacher, as he sought to apply what they had all heard from Scripture directly to their lives; active participants in the Eucharist. In this context, both preacher and congregation brought to their interaction minds which were already, to a significant extent, moulded by their faith, their Christian lives, and their previous exposure to Christian teaching and catechesis. In other words, both inhabited a shared thought world of presuppositions and expectations, which enabled what was said and heard to be understood, and to take effect in forming—or, if need be—reforming, the images which they already carried in their souls. As Mary Carruthers has observed, *textus* or text, comes from the verb meaning 'to weave'; texts have a social function, creating a 'textual community'. This is the case whether the 'text' is oral or written, for, she writes, 'it is in the institution-alising of a story through *memoria* [memory] that textualising occurs. Literary works become institutions as they weave a community together by providing it

---

[5] Notopoulos (1938) comments on the way in which oral poets memorized and repeated a vast system of fixed formulas, epithets, traditional sayings or word groups, which, as it were, provided the essential framework and structure for their extemporary recitations, and without which their spontaneous, natural creations would be impossible. See Love (2008) for reflections from a musicological standpoint. He emphasizes that we must always look beyond 'products' (finished pieces of music or doctrinal definitions) to their temporal 'process' (their re-performance and re-reception in a series of ongoing contexts so that they are interpreted and applied anew). It is the latter which leaves room for improvisation—and hope.

with shared experience, the language of stories that can be experienced over and over again through time and as occasion suggests. Their meaning is thought to be implicit, hidden, polysemous and complex, requiring interpretation and adaptation.'[6] As we will see in Chapter 7, this can be expressed in sociological, or cultural anthropological, terms as the formation of a Christian culture;[7] the gradual formation in the mind of the hearer of the tacit, habitual, thought patterns and presuppositions which create a person's identity and relation to the world.[8] In this chapter, however, I would first like to concentrate on how the oral 'text' of preaching upon the written text of Scripture created just such a Christian community of highly literate listeners.

It is significant, I think, that when Augustine turns to consider the relation between pagan and Christian culture in book two of *On Christian Doctrine* he does so in the context of preaching and the interpretation of Scripture: what might legitimately be used or taken over from pagan culture is identified and assessed solely on the grounds of whether it is useful and necessary for the task of preacher and exegete. None of the fathers would disagree with Augustine's basic intuition that it is Scripture—its interpretation and the communication of it through teaching and preaching—that shapes and identifies Christian culture.

When we read or 'hear' early Christian sermons we miss a great deal if we are not aware of how much is left 'unsaid' because it could simply be taken for granted, and was part of the complicit understanding, the common memory or 'symbol-system', shared by those whose conversation we are overhearing. In Chapter 4 we identified the basic grammar of the faith which all early Christians would recognize, accept as normative, and which increasingly functioned at the level of tacit agreement between speaker and hearer: the rule of faith, the narrative of salvation, the double commandment, the Creed. What we intend to do in this chapter is to consider the way in which this shared grammar was deployed, or 'played out' by early Christian preachers in their interpretation of Scripture, so that it at once confirmed it, was discovered in it, and, most importantly, was applied to the lives and minds of their hearers in such a way that it both resonated with them and transformed them.[9] In the process, we will see that Scripture too was transformed, as its images, stories, people, and events became part of early Christian imagination through the daring and creative improvisations and extemporizations of its preachers.

---

[6] Carruthers (1990), 12.
[7] Scholars regularly cite the work of Geertz (1966) and Berger and Luckmann (1967) in this context.
[8] See Tanner (1997).
[9] Young (2007).

TACIT PRESUPPOSITIONS

Before we do so, however, it would probably be helpful to at least remind ourselves of a number of other, also largely tacit—but, for that very reason, also enormously influential—presuppositions which Christian preachers shared with their hearers, and which affected both how they preached upon Scripture and how they were heard.

Rhetoric revisited: the eagle's flight

As we saw in Chapter 2, the culture to which educated Christian writers belonged was, above all, a rhetorical culture, shaped by the classical curriculum of the liberal arts. This training naturally involved close attention to texts—from annotating them to being able to analyse their grammar, language, and rhetorical strategies, to elucidating their arguments and interpretation.[10] Clearly, this education, which formed and defined an homogenous, educated elite throughout the Empire—one to which early Christian bishops firmly belonged—had an incalculable impact on the way in which Christian writers went about the exegesis of Scripture, and this has been well analysed in a number of recent studies.[11] When Christian bishops turned to the task of preaching, then, they would instinctively approach Scripture as a text to be first of all annotated,[12] then grammatically and linguistically analysed, and then, most importantly, interpreted and made applicable to their hearers through rhetorical figures and devices—in other words, through the effective, artistic, emotive use of the spoken word. Having been read (or sung) simply and clearly by a lector, Scripture would no doubt then appear curiously transformed as it was sounded again by the preacher, for all intents and purposes in the manner of a classical text, dressed in all the informative, attractive, persuasive finery of classical rhetoric, in order to teach, move, and persuade the congregation of its truth. Of course, this is a generalization, and the reality was much more complicated and ambiguous: we have seen that the fathers are often acutely aware, and highly critical, of their classical training and culture and its possible dangers and inappropriateness in a Christian context, but the fact remains that this did not usually stop them from rhetorically and emotively condemning the use of rhetoric in favour of simplicity, clarity, and the priority of teaching in preaching. Furthermore, it was no doubt the experience of both preacher and congregation that the teaching of

---

[10] For an excellent treatment of this education and culture, see Kaster (1988).

[11] Cameron (1991); Young (2007).

[12] As we noted in the Introduction, most texts would simply appear as a continuous block of letters, with no punctuation, paragraphs, or indeed, space between words. Gamble (1995), 48.

Christian truth was more effective (because more enjoyable) when it was communicated through the rhetorical use of language, simply because both belonged to a culture in which rhetorical expression was presupposed and expected when a speaker addressed their audience, and when a writer addressed their readers. If it was not used, then the hearer or reader would no doubt immediately sense that something was amiss, sensibilities would be offended, its very absence would put obstacles in the way of the communication of truth, such that the audience would became even more preoccupied, distracted, and diverted by the speaker's use of words than it would have been if he had simply followed accepted rhetorical practice.

This created a somewhat odd situation, and a good deal of tension for early Christian speakers and hearers: we have already observed that Scripture itself fell a long way short of classical eloquence, being a somewhat crudely written, rather vulgar text, belonging to an alien culture which did not recognize or value such rules or practices. Its translators had not helped matters either.[13] When it was communicated to the congregation by the preacher, however, it was somehow miraculously rehabilitated and transformed into a supremely eloquent text which, far from offending their cultural sensibilities, was presented and heard with all the rhetorical devices, figures, and fireworks necessary to enable them to be informed, moved, and persuaded by it. The preacher was therefore like Midas, transforming the crude metal of Middle Eastern scribes and peasants into Greek (or Latin) gold. What happened to Scripture in the process is clearly something to which we need to be sensitive.

We possess a number of treatises which were primarily intended to give advice to clergy on their various duties: Ambrose of Milan's *On the Duties of the Clergy*; Chrysostom's *On the Priesthood*; Augustine's *On Christian Doctrine*. It is worth noting that all three treatises devote a significant section to preaching and that, for all three authors, what is foremost in their minds is the rhetorical context in which any sort of public speaking in antiquity was inevitably approached. Ambrose's finicky concern to get the level of Christian preaching just right—neither too long or too short, too refined or too rough—demonstrates quite clearly his own acute sensitivity to rhetorical speech and his awareness that it will be shared by any Christian audience: 'Our exposition should not be excessively lengthy, but nor should it be broken off too soon: it ought to leave behind neither a sense of distaste nor an impression of

---

[13] Translations into Latin were commonly very literal and full of vulgarisms, making no attempt to observe the rules of correct speech or writing. As Kennedy (1980), 128, comments, 'The gospels are unique works which do not exactly fit any classical literary genre and which have a subtle internal rhetoric of their own.' He uses Wilder (1964) to summarize the characteristics of this rhetoric as: a creative novelty in style (including imagery); a dramatic immediacy with dialogue features; a use of common idiom and media; an addiction to narrative; a subordination of the personal role or talent of the writer to the spirit in the community; inseparable form and content.

carelessness and inattention. Our language should be pure, simple, clear, and plain, full of seriousness and dignity; it should not be studied with elegance, but nor should it be bereft of a touch of appeal.'[14] In short, Ambrose required his priests to be accomplished rhetors, able to pitch what they wanted to say at just the right level to make the correct impression on their listeners, so that their message would carry due weight and authority: they should not overdo it, but they could not afford to 'underdo' it either.

Chrysostom is likewise aware that there is simply no room for second-rate preaching. If Christian congregations were used to hearing accomplished public speakers at every turn—in the theatre, the forum, the law courts—then it was crucial that the Christian preacher should be a match for them in order to persuade their listeners of the truth of their teaching, and to counter that of rival speakers. A preacher's hearers were used to being entertained and swayed in their opinions by pleasure; what was he to do but, at least to an extent, to play the same game or to lose them? What use was a rough, unaccomplished, faltering preacher who could not command the attention or the respect of his hearers?[15] Chrysostom observes with some feeling: 'For most people usually listen to a preacher for pleasure, not profit, like adjudicators of a play or a concert. The power of eloquence, which we rejected just now, is more requisite in a church than when professors of rhetoric are made to contend against each other! Here, too, a man needs loftiness of mind . . . if he is to correct this disorderly and unprofitable delight of ordinary people, and to divert their attention to something more useful, so that church people will follow and defer to him and not that he will be governed by their desires. It is impossible to acquire this power except by these two qualities: contempt of praise and the force of eloquence.'[16] The combination of 'loftiness of mind' or 'contempt of praise' and the ability to make an audience yield by accomplished speaking, proved to be an almost impossible one to sustain in Chrysostom's experience—and no doubt that of his fellow preachers. The motivation, means, and goal of public speaking had always been to please an audience and win their praise, not least because this indicated that the speaker had been successful; he had won them over, persuaded them, and secured their assent. Chrysostom was requiring the Christian preacher to be a performer—a consummate rhetor who could not afford to fail in any respect—but to be immune to his audience's response; to continue to behave according to his hearers' cultural and social expectations but to cease to be affected by their natural responses (whether this was praise when he succeeded or jeers and censures

---

[14] *On the Duties of the Clergy*, 22.101 (Davidson, 177).
[15] *On the Priesthood*, 5.3 (Neville, 128–9): 'For only when he is himself beyond reproach in everyone's eyes will he be able, with all the authority he desires, to punish or pardon all who are in his charge.'
[16] *On the Priesthood*, 5.1 (Neville, 127–8).

when he fell short[17]). How could he achieve this? Congregations were clearly unaware of their preacher's dilemma: they continued to treat him like any other public speaker, applauding and jeering as they saw fit, and although Chrysostom remonstrates with them in this respect, they could not really be expected to understand his real reasons. He tells them they are behaving more like an audience in a theatre than a church,[18] but in fact his real objection is they are touching the acutely sensitive nerve of his desire for praise. One senses that he would find it just as difficult if they failed to applause and respond in the traditional way.

Chrysostom is clearly incapable of leaving this problem to one side; it determines everything he has to say about the preacher's task, no doubt because it was a problem which he was more than aware, from his own experience, he had not resolved for himself. One passage should be enough to give a sense of his painful dilemma:

> People who enjoy being wealthy take it hard when they fall into poverty, and those who are used to luxury cannot bear to live frugally. So, too, men who are in love with applause have their spirits starved not only when they are blamed off-hand, but even when they fail to be constantly praised. Especially is this so when they have been brought up on applause, or when they hear others being praised. What troubles and vexations do you suppose a man endures, if he enters the lists of preaching with this ambition for applause? The sea can never be free from waves; no more can his soul be free from cares and sorrow.[19]

Chrysostom's attempted solution—to urge that the preacher should be immune to the praise or blame of his listeners, and aim only to please God[20]—was clearly no answer at all. The congregation still had to be addressed, and they continued to respond as they had always done: How could he ignore them? That Chrysostom ends this section of his work with a description of the preacher's abject dejection when he fails to evoke a response from his audience is a clear indication that they simply cannot be ignored in favour of pleasing only God:

> How, then, can anyone endure the deep disgrace of having his sermon received with blank silence and feelings of boredom, and his listeners waiting for the end of the sermon as if it were a relief after fatigue; whereas they listen to someone else's sermon, however long, with eagerness, and are annoyed when he is about to finish and quite exasperated when he decides to say no more?[21]

These might seem like small matters, Chrysostom observes, but this is only because of inexperience: the beast of public fame must be slaughtered before the preacher can find any rest.[22]

---

[17] *On the* Priesthood, 5.6, 5.7 (Neville, 131–3).   [18] *Homily* 30.4 (PG 60.225).
[19] *On the Priesthood*, 5.4 (Neville, 130).   [20] *On the Priesthood*, 5.7 (Neville, 133).
[21] *On the Priesthood*, 5.8 (Neville, 135).   [22] *On the Priesthood*, 5.8 (Neville, 135).

The experience of preaching in a rhetorical culture was clearly a highly ambivalent one, which raised dilemmas not only about the nature of Scripture, or of appropriate level and style, for the Christian preacher, but also sensitive questions of self-identity, self-worth, and motivation. The tacit presupposition of rhetorical language was one which both preacher and congregation shared; its use was unavoidable and taken for granted, but when it became a matter of conscious reflection, it remained a raw and difficult question.

That these dilemmas are evident not only in theoretical treatises on preaching, such as we have just examined, but in actual practice, is clear even in the most overtly and extravagantly rhetorical of preachers, such as Gregory Nazianzen. As one of his recent biographers and editors has put it, 'Gregory's orations clearly are meant to respond to the tastes and expectations of a cultivated society, for whom a rich and florid style and verbal wit and learning were both persuasive and aesthetically satisfying.'[23] In this context Gregory's highly wrought rhetorical disavowals of rhetoric would be almost comical, if it were not for the fact that he is generally sincere in making them, or at least self-conscious about his use of rhetoric in the service of Christian truth and anxious that his listeners should appreciate this too, and not think that he is overly concerned with words rather than meaning: he wants to please and persuade them but not give the wrong impression in doing so.[24] Thus, we frequently find direct observations on what he is going to say and how he intends to say it with his listeners in mind, such as the following comment on a sermon on the Theophany: 'It will be at once both as full as possible and as concise as possible, so that it may not disappoint you by lacking substance, nor be distasteful through sheer excess.'[25] Gregory's simultaneous use of rhetoric, his self-consciousness unease with, and disavowal of it, and his desire to make this clear to his congregation and bring them to share it, even as they are persuaded by his eloquence, are clear in the opening remarks of his set piece funeral oration on the death of his sister, Gorgonia. He observes:

> No place will be given here simply to what delights the ear, even if we should wish to do so; for the listener stands here, like a skilled umpire, between my speech and the truth, giving no praise to words that are undeserved, but demanding what is deserved—and that is only just. So we shall take the truth as our norm and measure; and look to it alone, not regarding any other considerations that might

---

[23] Daley (2006), 62.

[24] In this he is simply representative of the attitude of almost all of the fathers. As Kennedy (1980), 143, comments of Gregory and his fellow Cappadocians, Gregory of Nyssa and Basil of Caesarea, 'virtually every figure of speech and rhetorical device of composition can be illustrated from their sermons, treatises, and numerous letters . . . yet all three are repeatedly critical of classical rhetoric as something of little importance for the Christian'. For the Cappadocians' use—indeed supreme mastery—of rhetoric, and for an extensive bibliography on the subject, see Kennedy (1980), 143–6.

[25] *Oration* 38.6 (Daley, 119).

sound attractive to the lowly crowd...We will spurn all attempt to make our language elegant and graceful, since the one we are praising went unadorned, and her very lack of ornament was her beauty.[26]

The highly wrought, vivid, emotive description of Gorgonia's death which follows rather belies his words.[27]

Gregory's emphasis on unadorned, simple prose is a familiar one in the fathers. We have already seen Ambrose and Augustine attempting to argue the same point in relation to Christian preaching, and it can really only be read as a reaction to the excesses of rhetoric, with the rather plain, not to say, crude, prose of the Scriptures in mind, and the classical argument that wisdom possesses a power and eloquence of its own, and does not need the additional adornments of rhetoric. We noted in Chapter 2 that most of the fathers explicitly acknowledge the desirability of simplicity, and often implicitly pursue it in their genuine attempts to avoid the unnecessary distractions of rhetorical excess in communicating the important truths of the gospel directly to their congregations.[28] But, more often than not, they adopt a middle way, and we find them using the grammar of rhetoric—antitheses, rhythmic closings, rhyme, word play, assonance, alliteration, parallelism repetition, question and answer, imaginary dialogue, vivid examples, digressions, topical references, images and stories, metaphors and similes, proverbs, jokes, and riddles, the simple, middle, and grand styles—just as they increasingly used the grammar of the faith—in a habitual, customary way which represented a perfectly natural form of speaking and hearing for both themselves and their congregations.[29] Thus, a simple, natural, unadorned style more often meant taking rhetoric for granted than avoiding it completely. It was only when, for one reason or another, early Christian writers and preachers became self-conscious about it that they started to falter and to try to justify and explain themselves. Gregory tells the story of the birds, disputing who should rule, and how each one of them came forward and congratulated himself for a different reason, 'but the most beautiful thing,' he comments, 'about the eagle was that

---

[26] *Oration* 8.1–2 (Daley, 64).

[27] *Oration* 8.22 (Daley, 74–5).

[28] Arnobius of Sicca's observations are pretty representative: 'When the question at issue is far removed from mere display, what is said should be considered, not with how much charm it is said, nor how it soothes the ears, but what profit it brings to those who listen, especially since we know that some who devote themselves to philosophy not only threw away refinements of style but even, when they could have spoken with greater elegance and richness, zealously strove after a commonplace and humble style, lest perchance they might spoil the stern gravity and revel rather in sophistic display.' *The Case against the Pagans*, 105, quoted by Auksi (1995), 166.

[29] As MacMullen (1989), 504, observes, 'Our first impression is that they [i.e. the fathers' audiences] were remarkably patient of rhetoric pitched at a high level of stylistic and exegetical sophistication.' Similarly, Barkhuizen (1998), 198, argues, in relation to Proclus of Constantinople, that we need to revise the view that 'homilies composed in a high-flown style were per se ineffective in influencing the lives of their audiences'.

he did not consider himself a beauty'. Gregory adds that one should especially aim at this in letters (but one might just as well say, in sermons, too): 'to be unadorned and near as possible to what is natural'.[30] The eagle possessed a natural and unselfconscious grandeur: that is the ideal for the Christian preacher who wishes to impress the truth upon the minds of his listeners.

The preacher as therapist

The fathers and their congregations not only brought with them ingrained assumptions and expectations about rhetorical practice, but, perhaps even more importantly, they brought a long-established familiarity with the content and goals of rhetorical speeches and would anticipate certain themes, concerns, and types, just as much as particular methods and techniques.

From the time of Socrates/Plato, rhetoric had been understood as employing different types of speech to address different types of listening souls according to their different needs.[31] In the law court this could be useful to persuade a jury of a particular argument; in the theatre it would enable the performer to play on an audience's feelings and reactions. In an educational context, it enabled the teacher to best suit their instruction to the needs of their pupil; to lead them into wisdom and virtue. Recent scholarship has done much to draw attention to the latter—the long-standing, deeply influential tradition of 'philosophical' or 'therapeutic' rhetoric—and to demonstrate its immense significance in relation to patristic preaching and teaching.[32] Originating as early as Homer, given classic definition in Plato's *Phaedrus*, and classic form in the Sophists,[33] it saw a hugely popular revival which lasted through the first four centuries AD, in what became known as the Second Sophistic.[34] The philosopher/rhetorician, or philosopher/preacher was, for the fathers and their congregations, a figure ingrained in their earliest experiences, their imaginations, their educational formation, and, above all, their habits of active and effective listening. His voice sounded in the schoolroom, in the theatre and amphitheatre, at the street corner, in the imperial court, in political propaganda and debates, and in civil speeches, where he appeared as teacher, preacher, politician, or civil servant. At every turn, in a wide variety of contexts and roles, he addressed a crowd of hearers, rhetorically inculcating his philosophy in order to provide intellectual and spiritual guidance, to form the soul

---

[30] *Letter* 51 (Daley, 178).
[31] *Phaedrus*, 270b (Waterfield, 61–2).
[32] Malherbe (1987); Maxwell (2006), ch. 1; Kolbet (2010).
[33] Philosophers—including not only the Platonists, but the Stoics, Epicureans, Cynics, and Peripatetics—who used rhetoric to expound their teaching.
[34] Anderson (1993).

in virtue, and to heal it from any disease. Figures such as Themistius, Maximus of Tyre, Dio Chrysostom, Lucian, Seneca, and Plutarch (who we encountered in Chapter 4 in precisely this context) embodied the philosopher–teacher–rhetor–statesman–therapist, intent, above all, on healing the souls of their hearers through their rhetorical preaching. As Kolbet writes of Dio Chrysostom,

> He presented himself as a physician who brought with him medicine truly curative of soul and productive of the moral good . . . Instead of providing mere entertainment, Dio claimed that discourses like his own, 'make people happier and better and more self-controlled and more able to administer effectively the cities in which they dwell'.[35]

These figures characteristically resisted the stereotype of the reclusive, erudite, and difficult philosopher, insisting instead on clarity of teaching which was intended for all levels of society, and which was essentially practical.[36]

This brief overview of philosophical rhetoric is, of course, rather generalizing, but one cannot avoid the conclusion that, however impossible it might be to accurately differentiate between sophists, rhetors, philosophers, or holy men,[37] there was a significant strand in classical philosophical rhetoric that cannot but have influenced the attitudes and expectations, thinking and practice of Christian bishops and their congregations. Bishops would join the ill-defined, but tremendously influential ranks of sophists, rhetors, philosophers, and holy men who had attempted to change the lives and heal the souls of their hearers by rhetorically preaching their philosophy to large audiences; their congregations would join the ranks of those who had long lent an ear to such preachers and (hopefully) been healed and transformed by them. The similarities between the pagan and Christian traditions of philosophical preaching are striking, if not at all surprising: the texts and authorities might be different (significantly different, as we shall see) but the attempt to inform, reform, exercise, and heal the minds and souls of their listeners was very much the same, and was another tacit presupposition which shaped not only what the Christian preacher said but how he said it, and how he was heard. There is no image more commonplace in the fathers' preaching than that of the doctor who acts, or prescribes remedies, to heal his patients, whether he is understood to be the preacher himself, or Christ.

---

[35] Kolbet (2010), 21–2, quoting Dio Chrysostom, *Oration* 32.7 (Loeb, 358.178).

[36] Maxwell (2006), 13–16, 21–9 for references.

[37] Maxwell (2006), 15–16, who comments, 'Then and now, one observer's popular philosopher is another person's "sham philosopher", or "sophist"—the act of speaking in public and attempting to hold listeners' attention with rhetoric or humour often leads to a fall from the category of "philosopher".'

Audience interaction

Whilst the experience of hearing a public speaker was one which was familiar to all Christians, what was also familiar—indeed, second nature—was an experience of what it was like to belong to a crowd, a group of listeners, an audience; to listen to a speaker, and to articulate one's reaction to what one heard. Most importantly, as we shall see in more detail later in this chapter, Christians were used to being able to participate and to interact with the speaker; to demonstrate their approval or disapproval, their understanding or confusion, their enthusiasm or disaffection, their hopes, fears, loves, and hates. In short, they were used to being treated not so much as an audience as a conversation partner; someone who could influence the speaker by their expressions, gestures, applause, laughter, and groans, or, indeed, their silence. They were accustomed to being addressed directly and personally, not in the abstract; drawn into what they heard such that they could not hide their response, and to being able to influence the subsequent course of the speech. They were certainly not used to being silent, passive listeners.[38] This was due partly to rhetorical convention and practice, partly to the legal system which required a jury, partly to the popularity of the theatre and acting/rhetorical contests, and partly to the way in which civic life was conducted in antiquity. Individual citizens found themselves treated as an audience, a group to be addressed on public occasions by an official speaker—whether it was the emperor's birthday, his entry (or *aduentus*) into a city, the dedication of a building, a religious festival, a spectacle financed by a local noble, the election of local officials—and were expected to demonstrate their loyalty and support by responding with applause or chanted acclamations (though they could also use the occasion to register their opposition and discontent).[39] Their reaction as an audience was effectively their way of voting with their voices. As noted in the case of Chrysostom, the fathers were acutely conscious of their congregation's response. Like the emperor and imperial officials, they were often elected by public acclamation. When Augustine proposed the priest Eraclius to his congregation as coadjutor Bishop of Hippo they initially called out 'Deo Gratias! Praised be Christ' twenty-eight times, 'Christ, hear us! Long live Augustine!' sixteen times, and then 'Father, Bishop' eight times. When Augustine continued to recommend Eraclius, to pray for unanimous agreement, and to remind the congregation that everything that both he and they said was being recorded by scribes (*notarii*), they responded with even more acclamations. As van der Meer describes it, 'Hereupon the congregation called out thirty-six times, "Deo Gratias! Christ be praised! Christ, hear us! Long live Augustine!", the

---

[38] Maxwell (2006), 5 n. 9, refers to Van Dam (2003), 101–50, on late antique sermons as dialogues between preacher and audience.

[39] Maxwell (2006), 56–63. On acclamations in antiquity, see Roueché (1984).

last being again repeated thirteen times, then eight times, "Father, Bishop!", then twenty times, "Worthy is he and righteous", then five times, "Well deserved! Most worthy!", then six times, again "Worthy is he and righteous!" ... When all was quiet again, Augustine asked for a prayer and again they began to shout—sixteen times, "Father, Bishop Eraclius!" [40] This was real audience participation!

Quite apart from contexts in which acclamations were traditionally expected, and the congregation, as we have just seen, rose to the occasion as any crowd in antiquity would have done, early Christian preachers were just as culturally wired to expect a reaction from them in response to their everyday sermons (even though, as we have seen, this could so easily militate against their determination to be immune to praise and to seek to please only God).[41] We therefore often find them commenting on their congregation's various responses—their beating of their breasts,[42] their groans, weeping, laughter, and especially their applause (clearly, they would applaud at every turn, to signify understanding, the fact that they had recognized a scriptural reference, to demonstrate approval and assent, to express admiration of a preacher's performance and efforts).[43] Indeed, so anticipated was the congregation's response that silence was interpreted as their failure to understand and an indication that further explanation was needed. If they had understood, their bishop would know about it; they even capped a quotation, cheered a familiar allegory, or identified a story before he had concluded it.[44] But the preacher was also careful to make clear to his audience just how his own role as bishop differed from the other speakers with whom they were accustomed to respond

---

[40] *Letter* 213, 1–7, cited by van der Meer (1961), 270–1.

[41] As we have seen above with Chrysostom. Augustine too makes clear his real ambivalence in a sermon on the anniversary of his consecration. It is quoted by van der Meer (1961), 430, 'Certainly, I like applause ... if I were to say that I do not wish for that, you would, I fear, think me a boaster rather than a righteous man. What, then, am I to say? I do not altogether wish to have it nor to do without it. I do not desire to have it, lest I be brought to fall through human praise; I do not desire to be without it, because I do not want to have an audience that is wholly unappreciative; but I think of the burden of my responsibility, for I must render an account even for your applause. Time and again I am praised, but I am anxious about the manner of life of those who thus praise me' (Augustine, *Frangipane Sermons X*, 2.1) ... 'How many people say, he preaches for applause and that that is the only reason for his preaching' (*Enarrations on the Psalms*, 141.8).

[42] For references, see van der Meer (1961), 339–40. As Robin Lane Fox (1994), 145, observes of Augustine's congregation at Hippo, 'Their participation was every bit as noisy as a jury's in classical Athens: they acclaimed, applauded and interrupted their preacher and beat their breasts in a great rumble of fists at the mention of deadly sins like adultery. However they also applauded, or even capped, concealed quotations from a Psalm in a sermon ...' See also McClary (2003), 427–34, for suggestive parallels with player/audience interaction in blues' singing.

[43] See A. Olivar (1991), 834–67, on applause, referred to by Maxwell (2006), 52 n. 54. van der Meer (1961), 427–32; Harmless (1995), 168–70.

[44] For examples and references, see van der Meer (1961), 427–32.

in this manner, and, above all, how the Church itself differed from the other contexts in which they normally behaved in this way. This was not least because their congregation's behaviour resembled nothing more closely than that of the average audience in the theatre, and it was the theatre which was the target of some of the preachers' most vitriolic attacks—for its immorality, its pagan superstition and promotion of the gods, its rival attractions and its sheer popularity.[45] They were eager that the Church should replace it in their congregations' affections and lives, and that preaching should become 'the theatre of the soul'.[46] Like every other aspect of their lives, the congregation's behaviour as an audience had to consciously be re-evaluated in a Christian context.

Jewish and New Testament preaching

The exegetical, liturgical homily was, of course, already extremely familiar to Jewish Christians from their worship in the synagogue, where it was established practice for lessons from Scripture to be read and then followed by an interpretation, which usually included an exhortation to moral conduct in accordance with the law (just as Jesus had preached on Isaiah in the Synagogue at Nazareth (Luke 4:16–21)). In a Greek context synagogue preachers were no doubt as influenced by the traditions of philosophical rhetoric as early Christian preachers were to be—indeed, the latter probably inherited the tradition partly from its influence on Jewish practices.[47] In fact, the Jewish evidence suggests that the homily was probably one of the earliest features of the Christian liturgy,[48] just as it appears to be the earliest form of spreading the Christian *kerygma*: the first summaries of the faith occur in the missionary preaching of the apostles—including Stephen's, Peter's, and Paul's speeches in Acts and Paul's preaching across the Empire. This was what Pope Leo, preaching himself on the Transfiguration, identified as God's providential design: 'These things, dearly beloved,' he comments to his congregation in Rome, 'were not enunciated for the sake of those who heard them with their own ears, but in the three apostles (Peter, James and John) the whole church

---

[45] Markus (1990), ch. 8; Leyerle (2001).

[46] Chrysostom, *New Homily* 10 (Allen and Mayer, 140–2). The fathers often attempt to set the rival attractions of the Church over against those of the pagan entertainments which lured away, and polluted the minds of their congregations.

[47] Kolbet (2010), 7.

[48] Lienhard (1989), 37, refers to Justin Martyr, in the second century, who observes that the Eucharistic liturgy begins with a reading from the OT or gospels and then a homily: 'When the reader has finished . . . the president in a discourse urges and invites us to the imitation of these noble things' (*Apology*, 1.67).

shared in what they experienced by sight and received by hearing. Thus, the faith of all is to be confirmed by the preaching of the Holy Gospel.'[49]

From both their Jewish roots and their first encounter with the faith, early Christians were accustomed to thinking of faith as something expounded, sounded, preached, and communicated to their ears through the text of Scripture and the 'text' (in Carruthers' sense) of the preacher's words.

Early Christian preaching

In the early Church (at least from the third century onwards) it was the duty of the bishop to preach, and in the absence of a bishop, it fell to a priest to perform this duty. It was an onerous one, as a sermon on one of the Scriptural readings appointed was expected at each liturgy/Eucharist, and often at morning and evening non-Eucharistic services.[50] This meant that bishops could find themselves preaching almost daily, but is also clear that preaching was tremendously popular: a longish sermon was anticipated and generally provided.[51] As Chrysostom comments (in observing how demoralizing it can be for a preacher to have an unresponsive audience): '. . . do you not know what a passion for oratory has recently infatuated Christians? Do you not know that its exponents are respected above everyone else, not just by out-siders, but by those of the household of faith?'[52] The sermon is indeed the most common genre among the fathers' writings, and for most of them, it represents at least two-thirds or more of their literary output. This is, first and foremost, because they thought of themselves as pastors rather than academic theologians; that any theology was generally done through exegesis of Scrip-ture within a sermon, rather than apart from it (and congregations were, as a result, much more theologically literate than contemporary ones); that biblical commentary often took the form of a series of sermons rather than an independent work; and that other concerns (such as the suppression of heresy) were met most effectively through the sermon. The prominence of the sermon was, as we can now appreciate, in large part a cultural phenomenon: public speaking (or at least public delivery of one's work, rather than just a written composition) had long been the way in which to engage a wide audience and communicate ideas. In a religious context, interpretation of Scripture had traditionally been done in the context of the exegetical homily. In philosoph-ical terms, or the pursuit of wisdom, dialogue between teacher and pupil had

---

[49] *Sermon*, 38 (li) 8 (SC 74b.34), referred to by Murphy (1989), 191–2.

[50] Cunningham and Allen (1998), 13–15.

[51] As van der Meer (1961), 419, comments in relation to the ancient audience's expectation of *copia*, or amplitude, in a sermon, 'brevity was accounted as the sign of a poor and ill-fashioned mind and was looked upon as a mark of weakness'.

[52] *On the Priesthood*, 5.8 (Neville, 135).

long been the established norm (indeed, until the end of the second century the early Christian preacher was simply called a *didaskalos* or teacher).[53] In practical terms, the sermon proved to be the most convenient and practical way of engaging and instructing a largely illiterate congregation in the Scriptures and the faith.

We cannot, of course, be at all sure of the status of the homilies we now possess, and to what extent they record the actual words which were spoken and heard. Many patristic sermons were, indeed, delivered *ex tempore*, following private reflection on the text appointed to be read in the service in which the sermon was to be preached.[54] The bishop would deliver it with the codex which the lector, having read the appointed text from Scripture from a raised pulpit (*pulpitum*/stage),[55] had passed over into his hands. He would be seated in his *exedra* (chair or throne) in the centre of the apse, probably flanked by his priests, and facing a standing congregation. His sermon was then likely taken down by secretaries, as was the normal practice for any public speech, and in some cases revised for publication; in others, perhaps left as it was originally recorded. Scribes (*notarii*) were employed in the many contexts in which speeches were delivered or works were composed by dictation (much more common than an author actually writing in their own hand), were highly trained, and generally quite accurate in taking down what had been said *uerbatim*, in their own form of shorthand.[56] But they were only human, and what effect the transcribing, or indeed any subsequent revision may have had, we can only guess. Other homilies were originally written/dictated and then subsequently delivered, or were never intended for delivery,[57] but were written more as treatises for instruction, or as sustained commentary on Scripture.

The social make-up of the congregation that confronted the bishop has recently exercised scholars:[58] were they predominantly well to do, with time and leisure to attend frequent services and follow extended series of sermons?[59] Were they representative of society as a whole?[60] I do not think

---

[53] Lienhard (1989), 42, in reference to Origen.

[54] See Deffarari (1922); Cunningham (1997), esp. 24 n.15, for bibliography on this question. Cunningham makes the important point that, even when a sermon seems to be extemporary, we should be alert to the fact that 'many exclamations and remarks to the audience in early Christian sermons may represent purely rhetorical devices, designed to lend orations an appearance of excitement and spontaneity' (22).

[55] Paoli-Lafaye (1986), 59–74.

[56] Haines Eitzen (2000). Houghton (2008), 27–30, 37–9, on stenographers; Marrou (1948), 212–13. Other scribes, known as *librarii*, would transcribe these notes to create the texts we now have.

[57] See Houghton (2008), 39l.

[58] For a good summary of different views, see Maxwell (2006), ch. 3, who concludes that 'middling classes' were more prominent in late antique society than is usually assumed. See also Cunningham and Allen (1998), 12–15.

[59] As argued by MacMullen (1989), 503–11.

[60] As argued by Cunningham (1990); Philip Rousseau (1998); Mayer (2000).

that in this context we need to be too concerned with these questions or distinctions; it is, anyway, very difficult (if not impossible) to generalize concerning different preachers with different styles and methods, their diverse congregations spread across the length and breadth of the Empire, in towns and villages, in house churches, cathedrals, or monasteries, on many different occasions.[61] Moreover, we have established that whether originally written or spoken the fathers generally tend to write in an accessible spoken style, as if for a listener, and attempted to reach the widest audience possible. What is important is how they and their hearers/readers understood this practice and how it both affected and effected their reception of Scripture.

THE TRANSFORMATION OF SCRIPTURE IN EARLY CHRISTIAN PREACHING

Having examined the presuppositions with which both the early Christian preacher and his audience would approach the interpretation of Scripture in a homiletic setting, and having considered aspects of this setting, we can now return to the nature of Scripture itself, for it was *the* text, the definitive, inspired, authoritative text on which all preaching was based. To a large extent it therefore functioned—on a grand scale—in very much the same way as the rules or summaries of the faith which we identified in Chapter 4. As we noted there, these rules were both drawn from Scripture and confirmed by it, and served not so much as independent summaries of Christian history, teaching, or revelation, but as summaries of Scripture itself. It was only in this sense that they possessed authority and could function as the necessary rules or constraints which made interpretation possible.

Early Christian preaching thus resonates with the words of Scripture: it was the text which had been read aloud to the congregation following an established lectionary;[62] the text on which the homily was always based; the authority which gave weight to anything the preacher said; the Word of God which the preacher aimed, above all else, to impress upon the hearts and minds of his listeners in order to transform their lives. Most importantly, in liturgical reading and preaching the text of Scripture was made accessible to

---

[61] On these various imponderables, see the excellent article by Mayer (1998). She points out that for each homily we read we should be asking ourselves a series of questions concerning the Who? Where? When? How? Why? in order to fully understand what is actually said.

[62] Although we are not always in a position to be certain what order each church adopted. For an attempted reconstruction, see Willis (1962). See Gamble (1995), 217, for *lectio continua* of Scripture in the liturgy, which formed the basis of patristic sermons.

the illiterate majority of Christians who, hearing it read and expounded on a regular basis, made up for their functional illiteracy by becoming impressively literate in the faith.

We must not forget that what the preacher tried to communicate to his listening audience was not, in fact, his own words. As we will see in more detail later in this chapter, the preacher was himself first and foremost a listener, before he could become a speaker: to Christ, the inner teacher; to Scripture, the Word of God. Between himself and his listeners there was always an inspired text which he attempted to communicate, through spoken words, to his congregation. The elusive, but crucial, moments, first, of the 'voicing' of Scripture by the preacher, and then of the hearing or imprinting of Scripture on the minds of his hearers, are the ones we need to pay attention to, for in them Scripture speaks; it is no longer a text to be read, but becomes a matter of speaking and listening, of communication, conversation—in a real sense it comes alive and enters the realm of time, change, and the senses, demanding a response, interpretation, imaginative appropriation, and ethical action. It is in this live, interpersonal context that we can speak of Scripture creating a distinctive Christian culture of understanding and action for its listeners.[63]

When we begin to listen to patristic sermons, then, we are entering a conversation which is already in progress, a rather privileged conversation between people who share a world of complicit understanding based on their shared community and faith. Above all, it is based on their hearing of a common text—an inspired, inerrant, unified, and authoritative text—the resonances of which provide the harmonies which make their conversation meaningful: 'for he knows all Scripture is the one perfect and attuned instrument of God producing from its various notes a single sound of salvation for those willing to hear'.[64]

A good deal of recent (and indeed not so recent) work on meaning stresses the role of the community, of tradition, or the interpersonal context in which something is said, rather than transcendental norms, absolute truths, or the words/text itself.[65] Dale Martin, introducing Elizabeth Clark's Festschrift, *The*

---

[63] See Dawson (1992), 184–6, on what he calls Clement of Alexandria's 'voice-based hermeneutic' based upon his conviction that the 'divine voice is heard through all sorts of writings' and that hearing this 'divine discourse' is, first of all, a matter of hearing: 'Just as scripture is the recorded speech of God so faith—as both goal and presupposition of scripture reading—comes from hearing rather than reading' (186).

[64] Origen, *Commentary on Matthew*, book 2, from the *Philocalia*; SC 302, 308, cited by Young (2007), 22.

[65] E.g. Polanyi and Prosch (1977), for whom metaphor only has meaning within the personal context in which it is spoken and heard. Similarly, Soskice (1985). Tanner (1987) suggests that the 'plain sense' is the way in which text is understood by the community, not something that is absolute or fixed in itself. Eliot (1950) makes the same point in relation to the role of tradition in reading poetry. Similarly, Elsner (1995), emphasizes the importance of context, tradition, and of the viewer's subjective appropriation of what they see, rather than the art object itself.

Cultural Turn in Late Antique Studies, and reflecting on this trend, therefore comments: 'The goal of the historian becomes not the conscious or even unconscious intentions of the author, but the larger matrix of symbol systems provided by the author's society and from which he must have drawn whatever resources he used to "speak his mind".'[66] This rather nicely echoes Augustine's observation in *On Christian Doctrine* book 2, that 'signs have meaning because they are agreed upon'. In the first part of this chapter we have noted the various aspects of the early Christian preacher's and the early Christian audience's culture and tradition, which might help us understand the way in which they went about reading, preaching, and hearing Scripture. As we turn to consider the meaning which Scripture had for the early Church, we must also be alert to its unique and distinctive role, as a text that was believed to be inspired, inerrant, and authoritative, in actually *defining*, as well as being influenced by, Christian culture and tradition.

The task which the early Christian preacher faced was somehow to ensure that Scripture did indeed exercise this determinative role, and to ensure that its authoritative truth and relevance in all situations and contexts was defended and observed. This explains their constant allusions to Scripture,[67] and a good deal of their exegetical practice—especially their use of allegorical, typological, or figurative exegesis in order to unify the Old and New Testaments, to overcome any apparent contradictions or immoral elements in Scripture, and to relate it to their own historical context and the concerns and lives of their listeners.[68] While we will be examining these various strategies when we consider some particular examples of early Christian preaching in more detail below, the overriding question must be: What difference does the oral/auditory context of exegesis of Scripture in a homiletic setting make?

---

[66] Martin and Cox Miller (2005), 16. Young (1990), 1–22, discusses the challenges of structuralism, which makes meaning depend on the system/structure of which words and sentences are a part, and therefore upon the culture, religion, and conventions of the author. Like the other authors we mentioned note 65, it is an approach which shifts the focus away from an 'original meaning' and instead concentrates on sociological, anthropological, and literary analysis.

[67] As Daley (2006), 62, observes of Gregory Nazianzen, he makes constant allusions to the Bible 'as a pagan orator might color his arguments and establish his own credentials as bearer of a cultural tradition, with allusions to Homer, Plato or tragedians'.

[68] Snyder (2000), esp. 1–121. The philosophers treated Homer in the same way: Lamberton (1986). Nauroy (1985), 379 n. 31, refers to Savon's comments that allegory was not a luxury for intellectuals but a necessity for the *infirmi* who needed to be reassured that each word of Scripture had a meaning and that nothing was otiose or redundant.

VOICING SCRIPTURE

One of the most striking effects of what we have called the 'voicing' of Scripture must be the influence which Scriptural language, imagery, and types had upon early Christian preaching and, as a result, on the culture which shaped the ears and expectations of the early Christian listener.[69] We have had occasion to note on a number of occasions that Scripture generally fell far short of the canons of classical eloquence and tended to strike those who heard or read it as at once direct and immediate, but also somewhat crude and vulgar. The fathers' frequent appeals for simplicity and clarity in communicating the truth of Scripture, rather than elaborate, mannered prose, were, no doubt, in part influenced by the nature of Scripture itself. On other occasions, they try to dress up the naked vulgarity of Scripture so as not to offend more sensitive and cultivated minds (including their own),[70] and to demonstrate that it can indeed meet the cultural canons of rhetorical expression if need be. More generally, Christian language, rhetoric, and imagery inevitably became, in large part, those of Scripture: Old Testament proverbs, the utterances of the prophets, the poetry of the Psalms, Christ's words in the Gospels, exemplary figures, memorable stories, dramatic events, pithy sayings, the strikingly non-classical prose of Scripture, with its own distinctive rhythms all became part of Christian language and the Christian imagination. They lent authority and weight, the reassurance of familiarity, a sense of identity and belonging, and, as we shall see, carried with them a sense of tacit understanding, a freight of implicit meaning, and endlessly rich resonances, which made possible both an effective shorthand and the possibility for infinite variations and imaginative improvisations for Christian preachers. In short, they built up a Christian tradition and culture based firmly upon Scripture and the speaking and hearing of it in community.

CONVERSING WITH SCRIPTURE

When we read early Christian homilies we can immediately appreciate the original meaning of the word homily (*homilia* (Greek)/*sermo* (Latin)): it means a conversation.[71] The conversation is, however, many-sided, and the

---

[69] Mohrmann (1958).

[70] E.g. Augustine, *On Christian Doctrine*, book 4 (Robertson, 117–69).

[71] Lienhard (1989), 36, comments, 'Its distinctive characteristic was its apparent artlessness, which marked the homily off from the studied and stylized speech.' Douglas Burton Christie (2001) has written on the significance of oral communication, the power of words, conversation, or spoken dialogue, and the practice of listening in the literature of early Christian monastic spirituality and its 'negotiation of meaning'. Unfortunately, we do not have space to cover this

voices (heard and unheard) create a complex polyphony of sound: the preacher is in dialogue with God, with the text of Scripture (and its multitudinous voices), and with his congregation. We also 'hear' the congregation's response through the preacher's comments on, and reaction to their moods, gestures, and exclamations; the way he adapts what he says to who they are, what he can expect them to comprehend, what he thinks they need to hear, and how they need to hear it, in order to be formed and reformed in the image of the divine Word. Indeed, we perhaps learn more about the congregation, the invisible interlocutor in these early homilies, than we do about the preacher himself. They are the object of the preacher's words and it is upon them that he impresses and imprints the words of Scripture.

The fact that the preacher was able to articulate the message of Scripture orally, face to face, for his congregation, allowed for an immediacy which a reading of the written text (even supposing that they could read it, which, as we have seen, is unlikely) could not possess. Scripture could be adapted to their needs and specific circumstances, in a personal, direct way that took account of their individual characters, backgrounds, and abilities, their hopes and fears, their foibles and failings. In this way, the preacher did not just address his congregation, but was able to enter into a meaningful conversation with them. They became not just passive hearers but participants in his attempt to convey the truth of Scripture to them; they were encouraged to relate it to themselves, reflect on it, take it to heart, and allow it to transform their lives. In this respect we often encounter an intense, passionate relationship between speaker and hearer in the communication of Scripture: the preacher knows his congregation, cares for them as a parent does their child, loves them as a lover loves their beloved, and is aware that what is at stake is their eternal salvation. The impassioned, emotive pleas which we encounter in patristic homilies are not, one senses, merely rhetorical devices to move and persuade, but genuine cries from the heart—and are obviously all the more moving for that. Through the preacher's words Scripture becomes personal, immediate, and irresistibly invites participation and response. This is not exegesis, in the academic, scientific sense of the word, but interpretation in order to impress upon the heart and mind of the listener the purifying, sanctifying Word of God.

Thus, as we shall see later in this chapter, when a preacher takes up the text appointed for the day he does so, not only as a grammarian and critic (though he does do this) but as a pastor, friend, and lover who shares a close understanding, indeed a degree of complicity, with his listeners. This close relationship between speaker and hearer means that the speaker's admonitions, exhortations, and attempts to shame or humble are all the more effective.

rich area of early Christianity here but will touch upon it in Chapter 6 in relation to early Christian practices of prayer.

He knows his hearers; he knows precisely what will move and persuade them to a particular course of action; he knows what is needed to instil a particular lesson or to communicate a particular idea. He therefore uses Scripture as a medicine chest, from which, as a doctor, he can select and prescribe what is needed in order to heal their souls;[72] as a collective oral memory of stories, songs, characters, or events, which, as a bard, he can repeat and perform in order to reinforce their shared, imaginative, thought world.[73] In short, Scripture provided a collection of types or images which could be impressed upon the minds of the congregation, through preaching, in order to form or reform them to the image of God. This creative and imaginative reappropriation and re-presentation of the text of Scripture lends itself uniquely to the homily rather than the written treatise; it works by means of participation and response; it requires a conversation. Only so could what Scripture contains be applied to the individual, their specific needs, and circumstances, and effectively be received by them. From being a mute text, which could only say one and the same thing, it was given a voice in the words of the preacher, which meant that it could enter into dialogue with the hearer.

So, by being voiced by the early Christian preacher, Scripture underwent a number of significant transformations: first of all, it was allowed to speak, and, above all, to enter into a dialogue with a listener; secondly, it became part of their culture and not only spoke directly to their ears, but did so eloquently, persuasively, and in terms which resonated, rather than jarred, with their cultural expectations. The transformation of Scripture by the preacher was also, in turn, the transformation of the listener into the image of God, and of pagan, classical culture into a distinctive Christian culture.

THE CASE OF CHRYSOSTOM

The text of Scripture

Let us briefly see if we can glimpse these transformations in practice in some of Chrysostom's homilies. I have selected examples from Pauline Allen and Wendy Meyer's superb translations.[74] They are all homilies delivered at Antioch on New Testament texts (*Homily* 3 on Acts 1:12; *Homily* 11 on Eph. 4:4–7; *Homily* 21 on 1 Cor. 9:1–12). In each of them Chrysostom reveals his classical education in his customary exposition of the text, which forms the

[72] One of the most common images—if not the most common—used by the fathers of their own work, and, above all, of the work of the incarnate Christ. It is omnipresent.
[73] E.g. Chrysostom, *Homily* 7 On Colossians (Allen and Mayer, 80–1).
[74] Mayer and Allen (2000).

first part of the homily. Following the order established by the schools he comments on punctuation, carefully reflects on each phrase, explains unusual words, expressions, and grammar; elucidates the author's intention and meaning,[75] then reflects on its impact on its audience and suggests how it might apply to his own hearers. This could be an extended process, taking up most of the homily, as in *Homily* 11 on Ephesians—an example of one of the many homilies in which Chrysostom presents Paul's pastoral admonitions and advice to various communities (in this case, concerning divisions within the Church) in such a way that it speaks directly to the situation and needs of his own congregation, who are encouraged to overhear it and apply it to themselves: he sets out Paul's strategies, techniques, tone of voice, rhetoric, arguments, and examples; he discusses why and how Paul uses them, thus bringing them directly to the attention of his congregation in order, implicitly, to make the same points to them.[76] In this dialogue between the text in hand and other texts from Paul, between Paul and his original audiences, and between Chrysostom and his hearers, Paul, as Scripture, is effectively brought into the present and allowed to address the concerns of Chrysostom's fourth-century audience with great effectiveness and authority.

In other sermons, the exposition of the text could be a process which was quickly dispensed with in order to move on to a particular moral lesson suggested by it, which Chrysostom wants to develop and apply to his audience and their current situation, as in *Homily* 21 on 1 Corinthians, which is an example of one of Chrysostom's many homilies on almsgiving and Christian care of the poor. In both cases Scripture is given a voice by the preacher: it is made to speak to a particular audience, in a particular situation, and is presented in such a way that it is impressed on the hearts and minds of those who hear it so that they might be taught, moved by, or persuaded to act upon it.

The voices of Scripture

This is effected, as we have suggested above, by allowing Scripture to enter into conversation with the congregation. In *Homily* 21 on 1 Corinthians 9:1–12, for example, Chrysostom draws his congregation into dialogue with Scripture by deploying a veritable cacophony of 'voices': Paul's words to the Corinthians; Paul's imagined words; Christ's words; words that Christ might have said, but

---

[75] Young (2007), 243–8, on this practice.

[76] Young (1986), 349–52. As she puts in it relation to Chrysostom's homilies on 1 and 2 Corinthians, Chrysostom does not need to explicitly draw any morals, rather, 'the empathy of Chrysostom the pastor with Paul the pastor produces a creative but non-explicit interplay between the two audiences who, by implication, share the same shortcomings. So there is an entirely unconscious "hermeneutic of retrieval"' (1986), 351. Cf. Young (1990), 144.

didn't; the voice of an imaginary commentator or observer; the imagined response of Paul's congregation; the imagined response of Chrysostom's hearers; Chrysostom's own words, questions, exclamations, and imagined conversation with himself; the response of an imaginary detractor or critic; popular sayings; 'someone's' question. This was, of course, standard rhetorical practice, in which a hearer's attention was maintained, and their thoughts informed, by the changes of 'voice' and the different viewpoints they represented: by being encouraged to identify with a particular speaker and to react against another; by considering possible difficulties or objections; by 'overhearing' and perhaps learning from, being moved by, or persuaded to act upon, the comments and conversations of others.

The mysteries of Scripture

Moreover, by means of these voices Chrysostom not only aims to keep the attention and inform the thoughts of the members of his own church in Antioch, but to induct them into the mysteries—or what we have referred to above as the 'grammar'—of the faith. All of the voices are either the voices *of* Scripture itself—direct quotations, allusions, resonances—or voices which are in dialogue *with* Scripture—responding to it, questioning it, discussing it, applying it. In this way the message and meaning of Scripture could be discovered and elaborated—both by hearing it and then being able to enter into conversation with it, in dialogue with others, in order to further investigate its meaning. In one sense, this was no more than what a teacher did in relation to whatever texts he studied, in dialogue with his students, in the schoolroom. For the preacher, it meant that not only the literal meaning of Scripture could be expounded, but its ethical implications could be drawn out and applied to their listeners. It also meant that Scripture's spiritual depths could be plumbed, so that listeners might be instructed in the mysteries of the faith which it implicitly contained. In short, by enabling their congregations to listen to Scripture, and by inviting them to enter into dialogue with it and hear its polyphony of voices, the preacher enabled them to hear not only its surface teaching but to explore its depths, and to allow their faith to echo and resonate with it. Thus, in the course of a single sermon on Ephesians 4:4–7 Chrysostom touches on the relation of faith and merit, Christian humility, grace, the Incarnation, the mystical body, God the Trinity, and the resurrection. It is a method which was familiar to him from Paul, and one which he explains to this congregation in his exegesis of Colossians 2:16–19: 'Such is Paul's custom—by preparing one aspect to jump to another. For example, just while speaking about those who are anticipating a feast, he suddenly falls into the observation about the mysteries. For the argument is weighty when it happens unexpectedly. It "is hidden" he says, from you. "Then you also will appear with him." So that now you don't appear. See how he transfers them to heaven itself. For, as I said, he's always keen to show that they have the same things as Christ. And throughout all his letters (there is) the same reasoning: to show that they have everything in common with Christ. Therefore he speaks of the head, and the body, and he does everything to describe this.'[77] In the same manner as Paul, Chrysostom, like Origen's exegete, lays bare not only the body of Scripture (literal meaning), but its soul (ethical teaching) and its spirit (teaching on the mysteries) for those who are ready to advance from milk to meat;[78] or, like Basil of Caesarea's teacher, he not only openly proclaims the message of the faith as set forth in written texts such as Scripture (*kerygma*) but draws out its mysteries, given through unwritten tradition (*dogmata*),[79] for the initiate.

The unity of Scripture

One of the ways in which the depths of Scripture were revealed by the fathers was by allowing their congregation to hear Scripture speaking to itself, as it were—by setting one passage alongside another (especially passages that appeared, at first sight, to be contradictory, or simply totally disparate and unrelated). Its inspiration and inerrancy meant that the voices of Scripture could—indeed, should—ultimately be harmonized to illuminate each other. In the often elaborate process of finding the key to harmonize the apparently discordant passages of Scripture, the preacher could attune the ears of his congregation to its different voices and the ways in which they could be played out in order to resonate with each other, and with the faith as a whole; for the 'key' was, more often than not, identified as one of the rules we identified in Chapter 4, which made up the rules or creeds of the faith. Indeed, more often than not, it was simply the double commandment of love of God and love of neighbour, which was found to harmonize the discordant voices of Scripture and to allow the congregation to hear its fundamental message, and be admonished to adopt it in their lives.[80]

Scripture as intertext

In this respect Scripture was given, in homiletic practice, the role which it was believed to have in theory: that of an inspired, inerrant, authoritative, unified

---

[77] *Homily* 7 On Colossians (Allen and Mayer, 76-7).
[78] *On First Principles*, book 4 (Butterworth, 256-328).
[79] *On the Holy Spirit*, 27.66 (Anderson, 98). See de Mendieta (1965).
[80] For an example, see the Third Impromptu.

witness to the mysteries and truths of the faith. Just as quotations and allusions to the classics had traditionally been used to lend authority to a classical text, Scripture became, as it were, the definitive 'intertext', in the sense that its voice—in quotations, allusions, or just a single word or image—gave authority, weight, and meaning to whatever the preacher said and his congregation heard. As Brian Daley comments of Gregory Nazianzen, he constantly alludes to Scripture as a 'pagan orator might color his arguments and establish his own credentials as bearer of a cultural tradition, with allusions to Homer, Plato or the tragedians'.[81] Sometimes a sermon could become simply become a collage of Scriptural quotations, one text juxtaposed with another: they might not appear to be related or coherent, but each would carry the authority and truth of the whole and would inevitably invite interpretation which would demonstrate this unity and draw out their inherent resonances and harmony, such as typological or allegorical exegesis. One text, indeed, one word or image from Scripture, could evoke infinite echoes, set up profound resonances, and be open to a multitude of interpretations in relation to other texts. As we shall see when we examine Augustine's preaching on the first epistle of John, later in this chapter, the fathers exploited this to the full in their preaching—transposing, elaborating, and improvising on its images, metaphors, stories, precepts, and themes, which, as a result, became readily familiar to their hearers and thereby carried an even greater resonance and depth of meaning, derived from the different ways in which they had been used, and the different contexts in which they had been previously encountered.[82]

Translating Scripture

Chrysostom's sermons are punctuated at every turn by similes and metaphors drawn from the everyday lives and experiences of his congregation—from nature, personal relations, business—which, in a certain way, 'translate' what Scripture has to say for them, so that they can make the imaginative or empathetic leap to apply it to themselves. The expression 'just as' (*ōsper*) occurs at regular intervals. In a sermon celebrating the martyr Ignatius, for example, Chrysostom compares his own ministry with that of the earlier bishop, and comments: 'For it is not the same to administer a church now as it was then, *just as* to travel in the steps of numerous travellers a road that's compacted and well constructed is not the same as [to travel] one that's right

---

[81] Daley (2006), 62.

[82] Nauroy (1985) on Scripture in Ambrose's pastoral work, refers to what he calls a 'mimétisme scripturaire' (402) in which multiple fragments, echoes, allusions, or single words from Scripture are interworked and interlaid so that it becomes difficult to identify or separate them out. See Young (2007), 116, who refers to an 'intertextuality of creative and imaginative play'.

on the point of being cut for the first time and has chasms and rocks and is full of wild animals and hasn't yet received a single traveler';[83] 'And so, *just as* we marvel at a captain not when he is able to save the passengers when the sea is calm and the ship is being carried along by a fair wind, but when he is able to set the vessel to rights with complete safety when the sea is raging, the waves are towering, the marines on board are mutinying, a great storm is besieging the passengers from without and within; so too should we be struck with far greater amazement and wonder at those entrusted with the Church at that time than at those who govern it now.'[84] Later on he likens the reception of Ignatius' relics in the cities they passed through on the way back to Constantinople, to that of a victorious athlete in the arena: 'For *just as* spectators immediately welcome a noble athlete who has wrestled down all his competitors and exited the arena with magnificent glory, and don't allow him to set foot on the ground but escort him home in a litter and bombard him with countless words of praise, so at that time too in succession the cities welcomed that saint from Rome, and carrying him on their shoulders sent him along as far as this city, praising the crowned victor.'[85]

In addition to similes and metaphors drawn from everyday life, Chrysostom also commonly draws analogies from secular learning and culture; from science,[86] Roman practice and law,[87] historical events.[88] A Christian world picture, woven from a tissue of Scriptural voices, is thereby brought into dialogue with the congregation's specific situation, their everyday experiences, secular learning, and pagan culture, and allowed to comprehend and transform them.

Dialogue with Scripture

Chrysostom's constant bombardment of his congregation with questions—direct, hypothetical, imaginary, through an interlocutor—meant that they could never settle into the role of passive hearers or lose attention for a second—rather they were forced to listen, to pay attention, to think, to examine their consciences, to weigh up different opinions, to see someone else's point of view, to assent or dissent—in short, to converse with Scripture. Again, this was, of course, standard rhetorical practice, and one does not have to look far to find examples of it in practice in patristic homilies. On occasion,

---

[83] *On the Holy Martyr Ignatius*, 7 (Mayer and Neil, 107).
[84] *On the Holy Martyr* Ignatius, 8 (Mayer and Neil, 108).
[85] *On the Holy Martyr Ignatius*, 17 (Mayer and Neil, 115).
[86] E.g. sense perception (*Homily* 11 On Ephesians, 220 D-221 B), the body and its organs (*Homily* 11 On Ephesians, 221 C–222A).
[87] *Homily* 11 On Ephesians, 224F–225B.
[88] *Homily* 17 On the Statues.

Chrysostom gives answers to the questions—sometimes his own, sometimes on the part of another interlocutor who might represent a different position or opinion, more often than not, from Scripture, and rehearses a sort of dialogue, into which the congregation are drawn and invited to take part, to learn from what is rehearsed in the course of the conversation and to come to their own conclusions. Reflecting on the response of the rich when they are asked to give to the poor, for example, Chrysostom asks his congregation, 'But what's their constant talk? "He's got the common church allowance" they say. And what's that to you? I mean, if I give, you're not saved; if the church gives an offering, you haven't blotted out your sins either. For if you don't give on account of the fact that the church is obliged to give to the needy, (then) because the priests pray, will you refuse ever to pray? Don't you know that God laid down laws about almsgiving not so much for the sake of the poor as for the sake of those very people who make an offering?'[89]

Attending to Scripture

On many occasions Chrysostom simply calls upon his congregation to listen: to attend to and to learn from what they hear. *Homily* 21, among those we are considering, is as good an example as any, as Chrysostom tries to make his congregation aware of their shameful neglect, self-centredness, and hypocrisy in relation to the poor and needy. He constantly admonishes them to listen: to 'listen to the words of a prophet', to 'listen to Paul'[90]—in other words, to listen to the voices, inspiration, and authority of Scripture. Elsewhere, he exhorts them to listen to reason, to listen to their own hearts, to listen to him. He is especially delighted when, having listened to his harsh, painful words concerning their attendance at the theatre/hippodrome, they demonstrate by their return the next day their willingness to be corrected, and their trust in him; these are the sort of listeners he wants! 'It's on this account that I'm jumping with excitement and flying under the influence of pleasure and call myself blessed as I struggle [to preach] among so many people who love me, having you hanging like this from my tongue. This is sweeter to me than sunlight, this is more pleasurable than light, this is life—to have favourable listeners like this who don't simply applaud but wish to be corrected, who are censured and don't recoil, but take refuge in the one who censured them.'[91]

---

[89] *Homily* 21 On 1 Corinthians (Mayer and Allen, 173–4).
[90] *Homily* 21 On 1 Corinthians (Mayer and Allen, 169).
[91] *New Homily* 10 (Mayer and Allen, 145). Chrysostom often comments on his congregation's great zeal for listening—e.g. On: I Opposed Him to His Face (Gal. 2:11) (Mayer and Allen, 141–2).

Teaching Scripture

And when they did listen, Chrysostom's congregation would hear an assidu-
ous, painstaking teacher, who was always concerned that what they heard they
should also understand. So much of what Chrysostom has to say is prefaced by
expressions such as, 'I meant that', 'the point is that'. He constantly reiterates
and explains; anticipates any misconceptions or confusion; provides illustrations or examples, in order to ensure that they are following everything he
says. Almost all the 'just as' passages we mentioned earlier in this chapter, in
which he gives a vivid simile or metaphor to illustrate his point, are therefore
followed by an 'I meant that', or 'the point is that' passage, in which he makes
absolutely certain that his congregation has grasped the point of the simile
and are able to apply it. He is sensitive to the capacity of his hearers, and how
much he can expect them to take in and remember. On one occasion he had
taken several days to explain a parable and then observes, 'So that you do not
spit out what you are given, I have not tipped the cup of education for you
all at once, but I have cut it up for you into many days, providing you with
a break from the work of listening on some days, so that what is put
down should stick securely in your thoughts, my friends, and that you should
receive what I am going to say next with a relaxed and mature soul.'[92] He is
likewise aware when he has lost them and they need more explanation.
When he does this he attempts to do so from as many different angles
as possible,[93] using a wide variety of texts and illustrations, making clear
precisely who he is addressing his comments to,[94] in order to meet their
different needs.

Acting on Scripture

The texts and illustrations are not always simply explanatory, however: Chrysostom's aim, like that of every early Christian preacher, was not only to teach
his congregation the truths of the faith, but to move them to act upon them, to
purify and reform their lives. The citations and examples, therefore, often also
serve the purpose of setting the congregation before themselves, of allowing
them to recognize themselves and to see their behaviour and responses for
what they are (sinful, wanting, contradictory, hypocritical . . .), and of provoking a response and a desire to reform. Like any classical rhetor, Chrysostom tries to appeal to the emotions of his congregation, to make them *feel*

---

[92] *On Lazarus*, 3.1 (PG 48.991), cited by Maxwell (2006), 92.
[93] E.g. *Homily* 11 On Ephesians (Mayer and Allen, 66).
[94] *Homily* 11 On Ephesians (Mayer and Allen, 68).

what he is saying. On those who cannot stay away from the theatre, for
example, he remonstrates,

> Old men brought shame on their grey hair, and young men threw their youth
> down a precipice, and fathers took their sons there, from the beginning leading
> youth without experience of evil into the pits of wickedness, such that one
> wouldn't be wrong in calling such men child-killers instead of fathers, who
> destroy their offspring's soul by evil. 'What evil?' someone asks? . . . The man
> who isn't strong enough to stay away from spectacles . . . how will he be able to
> remain spotless after watching [adulterous scenes]? Surely your body isn't stone?
> Surely it isn't iron? You are encased in flesh, human flesh, which is ignited by
> desire more quickly than hay is.[95]

His direct, uncompromising language can sometimes take the modern reader
aback. In *Homily* 11, where he is dealing with divisions within the congregation, for example, he attempts to move them to share his horror, repulsion,
and disgust at what amounts to their attack on Christ's body: 'Beat me, spit
upon me when you meet me in public, and get in some good blows! Do you
shudder when you hear these words? If I say: "Beat me!", you shudder with
horror; and yet you don't shudder when you rip apart your Master!'[96] He
certainly does not spare their feelings, but rather plays upon them for all he is
worth when he gets angry at their behaviour, threatens and frightens them
with punishments, ridicules their failings, or invites them to join in his
vilification of heretics. Scholars have commented on the rhetoric of vituper-
ation which can be so shocking for the modern reader when Chrysostom
directs it against the Jews, but we should note that he just as often uses it
against his own congregation.[97]

    Similarly, when he makes an exclamation he clearly intends the congre-
gation to identify with his exclamation and to share it. As Niki Tsironis
observes, 'we could imagine that the exclamations play the role of the words
of the chorus in ancient Greek tragedy. They represent the common feeling
that is pronounced by the preacher. At the same time, during the

---

[95] *New Homily* 7 (Mayer and Allen, 121).   [96] *Homily* 11 (Mayer and Allen, 71–1).
[97] A point made by Mayer and Allen (2000), 149. Chrysostom does have particularly harsh things
to say about the Jews—in *Oration* 1 Against the Jews (Mayer and Allen, 148–67), e.g. the synagogue is
likened to the theatre, a brothel, a robbers' cave, a place for demons; Jews are condemned as gluttons,
drunkards, murderers, stubborn, proud, licentious, deceitful, impious, cruel, inhuman, more savage
than wild beasts, thieves, cheats; Judaism is described as a disease, a sickness, and a weakness, but as
Wilken (1983), 112–23, makes clear, this was standard rhetorical practice—a rhetoric of abuse (or
psogos—invective). For the same sort of language directed against his congregation, see *Homily* 7 On
Colossians (Mayer and Allen, 81–2); *New Homily* 7 (Mayer and Allen, 120–1, 124), which are, in
addition, full of ultimatums and threats of punishment, intended to cajole and force his congregation
to reform their ways—'for the place where God is present [the church in contrast to the synagogue],
possessing power over life and death, is a frightening place—where homilies are delivered on
everlasting punishments, on rivers of fire, the poisonous worm, chains that can't be broken, external
darkness'. *Oration* 1 Against the Jews (Mayer and Allen, 155).

exclamations, the preacher sets aside his position of authority, sharing and voicing the common feeling of his congregation.'[98] For example, in a sermon preached following a procession by the Empress Eudoxia with the remains of the martyrs, from the Great Church in Constantinople to the martyrium, he can hardly contain his excitement, but opens his homily by voicing it in exclamations which he no doubt hoped would resonate with the feelings of his congregation and with which they could identify: 'What can I say? What shall I speak? I'm jumping with excitement and aflame with a frenzy that is better than common sense. I'm flying and dancing and floating on air and, for the rest, sunk under the influence of this spiritual pleasure. What can I say? What shall I speak?'[99] His appeal to their emotions is reinforced by his insistence on his own sincerity (he is not trying to be ironic, or to speak in generalities/small talk, but to say what he really thinks and feels)[100] and on their mutuality of purpose, their common love,[101] in order to place himself on their side and to win them over to his point of view. Like so many of the fathers, he therefore more often uses the plural rather than the singular, referring to 'we' and 'ours', rather than to 'I' and 'mine'. Thus, he effectively shares his emotions with the congregation and identifies with theirs.

Above all, as we see in *Homily* 3, where Chrysostom describes (and exasperatedly complains) about the well-nigh impossible vocation of the priest/bishop, they would hear someone who knew them almost better than they knew themselves, who was completely and absolutely devoted to them and their salvation; a father, a brother, a friend, a lover, who took them into his confidence, allowed them to share his secrets, who felt a real responsibility, as well as a deep passion, for their well-being:

> Nothing is dearer to me than you, not even this light. I would pray to be blinded a thousand times if in this way I could convert your souls. This your salvation is sweeter to me than light itself. What use to me are the sun's rays when the despondency caused by you spreads darkness over my eyes? What despondency can there be if you're in good repute? I have the impression I'm flying when I hear something good about you . . . I desire your progress. I strive for this with regard to you all, because I love you, because I hold you close, because you are everything to me—both father and mother, and brothers and children.[102]

What congregation could resist such a plea?

---

[98] Tsironis (1998), 307–8. Tsironis (1998), 314, refers to Mondzain, who describes Chrysostom in this context, as 'un remarquable manipulateur sacré qui pratique le shamanisme du verbe'.

[99] *New Homily* 1 (Mayer and Allen, 86).

[100] *Homily* 11 On Ephesians (Mayer and Allen, 71).

[101] *On: I Opposed Him to His Face* (Gal. 2:11) (Mayer and Allen, 142).

[102] *Homily* 3 (Mayer and Allen, 182–3). Cf. *On His Return* (Mayer and Allen, 100) where he talks of being a slave to his congregation's love; *On: I Opposed Him to His Face* (Mayer and Allen, 141) where, having been obliged to preach at another church, Chrysostom tells his congregation that he has missed them as child misses its mother.

In all these ways we see Chrysostom drawing on the techniques of classical rhetoric in order to expound the text of Scripture to his congregation so that it might converse directly with them, and address them in such a way that it was impressed upon their minds and hearts—their thoughts and action. Chrysostom can, therefore, be seen exercising his Midas touch, simultaneously transforming his congregation, and the very culture and language he has used to effect that transformation, through Scripture.

Listening to Scripture: The Preacher as Mediator

But there is another side of the multifaceted conversation that took place with Scripture in early Christian preaching which we must not ignore, even though we can now hear it only by inference and guesswork: the preacher himself was also, first and foremost, a listener. He first had to attend to Scripture and allowed it to impress itself upon him, before he could speak from it. As Augustine puts it in *On Christian Doctrine*, he had to be a hearer before he could be a speaker; someone who prayed (*orator*), before he could be someone who spoke (*dictor*).[103] In this sense, the practice of listening was just as influential on how Scripture was read and interpreted as on how it was presented and heard. Listening implies attentiveness, receptivity, openness— what Augustine describes as prayer, and prayer is, as we shall see in more detail in Chapter 6, a conversation. But like the conversation we have described in early Christian homilies, it is at the same time both multifaceted and one-sided: God does not need our words, but we need to enter into conversation with Him, in order to be formed and informed by Him. And what is Scripture but the Word of God, the inspired, authoritative Word of God, where God approaches human beings through human authors, and in the human Christ; where God acts and speaks, and can be encountered by fallen human beings who have obscured and darkened the image of God within, and can no longer know or hear Him speaking directly? The preacher, like all human beings, must first listen, and attend to God's revelation of Himself in Scripture, before he can communicate it to others.[104]

In many respects the fathers understood the role of the preacher as a mediator between God and humankind; someone who followed the pattern

---

[103] Augustine, *On Christian Doctrine*, 4.15.32 (Robertson, 140).

[104] As Gregory Nazianzen puts it, 'One must first be purified, and then purify others; first be made wise, and so make others wise; first become light, and then enlighten; first draw near to God and then lead others forward; first be made holy and then sanctify others, lead them by the hand, offer them understanding counsel' *Oration* 2. 71–2 (Daley, 56). Cf. *Oration* 39.10, 20 (Daley, 132, 138). In *Oration* 20. 1 (Daley, 98) he observes that this comes about by conversation with the divine: the preacher must first 'long for the philosophy which is from above . . . and so, in conversation with himself and with God, . . . live above the level of the visible, and always . . . bear the images of the divine things within himself '.

of God's descent to human beings in order to speak in temporal, mutable, sensible words. He did not speak from himself, but mediated God's Word and truth as he heard it in his prayerful reading of Scripture. His language was not his own, but resonated with Scriptural quotations, allusions, images, and types, which set up multiple echoes in the minds of his hearers. The preacher followed the example of Christ in descending from an inner 'word' or conception of truth, gleaned from his own listening to the inspired words of Scripture, to 'incarnate' it, or communicate it to his congregation; he mediated between the divine words of Scripture and the hearts and minds of his listeners, in order to impress the former upon the latter. A philosopher, he became a rhetor and exegete for the sake of his audience. In other words, his prayerful, imaginative reading and hearing of Scripture; his transposing of it for his congregation; his figurative interpretation, allowed what we have seen Carruthers describe as Scripture's necessarily 'implicit, hidden, polysemous and complex meaning',[105] to be uncovered, interpreted, and adapted—in other words, to speak—to his hearers. It is this process which, as we have noted, Augustine seems to be describing in *On Christian Doctrine*—his attempt to write a handbook for Christian preachers—and which he likens in the prologue of the work to learning a language through listening.[106] Hearing Scripture, then, is not a matter of formal rules, but of the unconscious reception and imprint on the mind/memory of the complicated web of imitation, convention, and tacit understanding in which language functions. Above all, it is a listening, and attentiveness, to the voice of God, which resonates throughout it. In this sense, both the preacher and the hearer are fellow pupils in the school of Christ; both listen to, and thereby learn, the language of the faith—the preacher from Scripture, and the hearer from Scripture, mediated through the words of the preacher.[107] Reflecting on the expression *diapsalma* in his *Inscriptions of the Psalms*, Gregory of Nyssa describes how the Holy Spirit was always speaking in the mind of David, inspiring his words and music, but that there were moments when David needed to pause, to concentrate, as it were, on listening to the Spirit's voice, which was always resonating within. He had to stop and listen to what the Spirit was saying, to receive it, and only then could he continue, relating what he had heard in song: 'when the great David served as interpreter for the Spirit, he related in his song the

---

[105] Carruthers (1990), 14.

[106] *On Christian Doctrine*, Prologue, 5 (Robertson, 4–5).

[107] As Augustine urges his congregation: 'Lend your ears to me, your hearts to him, that you might fill both', *Tractates on the Gospel of John*, 1.7 (WSA III.12), cited by Harmless (1995), 210. Szendy's (2008) reflections on musical arrangement are interesting here: listening to an arrangement of an original piece of music we are able to hear someone else's listening; just so, in sermons, the congregation were able to hear the preacher's listening to God. He comments, 'To hear listening [of the arranger]: it is from this reduplication that something like a critical moment of listening arises' (60).

things which he had previously learned, and if he was taught something additional while he was speaking, he submitted to the Spirit who was making the hearing of his soul resound and stopped the music, and when he was filled with these thoughts he related these matters, again entwining the words with the melody'.[108]

In order to illustrate this attentive listening to the resonating voice of the Spirit, this prayerful hearing of Scripture and the illumination of the mind of the preacher, which precedes any attempt to preach on it and to communicate it to his congregation, I would like to examine Augustine's treatment of the figures of John the Evangelist and John the Baptist in the first two of his homilies on St John's Gospel.

John's Prologue naturally prompts Augustine to reflect on communication, on the nature of language, the Word of God, Scripture, and divine illumination. That a human being could write the opening words, 'In the beginning was the word . . .' is only possible, Augustine insists, because of divine inspiration: if he had not been inspired John would not have been able to speak at all; insofar as he was inspired, he spoke, and communicates to us as much as a human being can articulate.[109] As is his customary practice, he illustrates this truth by quoting, and then reflecting on, a verse from the Old Testament, in this case Psalm 72:3: 'Let the mountains receive peace for thy people, and the little hills righteousness.' The mountains, he comments, are 'lofty souls', those who preach and teach God's word; the hills are 'ordinary souls', those who hear and receive their teaching. In order to 'receive peace and proclaim it to the people' Augustine observes that the lofty souls 'contemplated Wisdom herself, insofar as human hearts can reach that "which no eye has seen nor ear heard, nor has it entered in the heart of man"'.[110] That they *are* capable is, of course, a divine gift; wisdom ascends into their hearts insofar as they move beyond being simply human beings, and begin to be 'angels' or messengers of God. In other words, the authors of Scripture, and those who preach upon it, are only able to speak of divine truth because they have first been illuminated, and allowed to contemplate it, by divine inspiration and grace.[111] John is

---

[108] *Inscriptions of the Psalms*, 2.115 (Heine, 158). Cf. 116–30 (Heine, 158–63). Chrétien (2003), 57, cites similar reflections by Cezanne, who said of the painter, 'All his will must be silence. He must make silent within himself all the voices of preconceptions, forget, forget, make silence, be a perfect echo.' When we 'see' a work of art, then, we are also 'hearing' the painter's inspiration.

[109] 1.1 (WSA III.12 39).

[110] 1.4 (WSA III.12 41).

[111] This is similar to what Chrysostom describes as the work of the Holy Spirit at Pentecost, engraving the truth directly upon on the minds of the apostles, in contrast to the old law which was engraved on stone. The revelation is internal, rather than external, and works in the same way as hearing: by engraving or impressing the truth upon the mind. It is this which the apostles then subsequently shared in their preaching. *On Eleazer and the Seven Boys*, 7 (Mayer and Neil, 10).

simply a mediator, an 'angel' or messenger of God,[112] who has been allowed to 'ascend' and come closer to the divine mysteries than is ordinarily possible for human beings. He has heard, and can therefore speak; his hearers must, in turn, attend to him, or, in the words of another Psalm, lift up their eyes to the mountains: 'I lifted up my eyes to the mountains, from whence cometh my help' (Ps. 121:1). In doing so, Augustine warns them that they should remember that their help comes, ultimately, not from the author of Scripture, or the preacher, but from God, who has Himself illuminated and inspired them:[113] 'When we lift up our eyes to the scriptures, because the scriptures have been provided by human beings, we are lifting up our eyes to the mountains from where help will come to us. Even so, because those who wrote the scriptures were human beings, they were not shining on their own, but he "was the true light who enlightens everyone coming into this world" (Jn. 1:9).'[114] So, whilst divine illumination allows some lofty souls to contemplate the divine mysteries and become mediators or messengers, and, whilst their words, in Scripture or in preaching, allow their listeners to hear what they would not otherwise be able to hear, both lofty and ordinary souls must be aware of the source of what they hear. Both are fellow listeners or pupils in the school of Christ; both drink from the same fountain,[115] and the ultimate source of what they hear and imbibe is not human words, but divine truth. So, Augustine comments to his own congregation,

> when you raise your hearts to the scriptures at the sound of the Gospel, 'In the beginning...' you should realize that you have lifted up your eyes to the mountains. For unless the mountains were saying these things, you would not find anything at all for your minds to come to grips with. So, then, help has come to you from the mountains, so that you might at least hear things; but you still cannot understand what you have heard. Call for help from the Lord, who made heaven and earth; because while the mountains have been able to speak, they are not themselves able to enlighten since they too have been enlightened by what they heard.[116]

---

[112] 1.4 (WSA III.12 41). As Niki Tsironis (1998), 295, comments, 'in Byzantium, as well as in other civilisations and cultures, from the Jewish congregation to primitive shamanism and the Maori, the preacher played the role of the intermediary between God and the community, leading its prayers, interpreting the word of God, making the eternal revelation relevant to the present reality of the community, and teaching the rudiments of faith and the social and ethical implications of the sacred writings'.
[113] 1.5 (WSA III.12 42).   [114] 1.6 (WSA III.12 43).
[115] 1.7 (WSA III.12 43). Cf. *Expositions of the Psalms*, 34.1.1 (WSA III.16 45): 'we are indeed all listening to Christ. We all learn from Him, and in His school all of us together are students', cited by Dowler (2006). Augustine may be recalling Ambrose, *On the Duties of the Clergy*, 1.3 (Davidson, 119): 'For there is only one true Master, who never had to learn all that he taught everyone else: in this he is unique. Ordinary men must learn beforehand what they are to teach, and receive from him what they are to pass on to others.'
[116] 1.7 (WSA III.12 43).

Or, as he puts it in *On Christian Doctrine*, 'the benefits of teaching profit the mind when they are applied by men, when assistance is granted by God'.[117] The preacher is therefore simply a mediator, a messenger, who, as Augustine puts it, offers to the faithful, as it were, a 'chalice of words' from which they might partake of divine truth.[118] I have said 'simply a mediator', but for Augustine (as we saw for Plato at the beginning of Part One) it is of supreme importance that divine truth is mediated, not by angels, which God could so easily have done, but by ordinary human beings to their fellow beings. As Augustine comments in the Prologue to his treatise on Christian exegesis and preaching, *On Christian Doctrine*,

> All of these things [he has just referred to Paul's conversion and his being sent to a man to receive the sacraments, as well as to Cornelius' conversion and his being sent to Peter to receive instruction] might have been done by an angel, but the condition of man would be lowered if God had not wished to have men supply His word to men through men . . . for charity itself, which holds men together in a knot of unity, would not have the means of infusing souls and almost mixing them together if men could teach nothing to men.[119]

Both preacher and hearer are therefore joined together in prayer, or worship, united in their common listening to God.

---

[117] 4.16.33 (Robertson, 142).

[118] 1.7 (WSA III.12 44): *tamquam calicem, id est, uerbum propinatum acciperes*. Augustine often expresses these ideas in relation to 1 Cor. 3:7: 'Neither he that plants nor he that waters is anything, but it is God that gives the increase'—i.e. all growth comes from God, albeit through the preacher's efforts. In *Instructing Beginners in the Faith* he therefore stresses that the listener is 'listening to God through our agency' rather than placing 'hope in a human being' (7.11 (Canning, 79)). We find similar observations in almost all of the fathers. As Origen puts it, 'It is not my voice, but Christ's' (Hom. Ios. 5.2, cited by Monaci Castagno (1998), 65 n. 25). Gregory Nazianzen, like Augustine, does so in sacramental terms in *Oration* 39.2 (Daley, 128): 'Hear then, the voice of God, echoing strongly in me, a participant in and leader of these Mysteries, and perhaps also in you: "I am the light of the world." Do you see the grace of this day? Do you see the power of this Mystery? Have you not been raised up from the earth? Have you not been placed clearly on high lifted up by our voice and our instruction?' Cf. *Oration* 14.1 (Daley, 76): 'and pray that we may bestow these words on you richly, and nourish your souls with our discourse, breaking spiritual bread for the poor'.

[119] *On Christian Doctrine*, Prologue, 6, 8 (Robertson, 5, 6).

Third Impromptu

Singing the Blues

In this impromptu I would like to take one illustration of what we have described of the process of preaching in practice. It is the ninth of Augustine's *Homilies on the First Epistle of John*,[1] on 1 John 4:16–21:

> God is love, and he who abides in love, abides in God, and God abides in him. This is how love is perfected in us, that we have confidence regarding the day of judgement, because, as he is, so also are we in this world. There is no fear in charity, but perfect charity casts out fear, because fear has torment. Let us love because he loved us first. If anyone says, I love God, and hates his brother, he is a liar. For how can he who does not love his brother, whom he sees, love God, whom he does not see? And we have this command from him, that he who loves God must also love his brother.

Augustine opens the homily in his customary manner by reflecting on the relationship between himself, as preacher, and his congregation, as listeners, on their mutual participation and responsibility in speaking and listening to Scripture, and attempts to establish a relationship in which they will be predisposed to attend, take to heart, and be transformed what he has to say. In this instance, given that the lesson is about love, his task is easy: his homilies on the first epistle of John had been interrupted and he is in now in their debt and owes them a conclusion; they are creditors and must exact their debt. But charity is not a matter of debt and of credit, rather it is a matter of mutual affection and delight. Taking Cicero's advice that the speaker should first aim to make his audience 'benevolent, attentive and docile',[2] Augustine appropriately takes up the analogy of a cow and its calves to initiate his reflections on love. In a very mundane, somewhat bathetic manner (and perhaps all the more engaging for those reasons), which would nevertheless resonate with Paul's teaching on milk and meat, he likens the exalted, hieratic prose of the lesson they are about to engage with to a cow's milk: the preacher and his congregation are like a cow and its calves; the bond of love makes the 'debt', or burden, of suckling eager, butting calves one which is lightly and willingly

---

[1] All references are to WSA III. 14 (edited and translated by Boniface Ramsay, 2008).
[2] Cicero, *De Oratore*, 2.80, cited by Harmless (1995), 178.

born by the mother, whilst the sucking of milk by the calves becomes a matter of sweet affection rather than bitter exaction. Indeed, such is the cow's desire that its calves demand food that it will bellow if they don't. An 'intertext' from Augustine's favourite dialogue partner, Paul, caps the preface and gives his observations *the* Apostle's authority, 'I became a little child in your midst, like a nurse caring for her children' (1 Thess. 2:7). The preface is therefore rather like a well-known folk song, which reassures the listener by the familiarity of both the song and the singer. But Augustine's congregation would also know that, once their preacher had got them on his side, they needed to be prepared for a change of register.

The transposition is swift: Augustine immediately sounds the main theme of the sermon: it is 'brief in words and great in intellectual depth': 'God is love!' The theme is then elucidated a little, 'God is love, and he who abides in love, abides in God, and God abides in him' (4:16). As so often, Augustine proceeds to engage his listeners in his theme by a counterpoint of memorable parallelisms:

> Let God be your dwelling, and let your dwelling be God's.
> Abide in God, and let God abide in you.
> God abides in you so that he may contain you; you abide in God lest you fall.

And again, he caps what he has to say with an 'intertext' from the Apostle: 'Charity never fails' (1 Cor. 13:8).

Having been rendered 'docile and attentive' the congregation would now have the main theme of the homily ringing in their ears; it would have been imprinted on their minds by parallelisms, and further impressed by the authority of the Apostle. It no doubt resonated with much that they had already heard, and it was up to Augustine to creatively evoke these resonances so that they could build upon what they knew and explore what was unfamiliar to them. The parallelisms in paragraph one, for example, must have immediately resonated with the rules or summaries of the faith which had shaped their understanding as catechumens: God is love; God is the Creator on whom we are wholly dependent for our being; if we turn away from God we fall.

In paragraph two Augustine proceeds to work through the lesson from 1 John, 'This is how love is perfected in us, that we have confidence regarding the day of judgement.' Here is a further development of the main theme and another lesson in love: our progress in love can be measured by how much confidence we have in the day of judgement. Like any good composer or performer, Augustine therefore restates the theme and then elaborates on this variation of it: 'God is love', but, of course, God does not progress or regress, we do—so love is perfected in us insofar as we either advance towards him or fall away from him. This comes about, as we saw in Chapter 5, by faith, which inspires love, which in turn inspires good actions. Augustine reasons carefully, taking his congregation step by step into his argument: faith in the day of judgement inevitably gives way to fear because of our sinfulness; fear, however, causes us to refrain from evil deeds and reform ourselves; we are therefore purified and our faith bears fruit in good works; on the basis of our good works we can then look towards the day of judgement with confidence, hope, and desire, and progress in love of God rather than fall away from Him in fear; we become patient with life while we anticipate death and being dissolved with Christ, rather than struggling patiently with death while we try to hold onto life. These points are made by means of an intricate counterpoint of Scriptural 'intertexts' and allusions, which are generally introduced as answers to a question Augustine has posed in relation to the text or without any preface, simply in juxtaposition to it: Sirach 1:16: 'The fear of the Lord is the beginning of wisdom'; Colossians 3:5: 'mortify your members [evil deeds] that are on the earth'; an allusion to Song of Songs: 'Since the chaste soul, which desires the bridegroom's embraces, has now begun to desire Christ's coming, she becomes a virgin through faith, hope and charity. Now she has confidence concerning the day of judgement'; Matthew 6:10: 'Thy kingdom come'; Psalm 6:3–4, which voices the reformed believers newly found confidence and their groans at any delay in the day of judgement, 'And you, Lord, how long? Turn, Lord and rescue my soul'; the Apostle in Philippians 1:23–24 where he prays 'to be dissolved and to be with Christ'.

As we noted earlier, such 'intertexts' serve a number of purposes: first and foremost they gave Scripture a voice, indeed, they allowed it to address the listening congregation with a rich polyphony of harmonious voices. Moreover, they enabled the preacher to converse with Scripture; Scripture to interpret Scripture; one verse to interpret another. In a homily such as the one we are considering, intertexts are therefore cited in relation to the text in hand in order to elucidate it, confirm it, to provide answers to questions it has raised in the minds of the preacher and his congregation, or to raise more questions which might help clarify it further. As Scripture they provided an authoritative voice which the preacher could adopt as his own; its voice became his voice, as its language resonated and echoed with his own. Its inspired harmony and unity gave him a unique freedom as he alluded to, paraphrased, transposed, elaborated, and improvised on it in endless variations. In these variations on the theme of Scripture his listeners would hear not only his own voice but, like those whom Plato describes as listening to poetry inspired by the gods, they would be drawn, as by a magnetic field, into the unified harmony of Scripture sounding through it at every turn, giving it weight and meaning. And, as we shall see later in this impromptu, inspired and unified by the Holy Spirit intertexts also allowed for a provocative diversity in unity and prompted highly imaginative and creative attempts to reconcile and harmonize apparently dissonant and disparate texts.

Paragraph three reveals another example of Augustine's characteristic methods as preacher in interpreting a text for his listeners: the use of questions that he addresses to the text, which he then proceeds to answer, either by using an 'intertext' from another part of Scripture, by giving a story or analogy, or by conducting a dialogue with an imaginary interlocutor. In all these cases the congregation would be implicitly invited to share the question, to ask it themselves, to become involved in the search for an answer, and to evaluate the different types of answer which they heard their preacher offer. Questions demanded participation and response, and were therefore a good way of keeping an audience alert, interested, and involved. So, in paragraph three, Augustine takes the next phrase of the text from 1 John, which seems to suggest an answer as to why we should have confidence on the day of judgment: 'Because just as he is, so also are we in this world' (4:17). But the meaning of these words is not immediately obvious and Augustine proceeds to share the questions which he senses must be in the minds of his listeners by formulating them himself: 'Doesn't he seem to have said something impossible? For can a human being be just as God is?' In an attempt to clarify matters he reminds them that he has previously explained that 'just as' means 'being in the image of God'. But this provokes another question: 'If, then, we have been made to the image of God, why aren't we just as God is?' He answers that '[We are—yet] not in terms of equality but according to our measure.' The question, 'Where, then, is confidence given us regarding the day of judgment?' is recapitulated in this context. His answer this time is to revert to the theme of the homily and the epistle—to charity—and to an intertext from Matthew 5:44–6, which, elucidated by further question and answer,[3] suggests that likeness to God—'just as He is, so are we in the world'—consists in our forgiveness of our enemies and our willingness to pray for those who persecute us. 'Just as' 'God makes his sun to rise on the good and the bad and his rain to fall on the righteous and the unrighteous' (Matt. 5:45) so, too, we offer our enemies 'our tears when we pray for them'. Thus, by a series of questions directed to the text of John, by elucidations, quotations, or intertexts from other parts of Scripture, questions directed to the intertexts, and recapitulation and development of the main theme, Augustine finally explains John's rather enigmatic words.

The to and fro pattern of text–question; intertext–question; elaboration–recapitulation; punctuated by memorable antitheses, parallelisms, or alliteration is a characteristic one, and one which his congregation would be both accustomed to, and, to a large extent, anticipate, just as a listener to a piece of classical music would anticipate the general structure of theme, development, variations, recapitulation, and coda. The particular intertexts, language, images, and examples were like familiar chords or themes, which the congregation had heard over and over again, in many different contexts, in relation to

---

[3] 'From whom does he give an example?'; 'How does God do this.'

innumerable passages of Scripture, to elucidate a wide range of points. They would inevitably resonate with the text in hand, and the mere fact of voicing them again would sometimes suffice to convey the preacher's meaning.[4] This familiarity with the preacher's methods, and the tacit understanding it created, would, of course, also help the congregation to follow the otherwise challengingly swift staccato of his questions, his frequent juxtaposition of apparently unrelated texts, his extended antitheses, and his constant reversion to certain key aspects of the faith to resolve any difficulty or problem. For the preacher, it enabled him to appeal to a sort of complicit shorthand, which often meant that he did not have to explain a reference, or expound an image, but could rely on the fact that a simple allusion would be sufficient for it be recognized by his hearers and for it to carry with it a rich multiplicity of resonant meanings.[5]

These techniques for building up a shared understanding are clearly at work as the sermon progresses: Augustine is careful to constantly remind his congregation of what has gone before, to repeat conclusions, recapitulate key intertexts, and generally allow what has been established earlier on to resonate with, and inform, the text in hand.[6] So, when he moves on to reflect on 1John 4:18—'There is no fear in charity, but perfect charity casts out fear'—he is able to recapitulate his observations about the relationship between fear and charity in paragraph two, reiterate his citation of Sirach 1:16—'the fear of the Lord is the beginning of wisdom'—and develop the point that as charity increases so fear decreases. In order to drive home the fact that 'if there is no fear, there is no way that charity may come in', he gives an extended example, rather like one of Chrysostom's 'just as' passages, taken from everyday life and experience, which is obviously intended to create a vivid, easily remembered image by which his observations might be inscribed on the minds of his

---

[4] The intertexts, themes, and images were therefore rather like jazz riffs—a musical phrase or figure which forms a sort of ground bass or *ostinato*, and is taken up, and improvised over, by the different sections of the band in 'head' arrangements. The players don't need to be able to read music, or to know anything about music theory; they just need to be familiar with the riff and its rhythms and chords. Thus, Count Basie's famous twelve-bar blues, 'One O'Clock Jump', came about when the radio show, in which the riff was used as a theme tune, had a couple of spare minutes on air and different players or sections of the band took up the riff and improvised on it to fill the time.

[5] For philosophical reflection on this, see Polanyi (1958), 57: we are able to read a text because of agreed convention, tacit skill, and practice; we are aware of the meaning, not the words themselves.

[6] Gregory Nazianzen notes that this is precisely what the Spirit itself does in inspiring the authors of Scripture in order to instil the most important truths: 'For the instruments of the Spirit have not simply spoken once or twice about the needy [the homily is on love of the poor/neighbour] and then fallen silent; nor was it simply some of them and not others, or some more and others less, as if they were dealing with no great matter, with nothing of pressing importance. No—all of them laid this command on us, each with the greatest urgency, either as the first of our duties or as one of the first. Sometimes they exhort us, sometimes they threaten, sometimes they rebuke; and there are times, too, when they give recognition to those who have done well as a way of making the command efficacious by keeping it constantly in our memory', *Oration* 14.35 (Daley, 95).

hearers and easily recollected by them. In order to demonstrate that charity
cannot enter unless fear has made way for it, he gives the example of sewing;
the needle must first go in, make the hole, and then come out, for the thread to
be drawn through the material, 'similarly,' he comments, 'fear occupies the
mind first, but fear doesn't remain there, because it has entered in order to
introduce charity'.

As he continues to reflect on the remainder of the sentence—that 'There is
no fear in love, but perfect love casts out fear, *because fear has torment*'—he
offers (by way of an intertext from Psalm 30:11–12 and a questioning of it)
another everyday analogy in order to explain how the torment and suffering of
fear in the mind of the sinner is a salutary, as it were, medicinal experience,
which prepares it for the healing salve of charity. We observed earlier that the
image of the doctor, whose treatment involves pain and suffering in order to
heal his patients, was one of the most common images used by the fathers to
describe the way in which God heals the soul. Augustine's congregation would
no doubt bring all their previous encounters with this image, in many different
contexts, to their understanding of fear and charity, so that it hardly needed
further explanation: 'fear is the medicine, charity is the health'. They knew
who the doctor was; they knew who the patient was; they knew what the
remedy was; they knew that healing involved suffering. It was enough to
mention the doctor and the patient for all these tacit understandings to
come to mind and be applied to the text in hand (though Augustine cannot
resist a little elaboration, or a few appropriate intertexts (Sir. 1:28: 'For he who
is without fear will not be able to be made righteous')).

In the next paragraph (5) Augustine demonstrates another common tactic
in patristic interpretation, and one we noted briefly earlier in this impromptu:
whereas he often uses intertexts to allow Scripture to converse with itself, and,
as it were, interpret itself, in some contexts he uses them to make Scripture
contradict itself, and interprets the text in hand by establishing how an
apparently contradictory text might be reconciled with it. In this instance,
John's statement, 'There is no fear in charity, but perfect charity casts out fear',
is set alongside David's words in Psalm 19:9: 'The fear of the Lord is chaste,
abiding forever.' Discord and dissonance are used to bring about harmony and
consonance. It is an effective technique, used by almost all the fathers to
entertain their congregations with a familiar but evidently much-loved inter-
pretative ploy/game, on the one hand, and to demonstrate the divine unity,
harmony, and inspiration of Scripture, on the other. Both they and their
congregations knew the rules of the game and how it would eventually play
out. They tacitly shared a belief in the inspiration and unity of Scripture and
knew that however dissonant the discords they would eventually be reconciled, and, in their reconciliation, reveal their unique source: the one breath,
the one tongue, the one inspiration of the Holy Spirit. There might be two
apparently dissonant testaments, two conflicting voices, two contrary hearts,

two disagreeing tongues, a double flute, but there was ultimately only one breath breathing through both. As Augustine comments, 'There is, then, a certain harmony, there is a certain concord, but it seeks a listener'; 'Open wide your ears, listen to the melody.' What he is appealing to is their tacit understanding, their previous experience, their common knowledge, their shared faith in the unity and inspiration of divine Scripture. This was a rule, which, as we have noted on a number of occasions, worked in the same way as a key signature for a composer, or grammar for a writer, and which informed all their speaking and listening. It might often be presumed rather than overtly stated, but it was all the more forceful for that, and is but a notable example of the vast store of tacit understanding which they shared and which made their communication possible and meaningful. Without it, what was said and heard would fragment into meaningless noise. As Augustine stresses, what is required is an 'ear' for the harmonies of Scripture, an 'attentive' listening to its melodies, an opening of the ears in order to hear divine truth.

In this instance, the two texts are reconciled by the identification of two different types of fear: the sort of fear the homily has so far been describing—the fear of punishment and of judgement which precipitates reform, good works, confidence, love, and desire for God, so that, ultimately, it is cast out by perfect charity. The other fear is the fear of losing God's presence, and is effectively an embracing and enjoying of God: this is the chaste fear of the psalmist, which abides forever. In paragraph 6 Augustine, as it were, transposes the theme of fear into everyday terms, and into the language of common human experience, by illustrating the two different fears by means of two different married women. It is as if he is changing into another key—one that is more familiar to his hearers than even the language of Scripture—which can resonate directly with their lives and experiences so that that they can immediately relate to and identify with it; so that it can address their hearts as well as their minds and bring about a transformation of both. As any musician knows, transposition into a different key can have dramatic effects, as each key has its own mood and character; transposition between Scripture and everyday language and life was a similar device for the fathers. It was as if they moved from the grand, mysterious, and somewhat forbidding scale of B flat to the more accessible and direct scale of C major.

The two wives, one adulterous (or tempted by adultery) and one chaste; one fearing her husband's arrival, the other fearing her husband's departure; one sinful, the other righteous; one motivated by fear, the other by love, are set forth as figures of the two types of fear: one which gives way as charity perfects it whilst the other is eternal. Augustine addresses his congregation (men and women) on the part of the first wife, who fears being discovered by the arrival of her husband: 'O soul that fears God in that way...just as the woman displeases you, so you also be displeasing to yourself.' A string of observations, a string of questions, and a string of intertexts follow, to provoke them to self-recognition, confession, and reform—the intertexts giving Augustine's admonitions for change weight and authority. By voicing Scripture his words become the Word of God and God speaks through him. Who could disobey?

When Augustine turns to address the second, chaste wife, who fears that her husband might leave her, he is literally lost for words. He is at a loss, first of all, to think who she might be; he evidently knows no one like her: 'Let us also address her who now has chaste fear, abiding forever. Do we think we have found her, so that we may address her? Do you think that she is in this congregation? Do you think that she is in this hall? Do you think that she is on this earth? She cannot but be, but she is hidden.' He observes that she is like a hidden root in winter, waiting for the spring, and then wonders whether she can hear him, whether he has her ears. If he did, he insists that she wouldn't listen to him, he would listen to her: 'She would teach me something, rather than learning from me.' Meanwhile, while she lives patiently on the earth, he does not possess the words to address her, but rather it is God Himself who consoles her. In a daring move, which marks a significant transition in the sermon into the new, uncharted, and exciting territory Augustine is to explore until its end, Augustine hypothetically improvises God's voice and words to her, taking on the role of the absent but impassioned husband and lover: 'You want me to come now, and I know that you want me to come now. I know how you are, that you are awaiting my coming in peace. I know that this is irksome to you, but continue to wait and to endure. I am coming, and I am coming quickly.' In response the woman does not just speak, she 'sighs' and 'sings', and her language is not human language but the divine language of Scripture: 'Listen to her singing like the lily in the midst of thorns. Listen to her sighing and saying: "I shall sing and I shall understand on the unsullied way. When will you come to me?"' (Ps. 101:1–2). His congregation must indeed have wondered what they were listening to: questions directed to the text, questions addressed to an imaginary (if silent) interlocutor, intertexts, vivid everyday analogies, antitheses . . . all these they were accustomed to; but God speaking to God, as man to woman; husband to wife; an improvised God, as impassioned husband and lover, responding to the sighing and singing of God in Scripture, as longing wife? This was something new. But there was more . . .

Augustine turns in paragraph nine to the acme of John's epistle, which begins: 'Let us love, because he loved us first' (4:19). In one respect he returns to his classical roots in his repeated insistence that love of the beautiful makes its lovers beautiful; in another respect he transplants them and places his observations firmly in the soil of Christian Scripture and tradition. He first of all gives the everyday example of an ugly man, with a twisted face, who loves a beautiful woman. Piling up question after question he establishes the futility of the unfortunate man's love and the similar situation of his sinful hearers, except that even in their loathsome sinfulness God, who is always beautiful, has astonishingly loved them first, so that they might become beautiful as a responsive love of Him grows in them. Like one jazz player turning to another to allow him to take over the theme and improvise, Augustine turns to Paul and directs his congregation to 'Listen to the apostle Paul.' An intertext from Paul secures these observations, 'God showed his love for us because, when we were yet sinners, Christ died for us' (Rom. 5:8–9).

Paul then prompts Augustine to another daring improvisation: the crucified Christ was far from beautiful; having taken on the loathsome sinfulness of human beings he was the epitome of ugliness as he died in order to redeem it. The dissonance, discord, and ugliness of sin is set alongside the beauty of God; the human, crucified Christ alongside the eternal Son of God; the besotted, ugly lover alongside the supremely beautiful eternal Word. Augustine sets Psalm 45:2 ('Splendid in form beyond the sons of men, grace is poured forth on you lips') and John 1:1 ('in the beginning was the Word, and the Word was with God, and the Word was God') alongside Isaiah 53:2 ('And we saw him, and he had neither splendour or comeliness'). Again there are two discordant pipes, two tongues, two mouths at odds with each other, apparently contradictory. They are reconciled this time by a third voice: that of the Apostle in Philippians 2:6–7: 'Splendid in form beyond the sons of men: Who, although he was in the form of God, did not consider it to be robbery to be equal to God...We saw him, and he had neither splendour nor comeliness. He emptied himself, taking the form of a slave, having been made in the likeness of men, and having been found in appearance as a man.' The Son of God is set alongside the Son of Man; the form of God alongside the form of a servant; the supremely beautiful alongside a heap of broken images, but the love of God become man shatters the ugliness of sin in order to redeem and reform human beings and make them, too, love-worthy and beautiful. The message is too profound and too sublime for words, and prompts Augustine into what must count as one of the wildest passages of daring alliteration, relentless repetition and restatement, dizzying assonance and ecstatic exclamation in patristic literature, in order to convey in words (or at least in sound) to his listening congregation the love of the transcendent God who became man, and died as man, in order to save and redeem them, so that they too might be caught up in his words and be inspired to a responsive love of the one who had first loved them. Carefully chosen intertexts, well-judged examples, patient explanations, and precisely weighed questions give way to passages which might well be a verbal transcription of some of the most daring and sublime jazz improvisations (they break too many rules to be likened to classical music), as Augustine draws out the lesson of Christ's love for us and relates it to *the* paradigm for the interpretation of Scripture—the double commandment of love of God and neighbour—in the concluding passage of John 4:20. He is well aware that a reasoned exposition of the fact that 'God is love' simply isn't possible; it transcends human reason. He has tried to 'tell it slant'[7] and make it strange, through juxtaposed texts, unsettling images, analogies, antitheses, moving in and through words towards what transcends linguistic formulation. The images/words are meant to be iconic or sacramental: they are not the divine but re-present it, pointing towards that which they signify. They must therefore be opened up, broken apart, and the listener must move through and beyond them in order to grasp their inspiration and source. In this case, it is as if the definitive rule of love of God and love of neighbour somehow gives Augustine the liberty to leave behind careful exegesis, to take risks, abandon himself to an impassioned dialogue with his listeners, and to break through the words in which the double commandment is formulated to capture its sublime truth: 'If anyone says, I love God, and hates his brother, he is a liar. For how can he who does not love his brother, whom he sees, love God, whom he does not see?' 'What then?' Augustine asks in paragraph 10, rather as Miles Davis' *Kind of Blue* asks, 'So what?'

Does he who loves his brother also love God? It must be that he loves God; it must be that he loves love itself. Can he love his brother and not love love? It must be that he loves love. What then? Does he love God because he loves love? Precisely. By loving God he loves love. Or have you forgotten that you said a little earlier, *God is love*. If God is love, whoever loves love loves God. Love your brother, then, and be secure. You can't say, 'I love my brother, but I don't love God'. Just as you are lying if you say 'I love God' when you don't love your brother, so you are mistaken when you say 'I love my brother' if you are aware that you don't love God. It must be that you who love your brother love love itself. *Love is God*. It must be, then, that whoever loves God loves his brother. But if you don't love the brother whom you see, how can you love God, whom you don't see? Why doesn't a person see God? Because he doesn't have that love. He doesn't see God because he doesn't have that love. He doesn't have love because he doesn't love his brother. Therefore, because he doesn't have love, he doesn't see God. For if he has love, he sees God, because *God is love*, and his eye is ever more cleansed by love, so that he may see that unchangeable substance in whose presence he may always rejoice, which, once he has been united to the angels, he may enjoy forever.

[7] Emily Dickinson:

'Tell all the Truth but tell it slant—
Success in Circuit lies
Too bright for our infirm Delight
The Truth's superb surprise

As Lightning to the Children eased
With explanation kind
The Truth must dazzle gradually
Or every man be blind—'

Having followed him through this extended improvisation on the double commandment, Augustine's listeners no doubt reacted like any jazz audience—with applause. As they applauded, what they had heard—love of God and love of neighbour; God is love and love is God; the very word 'love' itself—would echo and re-echo with everything they had previously heard about love: with the teaching on fear and love they had just received; the images of the needle and thread; the two different wives; the ugly lover and the beautiful woman; the disfigured, crucified Christ and the splendour of the Word; the voices of God as husband and wife, of Paul, David, Wisdom . . . ; with the insistent questions and memorable parallelisms and antitheses of their preacher. These resonances would mean that next time they came to hear him they would be better attuned to hear the harmonies of Scripture, to attend to its melodies, to open their ears to hear divine truth echoing throughout it, and to be transformed by it.

Part Three

From Listening to Hearing

6

The Polyphony of Prayer

something understood
George Herbert, *Prayer*

Prayer is perhaps one of the most intriguing examples of the practice of listening in the early Church, for it is not at all clear who is doing the listening and who is speaking. Following Christ's example, the early Christians prayed with confidence to God the Father, whom they were unanimously persuaded was a willing and gracious listener. But this seems very odd: the transcendent, omnipotent, and omniscient God certainly doesn't need our prayers to be informed about our needs or failings. Rather, it seems that the one who *needs* to hear is the speaker: they need to articulate their prayer—to speak, and, above all, to listen and then to hear the words they address to God. This is because, in reality, it is not God who is moved, informed, or, indeed, transformed by our prayers, but us. How and why this is will be the subject of this chapter.

It has been rightly noted that there is no in-depth study of prayer in the early Church.[1] This is also odd. Of course, in one respect prayer is something that is simply done, and is a matter for the individual (or assembled group) and God. It is a direct communication between the speaker and God and is not intended for the ears of anyone else. Or is it? I suspect that part of the reason for the relative neglect of prayer in scholarly work is the fact that it is not, usually, concerned with the sort of things that scholars tend to find worth considering: doctrine, polemic, or even exegesis. Rather, it is essentially personal: an intimate conversation about everyday events and feelings; a confidential confession of sin and failing; a trusting, direct request for help; a grateful offering of thanks. Insofar as this conversation appears in a public, liturgical context it has received a good deal of attention, focused largely on the precise form and order it assumed in different times, places, and traditions. But insofar as it appears in an individual, personal context, it has been left

---

[1] Coyle in Allen, Meyer and Cross (1999), 25.

unheard by anyone other than the original speaker. To listen would be to eavesdrop, and although this might have a certain human fascination, and perhaps give us a glimpse into personal piety in the early Church, it has not been thought worth much scholarly time.

The fathers themselves do not help matters. The only formal occasions on which they turn to reflect on the nature of prayer are almost always (the only exceptions I can think of are in monastic literature) in relation to exegesis of the Lord's Prayer. This prayer, given by Christ and set forth in Scripture, had become an important part of Christian initiation, and it was expected that it would be repeated (at least) daily by the devout Christian. It therefore had a unique and highly influential position in early Christian practice, and we possess important treatments of it by Cyprian, Tertullian, Origen,[2] Theodore of Mopsuestia, Gregory of Nyssa, and Augustine.[3] But apart from a letter by Augustine,[4] and some important asides in sermons and treatises on other subjects, there is very little else that one can turn to in order to investigate an early Christian understanding of prayer. Rather, I think it would not be unfair to say that the early Christians seem to have instinctively got on with the business of prayer, naturally giving voice to their faith in supplications, intercessions, and thanksgivings addressed to God rather than formally reflecting on it.

The large body of literature on prayer in an ascetic, monastic setting, is, of course, a special case. It has received far more scholarly attention, not least because the desert fathers and ascetic writers thought of their lives as first and foremost ones of prayer: they did not pray to live, they lived to pray. The notion of continual prayer is one that exercised the early Church as a whole, as early Christian writers seem to have been generally preoccupied with how to implement the various Scriptural injunctions to 'pray ceaselessly'.[5] In this chapter I hope we will see that monastic reflection and practice was not as far removed from that of the rest of the Church as scholarly literature on it might at first suggest, and that the ascetics' more concentrated attention on prayer—in practice and in theory—will help us to understand wider practice and presuppositions.

So, in private and in public, alone and in company, silently and aloud, in the monastery and in church, in set forms and informal conversation, in prose and in verse, in speech and in song, the early Christians offered prayer to God.

---

[2] Actually, Origen's treatment is in the context of a wider treatise on prayer itself, defending its practice against doubters and critics.

[3] Cyprian, *On the Lord's Prayer*; Tertullian, *On the Lord's Prayer*; Origen, *On Prayer* (all Sykes); Theodore of Mopsuestia, *On the Lord's Prayer* (Mingana); Gregory of Nyssa, *The Lord's Prayer* (ACW 18); Augustine, *Epistle*, 130 To Proba (FC 18).

[4] *Epistle*, 130 (FC 18).

[5] E.g. Luke 18:1; 1 Thess. 5:17; Eph. 6:18.

Words were voiced by the tongue or heart in order to reach His ears. What was going on here?

'God's breath in man returning to its birth'[6]

When we turn to the subject of early Christian prayer we no doubt think, first of all, not of hearing but seeing. We have a mental picture of the raised arms and flat palms of the 'Orant',[7] depicted in so many scenes of early Christian art; of the three young men in the burning, fiery furnace, standing confidently amidst the flames, decked out in rather exotic-looking doublet and hose and cocked hats, their arms uplifted, calling upon God for deliverance, as they appear on the walls of the second- to fifth-century Catacombs of Priscilla in Rome. This was a pose which pagans and Jews, as well as Christians, would immediately recognize as one of prayer. As Origen puts it, with extended hands and upraised eyes 'one thereby wears on the body the image of the characteristics which are becoming to the soul in prayer'.[8] When the direction of the soul is transposed into words, it is more often than not described by the fathers as conversation (*homilia*) with God—most famously, perhaps, by the fourth-century master of monastic prayer, Evagrius: 'Prayer is a conversation of the mind (*nous*) with God',[9] though Clement, in the second century, similarly observes, 'Prayer is then, to speak more boldly, converse with God.'[10] It is not surprising that Clement felt that it was a brave move, not just to lift up one's hands to God in supplication but actually to engage in conversation with Him. The familiarity and immediacy which conversation implies is indeed an extraordinary move when one's interlocutor is the invisible, transcendent God. How is this possible? This is, of course, the real question with prayer: are human beings just babbling away to someone at the end of the line, exchanging gossip with the transcendent and passing time with the eternal, or is there really something worth saying—and, above all, something worth hearing? Gregory Nazianzen puts this problem eloquently in one of his many poems/hymns, which are almost all, as it were, couched in the form of prayers to God:[11]

---

[6] George Herbert, *Prayer*, from which the titles of the subsections in the first part of this chapter are taken.

[7] The 'prayer', from the Latin *orare*—to pray.

[8] *On Prayer*, 31.2–3 (Sykes, 207–8). This characteristic position, as well as kneeling, is one that Basil assigns to *dogmata* (*On the Holy Spirit*, 27.66 (Anderson, 100–1))—to the unwritten tradition handed on by the apostles, with equal authority to Scripture.

[9] *On Prayer*, 3 (Tugwell, 30).

[10] *Stromateis*, 7.7 (ANCL 12, 434).

[11] He wrote over three hundred, all of which can be accurately described as prayers.

> O All Transcendent God
> (what other name describes you?)
> what words can sing your praises?
> No word at all denotes you.
> What mind can probe your secret?
> No mind at all can grasp you.
> Alone beyond the power of speech,
> All men can speak of springs from you.

The last phrase provides the answer to Gregory's opening questions. How can he address, speak to, and engage with the transcendent God? He can do so because 'all men can speak of springs from you'. In other words, it is because God has *first* spoken to us that we can begin to speak to Him; our speaking is simply a response to our having first *heard* Him address us. So, yes, indeed, prayer is conversation, but it is one that is always initiated by God: God speaks to us, and hearing Him, we respond. Prayer is therefore first and foremost a listening to God, and only then a response to Him. Gregory continues his prayer, in order to set forth just how the transcendent God speaks to us, and how we can hear Him. He writes:

> All things proclaim you—
> things that can speak and things that cannot . . .
> All things breathe you a prayer,
> a silent hymn of your own composing . . .
> What mind's affinities with heaven
> can pierce the veils above the clouds?
> Mercy, all transcendent God
> (what other name describes you?)[12]

So, for Gregory, God first speaks to us, and we first hear Him, through His works—through all things animate and inanimate, which are His composition, and return His creative breath with a prayer. He also speaks through His mercy, which allows the human mind to hear and grasp Him who would otherwise remain veiled to human understanding.

Gregory's questions and answers deserve more detailed consideration: How exactly can God be said to speak to us, and how exactly can we be said to hear Him, in order to respond to Him in prayer?

'Heaven in ordinary': how does God speak?

'You made me and, when I forgot you, you did not forget me . . . Before I called to you, you were there before me. With mounting frequency by voices of many

---

[12] Gregory Nazianzen, *Poemata Dogmatica* (PG 37:507), cited in Hamman (1961), 162 no. 246.

kinds you put pressure on me, so that from far off I heard and was converted and called upon you as you were calling to me . . . I serve and worship you so that from you good may come to me. To you I owe my being and the goodness of my being' (*Confessions*, 13.1.1).

The transcendent, eternal, immutable God does not 'speak' as we speak; He does not have a mouth, tongue, lungs, and vocal chords. God speaks and we hear Him metaphorically, but no less forcefully, as Gregory suggests, through His works and merciful actions. To list them is, effectively, to rehearse the rule of faith, or the Creed, which, as we saw in Chapter 4, all Christians receive when they are initiated into the Church at baptism. God's works and actions were the substance of the faith, and a summary, or narration, of them was impressed upon the mind of every devout Christian so that he or she could subsequently hear them, or listen out for them, as it were, as they encountered them at every turn. To hear God, in this context, is effectively to be aware of, and responsive to, his revelation of Himself in creation, the Incarnation, the Holy Spirit, sacred history, the Scriptures, preachers, and teachers.

It is significant, I think, that almost all early Christian prayer contains some appeal to God as Creator (one need only think of Ambrose's *Deus Creator Omnium*),[13] as if the interlocutor is thereby being identified, and the grounds for prayer validated: the one to whom the prayer is addressed is the one who has first addressed us, who is all-powerful, and who, having called us into being, invites our response, and can in turn be trusted to respond to our requests for help or mercy.[14] One example will suffice: the opening of a prayer for use on Saturdays, which appears on a fourth-century papyrus:

> On you we call, Lord God,
> all-wise, all surveying, holy
> the only true Sovereign.
> You created the universe,
> you watch over all that exists.

[The author can therefore confidently respond to God with praise, and acknowledge his mercy] . . .

> With one voice we offer you
> praise and thanksgiving;
> full-hearted, full throated we sing you
> the hymn you have a right to at this hour.
> In your mercy you called to us

---

[13] Fontaine (1992), 236–9, and commentary 241–61. Cited by Augustine in *Confessions*, 9.12.32 and 11.27.35.

[14] The Lord's Prayer, which we will discuss in more detail later in this chapter, might well be said to be a notable exception to this statement, but the opening appeal to 'Our Father' is usually read by the fathers as addressed to the one who is our Creator—our Father—to whom we are related as to kin.

> (holy the calling!),
> taught us and trained us,
> gave understanding, wisdom, truth to us, life eternal.[15]

Creation itself, and especially its order and beauty, is therefore often described as God's 'voice'. As Augustine famously puts it, when contemplating creation in *Confessions*, Book 10, 'My question was the attention I gave to them, and their response was their beauty', or, as a third-century hymn, discovered at Oxyrhynchus, exclaims, with almost Franciscan piety:

> May none of God's wonderful works
> keep silence, night or morning.
> Bright stars, high mountains, the depths of the seas,
> sources of rushing rivers:
> may all of these break into song as we sing
> to Father, Son and Holy Spirit.[16]

We need hardly explain how God was understood to speak to humankind through his incarnate Word—His words, example, and actions—but we might dwell on one aspect which sheds an important light on a particular aspect of the fathers' understanding of prayer. In the Son, God was understood not only to speak to human beings and to reveal Himself to them, but to reconcile humanity which had fallen away from Him. He was heard not only as Creator but as Redeemer, who had offered himself as a sacrifice for sinful humanity, so that a broken conversation could be renewed. As Origen puts it, Christ is our High Priest, who mediates for us in prayer and prays on our behalf; we need to pray not *to* Christ, but *with* and *through* Christ, who is, as it were, our advocate and interpreter before God.[17] Despite our sinfulness, therefore, Christ enables us to be reconciled to God and to hear and speak to Him directly once again. In this sense, our prayer is, first of all, God's offering or sacrifice before it is ours; He has offered Himself for the sake of sinful human beings so that they might once again converse with Him. Human beings therefore need to hear Him, in His Son, and align themselves with His offering, through prayer in His name, in order to hear and speak to Him once again as Father.[18]

It is in this context that God's revelation and work in the Spirit becomes important in the context of prayer, since the fathers maintain that it is the

---

[15] *Patrologia Orientalis*, 18.442, cited in Hamman (1961), 66–8 no. 94.

[16] Third-century hymn, discovered at Oxyrhynchus, printed by A. Gastoué in *La Tribune de Saint-Gervais* (September–October 1922), cited in Hamman (1961), 69 no. 98a.

[17] *On Prayer*, 10.1–2 (Sykes, 132–3).

[18] As we will see later in the chapter there is a strong patristic tradition, in both East and West, of prayer of the heart, in which prayers are understood to be offered to God upon the altar of the heart as an interior sacrifice. A pure heart can thus make a pure offering/prayer which ascends to God. See Brock (1987), 109, on the Syriac tradition, e.g. Aphrahat and Ephrem; Bradshaw (1981), 64, on Tertullian, Clement, and Origen on prayer as sacrifice.

Spirit of God who effects our adoption as sons,[19] through Christ's saving work, and who (as we shall see in more detail later in this chapter) prays within us, inspiring our delight, love, and longing for God the Father. In this respect, once again, God first speaks and addresses us, through His grace, before we can hear and respond to Him. As Origen, once again, reflects in his treatise *On Prayer*, commenting on 1 Cor. 14:15, 'I will pray in the Spirit, and I will pray in the mind also. I will sing out in the Spirit and I will sing out in the mind also.' 'For our mind [he comments] cannot pray unless the Spirit pray first, as it were within earshot, just as it cannot sing out with rhythm and melody and tempo and harmony, hymning the Father in Christ, unless the Spirit which searches all things, even the depths of God, first gives praise and hymns him whose depths he has searched out and, as he is able, comprehended.'[20] Indeed, what Origen identifies as necessary in his task of writing *about* prayer is actually a very good summary of what is needed to pray: 'The illumination of the Father is needed,' he observes, 'as well as the teaching of the firstborn Word and the inner working of the Spirit.'[21] God's Trinitarian work as Creator, Redeemer, and illuminator/inspirer therefore provides the grounds for prayer; for human beings to hear and respond to Him. He first of all speaks by revealing Himself as Father, Son, and Holy Spirit, and only then, as so many early doxologies make clear, can human beings hear Him, and respond by praying *to* Him, *with* Him, and *through* Him as God the Father, Son, and Holy Spirit respectively.

Of course, as we have seen in Chapter 5, God was also believed to speak and to be heard through His inspired Scriptures and the words of His preachers and teachers. Their witness (like that of the saints and martyrs) similarly provided the grounds for prayer—not only as a response to what was heard, but the language and understanding with which to pray. Above all, they inspired and informed the faith of the believer, without which they would never be able to hear God, let alone respond or pray to Him.

Prayer is, therefore, first and foremost God's gift: it is our response to His work in Creation, revelation, and providence; to His offering of Himself for our redemption through His Son; to His adoption of us as sons through the Holy Spirit; to His inspiration of his prophets, saints, and martyrs, priests, and teachers.

---

[19] They cite Gal, 4:6: 'And because you are sons, God has sent the Spirit of his Son into our hearts, crying "Abba, Father"', and Rom. 8:26–7: 'for we do not know how to pray as we ought, but the Spirit himself intercedes for us with sighs too deep for words'—e.g. Origen, *On Prayer*, 2.3 (Sykes, 114–15).

[20] Origen, *On Prayer*, 2.4 (Sykes, 115–16).

[21] Origen, *On Prayer*, 2.6 (Sykes, 117).

'Heart in pilgrimage': how do we listen?

As we have just seen, in the conversation of prayer God is the first one to speak, but in order to hear Him and respond to Him we need the ears of faith. The transcendent God's manner of speech, is, to say the least, challenging: we must believe that what He says to us in Creation, the Son, and the Spirit; through Scripture; through other human beings or in our own hearts, is, indeed His Word, and that it is true. Without faith, it would be impossible to hear or comprehend Him, never mind respond in confidence and trust. We have seen, in Chapter 4, that the fathers held that faith was, above all, acquired through the gift of the Spirit at baptism, which sealed, or impressed the instruction which the candidates had received through catechesis firmly upon their hearts and minds. Henceforth, the elements of the rule of faith or creed, which consisted of no more and no less than a summary of the ways in which God has spoken to human beings in creation and redemption, were imprinted not just on the memories of the candidates who had learnt and recited them before baptism, but on their hearts and minds. They became one of the 'faithful', able to hear and respond to God in prayer with the confidence and trust which a son has in his father. As we noted in Chapter 4, the fathers turned to Romans 10:14, 'How can they call on him in whom they have not believed?' to illustrate that it is faith alone which makes prayer possible. As Augustine puts it, 'If faith falters, prayer perishes. I mean, who are going to pray to what they don't believe? Which is why the blessed apostle, in urging us to pray, said, *Everyone that calls upon the name of the Lord shall be saved.* And to show that faith is the fountainhead of prayer, and that the stream can't run when the head of water dries up, he went on to add, *how, though, shall they call upon one in whom they have not believed? (Rom. 10:13–14).* So in order to pray, let us believe; and in order that the very faith by which we pray may not fail, let us pray. Faith pours out prayer, prayer being poured out obtains firmness for faith.'[22] What Augustine suggests in his closing comments Origen endorses: that we effectively become one of the faithful through prayer, and that the act of praying, as it were, bears its own fruit: 'For souls that had long been barren have realized the sterility of their own motivation and the barrenness of their own minds, and have become pregnant from the Holy Spirit through constancy in prayer, and have given birth to words of salvation filled with perception of truth.'[23] All good conversations do, in fact, have this effect on those who participate in them; they are transformative. It is this aspect of prayer which I would like, above all, to consider in the rest of this chapter, for it seems clear that the fathers are persuaded that one cannot listen to God or talk to God without somehow being changed by the conversation.

---

[22] *Sermon*, 115.1 (WSA III.4 198).   [23] *On Prayer*, 13.3 (Sykes, 139–40).

The very fact that one has listened and responded, which prayer witnesses, is in itself both informative and transformative. It is in this sense, perhaps, that we might interpret Evagrius' famous description of the theologian as 'one who prays': we only come to know God through listening and responding to Him in prayer. Prayer makes us theologians—those who, having talked *with* God in prayer, can talk *about* Him.

The salient features of early Christian prayer, such as the fathers categorize them[24]—supplication/confession, intercession, thanksgiving, prayer/praise—should all be understood as indications of the transformative effect which listening and speaking to God have upon the individual: they are made aware of their created dependence; their failings and sinfulness; their privileged status as sons; their confidence to intercede for others; their gratitude for God's gracious benevolence; their love of God who has first loved them. As we saw in our First Impromptu, in comparing Plutarch and Augustine, listening to someone requires participation and a change within ourselves: we must align ourselves with them in order to listen and respond to them aright. We cannot converse with someone unless their words kindle within us a conversion of our attention and will/love towards them. Theodore of Mopsuestia gives a good illustration of this in his commentary on the Lord's Prayer, 'As we are pleased at all times to meet, and to deal and converse with a person whom we love most . . . so those who possess God in their mind and are very anxious to do the things that please Him are wont to make use of frequent prayers, because they believe that they work and converse with Him when they pray.'[25] Like faith, the ability to listen and respond in love is God's gift. As Theodore put it, we converse with God because we possess Him in our mind. Augustine sums up his doctrine of grace in this context, in reference to Romans 5:5: 'So in order for you to love God, let God dwell in you, and love himself by means of you; that is, let him prompt you to love him, kindle you, enlighten you, rouse you.'[26]

There is, then, a real sense in the fathers' reflections on prayer that we can only pray, or hear and respond to God, if we first believe and love him, and that both faith and love are his gifts. God, as it were, speaks to, in, and through us, so that we might listen and respond to, in and through Him. Prayer, as we have seen George Herbert so aptly observe, is therefore very much 'God's breath in man returning to its birth'—or, as Evagrius, in the fourth century, puts it, rather more bluntly: 'If you desire to pray, you need God who gives prayer to the one who prays.'[27]

---

[24] Based on 1 John 4:10 'I urge first of all that supplications, prayers, intercessions, and thanksgivings be made.' E.g. Origen, *On Prayer*, 14.1–6, 33.1–6 (Sykes, 143–6, 212–14); Cassian, *Conferences*, 9.9–15.1 (Ramsay, 336–8).

[25] (Mingana, 2).

[26] *Sermon*, 128.4 (WSA III.4 295).

[27] *On Prayer*, 58 (Tugwell, 36).

'Engine against the Almighty, sinner's tower': the Lord's Prayer

There was one prayer, above all others, which was universally understood by early Christians to be God's words, given to them so that they might offer them back to Him, and in the act of doing so, be transformed by them. This was the Lord's Prayer, which, having been transmitted by Jesus to his followers, was carefully recorded in Scripture (Luke 11:1f), handed over to catechumens preparing for baptism, learnt by heart, and handed back or delivered word for word, from memory, just before they became one of the faithful in baptism. It was, without doubt, *the* prayer. As Tertullian, in what was to be the first of a long tradition of commentaries on the Lord's Prayer in the early Church, puts this in the second century, 'Therefore, the practice of prayer is laid down by him, and when it was brought forth from the divine mouth it was animated by his spirit. By its own special right it thus goes up to heaven, commending to the Father the things the Son has taught.'[28] It is clear that the fathers can hardly find words adequate enough to express the unique nature of the Lord's Prayer. Tertullian clearly feels he must assure his readers at the outset that 'without exaggeration, a summary of the whole Gospel is to be found in the prayer'.[29] Other fathers agreed with him: for Augustine it is a 'rule of prayer' as the Creed is a rule of faith,[30] which contained in itself every possible type of prayer.[31] Cassian similarly refers to it as a 'schema' of prayer', which represents the culmination of the four main forms of Christian prayer we noted above.[32] Gregory of Nyssa calls it the 'science of prayer', which Christ has taught to those 'eager to learn to pray in such a way as to win the favour of the Divine hearing'.[33] It was therefore the definitive measure and yardstick for Christian prayer, just as the Creed was for the faith. Having learnt *what* to believe in the Creed, the Christian was then in a position to know *whom* to call upon in the Lord's Prayer.[34] No prayer could diverge from it, every prayer should emerge from it, and it naturally formed the acme of all

---

[28] *On the Lord's Prayer*, 9 (Sykes, 70–1).

[29] *On the Lord's Prayer*, 1 (Sykes, 65).

[30] *On the Sermon on the Mount*, 2.26 (FC 11, 134): 'We have received a rule of prayer from the Lord. It would be wrong to transgress it either by adding something or by taking something away.'

[31] *Epistle* 130.22 (FC 18, 392–3): 'For whatever other words we may say . . . we say nothing that is not found in this prayer of the Lord, if we pray properly and fittingly.' Indeed, he elsewhere insisted that: 'You are not allowed to ask for anything else, but what is written here', *Sermon*, 56.4 (WSA III.3 97).

[32] *Conferences*, 9.18.2 (Ramsay, 340).

[33] *On the Lord's Prayer*, 1 (ACW 18, 21).

[34] Augustine, *Sermon*, 56.1 (WSA III.3, 95): 'So it's because he said, "How are they to call upon one in whom they have not believed?" that you didn't first receive the prayer and afterward the creed; but it was first the creed, where you would learn what you were to believe, and afterward the prayer, in which you would come to know whom you were to call upon.'

the different forms of prayer which Christians used to address God. Its unassailable centrality in early Christian faith and devotion is beyond question; it was inscribed not only upon the memories, but the minds, hearts, and lives of the early Christians in a manner which makes it a unique example of transformative listening.

Why listening? Is the Lord's Prayer not, in fact, the definitive example of the way in which the early Christians believed they should *speak* to God? What the fathers have to say in their commentaries on the prayer suggests otherwise. When we speak to someone—at least, when we speak to someone who we would like be able to hear, understand, and sympathize with us—we do so always with our hearer in mind. We accommodate what we have to say to them by drawing on everything we already know about them, and, if we can see them, their facial expressions and gestures. We, as it were, imaginatively enter into their reception of what we say, anticipating their reaction, aligning ourselves with them so that we, in turn, might be heard. Speaking, as well as listening, was therefore very much a matter of participation and imaginative empathy. The attempt to communicate inevitably changes the speaker, as he or she adapts and accommodates themselves to their listener. This is precisely what the fathers describe in their commentaries on the Lord's Prayer: they understand the prayer not as words which we simply recite in a precise form, as a sort of magical incantation, but as, above all, forming a relationship between God and the speaker, in which, by addressing their hearer, the speaker aligns themselves with Him—and, in this particular case, establishes their kinship with Him, their identity as His son. Everything that is said in the Lord's Prayer therefore depends on establishing this right relationship with God, of being worthy to call God 'Father'; to request that his kingdom, his will, his sustenance, his forgiveness, his deliverance, be given to the needy speaker so that they might be worthy to call Him 'Father'. In short, the prayer presupposes a gracious, benevolent listener for it to be meaningful and effective, and a speaker aware that they are only able to address their listener because He has made it possible for them to do so by first giving them the words that will enable them to approach Him, the otherwise transcendent God. He invites them to address him as Father, to call upon Him as sons, to align themselves, as adopted sons, with his own Son, who has given them the prayer and with whom they can pray in confidence, imagining a hearer who is well disposed towards them and whom they can freely importune for the grace to be worthy of being a son.

Beginning to pray by addressing one's hearer as 'Father' is, in itself, a dramatic example of transformative listening for the speaker. In using this form of address the speaker could not but be acutely aware of everything that was tacitly understood of the father-son relationship by both pagans and Christians in the ancient world. Fathers and sons were bound together by kinship, and by the formal, legal ties of duty and obedience, as well as the cultural and personal bonds of *pietas*, respect and love. As Gregory of Nyssa exclaims in response to the opening invocation of 'Our Father' in the Lord's Prayer, 'What spirit a man must have to say this word—what confidence, what purity of conscience.'[35] Speaking to God as 'kin' was unimaginable in pagan-ism, where the distance between the gods and human beings was always rigorously upheld, but for Gregory it means that, in adopting us as sons, God has given us the confidence (*parrhesia*) which, as fallen human beings, we could otherwise never possess, to address Him in this familiar and direct manner. Above all, it means that we must strive to be as 'akin' to God as possible. As he puts it, 'if we call our Father Him who is incorruptible and just and good, we must prove by our life that the kinship is real'.[36] This means, for Gregory, that the speaker must turn his attention from temporal to eternal concerns: we must first of all leave behind all mutable distractions—anything 'subject to flux and change'—so that we might, as he puts it, 'tranquilly rest in motionless spiritual repose, so as to be rendered akin to Him who is perfectly unchangeable'.[37] It would not be an exaggeration to observe that for Gregory, saying the Lord's Prayer effectively begins the transformation of the speaker into the image of his immutable, eternal, divine hearer. Tertullian demon-strates much the same concern for the spiritual transformation which praying to a divine hearer effects in the speaker when he sets out the basic principle that 'prayer . . . should be sent forth from the same sort of spirit as that to which it is sent'. He develops this insight by observing that 'a polluted spirit cannot be known by a holy spirit, any more than a saddened spirit may be known by a gladdened spirit, nor a shackled spirit by one that is free. Nobody opens his door to a foe, nor admits anyone except his peer.'[38] Theodore of Mopsuestia is likewise no less conscious of the transformation which calling God 'Father' brings about in the speaker, but he expresses it in more prag-matic, legal terms: a son (even an adopted one) is a free citizen, who shares the honour and status of His Father. He therefore urges the faithful to 'call Him "Our Father", so that when you have been made aware of your freedom and of the honour in which you have participated and the greatness which you have acquired . . . you will act accordingly to the end.'[39] Whether mystical, moral, affective, or legal, speaking to God the Father as one's hearer meant that the

---

[35] *On the Lord's Prayer*, Sermon 2 (ACW 18, 38).

[36] *On the Lord's Prayer*, Sermon 2 (ACW 18, 38). Cf. Cyprian, *On the Lord's Prayer*, 11 (Sykes, 72), who states that: 'We should remember . . . and realize that when we address God as our Father we should act as children of God, so that just as we have pleasure in having God as our Father, so he should have pleasure in us. Let us act as temples of God, so that it may appear that God dwells in us.'

[37] *On the Lord's Prayer*, 11.

[38] *On the Lord's Prayer*, 12 (Sykes, 73).

[39] *On the Lord's Prayer* (Mingana, 7).

one who prayed could not but be affected by conversing with Him on such intimate terms.

Confidence, or *parrhesia*, is often mentioned by the fathers as evidence of the fact that the one who prays is transformed by the assurance that their hearer is God, the Father. Confidence, or boldness of speech, comes, first of all, from the fact that it is the Holy Spirit, the spirit of adoption, who not only gives us the freedom to pray as sons but himself intercedes on our behalf.[40] It is also founded on our belief that God the Father is present and does, indeed, listen to prayer. In his treatise *On Prayer*, Origen is clearly preoccupied with those detractors (no doubt Christian, as well as pagan) who wonder why one should bother to pray at all, since God foreknows what we will pray anyway. His answer seems to be that our prayer should not be motivated by a desire to change what God's foreknowledge and providence does, indeed, already effect, but rather that prayer is valuable as effecting change within ourselves, by enabling us simply 'to be present to God, and to speak to him who is present as one who both looks upon us and who hears'.[41] 'Anyone who prays in this manner,' Origen urges, 'concentrating on the power of the one who listens and having cast away all discontent with providence, will, while he is still speaking, hear "Here I am".'[42] The assurance of God's presence as hearer and its frequent recollection in prayer has a dramatic, transformative effect, without the need to 'babble' any requests for earthly benefits: 'If the memory and recollection of a man who is renowned and who has found benefit in wisdom encourages us the more to emulate him and often restrains our impulses to do evil, how much more should the recollection of God who is the father of all, together with prayer to him, give advantage to those who believe that they are present to him, and that they are speaking to God who is present and who hears them.'[43] The simple assurance of God the Father's presence as the hearer of our prayer thus has a transformative effect in and of itself, without the need to 'pray' for anything else.

Despite the fact that the assurance of God's presence obviates unnecessary babbling, it remains the case that the Lord's Prayer not only places the speaker in God's presence, but consists mainly of petitions: 'thy kingdom come . . . thy will be done . . . forgive us our trespasses . . . give us this day our daily bread . . . lead us not into temptation . . . deliver us from evil'. However, these requests are interpreted by the fathers in very much in the same manner as Origen deals with the question of why we should pray at all: they are not meant to inform or bring about any change in God, the hearer, but are intended to inform and thereby transform the speaker; the whole effect of

---

[40] Origen, *On Prayer*, 14.5 (Sykes, 145–6); Theodore of Mopsuestia, *On the Lord's Prayer* (Mingana, 6).
[41] Origen, *On Prayer*, 8.2 (Sykes, 130).
[42] Origen, *On Prayer*, 10.1 (Sykes, 132).   [43] Origen, *On Prayer*, 8.2 (Sykes, 130).

the prayer is on the one who prays, not the one to whom it is addressed. As Augustine explains to Proba, in a letter on the subject of prayer, 'Words . . . are necessary for us so that we may be roused and may take note of what we are asking, but we are not to believe that the Lord has need of them, either to be informed or influenced.'[44] Similarly, he makes clear in a sermon on the Lord's Prayer that when we pray that God's name may be hallowed, we pray not for God but for ourselves, 'What you are asking for,' he comments, '. . . is that what is always holy in itself should be hallowed by you';[45] we pray that his kingdom should come in us; that his will be done by us.[46] As he succinctly puts it, '. . . from this point on until the end of the prayer, it's clear that we are asking God for things for ourselves'.[47] Of course, God already knows what we need, and what we pray for is only effected by God's grace,[48] but in giving us the words and the grace to pray persistently and repeatedly in the Lord's Prayer, God gives us what Augustine calls a 'framework of true desires':[49] he enables us to become aware of our needs, our failings, our responsibilities, and our dependence on Him—to convert ourselves to Him by conversing with Him, thereby making His will our own. As he puts it, '. . . when you pray, it's devotedness you need, not wordiness, "But your Father knows what is necessary for you, before you ask him for it" (Mt. 6:7–8).'[50] Cassian makes the same point in his ninth *Conference* on prayer: our 'confidence of being heard (*parrhesia*)' rests in the 'grace of being heard'—we must confidently persist in turning towards the one who we believe will graciously hear us, for in doing so our prayers answer themselves.[51] The Lord's Prayer is therefore a good example of the general truth that in praying we are transformed more by listening than by speaking; by attending to the words which God has given us to pray and to the One who graciously hears us. We will see this becoming more apparent in what the fathers have to say about other forms of prayer.

---

[44] *Epistle*, 130 (FC 18 391–2).

[45] *Sermon*, 56.5 (WSA III.3 97). Cf. Cyprian, *On the Lord's Prayer*, 12 (Sykes, 73): 'Next we say: "Let your name be hallowed." We say this not wishing that God should be made holy by our prayers, but asking the Lord that his name should be hallowed in us.'

[46] *Sermon*, 56.5–6 (WSA III.3 97–8). Cf. Tertullian, *On Prayer*, 3–5 (Sykes, 43–6).

[47] *Sermon*, 56.9 (WSA III.3 99).

[48] In writing to Pope Innocent, concerning Pelagius, Augustine observes that 'the Lord's Prayer is the clearest testimony of grace' (*Epistle*, 177.4 (WSA II.3 143)): we must pray 'lead us not into temptation' because it is only by God's grace that we can avoid it—'. . . it is clear enough that, though the choice of the will undoubtedly exists, still its power does not suffice for not sinning, that is, for not doing evil, unless its weakness is helped'. In *On the Sermon on the Mount*, 2.11.38 (FC 11, 146–8), he relates the seven petitions of the Lord's Prayer to the seven gifts of the Spirit and the seven stages of spiritual progress, observing that we need to pray for God's grace to attain each gift or stage.

[49] *Epistle*, 177.

[50] *Epistle*, 117.

[51] *Conferences*, 9.24.1–9 (Ramsay, 349–53).

The 'givenness' of the Lord's Prayer is perhaps its most important feature. It consists not of human words, but of words given by God, so that we might address Him as Father and become aware of what we need to ask and do. As Cyprian puts it,

> [The Lord] . . . himself gave the form (*orandi formam*) by which to pray, and himself guided and directed the purpose of our prayer . . . He had already said that the hour would come when true worshippers would worship the Father in spirit and in truth (Jn. 4:23) . . . what prayer could be spiritual other than that which Christ, by whom the Holy Spirit is sent to us, has given us? What prayer could be truer in the presence of the Father than that which was conveyed by the Son, who is truth, from his own mouth?[52] . . . Therefore let us pray . . . just as God the master has taught us. Imploring God in his own words, sending up to his ears the prayer of Christ . . . When we make our prayer let God the Father recognise the words of his own Son. May he who lives inside our heart be also in our voice . . . let us set forth the words of our advocate. For since he said that whatever we ask from the Father in his name he will grant us (Jn. 16:23), how much more effectively should we obtain what we ask in the name of Christ if we ask it using his own prayer.[53]

In saying the Lord's Prayer, therefore, we are effectively hearing God's own words being spoken back to Him. In this sense it does indeed contain a summary of the whole faith, and the substance of all other prayers, since it is nothing more than God's own summary and his own prayer. As such, it informs the faith of the one who prays it—God tells us what sort of listener He is, how we should relate to and address Him and what we need to ask of Him to align ourselves with Him. In short it establishes the believer's relationship with God, the willing hearer, and gives them a 'framework of true desires' so that, in speaking and in listening to Him, they are transformed.

The rule of faith, or the Creed, is the only other summary which fulfils the same function, and like the Creed, the fathers urge the faithful to memorize it, imprint it on their hearts, and continually repeat it. All subsequent prayers, like all other expositions of the faith, are simply variations on its paradigmatic themes. Just as constant repetition and practice of a theme can open up the freedom for endless improvisation and variations, so these can, in turn, give way to moments of transcendent insight. For Cassian, the 'schema' of the Lord's Prayer is not just the theme on which all other prayers are but variations, but, as we shall see in more detail later on in this chapter, the height and culmination of the variations. Petition, prayer, intercession, or thanksgiving, he writes, give way to 'a still more sublime and exalted condition . . . It is fashioned by the contemplation of God alone and by fervent charity, by which the mind, having been dissolved and flung into love of

---

[52] *On the Lord's Prayer*, 2 (Sykes, 65–6).
[53] *On the Lord's Prayer*, 3 (Sykes, 66).

him, speaks most familiarly and with particular devotion to God as to its own father.'[54]

'The Church's banquet': communal listening

The Lord's Prayer was primarily understood as a prayer offered not by the individual but by the body of Christ; the congregation of the faithful assembled for worship. As Cyprian comments (no doubt with Acts 4:32 in mind), 'we do not address God as "my Father" but "with one mind", as "Our Father"'.[55] Hamman's collection of early Christian prayer is not only an extremely useful resource,[56] it is also particularly interesting for the large number of examples of personal prayers it contains. He includes prayers found in inscriptions, on stone, papyri, and potsherds, extracts from sermons or treatises, as well as the very personal poems of the likes of Gregory Nazianzen. He could well have included Augustine's *Confessions* (if he had not judged Augustine too large to be encompassed by an anthology). Indeed, it could be argued that a large part of the fathers' writing should be regarded as personal prayer: it was generally dictated—being spoken aloud to a scribe— and the resultant text often reads more like a personal, direct address to God, the imagined hearer and interlocutor, than a composition for a listening audience or reader. This was, in part, because, as we saw in Chapter 5, the fathers first prayed for God's illumination and guidance before they spoke— they were *orators* before they were *dictors*—and believed that, in a real sense, it was God who was the author and inspiration of their words. This belief may have simply rested on the fact that, as their imagined hearer and conversation partner, the fathers were aware that it was God who was ultimately responsible for informing and directing what they said, but one gets the impression that it was more than this, and that, like Plato's poets, the speakers believed that what they were given to say was God's inspiration and gift, rather than their own words.

Their hearers similarly believed that, through their preacher, they heard God's authoritative voice. The congregation therefore both heard a conversation with themselves, in the context of their own particular circumstances, and also overheard the preacher's personal conversation with God. Both types of hearing were important: having examined the former in Chapter 5, the latter is

---

[54] *Conferences*, 9.18.1 (Ramsay, 340).
[55] Cyprian, *On the Lord's Prayer*, 8 (Sykes, 69–70); Theodore of Mopsuestia, *On the Lord's Prayer* (Mingana, 7): 'I do not wish you to say "my Father" but "our Father", because he is a Father common to all in the same way as His grace, from which we have received, is common to all.'
[56] Hamman (1961).

of interest here as being a prayer which the congregation, as it were, listened in on, and effectively made their own. The preacher's prayer could become their prayer; his direct conversation with God could be made their own through listening to him attentively; his words, which were at once God's and his own, could also become, through overhearing, the words of his hearers, uniting them in a single prayer.

The example we have just given, of a preacher speaking to God and being heard by his congregation, as a form of prayerful overhearing, is one that we can apply in a more specific way to the prayers which the congregation offered as a whole, in so-called communal prayer. I would like to suggest that communal prayer should, first of all, be understood as form of communal listening, or, more precisely, communal overhearing. Saying the Lord's Prayer, as we have just seen, was primarily understood as offering the words God had given back to God. The individuals who said this prayer together would thus hear not only their own voice, along with the common voice of the faithful, but God, as it were, speaking to Himself. As a result, they would become aware of their relationship to God as, on the one hand, the body of Christ, the Church, confidently speaking to the Father; and on the other, as that of sinful, needy human beings, who must seek reconciliation with God through offering up His own offering to Him.

What we have just described is a rather complicated polyphony of speaking and hearing: God speaks to Himself; the individual and the congregation speak to God; God hears His own words and those of the faithful; the faithful hear what they pray, overhear the words of their neighbour as they pray with them, and, above all, overhear God's own words. Even when the Lord's Prayer is not the prayer being offered, and the words are more extemporary, personal, and ad hoc, there is an argument that, at least in the prayers of the devout, the words that are voiced in prayer are formed by the fact that it is God who is their intended hearer—what we might call an indirect inspiration—and by the fact that God was thought to directly inspire what was uttered through the operation of His Holy Spirit. Indeed, insofar as prayer was true prayer—in other words, directed to God and informed by the rule of faith and the Lord's Prayer—God might, in some sense, be regarded as its author and source as well as its end. The question of who speaks and who hears in prayer remains, then, an unresolved, but ultimately illuminating one. This is especially the case when we take into account the fathers' reflections on communal prayer in the Church as the body of Christ, and their understanding of prayer as an offering made not only by human individuals, but, as it were, by the communion of saints.

Augustine is well known for interpreting the entire Psalter in terms of his understanding of the Church as the body of Christ. The person who prays in the Psalms must be heard and understood as either the voice of the head or the voice of the body: Christ the head or his body, the Church. Christ prays for and in us; the Church prays in him and to him: 'He prays for us as our priest; he prays in us as our head; he is prayed to by us as our God. Accordingly we must recognize our voices in him, and his accents in ourselves . . . In the form of God . . . he is prayed to, but in the form of a servant he prays.'[57] At one level, the fact that anything the Church prays must be understood to be the voice of Christ, does indeed make the question of who is speaking and who is hearing very much more complicated. At another level, however, it simply confirms the suggestion we made above—that anything that is said in prayer is ultimately the Word of God returning to itself—whilst at the same time allowing for a rich polyphony of voices emanating from the body or the head; the form of a servant or the form of God. 'If he is with us, then, he speaks in us, he speaks about our concerns, and speaks through us, because we also speak in him.'[58]

In his treatise *On Prayer*, Origen reminds us of a relatively neglected aspect of the early Church's understanding of communal prayer that also contributes to the question of who is speaking and listening. He notes that it is not only the faithful who offer prayer, or the Lord Himself, but also the 'angelic powers' and the 'holy spirits' of the departed: 'A place of prayer that has a particular blessing and benefit is the place where believers gather. It seems probable that angelic powers are in attendance at the assemblies of the faithful, as well as the power of the Lord and Savior himself, and indeed holy spirits—I think of those who have gone to their rest before us.' He thus speaks of what he calls a 'twofold Church': the human and the angelic.[59] When we pray together, therefore, our prayers are joined with those of Christ, the angels, and holy spirits. It is for this reason that Origen seems to recommend communal prayer rather than individual prayer: it unites our voices with those of the faithful—living and departed, earthly and heavenly.[60]

The understanding of the Church as the body of Christ, and as the communion of the faithful, therefore both enhances the polyphony of prayer whilst underlining the fact that prayer itself unifies the faithful. This is the case, not least, because communal prayer presupposes that particular prayers, or ways of addressing God, have been 'handed down', learnt, repeated, and become part of the customary practice of the community, so that all its members are able to recite them together, from memory. In other words, certain prayers and ways of praying must have become part of the community's collective

---

[57] *Expositions of the Psalms*, 85.1 (WSA III.18 220–1).
[58] *Expositions of the Psalms*, 56.1 (WSA III.17 104).
[59] *On Prayer*, 31.5 (Sykes, 209).
[60] *On Prayer*, 11.1 (Sykes, 134): 'Not only does the high priest pray alongside those who pray authentically, but those who are in heaven, the angels . . . and likewise the souls of the saints who have gone to their rest.' Cf. Nicetas, *Liturgical Singing*, 11 (FC 7, 73): 'let us have full confidence in carrying out our ministry of song. Let us believe that we have been given a great, a very great, grace by God who has granted us to sing the marvels of the eternal God in the company of so many and such great saints, prophets and even martyrs.'

memory, engraved on the minds and hearts of the faithful, in much the same manner as Scripture, the Creed, and the Lord's Prayer. They therefore functioned not only to create and identify the community, and to inform its faith, life, and worship, but enabled it to cohere as a community of listeners, who, by giving voice to God's Word in prayer, were simultaneously unified and transformed by listening to it.

I would like to examine a little further just how what we have called 'communal listening' worked, by investigating in what way early Christian writers are clearly aware of it and reflect on it (or exploit it) themselves in relation to the idea of 'overhearing'.

'Reversed thunder': overhearing

When we listen to a conversation in which we are not directly involved we effectively 'overhear' what is being said; we 'listen in', and, in some cases, might be said to 'eavesdrop' on a dialogue in which we do not participate but which we, nevertheless, by hearing, are aware of, and can be drawn into, very much as an audience observes what takes place in the theatre. Indeed, there is something about overhearing which draws the listener into a conversation more effectively than if he or she were participating in it themselves, and it is essentially on this basis that theatre works. Why is this? Is it because, as an onlooker, or overhearer, we can observe without being observed? Hear without being heard? Participate without having to become directly involved? We are in a privileged position—able to receive without having to respond. We therefore have a greater freedom, and more time, to take in what is happening. Since we are not part of the action we can observe, reflect, weigh up what is being said, take sides or change sides, as we wish. If the conversation is particularly involving, however, we might find ourselves involuntarily caught up in it, moved by what is said, drawn into sympathy with a particular speaker, for example, or angered by another. There is at once both an independence and freedom in overhearing, but also the risk—or potential—of becoming caught up in it. Beginning with Aristotle's reflections on the cathartic effect of Greek drama, the latter has always been identified as the very reason why good theatre works: the better and more effective it is, the more the audience is involuntarily moved by it, caught up in it, and changed by it.

Overhearing also works because it plays on natural human curiosity: our attention is often more readily engaged by what appears to be a private conversation between others than by someone addressing us directly. There is the frisson of 'eavesdropping'; of listening in on something not intended for our ears; of learning something we would not otherwise have access to and discovering the confidential thoughts and feelings of another. As a result, we can feel more involved as a covert 'overhearer' or 'eavesdropper', than if we were overtly taking part in the conversation.

It was perhaps on these grounds that the fathers felt able to address God directly in their sermons and treatises, aware that their congregations or readers were effectively being rendered overhearers or eavesdroppers on their prayers.[61] Even more obviously, they deployed the traditional device of an imaginary interlocutor, or a dramatic dialogue, in order to make their sermons a piece of theatre which the congregation, as audience, could over-hear and hopefully be caught up in: imaginatively identifying with the speakers, empathizing with their plight, sympathizing with their ideas, being moved to share their (noble) sentiments, and emulate their (righteous) behav-iour in their own hearts and lives. Early homilies or acts of the martyrs often took this form: the details of a martyr's life were set forth in dramatic detail, their conversation with their persecutors and their prayer to God being recounted *verbatim*.[62] Almost all the fathers use the device of an imaginary conversation partner to whom they can address questions, discuss the details of a story, reflect on the significance of particular events . . . and it is clear that this interlocutor is more often than not used to voice the responses and questions which they either wish to prompt in their congregation, or which they anticipate and imagine are going through their minds as they listen. In overhearing the conversation the congregation would, therefore, be very effectively invited to identify with the interlocutor and participate in the discussion in such a way that what they heard informed their own thoughts and responses and perhaps, even, transformed them.[63]

Mary Cunningham's work on eighth-century Byzantine homilies has made available some of the most interesting manifestations of this 'conver-sational' or dialogue genre.[64] Although they are rather later than our time-frame, the dramatic dialogues which structure the homilies of such preachers as Andrew of Crete and Germanos of Constantinople deserve mention as the culmination of a tradition that begins in a much more modest, restrained form in the works of the early fathers, which was extremely popular in fifth- and sixth-century Greek preaching,[65] and which reached its full theatrical

---

[61] E.g. Origen frequently adopts this practice—see Sheerin (1988), 200–14.

[62] For example, see Leemans et al. (1983), 331–4; Chrysostom, *Homily on the Holy Martyrs*, 1 (Mayer and Neil, 119).

[63] This was, of course, one of the exercises they would have been practised as part of the *progymnasmata*—Vickers (1989), 206.

[64] Kecskemeti (1993); Cunningham (1998), 267–93; Cunningham (2008).

[65] Kecskemeti (1993) mentions Amphilochius of Iconium (fourth century); Severus of Gabala (fourth/fifth century); Proclus of Constantinople (fifth century); Anastasius the Sinaite (sixth century); Romanos (sixth century). Uthemann (1998), 139–77, gives the example of Severus of Gabala, and demonstrates how he dialogues with his hearers, with God, with interjectors, and with Scripture, and thus allows God to address his listeners and his listeners to address God; Barkhuizen (1998), 179–99, refers to various homilies by Proclus of Constantinople (fifth

manifestation, as it were, in their extraordinary homilies, on, for example, the Annunciation. Their *dramatis personae*, God, Mary, Joseph, and the archangel Gabriel, come alive for their congregations as vividly as any character in a play; the very human—and yet divinely inspired—reactions and emotions of the latter three allowing the hearer to enter into Mary's stupefaction, Joseph's suspicion, and Gabriel's confusion, in a way which no narrative account could ever hope to achieve. In addition, their impressive, emotionally literate, psychological commentary on the reactions and deliberations of their characters, as well as soliloquial dramatization of their inward reflections, do help a lot in advancing the narrative sections. For example, Gabriel muses and soliloquizes, quite at a loss as to how to undertake the disconcerting task of making an entrance to deliver his message to the Virgin, 'How shall I begin to carry out God's purpose? Shall I enter the room at a run? But I will terrify the Virgin's soul. Shall I go in at a more leisurely pace? But then I shall be judged by the girl to have tricked my way in. Shall I knock on the door? But how? For this is not natural for angels . . . Shall I first open the door? But it is possible for me to be inside although the door is closed. Shall I call on her name? Yet I will disturb the maiden.'[66] When Gabriel does finally arrive, having decided just to appear, and to say 'Hail' as a suitable opening, Germanos of Constantinople's engaging dramatization of Mary and Gabriel's mixture of suspicion and seduction could not be heard without provoking the best eavesdropping instincts of the assembled faithful:

The Theotokos: 'Young man, I see the striking beauty of your elegant form and the splendid sight of your figure, and I am listening to your words [the like of which] I have never heard before, and I am rapidly beginning to suspect that you have come to lead me astray.'

The Angel: 'Understand clearly and be persuaded that it is rather I who, on perceiving such divinely portrayed beauty in you, have fallen into amazement; and seeing you now, I think I am becoming aware of the glory of the Lord.'[67]

The metrical, verse homilies of Ephrem the Syrian (fourth century) and Jacob of Serug (eighth century) (to mention just two examples from the

---

century) which contain fictitious dialogue between the homilist and various biblical characters, angels, and cosmic elements, and between biblical characters themselves; see Allen (1998), 201–25, on the abundant use of dialogue as a characteristic feature of sixth-century Greek homilies by Leontius of Constantinople, Timothy of Jerusalem/Antioch, and Gregory of Antioch. She comments, 'in the sixth century we appear to be witnessing an escalation in the use of this dialogue form which may be connected with its use in the kontakia [metrical chant]. It suggests that this manner of treating the biblical text appealed to a wide spectrum of the homilists' audiences' (144).

[66] Andrew of Crete, *Oration on the Annunciation of the Supremely Holy Lady, our Theotokos*, 6, in Cunningham (2008), 204–5. Such homilies therefore make abundant use of *prosopopoeia* and *ethopoiia* (speech in character or impersonation).

[67] Germanos of Constantinople, *Oration on the Annunciation of the Supremely Holy Theotokos*, 74 (Cunningham, 228).

relatively neglected Syriac tradition) both belong to this important genre of dramatic dialogue and imagined speech, in which the hearer's attention is caught up by the voices and situations of the interlocutors. In them we likewise encounter imagined soliloquies, conversations between biblical figures, biblical figures and God, the preacher and his congregation, the preacher and an imaginary interlocutor, the preacher and God. All of these interchanges come alive with an immediacy only direct speech can bring, so that the hearer, moved no doubt also by the verse and chant, could not but be drawn into them, and, in some sense, participate in them.

Of course, this might seem far removed from how we normally understand prayer, but tradition and human nature do not change: as trained rhetors and philosophers,[68] the fathers were more than aware of the way in which imaginary, dramatic dialogue served to complicitly involve their hearers, and their hearers, in their turn, would both anticipate this and have their ears and minds attuned for it. It is therefore just as important in examining the practice of prayer in the early Church as in helping us to understand the techniques of early Christian homiletics, and one will naturally illuminate the other. Both work on the basis of a speaker and an imagined hearer or interlocutor; a dialogue or conversation (even if, in prayer, one can only, tantalizingly, hear one side of it); a veritable polyphony of hearers and speakers; above all, an invitation to overhear, to eavesdrop, and to be caught up in the shifting voices and conversations—to identify with, be moved, and changed by them.

'The soul's blood': personal prayer

In his wonderful book on prayer in the patristic tradition, Gabriel Bunge, who continues that tradition himself, reminds us of what is obvious, but what we so easily forget: that in the early Church all prayer—individual and private, as well as communal and public—was, like reading, said aloud. It could be heard, or overheard, therefore, by the one who prayed, by anyone who was nearby, and, of course, by God (as well as by the demons[69]). He observes that when Hannah fell silent with grief, and prayed simply by moving her lips, in the temple at Shiloh, Eli the priest thought she was drunk (1 Sam. 1:12ff).[70] Personal prayer was therefore always, in one respect, 'public' prayer—it could be heard, or overheard by others. The examples of personal prayer

---

[68] One should not forget the long tradition of dialogue in philosophical teaching and writing, beginning with Plato. The fathers continued to compose dialogues, e.g. Gregory of Nyssa, *On the Soul and the Resurrection*, and Augustine's early works. They likewise continued the tradition of soliloquy—e.g. Gregory Nazianzen's *To His Own Soul*; Augustine's *Soliloquies*.

[69] Bunge (2002), 128—hearing prayer the demons tremble and are driven off!

[70] Bunge (2002), 123.

which we now possess are all, inevitably, unrepresentative, since they have been transcribed into written form, and—as with the majority of early Christian literature—their original context, intention, and immediacy have been lost. And yet one suspects that the fact that the particular examples we have were, indeed, transcribed, preserved, and handed on means that their author somehow understood them to be rather different from the words he or she might address to God in private. They were, to some extent, intended to be heard, not only by God, but overheard by others. We must therefore bear in mind, at least in the case of writers like Gregory Nazianzen and Augustine, that the very personal, conversational, intimate form which so often characterizes their work, whilst no doubt sincere, is also a self-conscious and contrived one, intended as much to engage overhearers more directly and immediately by appealing to their common human feelings—and failings— before God, as to express their own feelings. Indeed, such texts no doubt have a wide range of motives—from examining the very nature and effect of prayer itself and sounding out God as hearer, through self-examination and theological reflection, to explanation and exoneration in the eyes (and ears) of detractors or heretics. Sometimes—most notably in some of Gregory Nazianzen's poems/prayers—such prayers are simply an occasion to have a good complain about the human lot. It is difficult to choose examples, but Hamman's fine collection of early Christian prayers offers a good representative selection.[71] What we can say is that they are all multifaceted dialogues— between the speaker and God; the speaker and him or herself; the speaker and any intended or imagined (over)hearer (human beings, angels, and demons)—which are intended to be heard, or overheard, by others.

I intend to take an early example of individual prayer, offered by the martyr Polycarp, and then some fourth/fifth century texts (from Gregory Nazianzen and Augustine), in order to illustrate some of the points we have made above, as well as to examine what, if anything, is distinctive about the practice of listening in personal prayer.

The account of the martyrdom of Polycarp, bishop of Smyrna, sent from his church at Smyrna to another Christian community in Philomelium sometime between 154 and 177,[72] is punctuated by references to Polycarp's prayers, and includes the words of his actual prayer just before his martyrdom. Despite its early date (it is usually regarded as the first martyr act) it stands firmly within a well-established tradition of prayer, and includes references to Old Testament prayers and practices,[73] as well as early forms of

---

[71] Hamman (1961).

[72] Though, see Moss (2010) for a challenge to this traditional dating. (I owe this reference to the anonymous reader appointed by OUP to review this book.)

[73] Weidmann (1997), 286, notes references to Israelite cult practices, Isaiah's servant songs, Azariah's prayer, the prayer of the three young men in the furnace in the LXX version of Daniel.

Christian prayer.[74] Very much conforming to the early Christian ideal of continual prayer (which we will examine in detail later in this chapter) Polycarp himself, having retreated to a safe place before his arrest, is described as 'doing nothing else day and night but praying for us all, and for the churches all over the world, as it was his usual habit to do'.[75] Like Perpetua in the second/third century, indeed like any Christian called to witness to their faith by martyrdom, he would be regarded as being in a position in which he could intercede, or petition God, with a unique boldness (*parrhesia*) and confidence. When he was eventually arrested he asked his captors for time to pray undisturbed. Having 'got to his feet' (we must imagine him in the position of the *orans*, with hands uplifted), and 'full of the grace of God' the account tells us that '...two whole hours went by before he could bring himself to be silent again'.[76] So although he desired to pray undisturbed, Polycarp evidently prayed aloud. The observation that 'all those who heard him were struck with awe' confirms that he was overheard—by the Roman soldiers, as well as his friends—and that what he said in prayer had an effect on them: not only were they 'struck with awe' but we are told that 'many of them began to regret this expedition against a man so old and saintly'.[77] We are not given Polycarp's prayer at this point, but are simply told that it was again one of intercession: 'he remembered everyone whom chance had ever brought him into contact with—small and great, known and unknown—as well as the entire world-wide Catholic Church'. The fact that Polycarp is then mounted on an ass and taken to Herod makes it almost certain that Christ's high priestly prayer, in John's Gospel, was in the author's mind when he describes Polycarp's intercessions.[78] So far, Polycarp's practice and prayer have confirmed and followed early Christian tradition—and are no less interesting for that. His final prayer, as he is tied to the stake to be burnt, however, advances it. Bound (having refused to be nailed), he is described as 'like a noble ram taken out of some great flock for sacrifice: a goodly burnt offering all ready for God'.[79] His bodily sacrifice, however, is only one aspect of his offering, for he immediately begins to offer the sacrifice of prayer, too. The prayer contains many of the characteristic features of early Christian prayer: it is addressed to God, who is immediately identified as the 'Father of thy blessed and beloved Son Jesus Christ' and as the 'God of angels and powers, of the whole creation'. Polycarp

[74] Weidmann (1997), 286, notes probable allusions to 1 Clement (an epistle which contains one of the earliest Christian prayers), Ignatius, and the *Didache* (a handbook for Christian worship).
[75] *Martyrdom of Polycarp*, 5 (Staniforth, 126).
[76] *Martyrdom of Polycarp*, 7 (Staniforth, 127).
[77] *Martyrdom of Polycarp*, 7 (Staniforth, 127).
[78] As with so many martyr acts, the whole account seems to be modelled on the details of Christ's arrest and passion.
[79] *Martyrdom of Polycarp*, 14 (Staniforth, 129).

thus establishes the two fundamental grounds for early Christian prayer which we have already noted: first, God is the omnipotent Creator of all that is; secondly, He is one who is addressed as Father. The confidence and trust which Polycarp displays in his acceptance of his sacrificial death are based on this belief and relationship, which is at once established by prayer, and confirmed by it. Having offered an all-embracing intercession at his arrest, Polycarp proceeds to use the other main forms of early Christian prayer: thanksgiving—'I bless you for granting me this day and hour'; supplication—'may I be numbered amongst the martyrs, to share the cup of thine Anointed and to rise again unto life everlasting'; and prayer—'both in body and soul, in the immortality of the Holy Spirit'. He throws himself upon the givenness of prayer—upon God's foreknowledge and providence—and prays, as in the petitions of the Lord's Prayer, not that his lot might be changed, but that he might become worthy of it: 'May I be received among them this day in thy presence, a sacrifice rich and acceptable, even as thou didst appoint and foreshow, and dost now bring to pass.' The prayer comes to a close with words which would no doubt be familiar to all his listeners from liturgical prayer: 'I praise thee, I bless thee, I glorify thee'—the liturgical context being further evoked and confirmed by reference to 'our eternal High Priest in Heaven, thy beloved Son Jesus Christ'. An early doxology brings the prayer to an end: 'by whom [Christ] and with whom be glory to thee and the Holy Ghost, now and for all ages to come. Amen.' Polycarp's listeners would be left in no doubt that what they had heard were God's words offered up to God; that it was the Father and Creator, the Son and High Priest, the immortal Holy Spirit, who enabled Polycarp to offer up his life and his prayer with such confidence, assurance, trust, and hope. The faith which had been impressed upon them at baptism, re-presented in the liturgy, and repeated in the Lord's Prayer would be recalled, confirmed, and strengthened by its vivid enactment in Polycarp's life and death, and its confident statement in his prayer.

Gregory Nazianzen, the fourth/fifth century 'Cappadocian', and, briefly, bishop of Constantinople, was by temperament a recluse and man of prayer. His hundreds of poems and hymns often take the form of prayer—or, at least, they are directly addressed to God. They are highly personal works— often autobiographical[80]—which reveal his trials and tribulations, his faith and theological meditations, his culture and tastes, his insightful psychological musings as well as his rather grumpy, grudging sense of duty—in a manner which is only really paralleled by Augustine's *Confessions* in the early Church. As such, they are, as we noted, rather difficult to judge: he chose to write them down, and intended them to be heard and read.

---

[80] Especially his *Concerning His Own Life* (White, 10–153). White (1996), xxv, points out that section II.1 in Migne's *Patrologia Graeca* contains 99 poems about Gregory himself.

Moreover, he was an accomplished rhetor and poet. One therefore has to allow for a good deal of poetic licence and literary show—indeed, for a rather fastidious sense of correct style—but, even then, the impression that one is overhearing a heartfelt conversation with God, which resonates with one's own experiences, is difficult to avoid, and the reader or hearer cannot fail to be affected by them. This is, no doubt, in part attributable to Gregory's consummate skill as a writer, but it is also due to his genuine devotion to the God whom he addresses in such a familiar way, and it is this into which we are irresistibly drawn. Moreover, Gregory stands out as doing theology through prayer: the relationship which prayer both presupposes and creates is one that he specifically reflects upon. Prompted by the fact that prayer is possible at all, he reflects on how and why this is the case, what it tells us about the nature of God, the Trinity, His creation, redemption, and inspiration, about the nature of providence, and about the manner in which God can communicate with us, and we, as fallen human beings, should communicate with Him. His poems or prayers therefore sometimes read very much like theological or moral treatises. The combination of intimate conversation, academic theology, and asceticism, in highly accomplished classical verse form is characteristic of Gregory, and is a heady mix. A few brief examples, taken from Brian Daley's wonderful translations, must suffice:[81]

The first allows us to glimpse Gregory's intimate self-reflection, with which the hearer cannot but identify and sympathize:

> *A Prayer to Christ the Next Morning*
> Yesterday, Christ, turned out a total loss!
> Rage came upon me, all at once, and took me.
> Let me live *this* day as a day of light.
> Gregory, look—be mindful, think of God!
> You swore you would; remember your salvation![82]

The second reveals Gregory the Theologian at perhaps his most accessible (and allows us to see his classical background breaking through). It would be a prayer the listener could readily grasp, and whose language would no doubt prove memorable, although the element of dialogue is minimal, as Gregory swiftly moves into didactic mode after the opening invocations:

> *Prayer Before Reading Scripture*
> Father of Christ, all seeing, hear our prayers;
> Look kindly on your servant's solemn song.
> He turns his footsteps down a godly path,

---

[81] Though Gregory has found some excellent translators—McGuckin (1986); White (1996); Daley (2006).

[82] Carmina II.1 (*Poemata de seipso*), 24–6 (Daley, 170–1).

> Who knows, while living, the ingenerate God,
> And Christ, the king who bans all mortal ills.
> Once, out of pity for our hard-pressed race,
> Freely conforming to the Father's will,
> He changed his form, taking our mortal frame
> Though he was God immortal, freeing us all
> From Tartarus's bondage by his blood.
> Come now, refresh this soul of yours with words—
> Pure, godly sayings from this sacred book;
> Gaze here upon the servants of your Truth
> Proclaiming life in voices echoing heaven![83]

The third is more profoundly theological, but in a form which captures the hearer's imagination even if they are not able to fully plumb its depths. Gregory has hymned the Father as Creator, the consubstantial Son who, as the Word, God speaks to form us, and the Holy Spirit as the bond that embraces all. He then addresses the Trinity:

> So I name you living Triad:
> Single, archetypal power,
> Without source, unchanging always,
> All-unspeakable in nature,
> Mind of all-eluding wisdom,
> Power of heaven, all-unconquered,
> Without cause, and free from limit,
> Source of light, still undetected,
> Yet surveying all in brilliance,
> Before whom nothing lies hidden,
> From this earth to deepest heaven![84]

We observed earlier in this chapter that Gregory's acute psychological insights, combined with his very personal conversation with God, had no real parallel in the patristic period apart from Augustine's *Confessions*, and it would be difficult to have a chapter on prayer without at least mentioning this work. We saw that Hamman omitted Augustine entirely from his anthology of early Christian prayer because he judged him just too big to be encompassed by it. Of course, that is the case, but better, I think, something than nothing at all!

Augustine, the fourth/fifth century bishop of Hippo, began to compose his *Confessions* almost ten years after his conversion in 386. The thirteen books are all written in the form of a soliloquy with an imaginary interlocutor, if that is not a contradiction in terms: Augustine speaks to God—prays to God—and

---

[83] Carmina I, 1 (*Poemata dogmatica*), 35 (Daley, 168–9).
[84] Carmina I, 1 (*Poemata dogmatica*), 30 (Daley, 166).

harangues him to listen ('Listen, best of judges, God, truth itself, listen to what I say to this opponent, listen . . . Listen to what I say to him and see if it is pleasing to you')[85] but God remains silent and invisible, though perhaps more present in the imagination of the listener precisely because of his absence. The reader/hearer is therefore invited to eavesdrop on one half of an utterly engaging conversation—personal, revealing, animated, dramatic, meditative—and to imagine the response of the other half. It is as if, in laying bare his whole life, from infancy to his present job as bishop of Hippo, Augustine is attempting to make sense of it by going over each stage with God, who he believes is responsible for his very existence, the good that his fallen will has done, and the deep love and longing which drives him in search of the true, good, and beautiful. His relationship with God is therefore not only the trusting, confident one of a son to a father, which we have hitherto encountered, but the passionate, utterly devoted one of a lover for a beloved, whose presence they long, hunger, and sigh for. The same heady mix which we identified in Gregory, of autobiography, profound theological reflection, intimate conversation, and classical prose poetry therefore reaches its apogee in the *Confessions*. As with Gregory, we must also remember that the work is not a naive, disingenuous composition—even though it often aims to give that impression—but a highly crafted, calculated work of self-justification, exoneration, polemic, and theological apology and instruction, written by a master of the art. There is nothing that is not calculated to have a particular effect on its reader, or hearer, and the whole work was dictated by Augustine for a number of silent, invisible, imaginary interlocutors, as well as God: his friends, his family, his critics, his clergy, his congregation—even us, his future readers. All are called upon to listen: to engage with him, converse with him, understand his situation, take part in his reflections, and, above all, share his faith, hope, and longing love for his and our God. The devices Augustine uses to effect this include rhetorical art, psychological insight, a canny sense of appealing to common human experiences, love, and longing, and, above all, the genre of prayer—of conversation or dialogue which, when overheard, invites identification, participation, and relationship, which the author clearly hopes will ultimately transform his listeners as he is himself being transformed.

Again, it is difficult to give an example. The opening is perhaps as good as any:

> Great are you, O Lord, and exceedingly worthy of praise; your power is immense, and your wisdom beyond reckoning. And so we humans, who are a due part of your creation, long to praise you—we who carry our mortality about with us, carry the evidence of our sin and with it the proof that you thwart the proud.

---

[85] *Confessions*, 12.25.35—the work is full of these audacious *aude*'s.

Yet these humans, due part of your creation as they are, still do long to praise you. You stir us so that praising you may bring us joy, because you have made us and drawn us to yourself, and our heart is unquiet until it rests in you.

The elements of the prayer are familiar ones: God as Creator, our created relationship with Him, which is the grounds of our prayer—but the sense that God stirs and draws us, and our heart's restless longing for Him, are distinctively Augustinian. In this opening invocation Augustine obviously understands his prayer as a communal one—he borrows the language of Scripture so that his voice becomes its voice, and, as so often in the *Confessions*, he understands himself as speaking on behalf of the whole of humanity, who, hearing him, will identify with and share what he says.

He also intends them to share his more direct, personal conversation with God, and the theological reflections on the nature and possibility of prayer that this prompts, when he continues:

> Grant me to know and understand, Lord, which comes first: to call upon you or to praise you? To know you or to call upon you? Must we know you before we can call upon you? Anyone who invokes what is still unknown may be making a mistake. Or should you be invoked first, so that we may then come to know you? But how can people call upon someone in whom they do not yet believe? And how can they believe without a preacher? But Scripture tells us that those who seek the Lord will praise him, for as they seek they find him, and on finding him they will praise him. Let me seek you, then, Lord, even while I am calling upon you, and call upon you even as I believe in you; for to us you have indeed been preached. My faith calls upon you, Lord, this faith which is your gift to me, which you have breathed into me through the humanity of your Son and the ministry of your preacher.

In this short paragraph Augustine has summarized and answered the questions concerning the grounds for prayer which we spent the first half of this chapter addressing: the gift of faith, breathed into us through the incarnate Son and the Church's teaching, allows us to call upon God and to seek Him, seeking to find Him, and, finding, be moved to praise Him. Prayer works, and we are able to call upon God, because it is God's breath returning to God. If we had heard this paragraph, identified with Augustine's questions, and been persuaded by his answers, then we, as hearers, would not only be given the grounds for prayer but would have effectively prayed with Augustine and been aligned with God through his prayer. The fact that his theological reflections take the form of prayer—of dialogue with God—means that they effectively provide their own answers: Augustine is transformed in faith and understanding by speaking to and hearing God; his hearers are transformed by listening to the conversation and identifying themselves with it.

'Christ side-piercing spear': common prayer

Apart from individual prayer, from the very beginning there also existed 'set' times of prayer and, increasingly, 'set' forms of prayer in the early Church. This is not the place to consider what has become known as liturgical prayer,[86] but what we have said about the Lord's Prayer—as a 'given' or set form (rule/schema/science) of prayer comprehends a good deal of what needs to be said about liturgical prayer in relation to the practice of listening in the early Church. Although, at the outset, the prayers which were said by the faithful when they gathered together at set times were no doubt very fluid,[87] and resembled more what we have called 'personal' prayer, at least some of them would gradually, by dint of repetition at the same time of day, in the same context, and in relation to the same Scriptural readings and psalms, become more 'fixed', and thereby impress themselves upon the minds and hearts of those who prayed them very much in the same way as Scripture, the Creed, or the Lord's Prayer—thereby, in turn, providing the framework for the more personal, extemporary prayer we have considered above.[88]

'A kind of tune, which all things hear and fear': the Psalms

There was one particular form of prayer, both individual and common, which was perhaps just as influential in forming the faith and lives of the early Christians as the Lord's Prayer, and that is the Psalter. The 'songs of David' resonated in the ears of the early Christians at every turn, and were, beyond doubt, the most familiar and oft-cited book of Scripture in the early Church. If we are to speak of 'intertexts', as we did in Chapter 6, the Psalms were *the* intertext (the two short passages from Augustine we have just cited above, for example, contain four allusions or citations from the Psalms). The early Christians did theology, preached, and worshipped in the language of the

---

[86] I intend to examine how it functioned in relation to those who said and heard it, and especially those who sang various parts of it, in my next book.

[87] There are early references, no doubt following Jewish practice, to prayer in the morning and evening (Tertullian), as well as three times a day—morning, noon, and evening (*Didache*, Clement, Origen), or six times a day, including midnight (Hippolytus)—see Bradshaw (1981), chs 2–3, for references. These set times of prayer have become known in their post-Constantinian form as the 'cathedral office' in contrast to the 'monastic office' (which we will examine later in this chapter) though it is generally agreed that the latter increasingly influenced the former—see Bradshaw (1981), ch. 4.

[88] It is interesting to note, however, just how long the prayer of consecration remained one that was freely improvised by the celebrant.

Psalms; they celebrated, mourned, processed, ate, and went to sleep with the psalms on their lips. Like the Lord's Prayer, the Psalms were believed to be God's Word; to sum up the whole of the faith and the Scriptures. Moreover, they were thought to be appropriate in every context—ecclesial, monastic, and domestic—for every occasion and every human experience. As such, they were regarded as a sort of universal panacea, able to calm, heal, harmonize, and transform the soul of the one who prayed them, as well as unite souls into one.[89] Their omnipresence and multivalence are well summed up in the following (anonymous) text:

> In the churches there are vigils, and David [= the Psalms] is first and middle and last. In the singing of early morning hymns David is first and middle and last. In the tents at funeral processions David is first and last. What a thing of wonder! Many who have not even made their first attempt at reading know all of David by heart and recite him in order. Yet it is not only in the cities and the churches that he is so prominent on every occasion and with people of all ages; even in the fields and the deserts and stretching into uninhabited wasteland, he rouses sacred choirs to God with greater zeal. In the monasteries there is a holy chorus of angelic hosts, and David is first and middle and last. In the convents there are bands of virgins who imitate Mary, and David is first and middle and last. In the deserts men crucified to this world hold converse with God, and David is first and middle and last. And at night all men are dominated by physical sleep and drawn into the depths, and David alone stands by, arousing all the servants of God to angelic vigils, turning earth into heaven and making angels of men.[90]

The above list is clearly meant to be exhaustive of all aspects of early Christian life and practice, and is confirmed by a multitude of other patristic texts; the Psalms were simply everywhere: they even sounded wherever pagan music had sounded, driving out, and replacing, instrumental music and singing directed towards the gods, with Christian chant, inspired by and offered to God.[91] They punctuated everyday life as well as continuing throughout the night as part of vigil services,[92] and, at least by the fourth century, formed part of the Church's liturgy.[93] At the same time they also became prominent in ascetic circles, where they formed part of the cycle of prayer and psalmody which structured the monastic offices,[94] and accompanied the monk's manual

---

[89] Kolbet (2006); Harrison (2011).

[90] Pseudo-Chrysostom, *De Poenitentia*, referred to by McKinnon (1989), 90.

[91] See Quasten (1983) for a full consideration of this.

[92] Basil, *Letter* 207 (FC 28, 83–4); Nicetas of Remesiana, *The Vigils of the Saints* (FC 7, 55–64).

[93] McKinnon (1989), 8–10, however, notes that although there is evidence for the widespread use of psalmody at Christian meals, there is no evidence for their use in the liturgy until the fourth century, when he observes that there was a 'wave of enthusiasm for psalmody'. See also Bradshaw (1981), 43–5, who confirms this.

[94] See Dysinger (2005), 48–57. In Pachomius' rule, for example, there were six offices in which the entire psalter was recited during the course of the day. As McGuckin (1999), 80, comments:

labour, with the aim, as we shall see, of creating an unceasing cycle of prayer.[95]
As one observer put it, psalmody rose up from the monasteries at the ninth
hour in such a way that it allowed the hearer to imagine he or she was
participating in the heavenly choir.[96] In his *Institutes*, Cassian provides us
with a very good insight into the actual practice of alternate psalmody and
prayer, in which the monks sat to listen to the psalms being sung, fixing the
whole focus of their heart (*intentio cordis*) on the singing of the cantor,[97] and
then stood to observe a period of silent prayer, before prostrating themselves
and moving on to the next psalm. The integration of silent prayer, sung
psalmody, and Scripture, allowed the Word of God to continually echo and
re-echo within the ears, minds, and hearts of its hearers, one form resonating
with, and illuminating the other, so that they became one Word of God and
one prayer offered back to their source.[98] Indeed, he insists on the importance
of paying close attention to the lesson and listening attentively, not least
because, as he insightfully observes, 'prayer is improved if our mind has
recently fed on reading and is able to roam among the thoughts of divine
things which it has recently heard'.[99]

   Although the practice of alternating psalmody and prayer is generally
referred to as characteristic of the monastic office it was also increasingly
influential on the so-called cathedral office—the daily, public services in
Church—where prayer and psalmody and Scriptural readings punctuated
and informed each other. As Nicetas in the fourth century puts it, in reference
to church services, 'Can any joy be greater than that of delighting ourselves

---

'the first of all the Christian practices of prayer that emerged in the desert tradition was the
repetition of the Psalms. The Psalms, and all the biblical anthropology they taught, thus inevitably passed directly into the spiritual bloodstream of the desert.' Or as Bradshaw (1981), 94,
comments: 'in effect the hymn book of the secular Church became the prayer book of
monasticism'.

   [95] There are many references to unceasing psalmody in a monastic context, e.g. *Apophthegmata Patrum*, Epiphanius 3, cited by McKinnon (1989), 62; Eusebius of Vercelli, *Epistle*, 63.82,
cited by McKinnon (1989), 132, though it is not confined to that context. Gregory of Nyssa says
of his sister Macrina, 'She was especially well versed in the Psalms, going through each part of the
Psalter at the proper time; when she sat down to eat or rose from the table, when she went to bed
or rose from it for prayer, she had the Psalter with her at all times, like a good and faithful
travelling companion'—and of Macrina and their mother Emmelia, 'There was constant prayer
and unceasing singing of hymns throughout the whole day and whole night, so that this was for
them both their work and their rest from work' (*Life of Macrina*, 3), quoted by Giannarelli in
Allen, Meyer and Cross (1999), 120.
   [96] Palladius, *Lausiac History*, 7.5 (ACW 34, 41).
   [97] *Institutes* 2.5.5, referred to by Dysinger (2005), 54. More generally, see *Institutes* 2 and 3.
   [98] Though Bunge (1987) insists on the distinction between psalmody and prayer and stresses
that they are two separate entities. See Dysinger (2005), 71 n. 36, for references and comment on
this.
   [99] *Liturgical Singing*, 14 (FC 7, 76).

with psalms and nourishing ourselves with prayer and feeding ourselves with the lessons that are read in between?'[100, 101]

Continual prayer

Jesus' command to 'pray at all times' (Luke 18:1) and Paul's admonitions to 'pray without ceasing' (1Thess. 5:17); to 'pray all the time, asking for what you need, praying in the spirit on every possible occasion' (Eph. 6:18) were ones which the early Church felt it could not ignore. The problem was, how could they be observed? How could prayer be unceasing? We find two main responses to this difficult question, which might be summarized as 'life as prayer' and 'prayer as life' respectively. The whole of the Christian's life—their words and actions—could be understood as an unceasing prayer; alternatively, unceasing prayer could be understood as the sole occupation of a Christian's life. Clearly, the first relates to lay people, the second is only possible for ascetics, although, as we shall see, they are not mutually exclusive.

Life as prayer

Among the arguments which Origen rehearses,[102] in order to counter those who are sceptical about whether it is worth bothering to pray at all, is an appeal to the *effects* which prayer has: first upon the mind of the one who prays; secondly, upon their life and behaviour. By fixing the mind upon God in prayer, instead of upon worldly things, the images and memories that are imprinted upon the mind are not the confusing jumble received through sense perception, but those which allow the mind to 'be present to God . . . to have recollection of God' and for God to be present to it, penetrating and searching the heart. In other words, prayer allows the one who prays to become aware of

---

[100] *Liturgical Singing*, 12 (FC 7, 74). Bradshaw (1981), 123, comments, 'the dominance of monasticism in the Church was such that in the end the monastic office triumphed over the cathedral, and the latter became more and more conformed to the former, until ultimately it was supplanted by it altogether throughout the West'. Though Bradshaw thinks that this meant that the laity increasingly became 'spectators of the professional clergy and religious who sang the office' Nicetas' comments rather undermine this. He insists that *all* should sing and pray and *all* should remain silent in order to listen to the lesson. 'We need not wonder, then, if the deacon in a clear voice like a herald warns all that, whether they are praying or bowing the knees, singing hymns, or listening to the lessons, they should all act together. God loves "men of one manner" and . . . "maketh them to dwell in his house" (Ps. 67:7)', *Liturgical Singing*, 14 (FC 7, 76).

[101] There is much more that could be said about the Psalms, as well as the transformative effect which hearing and listening to music was thought to have in the early Church. My next book will take the subject further.

[102] *On Prayer*, 8.2 (Sykes, 130).

God: to effectively sense, impress, recollect, and be present to Him. The second effect follows from this, especially if prayer is frequently or continually repeated: God will inform not just the mind but the actions of the one who prays—keeping them from sin and moving them to righteous deeds.

We have encountered similar arguments to Origen's in relation to the Lord's Prayer: everything that it contains was intended to have an effect on the one who prays, not upon the one who is addressed. In saying it, the one who prays is made akin to God the Father, as a son, and prays to be made worthy of this kinship with the incorruptible, just, and good God by aligning their will and lives with Him. Hence, the prayer is full of petitions: that God's name may be hallowed in us, His will done by us, His kingdom come in us . . . Speaking to God in prayer, therefore, at once impresses the divine image upon the speaker and transforms their (fallen) minds and lives into his image. As Gregory of Nyssa comments, 'Do you realise to what height the Lord raises His hearers through the words of the prayer, by which he somehow transforms human nature into what is Divine? For he lays down that those who approach God should themselves become gods.'[103]

One way of putting this would be to say that prayer enables the mind to engage effectively in what, as we will see further in Chapter 7, is the creative, imaginative, drawing together, or recollection and representation of the images contained in the mind/memory, which allows them to be presented in a new, and perhaps transformative, way. When these are images created, not by sense perception, or by the rule of faith, or even by Scripture and preaching, but by being present to, and speaking and listening to God in prayer, then how much greater must the transformation be? Augustine attempts to articulate this when he describes the expansion or stretching out of the mind which such creative recollection effects, so that it is made more capable of 'comprehending' (*capaces*) God: 'not even I understand. But thinking about these things makes us stretch ourselves, stretching ourselves expands us, expansion increases our capacity.'[104] Gregory of Nyssa's understanding of prayer as a continual *epektasis* or 'stretching out', in order to seek (though never fully to comprehend) the eternal God, echoes this. Both Augustine and Gregory clearly have in mind Philippians 3:13, 'straining forward to what lies ahead'—a verse which, as we shall see in Chapter 7, was used to express the inherent tension, or *distentio*, between what the memory has heard in the past, what it is attending or listening to in the present, and what it must anticipate in the future. All prayer, insofar as it is an act of speaking and listening to God, must, by definition, also be caught up in this creative and transformative tension.

---

[103] Gregory of Nyssa, *On the Lord's Prayer*, Sermon 5 (ACW 18, 72).
[104] *Sermon*, 225.3 (WSA III.6 249), cited by Carruthers (1990), 199.

It was within this tension that life was to be lived, and those who prayed sought to ensure that their lives resonated with their prayers. We have noted Origen's insistence on the twofold effect of prayer: on the mind, and on life and behaviour. The two, had, of course, always been understood to be inextricable, both in a classical and a Christian context: as we saw in Chapter 4, the effect of hearing the apostle's preaching or of baptismal catechesis was first of all faith, then works or actions informed by faith, and then prayer to the One who was believed in; and as we saw in Chapter 2, the speaker's words only carried as much weight as their deeds, otherwise they were simply empty noise. This was also the case with prayer: the Christian could only pray if their life and actions were in harmony with their words.

Many of the fathers therefore insist that believers must first of all reform their lives so that they might be worthy of the One to whom they pray. In reference to the petition of the Lord's Prayer 'forgive us our trespasses as we forgive those who trespass against us', Gregory expresses this by observing that the root of the word for prayer (*proseuche*) is a vow (*euche*): we cannot ask for forgiveness unless we have first forgiven others, 'A vowed promise (*euche*) ought to have been made before approaching God in prayer (*proseuche*)' . . . thus the psalmist teaches us 'not to ask something from God without first having offered Him an acceptable gift'.[105] 'When therefore,' Gregory writes, 'we are about to offer to God the petition for mercy and forgiveness, we ought to give holy confidence to our conscience by putting forward our life as an advocate of our words, so that we can truly say "as we forgive our debtors".'[106] But the relation between works and prayer was not quite as straightforward as this passage might suggest—and Gregory would be the first to acknowledge this: he insists at the very beginning of his commentary that prayer, which reforms the divine image and unites us with God, should precede and inform works, since everything follows from it.[107]

Works and prayer are therefore very much caught up in the tension we have just described—a virtuous life was indeed made possible by prayer; but, equally, prayer was made possible by a virtuous life: one could not be had without the other. As Theodore of Mopsuestia observes in his commentary on the Lord's Prayer, 'He [our Lord] made use of these short words as if to say

---

[105] *On the Lord's Prayer*, ii.36–7, cited by Simpson (1965), 127. Cf. Cassian, *Conferences*, 9.12.1–2 (Ramsay, 337) who makes the same link, and identifies the vows as ascetic practices and renunciations which enable the mind to focus its attention wholly on God in prayer.

[106] *On the Lord's Prayer*, Sermon 5 (ACW 18, 83). Cyprian seems to have the same ideas in mind when he repeatedly insists on the importance of works or deeds in his commentary on the Lord's Prayer: 'Not only by words alone but by deeds does God teach us to pray' (*On Prayer*, 29 (Sykes, 86–7)); God will be a 'friendly listener' to the 'one who comes to him in prayer associated with good deeds' (*On Prayer*, 32 (Sykes, 89); 'The prayers that ascend quickly to God are those which the merits of our works urge upon Him' (*On Prayer*, 33 (Sykes, 89)).

[107] *On the Lord's Prayer*, Sermon 1 (ACW 18, 22–3).

that prayer does not consist so much in words as in good works, love and zeal for duty. Indeed, one who is inclined to good works all his life must needs be in prayer, which is seen in his choice of these good works.'[108] He is echoed by Cassian, writing in relation to monastic prayer, where 'bodily labour' (presumably fasting, mortification, and so on) is understood to be just as important as the prayer it both depends on and makes possible. He observes, 'Between the two there is a kind of reciprocal and inseparable link.'[109]

Clearly, the 'reciprocal and inseparable link'—as well as the creative tension—between prayer and works was what undergirded the early Christian conviction that all life and work could be understood as prayer, since both were a response to hearing God—to the reformation of the mind which listening to Him effected and which could not but affect the lives and actions of those who were thus transformed. Right living was a sign of right praying and right praying a sign of right living. Origen sums this up when he describes the whole of life as 'one mighty, integrated prayer'. He writes, 'Since works of virtue and the keeping of the commandments have a part in prayer, the person who prays "ceaselessly" is the one who integrates prayer with good works and noble actions with prayer. For we can only accept the saying "Pray ceaselessly" as realistic if we say that the whole life of the saint is one mighty, integrated prayer.'[110]

It is worth noting Origen's additional observation that part of this 'mighty, integrated prayer' is what we would normally call 'prayer'—the daily offices at set hours (for Origen there were at least three;[111] in other sources, such as the apostolic tradition,[112] there were four/six) which effectively became a liturgical expression of continual prayer—an integration of work and prayer.

That listening to God in prayer should affect the minds, as well as the actions and lives, of those who pray is inherent in the word for listening itself:

---

[108] *On the Lord's Prayer* (Mingana, 3).
[109] *Conferences*, 9.2.1 (Ramsay, 329): 'For just as the perpetual and constant tranquillity of prayer about which we are speaking cannot be acquired and perfected without those virtues, neither can these latter, which lay the foundation for it, achieve completion unless it be persevered in.' This is confirmed by Augustine in a rather more mundane, but just as cogent, manner when he writes to Proba, on the subject of prayer, that 'fasting and abstinence from other pleasures of carnal desire . . . and especially almsgiving, are great helps to prayer . . . How is it possible to see an incorporeal God who cannot be felt with the hands, unless he is sought by good works?', *Epistle*, 130 (FC 18, 395).
[110] *On Prayer*, 12.2 (Sykes, 137). Cf. Clement, *Stromateis*, 7.7 (ANCL 12, 432): 'during his whole life, the Gnostic in every place . . . honours God . . . persuaded that God is altogether on every side present, we cultivate our fields praising, we sail the sea hymning . . . '; Tertullian, *On the Lord's Prayer*, 24 (Sykes, 60–1): 'No rule whatever has been laid down concerning the times of prayer, except, of course, to pray at every time and place'; Cyprian, *On the Lord's Prayer*, 35–6 (Sykes, 91–3): 'God should be worshipped constantly and continually. There is no hour at which Christians should not pray; rather . . . we should spend the entire day in petition and prayer . . . and . . . we are not to cease from prayer in the darkness of the night.'
[111] *On Prayer*, 12.2 (Sykes, 137).
[112] *Apostolic Tradition*, 35, cited in Hamman (1961), 332.

in both Latin and Greek hearing (*audire/akoae*) was the root of obedient action (*obaudire/hypakoae*). Hearing was therefore at once a cognitive and an ethical/transformative act.[113]

Prayer as life

In an ascetic, monastic setting, prayer was believed to be the sole purpose and occupation of life: monks lived to pray, in the sense that their whole life was one focused on listening to God. The ascetic life was essentially one of single-minded and single-hearted attention to the incorporeal, eternal, immutable God. The ascetic therefore sought to avoid the jumbled distractions and temptations of bodily, temporal, mutable sense perceptions, in order to seek out solitude, to be in God's presence, listen to Him, receive His impress upon the mind and memory, recollect and meditate upon Him, and thus be trans-formed into His image.[114] This process of transformation by listening is one that we are now familiar with in relation to the theology of the image of God and the ancient's understanding of sense perception, and, in particular, in relation to hearing the rule of faith and preaching upon Scripture. Prayer, and especially ascetic prayer, builds on this, by placing the believer in God's presence and enabling them to listen to him directly. As Gregory Nazianzen comments, 'Nothing seems so important to me as for a person to shut off his sense, to take his place outside the flesh and the world—not to fasten on human realities unless it is completely necessary, and so, in conversation with himself and with God, to live above the level of the visible, and always to bear the images of divine things within himself in their pure state, free from the stamp of what is inferior and changeable.'[115] Or, as Basil of Caesarea, writing to Gregory, observes, 'Prayer is to be commended, for it engenders in the soul a distinct conception of God. And the indwelling of God is this—to hold God ever in memory. His shrine established within us. We thus become temples of God whenever earthly cares cease to interrupt the continuity of our memory of Him, whenever unforeseen passions cease to disturb our minds, and the lover of God, escaping them all, retires to God, driving out the passions which tempt him to incontinence, and abides in the practices which conduce to virtue.'[116]

Of course, as Basil's words indicate, the same tension between actions and words, between a virtuous life and the ability to pray, was present for the

---

[113] See Wannenwetsch (2006).
[114] Theodore of Mopsuestia, *On the Lord's Prayer* (Mingana, 2): 'our Lord showed great zeal for prayer . . . He used to go to lonely places in order to teach that it is necessary for the one who prays to be free from every care, so that he might extend the sight of his soul towards God and contemplate Him, and not be drawn to any other thing.'
[115] *Oration*, 20.1 (Daley, 98).
[116] *Epistle*, 2 (Loeb 13–15).

ascetic as for the laity, but the fact that ascetics devoted their whole lives to the work of prayer meant that the interrelation between the two was much more self-conscious and obvious. The ascetic life was, by definition, one of *ascesis*, or exercise and training—of what Evagrius, the great master of ascetic prayer, calls *praktike*—practising the virtues in order to avoid distraction and temptation, and to purify the soul of the passions so that it might be present to God: 'do you think that you need not put off every passioned thought (noema) from yourself, if you want to see him who is above all perception and all concepts and converse with Him'.[117]

When we examined how God might be said to speak to us at the beginning of this chapter we identified God's work in creation, His revelation in history, the Incarnation, Scripture, preaching . . . as ways in which God speaks to fallen human beings, as it were in their own terms: in time, through the body, through sense perception and physical hearing—and we have seen that hearing them as God's Word enabled the hearer to be transformed by responding to them in prayer. Ascetic prayer, however, seems to represent an attempt to move beyond simply *hearing* God through sense perception and the physical ears, to *listening* to Him as He is present within, in the mind, or, more often, the heart. It is not that God's speaking in time (and most especially in Scripture and the Psalms, which, as we have seen, the ascetic read, sang, and meditated upon) can be ignored, but that it is treated as a step towards a more inward, intimate listening which often moves beyond words and simply becomes a silent, wordless prayer of the heart in which the ascetic is present to God and God is present to them. This movement is often framed in terms of introversion and ascent in ascetic literature—from creation to the Creator; the senses to the mind; the temporal to the eternal—as Basil puts it in the same letter we referred to above, 'the mind is not dissipated upon extraneous things, nor diffused over the world about us through the senses, [but] . . . withdraws within itself, and of its own accord ascends to contemplation of God'.[118]

Ascetics took the command to 'pray at all times' both literally and metaphorically. Some attempted to pray 'unceasingly', through the night and day, at work (while doing something like weaving, which did not distract, but rather helped to focus the mind) and at the set times for prayer. Often, they

---

[117] *On Prayer*, 4 (Tugwell, 30). See Bunge (2002), 38. Cf. Gregory of Nyssa, *On the Lord's Prayer* (ACW 18, 38): 'First my mind must become detached from anything subject to flux and change and tranquilly rest in motionless spiritual repose so as to be rendered akin to Him who is perfectly unchangeable.' Cf. Origen, *On Prayer*, 9.2 (Sykes, 131): 'the eyes are lifted up from interest in earthly matters and from satisfaction with the perception of material things and are so lifted up that they look beyond whatever is begotten and contemplate God alone, and hold modest and solemn converse with the one who hears them. Such people afford the greatest benefit to their eyes, looking upon the glory of the Lord with face unveiled, and so being transformed into his image, from glory to glory (2 Cor. 3:18).'

[118] Basil of Caesarea, *Letter* 2 (Loeb, 14–15).

simply repeated the same prayer—the same form of words (*monologistōs*)—over and over again, in order to still and focus the attention of the mind, and impress the words of the prayer on the heart. We have an example of such a prayer from the lips of one of the old men of the desert: 'Have mercy on me, O God, according to your great mercy, and according to the multitude of your mercies blot out my iniquity.'[119] This did not mean, of course, that the ascetics did not stop to sleep or eat (as the Euchites claimed to do) but that this sort of undistracted, uninterrupted, continually repeated prayer would so hallow the mind and heart that it could rightly be understood both literally and metaphorically as truly continual prayer. As Cassian puts it, 'when the mind has been established in tranquillity and has been freed from the bonds of every earthly passion, and the heart's attention is unwaveringly fastened upon the one and highest good, it will fulfil the apostolic words: "Pray without ceasing".'[120] He himself recommends continual repetition of the prayer 'O God, incline unto my aid; O Lord, make haste to help me' (Ps. 70:1), like that of the old man of the desert, as a form of words that sums up the Christian's faith and comprehends every type of prayer, every human emotion, and every human circumstance or eventuality. He urges, 'You should, I say, meditate constantly on this verse in your heart. You should not stop repeating it when you are doing any kind of work or performing some service or are on a journey. Meditate on it while sleeping and eating and attending to the least needs of nature. This heart's reflection, having become a saving formula for you, will not only preserve you unharmed from every attack of the demons but will also purge you of every vice and earthly taint, lead you to the theoria [contemplation] of invisible and heavenly realities, and raise you to that ineffably ardent prayer which is experienced by very few.'[121]

Prayer of the heart

We have argued that prayer is first and foremost a listening to God, and, only then, a response to Him. We have also seen that the conversation of prayer—the listening and the response—could be a transformative one, as the one who prayed became aware of their relationship to God and responded in praise,

---

[119] *De uitis patrum* 5 (*uerba seniorum*), 12.9 (PL 73.942), cited by Ramsay (1985), 170–1. This tradition of so-called monologistic prayer finds its culmination in eighth-century Hesychasm and the practice of the Jesus Prayer: 'Lord Jesus Christ, son of God, have mercy on me, a sinner.' As Hesychius, the eighth-century abbot of Sinai wrote, 'Attentiveness is the stillness (*hesychia*) of the heart, unbroken by any thought. In this stillness the heart breathes and invokes, endlessly and without ceasing, only Jesus Christ, who is the Son of God Himself...' *On Watchfulness and Holiness*, 5 (*Philokalia*, vol. 1, 163), cited by McGuckin (1999), 85.

[120] *Conferences*, 9.6.5 (Ramsay, 334).

[121] *Conferences*, 10.10.14 (Ramsay, 382–3).

thanksgiving, petition, and intercession. But if God knows what is in our hearts and minds before we speak, then why speak or pray at all? In an ascetic context the conversation of prayer becomes a rather one-sided affair, or, one might argue, a more focused affair: the distinctive feature of ascetic prayer is its listening and attentiveness to God's presence rather than any spoken response. Words and images are generally seen as superfluous—indeed, as positively distracting and harmful—in the business of prayer: as we have just seen above in the case of monologistic prayer, the fewer words the better.[122]

But how can we talk about wordless or imageless listening and prayer? The answer, I think, lies in the fact that, for many early Christian writers, the process of prayer is a matter not of the mind but of the heart; not of reason but of desire and will. Prayer was a matter of comprehending God, not with the intellect—for He transcends human knowing—but with the affections. It was not so much a matter of grasping God with the mind but of being present to Him and being transformed by His presence. This understanding is clearly seen in Augustine's understanding of prayer as continual desire, and in the tradition which eventually became known as 'prayer of the heart'.[123]

The notion of prayer as the expression of desire or love for God, who is both present but still to be fully comprehended by the mind and heart, is one to which Augustine often reverts. Prayer, he insists, is not so much a matter of informing God of anything—He knows what is in our hearts—but of articulating our desires, 'the words we use in prayer are not intended for the instruction of God but for the construction of our desires'.[124] Prayer turns, or converts us, then, towards God; it brings us into his presence, enables us to stretch out towards Him and to 'be able to receive what He is preparing to give'.[125] We should pray, Augustine urges, not with our lips, but with our thoughts and affections, to which God's ears are inclined.[126] The fact that it is

---

[122] This is especially seen in the work of Evagrius, for whom the images (*noemata*) imprinted upon the mind by sense perception need to be set aside in prayer, though Stewart (2001) makes the point that Evagrius does not abandon words and images from the Bible, or spiritual perception, or feeling (*aesthesis*), even in the highest stages of prayer: 'Even at the highest stage of prayer, then, Evagrius takes the imagery of Scripture, hammered thin through spiritual interpretation, and wraps it carefully around his experience, itself shaped by exegesis' (201).

[123] In this chapter we will simply be touching on its antecedents, as it were. For an excellent survey of the later tradition, see McGuckin (1999).

[124] *Epistle*, 130 (FC 18, 389).

[125] *Epistle*, 130 (FC 18, 389).

[126] *Expositions of the Psalms*, 119.9 (WSA III.19 508) 'How many people there are who make plenty of noise with their voices but are dumb in their hearts! And how many others have no sound on their lips but shout with their love! God's ears are alert to the human heart. Just as a person's ears are open to the speech of another, so are God's ears open to a person's heart'. Cf 141.2 (WSA III.20 328) 'A person of interior life, one in whom Christ has begun to dwell through faith, must cry to the Lord with his own true voice, not with the noise of the lips but with the affection of the heart. God does not hear where humans hear . . . your inner thoughts are your clamor in the Lord's hearing.'

desire—love, longing, and groaning—that is expressed in prayer, is an indication both of God's gift and of His transcendence. Through the gift of His Holy Spirit He inspires love and desire for Himself in us, but He can never be fully comprehended or grasped.[127] Prayer is, therefore, not so much a matter of articulating words as of orientating the will, and of enlarging our capacity to receive and comprehend God. As Augustine puts it in a homily on the first epistle of John, 'By desiring you open up and expand the soul; by expanding it you make it capable of receiving more. Let us stretch ourselves to him, so that when he shall come he may fill our souls.'[128]

The understanding of prayer as a matter of the heart rather than the lips and tongue is one that has a long history. The tradition seems to have found its roots in one of the other Scriptural commands concerning prayer which the early Church felt impelled to observe: not only should one 'pray ceaselessly', but the believer should follow Matthew's injunction to pray 'to your Father in secret, with the door shut' (Matt. 6:6). This verse was often interpreted as closing the door of the senses in order to enter the chamber of heart, where God dwelt, so that one might pray in his presence.[129] As Cassian puts it, 'We pray in our room when we withdraw our hearts completely from the clatter of every thought and concern and disclose our prayers to God in secret and, as it were, intimately. We pray with the door shut when, with closed lips and in total silence, we pray not to the searcher of voices but of hearts.'[130] Matthew 6:6, in fact, proved to be a much more straightforward command to follow than the one 'to pray ceaselessly', as it was taken as a given that God, who knows our thoughts, does not need words to be informed of anything. As Tertullian observes, He 'is not a listener to the voice but to the heart'.[131] Clement of Alexandria, in the second century, was perhaps the first to fully pursue the idea of prayer as a movement of the heart, 'a continual inward conversation', as he puts it, which is 'uttered without the voice, by concentrating the whole spiritual nature within an expression of the mind, in undistracted turning towards God'.[132] This tradition reaches its fullest development in what has become known as the tradition of 'prayer of the heart'. Here, God is understood to be present—to dwell in the heart of the one who prays—so that the heart becomes, as it were, a sort of shrine; a place where

---

[127] *Epistle*, 130 (FC 18, 398–9) 'for we know not what we should pray for as we ought, but the Spirit himself asks for us with unspeakable groanings' (Rom. 8:25, 27). Therefore He makes the saints ask with unspeakable groaning, breathing into them the desire for this great thing, as yet unknown, which we await in patience. For, how could it be put into words when what is desired is unknown?'

[128] Cf. *Sermon*, 61.6: 'Ask, seek, insist, by asking and seeking you grow in your capacity to receive' (WSA III.3 144).

[129] Cf. Cyprian, *On the Lord's Prayer*, 4–5 (Sykes, 67–8); Origen, *On Prayer*, 20.2 (Sykes, 157).

[130] *Conferences*, 9.35.1 (Ramsay, 353).

[131] Tertullian, *On the Lord's Prayer*, 17.

[132] *Stromateis*, 7.7. See Graumann (1997), 589, on Ambrose on silent prayer.

God hears the thoughts and affections of the one who prays, and, above all, a place which He hallows, illuminates, impresses with His image, and ultimately transforms. In the Syriac tradition, for example in Aphrahat and Ephrem, where the body is understood as the temple of God, the heart, which is the spiritual centre of the human person, becomes an altar on which the sacrifice of prayer is continually offered.[133] Echoing what we have already found in Clement, Tertullian, Origen, Cyprian, Augustine, and Cassian concerning the voice of the heart rather than the lips and tongue, Aphrahat writes, 'Purity of heart constitutes prayer more than do all the prayers that are uttered aloud, and silence united to a mind that is sincere is better than the loud voice of someone crying out.'[134] Sebastian Brock notes that for the Syriac fathers such prayer is also transformative: 'pure prayer' based on a 'pure heart'—a heart which is clear, pure, and transparent—can reflect God's image like a mirror.[135]

Purity of heart was increasingly expressed in terms of the absence of all mental images, thoughts, or concepts—both those derived from sense perception, and, ultimately, any images at all. Basil, in the letter to Gregory we have already encountered, describes this process of purifying the mind of all temporal distractions, passions, and cares as like smoothing out wax, erasing any images that disturb its surface, so that is cleansed, ready to receive the impression of divine truth.[136]

The process of emptying the mind and heart, purifying and cleansing it, as it were, so that it might be brought into God's presence and impressed with the divine image, is described in various ways. In all of them, by moving beyond the senses, passions, and even conscious thought, prayer moves beyond the voice—the lips, tongue, and lungs—to become a matter of bringing the heart and mind into God's presence so that God might be present to them, and transform them. This is listening in its highest and purest form—a wordless, imageless, often silent, attentiveness to the God who transcends human words, images, and thought, so that, in Cassian's words, '[the mind purged of every carnal desire may daily be elevated to spiritual things, until] one's whole way of life and all the yearnings of one's heart become a single and continuous prayer'.[137] It is given its classical expression by Evagrius, the fourth-century

---

[133] Brock (1987), xxvi; McGuckin (1999), 105.

[134] *Demonstration*, 4, cited in Brock (1987), 5. Cf. Cyprian, *On the Lord's Prayer*, 31 (Sykes, 88), where he insists that the mind should offer prayer with the 'whole heart': 'Every fleshly and worldly thought should depart, nor should any mind dwell on anything other than the prayer it is offering . . . It is not the sound of our voice but the mind and the heart which should pray to God with sincere intent.'

[135] Brock (1987), xxviii–xxix. See Aphrahat, *Demonstration*, 2–10, for examples of the 'power of pure prayer . . . a pure offering' and the things effected by it. The notion of purity of heart is one that plays out in the Hesychast tradition as the absence or emptying of all mental images, thoughts, or concepts so that the divine light can illuminate the heart and mind. McGuckin (1999), 8.

[136] *Letter*, 2 (Loeb, 11).   [137] *Conferences*, 10.7.3 (Ramsay, 376).

desert father, who, with extraordinary psychological insight and subtlety, wrote in the form of short, pithy sayings, on the practice of prayer.[138] In conclusion, however, I would like to examine this tradition in a little more detail by turning to two Western writers of the fourth/fifth century, to Cassian and Augustine, not least to show that what is generally perceived to be characteristic of the tradition of Eastern, ascetic prayer is not absent from the West.

In his *Conferences* on prayer, Cassian, who had extensive first-hand experience of Eastern asceticism, having travelled extensively in the Egyptian desert to visit hermits and monastic settlements, before founding his own monastery in Marseilles, in southern France, records his conversations with some of the monks he had met. We have already encountered the idea that the mind can be enkindled, or set alight, by hearing. In his ninth conference, with Abba Isaac, Cassian seems to attribute much the same effect to listening to God in prayer. For example, the four different types of prayer,[139] culminating in the Lord's Prayer, can raise the one who prays, he observes, to a more 'sublime . . . fiery, wordless' prayer which, as he puts it, 'transcends all human understanding and is distinguished not, I would say, by a sound of the voice or a movement of the tongue or a pronunciation of words. Rather,' he adds, 'the mind is aware of it when it is illuminated by an infusion of heavenly light from it, and not by narrow human words, and once the understanding has been suspended it gushes forth as from a most abundant fountain and speaks ineffably to God, producing more in that very brief moment than the self-conscious mind is able to articulate or reflect upon.'[140] It is as if the mind, leaving behind words, images, or self-conscious thought, is simply placed in the presence of God's light, and overflows in ineffable, ecstatic prayer. Cassian describes this most directly in the tenth conference, in relation to what he calls 'incorruptible prayer': 'So it is that our mind will arrive at that incorruptible prayer . . . This is not only not laid hold of by the sight of some image, but it cannot even be grasped by any word or phrase. Rather, once the mind's attentiveness has been set ablaze, it is called forth in an unspeakable ecstasy of heart and with an insatiable gladness of spirit, and the mind, having transcended all feelings and visible matter, pours it out to God with unutterable groans and sighs.'[141] Hearing clear, earnest, well-modulated singing can have the same effect as the Lord's Prayer: 'the mind, ardent and enkindled [by it] is moved to pure and fervent prayers'.[142] Cassian calls these instances of listening 'various types of compunction'—in other words, various instances which kindle the mind to a more 'sublime' or 'perfect' prayer. Hearing a

[138] See, for example, *On Prayer*, 55–8 (Tugwell, 35–6); Stewart (2001).
[139] *Conferences*, 9.9.1–18.1 (Ramsay, 336–40).
[140] *Conferences*, 9.25.1 (Ramsay, 345–6).
[141] *Conferences*, 10.11.6 (Ramsay, 385).
[142] *Conferences*, 9.26.1 (Ramsay, 346).

'spiritual conference', becoming aware of our own negligence towards a brother, or simply experiencing 'an ineffable joy and gladness of spirit' can equally arouse in the mind an ardour to pray—in an exultant shout of joy, silent speechlessness, a stunned, wordless stupor, or unutterable groans and tears.[143] 'Sublime prayer', for Cassian, is therefore one that arises from the 'deepest recesses of the soul', and is a response to hearing intimations of the divine; to compunction enkindled by God's gracious prompting and presence—which can only be expressed in either inarticulate sound or silence.

Augustine's *Confessions* are punctuated with descriptions of very Neoplatonic-looking ascents of the soul to God: the stages of ascent—from creation, to the soul, to the mind and memory, to a fleeting encounter with God who 'deigns to dwell in the memory'—are carefully traced until words, images, and conceptual thought have been left behind and the soul experiences God in very much the same way as we have seen Cassian describe as characteristic of 'sublime' prayer: in a 'fleeting glance', a momentary eschatological foretaste, in sighs and groans, a gushing forth of the mind. The ascent in book 9, which he, unusually, shares with his mother, Monnica, is of especial interest here as it is framed, uniquely, both in terms of an intimate conversation between mother and son, and in terms of hearing the noise and din of creation, the soul, the imagination, and the memory progressively fall silent, until only God can be heard. The scene is described so that we can almost visualize it: mother and son have retreated from the crowded streets of the seaport of Ostia and are leaning against a window which looks out into a garden, resting and gathering their strength before the long sea journey back to Africa. They fall into conversation about the life to come, and what the 'eternal life of the saints would be like'. It causes them to wholly forget the past, to stretch out to what is ahead (again Phil. 3:13) panting with thirst for God, the fount of life (9.10.23). As they talk, the attractions and pleasures of sense fade away and they are gradually drawn upwards, from the earth to the heavens, from 'bodily creatures' to the sun, moon, and stars, through God's works, to their own minds, to momentarily touch eternal Wisdom: 'as we talked and panted for it, we just touched the edge of it by the utmost leap of our hearts; then sighing and unsatisfied, we left the first-fruits of our spirit captive there, and returned to the noise of articulate speech, where a word has beginning and end' (9.10.24).

The movement of Augustine and Monnica's souls is one which reaches out towards the eternal: leaving behind the past, passing beyond temporal

---

[143] *Conferences*, 9.27.1 (Ramsay, 346–7). Groans, sighs and tears are a common feature of 'prayer of the heart'. They are usually attributed to the work of the Holy Spirit within us, on the basis of Rom. 8:26: 'For we do not know how to pray as we should, but the Holy Spirit himself intercedes for us with unspeakable sighing (gemitibus)', e.g. Augustine, *Homilies on the Gospel of John*, 6.2 (WSA III.12 121–2): 'Nor is it a small matter that the Holy Spirit teaches us to groan; for he is reminding us that we are on pilgrimage and teaching us to sigh for our home country, and with that longing, we groan'; Cassian, *Conferences*, 9.15.2 (Ramsay, 339).

creation, they stretch out towards Wisdom, in whom 'there is no "has been" or "will be" but only being'; they thus move beyond words, and the temporal sequence of speech, to glimpse the eternal Wisdom of God.

In the second half of his description Augustine's prose becomes prose poetry (as Maria Boulding's inimitable translation makes clear) as he describes their ascent afresh in terms of the movement from sound to silence, movement to stillness, temporal to eternal. He describes every level of created, temporal reality—the body and soul, the earth and the heavens, the mind and the imagination—which have pricked the ear towards God, gradually, one by one, falling silent, until all that is present, unmediated by anything else, is the eternal Wisdom of God Himself. For he and his mother this proves to be an achingly transient thing—they 'touch' eternal Wisdom in a 'flashing thought' and 'know' it for a 'passing moment'. If their experience could be made permanent, however, he is convinced that it would be no more and no less than the eternal life of the saints.

It deserves to be quoted in full:

> Then we said,
> 'If the tumult of the flesh fell silent for someone,
> and silent too were the phantasms of earth, sea and air,
> silent the heavens,
> and the very soul silent to itself,
> that it might pass beyond itself by not thinking of its own being:
> if dreams and revelations known through its imagination were silent,
> if every tongue, and every sign, and whatever is subject to transience
>   were wholly stilled for him
> —for if anyone listens, all these things will tell him,
>
> 'We did not make ourselves;
> he made us who abides for ever'—
> and having said this they held their peace
> for they had pricked the listening ear to him who made them;
> and then he alone were to speak, not through things that are made,
>   but of himself,
> that we might hear his Word,[144]
> not through fleshly tongue nor angel's voice,
> nor thundercloud,
> nor any riddling parable,
> hear him unmediated, whom we love in all these things,
> hear him without them,

---

[144] Augustine may have had Plotinus' words in mind, 'as if someone was expecting to hear a voice which he wanted to hear and withdrew from other sounds and roused his power of hearing to catch what, when it comes, is the best of all sounds which can be heard; so here we must let perceptible sounds go . . . and keep the soul's power of apprehension pure and ready to hear the voices from on high' (*Enneads* 5.1.12), cited by Kolbet (2010), 84.

> as now we stretch out and in a flash of thought
> touch that eternal Wisdom who abides above all things;
> if this could last,
> and all other visions, so far inferior, be taken away,
> and this sight alone ravish him who saw it,
> and engulf him and hide him away, kept for inward joys,
> so that this moment of knowledge—
> this passing moment of knowledge—
> this passing moment that left us aching for more—
> should there be life eternal,
> would not *Enter into the joy of your Lord*
> be this, and this alone?
> And when, when will this be?
> When we all rise again, but not all are changed?
> (9.10.25)

The characteristically Eastern, ascetic tradition of leaving behind the temporal in order to be present to God, and to listen to Him directly, unmediated by words, images, or mental concepts is therefore by no means absent from Western reflection of prayer.

We have encountered many oddities in this chapter, and there is one last one: in concluding a chapter on the practice of listening in prayer, we are brought to realize that what is heard in perfect prayer is not, ultimately, sound or words, but God's unmediated presence. But we have also seen that sound— the articulation of words in prayer, the chanting of psalmody—is necessary to allow the speaker to respond to the one who has first addressed them, to turn their attention towards Him, to receive His impress, recall Him to mind, converse with Him, render themselves akin to Him in confession, petition, and thanksgiving, be hallowed by His grace, and stretched out in longing love towards Him. This was not least because the words that they articulated in prayer were more often than not those given or inspired by God Himself. As the speaker became more and more aware of the presence of their transcendent listener, words proved less able to comprehend him, and prayer increasingly found expression either in sound which defied verbal articulation—in groans and longing sighs of love for what could only be fully attained in eternal life; in weeping, or inarticulate shouts of joy or praise; in silent, wordless, imageless contemplation. Listening to God, responding to God in prayer, became a matter for the heart, arising from the 'depths of the soul', rather than for the mind or voice—an awareness both of God's presence and his transcendence. It is to this creative tension between listening to presence and transcendence that we will turn in Chapter 7.

7

From the Bottom to the Bottomless

Believers instead of logicians.'[1]

To be listening is always to be on the edge of meaning.[2]

In the course of this consideration of listening in the early Church we have gradually built up a sense of the distinctive characteristics of the physical sense of hearing, and have hopefully become increasingly aware that, far from there being a dramatic 'corporeal turn' in the years following Constantine's conversion, early Christianity had always been firmly and fully implicated in the body and the senses. In Part One we first of all observed just how auditory a culture late antiquity was; then, drawing upon anthropological reflections on the senses, and philosophical work on the phenomenology of perception, we noted that the way in which a culture understands or prioritizes the senses is one of the most influential factors in how its members understand themselves, express themselves, are conscious of and relate to each other and the world, as well as to the divine. Early Christianity, which gradually emerged from within Jewish and Hellenistic cultures, both of which gave speaking and hearing a very distinctive role—as part of the very substance of the divine, and as articulating and revealing the divine in the creation of the world, historical events, and in the insights and teachings of the philosophers, prophets, and poets—could not fail to be influenced by them. In fact, the early Christians took these cultures of the word to an hitherto unimaginable conclusion in affirming their belief that the divine had been finally and fully revealed in the incarnation of God, the Word, who lived, taught, suffered, and died as a human being.

The importance of the body, the senses, and of speaking and listening were confirmed for Christians by the rhetorical culture in which their leaders had been formed, and that they themselves instinctively anticipated in any context in which they were taught and admonished in the faith through their ears.

---

[1] Gregory Nazianzen, *Theological Oration*, 3 (29) 8 (Williams and Wickham, l).
[2] Nancy (2007), 7.

They were further emphasized by theories of sense perception, which understood hearing to be the result of a blow which, having struck the air, travelled through it to impact upon the ear, creating a sound that could then be impressed upon the mind or memory of the hearer. In contrast to the immediate, fixed, and direct nature of vision, hearing was invariably understood as something that was indirect and mediated in time, through a sequence of actions and events which demanded an active engagement and response on the part of the perceiver. Above all, an emphasis on the body, the senses, and especially the sense of hearing, was confirmed by early Christian reflection on the consequences of the Fall. Having turned away from the inner teacher who addressed the mind directly and gave it an inward grasp of truth unmediated by sound or words, fallen human beings now stood in desperate need of a mediator, an outward teacher, and of words spoken externally by the voice and received and impressed upon the mind, though the ears, in order to reform and restore the image, and retrieve the truth, they had once enjoyed directly and intuitively, within. Listening, for the early Christians, was therefore the means by which divine truth was communicated: externally, indirectly, mediately, physically, within the necessary and salutary constraints of the body and the senses, time and history, words and images, teaching and preaching, and which demanded of them an active participation and response in order to reform the fallen mind and transform the divine image within.

In this chapter I would like to dwell on some of these characteristic features of listening, first, in order to draw together some of the insights and observations which we have left scattered throughout this work, in different contexts, and, secondly, in order to draw out their implications for the transformative movement from listening to hearing, which we sketched at the end of Chapter 6.

LISTENING IN TIME

> Time present and time past
> Are both perhaps present in time future,
> And time future contained in time past.[3]

First of all, we have often had occasion to reflect on the way in which listening is bound up with time. Indeed, in exploring Augustine's *Confessions*, book 11, we saw that listening not only exemplified and illustrated the nature of time but, in a real sense, was identical with it: the unyielding elusiveness of time—ever moving from a past which no longer exists, through an unpindownable

---

[3] T. S. Eliot, 'Burnt Norton', *Four Quartets* (1944), 13.

present, to a not yet existent future—was captured corporeally for Augustine by the act of listening. In listening, the mind, as it were, incorporates time into itself: what has been heard in the past is imprinted as an image upon the memory; what is happening in the present is the focus of the attentive mind; what is to come is a matter for the operation of the will, in anticipation (and love). What Augustine describes as a *distentio animi*—the stretching out of the mind to comprehend time in its passing, is also the key to its reformation and its ability to comprehend the transcendent, eternal, and immutable God as He is revealed in the temporal sequence of words uttered in creation, Scripture, preaching, and the sacraments, as they physically strike the ear, impress themselves upon the mind, capture the attention, and motivate the will.

Time, in its elusive and precarious successiveness, is thus the context in which human beings can lose focus, forget their dependence on their Creator, and fall away from Him, but it is also the context in which they can gather its isolated moments into a meaningful pattern, turn towards Him, and be reformed. The process of listening is what makes possible this experience of time, and it carries within itself the potential for transformation. As we have seen, the early Christians expressed this insight in a number of ways: in terms of the providential action of God within time to recall and redeem His chosen people, stretching from Paradise, to the Church in the present, and forward to the life to come;[4] in the narrative of salvation which recounted this history across the vast panorama of Old and New Testaments; in the detailed miniature of this narrative in the rules of faith or Creeds; in the stories of individual lives which exemplified God's saving action and the ideal Christian life—from Abraham and Moses to Christ, to holy men and women, martyrs and ascetics;[5] in the liturgy, which dramatically re-enacted the history of salvation each time it was performed. Listening to these accounts allowed the hearer, as it were, access to a fully orchestrated version of God's actions towards humanity: it

[4] The first and most influential *History of the Church* was written by Eusebius in the early fourth century. His work was continued by Rufinus of Aquileia in the West and Socrates, Sozomen, and Theodoret of Cyrus in the East. One should also not forget Augustine's *City of God*. See Milburn (1954); Marrou (1968); Markus (1975); Chesnut (1986); Harries (1991), 269–79.

[5] Cameron (1994), 90–5, notes the importance of the genre of *Lives*: the Gospel account of Christ's life and passion; second- to third-century *Apocryphal Acts* which are full of direct speech, sermons, references to listening, language, and the power and effect of words; second-century stories of the life of Mary (*Protoevangelium of James*). Notable later *Lives* included the *Martyr Acts*, Athanasius' *Life of Antony*, the *Lives of the Desert Fathers*, Gregory of Nyssa's *Life of Macrina*, Gregory Nazianzen's *Life of Gorgonia* (Gregory Nazianzen, *Oration* 8). Cameron observes (143) that *Lives* could embrace all subjects—male and female, high and low—and all literary levels. There were, of course, many classical models for Christian lives, as the genre was a popular one in rhetorical training and practice, in *encomia* and *epideictic* (see Vickers (1989), 22–4)—speeches intended to celebrate a person's life and actions in order to encourage the audience to follow their example (e.g. Eusebius' *Life of Constantine*), as well as in philosophical works, where the individual was set forth for imitation and emulation as a model and exhortation to virtue or the ascetic life (e.g. Plutarch's *Parallel Lives* and Philostratus' *Uita Apollonii*). See Brown (1987); Lai (2010).

enabled them to trace its pattern, order, and outworking; to pick up its resonances in world history and in individual lives; to be caught up in it themselves and transformed by it. The memory, attention, and anticipation which were required to listen to any piece of music, poem, or recitation, were similarly involved in listening to God's revelation in time and history, transposed into the words of Scripture, carefully sounded by the catechist, improvised by the preacher, and resonating in the Church's prayers and hymns, as well as the lives of its members.

In all of these instances of listening to God, remembering what had gone before (or *anamnesis*) had the potential to become *mimesis*, or active representation and repetition, in the present. The listener could be moved to repeat and re-present, in their own lives, the revelation of divine truth, goodness, and beauty which had been so compellingly played out in the history of salvation or the lives of the saints, so that they too became part of the ongoing story, and their lives were transformed by it. Hearing (*audire*), in other words, had the power to compel and inspire; to lead to imitative action, or obedience (*obaudire*). *Anamnesis* and *mimesis*—remembering the past and representing it in the present—therefore had an important ethical dimension in the effective formation of habits of good moral conduct.[6] As Gregory Nazianzen puts it in a homily on the feast of the Holy Lights: 'And because the heart of any feast is godly recollection (*anamnesis*), let us remember God! For I believe that the ringing echo of those feasting there, in "the dwelling place of those who rejoice" is nothing other than this: God, praised and glorified by the people found worthy to live in his city.'[7] Chrysostom makes clear in a homily on Saint Philogonius that such praise is essentially a matter of *mimesis*: it is not God or the saint who needs remembrance and praise but the faithful, who need to remember and praise the saint so that they might 'be galvanised to emulate him'. 'This is why,' Chrysostom comments, 'some wise person said... "the memory of the just person is accompanied by words of praise".'[8] For the early Christians it was the lives of the martyrs which were especially recollected and set forth for imitation and praise, in such a manner that their bodily actions, and especially their martyrdoms, became dramatic performances which spoke to, and impressed themselves upon, the mind and heart of the hearer.[9] As

---

[6] Carruthers (1990), 68, refers to Aristotle, *Nichomachean Ethics*, 1103a17ff, 1104a 27–30, on *ethos*, in which he describes the formation of moral character by remembering and repeating particular virtuous responses from the past which will predispose the soul to the same virtuous responses in the future. Plato, *Republic*, 2–3, 396 (Russell and Winterbottom (1972), 33, similarly observes that after reading of a good man we desire to imitate him and identify ourselves with him. We saw in Chapters 2 and 5 that the rhetor's and the preacher's character was just as important as his words in convincing his listener.

[7] Gregory Nazianzen, *Oration* 39.11 (Daley, 132).

[8] *Concerning Blessed Philogonius*, 748 (Meyer and Allen, 185).

[9] They produced a *sermo corporis*. Shaw (1996), 278, referred to by Martin (2006).

Chrysostom comments on the Maccabean martyrs, they teach silently through their actions, 'uttering voice not with their tongue but with their deeds—a voice far superior to that which comes from the mouth. Through it they preach to humankind's whole nature.'[10] Of course, these silent 'bodily sermons' of the martyrs were only possible because the preacher had first recollected and recounted (*anamnesis*) the actions of the martyrs so vividly and effectively in his verbal descriptions (*ekphrases*) that they were impressed upon the minds of their hearers in an image so lifelike it was if it could be seen and heard—as if the martyrs' actions were actually being played out before their inner eyes and ears, allowing them to be caught up in it, as if they were actually present, and moved to imitate and emulate their example (*mimesis*).[11] As Augustine puts in relation to a reading of the passion of the martyr, Cyprian, 'We were listening with our ears, observing it all with our minds.'[12] This was an experience which, Chrysostom comments, was accessible to all people, not just the learned theologian, and could be effected by a bad example as well as a good one. Preaching on Eutropius he comments, 'Do you see how this man's flight here affords no small benefit for both rich and poor, both lowly and lofty, both slaves and free?' All could be equally affected by it and transformed by it—as was seen in their changed behaviour on hearing of it. As Chrysostom observes, 'Do you see how each person receives medicine and departs from here after being treated by this sight alone? Have I softened your passion and cast out your anger? Have I quenched your inhumanity? Have I drawn you into sympathy? I very much think so—the faces indicate it and the fountains of tears.'[13]

This was, of course, the main function and effect of the liturgy, in which every facet of God's revelation was recalled in a dramatic performance which was made all the more gripping as it was forever suspended, and caught up in, what we will see more fully towards the end of this chapter, was the creative, transformative tension between remembering the past (*anamnesis*), re-enacting, making it one's own in the present (through *mimesis* and participation in the sacraments), and anticipating the future which was yet to be revealed. The celebration of the liturgy, Scriptural readings, homilies, psalms,

---

[10] Allen and Mayer (2000); *Homily on the Martyrs*, 1, cited by Martin (2006).

[11] I owe these insights to my doctoral student, Elena Martin—Martin (2006). This process of *ekphrasis*, or verbal description, in order to create a vivid mental picture in the mind of the hearer, so that they effectively also became spectators, was, as we noted in Chapter 2, a common rhetorical technique, which the fathers were well aware of and used extensively, e.g. Asterius, *Ekphrasis on the Martyr Euphemia*, in Valantasis (2000), 464–8. Chrysostom often describes this painting of a mental picture, by the preacher, in the minds of his listeners, in his sermons on the martyrs, e.g. *On the Holy Martyr Ignatius*, 5 (Meyer and Neil, 106); *On Saint Barlaam*, 12 (Meyer and Neil, 188); *On the Holy Martyrs*, 8 (Meyer and Neil, 226). See Cox Miller (2009), esp. ch. 4 on *ekphrasis* in relation to the martyrs, 104–5.

[12] *Sermon*, 313A.3 (WSA III.9, 92–3) (referred to by Cox Miller (2009), 86 n. 25).

[13] *On Eutropius* (Meyer and Allen, 137).

hymns, and prayers culminated in the reception of God's redeeming Word Himself in the Mass. Here, words and actions, types and reality,[14] figures and fulfilment, resonated with, informed, and interpreted each other—their cumulative barrage upon the senses no doubt proving as effective as any piece of Renaissance polyphony in assaulting and seducing the worshipper to inform their memories, and transform their minds and souls, through their participation.[15] One only has to read a work such as Melito of Sardis' *On Easter (Peri Pascha)*[16] to get a sense of this in practice.

FAITH, POSTMODERNISM, AND THE
TACIT DIMENSION

But the grand, transformative symphonies of salvation history, performed in the liturgy, or even the delicate miniatures of individual lives, were only part of the story. We should not forget that history and biography are themselves the result of imaginative reflection and creative assimilation of the available facts, and reflect as much about their authors as they communicate about the events themselves. Moreover, they could affect and transform their listener only because he or she was able to hear them, and the fact that this was possible was due to the fact that they had effectively become what we have called 'literate listeners'. How this came about has occupied a large part of this book, but here we will try to draw some of the threads of our argument together by examining not so much the details or content of this literacy as the wider culture which informed it.

   The main point to note is that this was a culture based, not so much upon rational argument, logical deductions, scientific proofs, or philosophical statements of truth, as upon faith—faith in a transcendent, eternal, immutable Creator who could only be apprehended by his physical, temporal, mutable creation through his gracious revelation: directly and inwardly, to the mind, which, when pure, reflected his image; indirectly and outwardly, to the senses of fallen human beings, through physical, temporal, mutable signs and images. In short, as we concluded in Chapter 3, God could not be known directly, but

---

[14] On the role of typology in impressing the *typos* or seal of the faith on the soul of the hearer, through *mimesis*, see Young (2007), ch. 5.

[15] Though we must remember that all the senses are involved in the liturgy and are sanctified by it. Georgia Frank (2000), 175; Ashbrook Harvey (2006), 83–90.

[16] In Sykes (2001) or any of the other hymns devoted to Easter—e.g. Sedulius' *Carmen Paschale* (White (2000), 106–9); Asterius' *Easter Hymn* (Hamman (1961), 261); Hippolytus' *Easter Hymn—Homily* 6 (Hamman (1961), 44). All summarize salvation history, using typology or allegory, to illustrate prophecy and fulfilment. Of course, the Eucharistic prayer itself is perhaps the best, concise, example of this genre.

only through the images He impressed upon the mind and soul. This had endless repercussions for how Christians understood themselves, their place in the world, and their relation to each other and to God.

First of all, it meant that 'literate listening' signified something very different from mere functional literacy. It had more to do with an awareness (whether tacit and unarticulated, for the uneducated majority, or explicit, for the cultured elite) that words were simply signs; that signs were merely pointers; that images were not themselves reality; and that whatever they communicated was simply an indication of a reality beyond themselves, which could never be comprehended in its fullness. There was therefore nothing fixed or definitive about early Christian culture, but rather it was characterized by a general awareness of the significance of its images, which was, more often than not, a matter of tacit or complicit agreement, reached by convention, habit, and custom rather than one articulated in rules, definitions, and statements. We have seen how these tacit markers and this complicit agreement were gradually built up in examining the practice of catechesis, preaching, exegesis of Scripture, and prayer, and have seen that what was imparted in these contexts was indeed, in some senses, a 'rule', a statement, a definitive system of belief and behaviour. But we have also suggested that, in summarizing and imparting the *faith*, these rules, statements, and systems functioned more as grammar does for a writer, or notation for a musician: they were the necessary precondition for composition and creativity—for opening up and improvising upon the faith in order to explore and exploit its limitless possibilities and attempt to grasp something of its transcendent object.

Another way of putting this is that the Christian faith was not an unmoving, monolithic, perfectly finished object which could be placed on a pedestal to be admired and contemplated, but was something which demanded active engagement and participation, or performance. It was something one related to, rather than simply accepted; it was open-ended rather than complete; it consisted of shifting images rather than stationary objects.

In describing what she calls 'dissonant echoing' or an 'aesthetics of discontinuity', Patricia Cox Miller,[17] drawing upon Michael Roberts' work *The Jeweled Style*,[18] sets out a similar process, in which, by dwelling on a fragment rather than the whole, literature, as well as art and ritual practice in the fourth and early fifth centuries, transformed the fragment (be it an event, a person, or a pictorial or verbal image) into something which, by its repetition or juxtaposition, invited active participation, aesthetic appreciation, imaginative reception, and, by eliciting the whole, had the power to transform the one who perceived it. In other words, fragments could 'exceed their mere materialisation

---

[17] Cox Miller (2009), ch. 2.   [18] Roberts (1989).

as objects' by becoming religious values, and teach viewers to see 'that a material object might have a spiritual life'.[19]

Once again, the distinctive characteristics of listening—temporal, sequential, indirect, mediated, contingent, requiring relation and participation—suggest themselves as the most appropriate means to describe the sort of culture which emerges from such an understanding of the faith. We have already suggested that it was a culture made up first and foremost of 'literate listeners'; having now pinpointed the significance of faith in the formation of Christian culture, we are perhaps in a better position to examine just what this expression means.

In many respects, to say that Christian culture is based upon faith is a rather obvious statement—so obvious as to be almost empty of meaning. And yet, the work of someone like Kathryn Tanner,[20] who has attempted to confront the challenges of postmodern cultural analysis from a theological standpoint, enables us to see it again in all its disturbing, dangerous, and provocative ambiguities. It allows us to appreciate afresh the power of the conviction, which the fathers were acutely sensitive to, that God cannot be rationally defined and that the ways in which He reveals Himself are a matter of faith, open to interpretation, discussion, and creative improvisation—all of which have limitless possibilities for discovering new aspects of their transcendent object. Tanner observes that the theologian, if he or she is not to remain within the comfortable confines of academia, but be in a position to engage in the faith as it is currently held and practised,[21] must, like the postmodern critic, be willing to 'deal with what is not homogenous, clear, consistent, ordered, definable . . . but with what is complex, diverse and indeterminate'. She contrasts the 'totalising theories' of the academic with the 'polyvalent ambiguities' of popular practice.[22] Her antithesis is, of course, an artificial one, constructed for the sake of argument—at least one hopes it is—for the academic theologian at their desk, just as much as the layperson in the pew, does not have the privilege of certainty, but must confront a transcendent God who cannot be comprehended by rational, philosophical analysis, but only 'at a slant'. In other words, they must be prepared to confront and engage with the tacit beliefs which make up the Christian faith—indefinite, fragmented, elusive, and provisional as they often are—in order to work with and exploit the nature of the faith, rather than ignore it or attempt to theorize it into some sort of watertight, rational statement. It is significant that the image Tanner uses in order to capture this approach is that of listening:[23] the theologian must listen to the faith—in other words, be open and flexible in using what is there; approaching it with 'tact', 'good timing', a 'feel' for what is 'fitting';[24] with

---

[19] Cox Miller (2009), 54.   [20] Tanner (1997).
[21] Tanner (1997), 71.   [22] Tanner (1997), 86.
[23] E.g. Tanner (1997), 138.   [24] Tanner (1997), 87.

'artful attention' and 'tactical cleverness';[25] willing to make 'ad hoc ... adjustments';[26] and generally pursue a precarious 'balancing act' in their creative appropriation of it.[27] In short, the theologian must work like an artist, a poet, or a musician—aware, as Tanner puts it, of the 'subtle and ambiguous ... elusive and associative' character of the faith,[28] daring to exploit its relation to its wider culture, to 'different positionalities' and 'cross cutting differences', to tie them together (*religare*) and make of them something new, odd, and strange.[29] Above all, Tanner insists that theologians be 'willing to listen':[30] to be open and receptive to unresolved differences and disagreements, to engage in 'mutual hearing and criticism'[31] in their efforts to discover continuity and to make the transcendent God, rather than any human account of God, the focus of their attention.[32]

Tanner's reassessment of Christian culture and the task of the theologian in the light of postmodern cultural analysis is suggestive and exciting, but in arguing her case she predictably and understandably—though regrettably, I think—feels that she must dismiss the sort of creeds, rules, and tradition which we examined in Chapter 4, as too open to a diversity of reception and interpretation to be of any use in articulating the faith. In fact, she seems to reject them on the grounds that they are human accounts of God which ignore the vicissitudes of history and stand in the way of God's freedom to reveal Himself—as well as our freedom to receive His revelation—since He so often works by reversing human expectations rather than conforming to them. In taking this line, she seems to have overlooked the fact that Christian rules, creeds, and tradition have emerged precisely from within the 'vicissitudes of history' (138) and continue to be part of it; that they are themselves an expression of God's revelation and are, in fact, often radically subversive of human expectation in their teaching and message. Indeed, it seems that she has confused attempts to offer rational definitions of God (which are indeed impossible) with the creeds, rules, and traditions of the faith, and therefore dismisses them as unrepresentative of human experience; as restrictive,

---

[25] Tanner (1997), 81, 87.

[26] Tanner (1997), 92.

[27] Tanner (1997), 92.

[28] Tanner (1997), 91. Her distinction between academic theology and popular practice echoes Richard Viladesau's (2006), 3–4, contrast between what he calls 'theoretical or conceptual theology' and 'aesthetic theology'; the one is the province of the theologian, the other, the most common medium for receiving the faith by the average Christian (in the liturgy, preaching, art, architecture, poetry, music).

[29] Tanner (1997), 112–13, 116–17. Cf. Williams (2002).

[30] Tanner (1997), 125.

[31] Tanner (1997), 123.

[32] Tanner (1997), 125, 174. This resembles the approach of sociologist, Les Back, who describes sociology as a 'listener's art ... an aspiration to hold the experience of others in your arms while recognizing that what we touch is always moving, unpredictable, irreducible and mysteriously opaque' (Back (2007), 3).

unhelpful, and even idolatrous. But I would argue that if they appreciated for what they are—expressions of faith rather than statements of reasoned under-standing—then they can become positively helpful in articulating the faith's intrinsic ambiguity and its openness to a creative diversity of interpretation and practice, as well as its tacitly agreed parameters. As we saw when examin-ing exegesis of Scripture in Chapter 5, they provide the tacit 'mind', 'horizon', or 'skopos' of the faith, and thus enable the believer to hear it in all its rich and conflicting polyphony, without becoming deafened by its apparent dissonance and sheer multiplicity of reference. They provide the ears, as it were, with an 'oral literacy' and enable Christians to be 'literate listeners': able to hear the voices of Scripture, its preachers and teachers, and, through them, God. 'Literate listening' therefore means less an ability to process information and more a capacity, as Tanner indeed suggests, to tacitly discern and engage with the 'subtle and ambiguous . . . elusive and associative' character of the faith, in and through what comes to the ears in many different forms (though I would add rules, creeds, and traditions conveyed in catechesis, exegesis, and worship, to her willingness to engage in dialogue and discussion) in order to hear it for what it is—faith in a transcendent, ineffable God.

A crucial aspect of what we have loosely referred to as the 'tacit dimension' of a culture of literate listening, is that of participation. It is this element of relation or participation which Polanyi emphasizes (from whose work *The Tacit Dimension* I have borrowed the expression) when he essays a philosoph-ical analysis of how it is we come to know or simply recognize something. His premise is that 'we know more than we can tell';[33] for example, when we recognize someone's face we do so first of all on the basis of a prior, 'tacit' knowledge, but cannot explain how this works; we 'attend from' the features in order to 'attend to' the face; we move from dwelling in/participating in particulars to their joint meaning.[34] How we do this is by a tacit movement of personal recognition, an 'intimation of coherence' which is almost impos-sible to articulate or explain. Polanyi observes that this process appears to be just the opposite of modern scientific knowledge, which aims at detached, objective explanation,[35] and yet he argues that it too rests on just such tacit intuitions in order to frame its hypotheses: we know there is a problem, or we believe something to be true, but we cannot yet solve it or prove it be true.[36] As he puts it, in reference to Plato's *Meno*, 'if all knowledge is explicit, that is, capable of being clearly stated, then we cannot know a problem or look for its solution . . . if problems nevertheless exist, and discoveries can be made by

---

[33] Polanyi (1966), 4. (See Louth's (1983), 59–66, treatment of Polanyi's *Knowing and Being*, which prompted me to examine him in this context.)
[34] Polanyi (1966), 6.
[35] Polanyi (1966), 19.
[36] Polanyi (1966), 22–3.

solving them, we can know things, and important things, that we cannot tell'.[37] And just as the answer to a problem might reveal itself in what Polanyi terms 'an indefinite range of unexpected manifestations', so too with people: there is an inexhaustible profundity to our knowledge of them;[38] we can never fully know them, and they might be revealed to us in all sorts of unexpected ways in the future. Tacit knowledge, then, is very similar to what McGilchrist describes as characteristic of the working of the right hemisphere of the brain: it is capable of integrating particulars, of recognizing a face, solving a problem, composing a poem, inventing a machine, or making a scientific discovery. It is a cumulative process, building on and presupposing what has gone before, so that new things can emerge;[39] as literary composition presupposes style, style presupposes sentences, sentences presume words, and words presume a voice.[40] In this process Polanyi urges that we must trust a teacher or an authority. He quotes Augustine, 'Unless you believe, you shall not under-stand',[41] and observes, 'It appears then that traditionalism, which requires us to believe before we know, and in order that we may know, is based on a deeper insight into the nature of knowledge and of the communication of knowledge than is scientific rationalism, that would permit us to believe only explicit statements based on tangible data and derived from these by formal inference, open to repeated testing.'[42] There is therefore an openness to tacit knowledge, an ability to live with the implicit, the indefinable, and the inde-terminate; with hints and guesses; surmises and hunches. It prompts the imagination to stretch out towards the hidden, and holds out the potential for limitless discovery,[43] and creative originality.[44]

Just as we did not need to transpose McGilchrist's work on cognitive science into the language of theology, we do not, I think, really need to transpose Polanyi's philosophical reflections into the language of Christian faith in order to appreciate that what McGilchrist has to say about the characteristics of the right hemisphere of the brain, and what Polanyi has to say about the workings of tacit knowledge, are very similar to what we have been attempting to describe as the role of faith in a culture based upon 'literate listening'.[45] One illustration might suffice: when Basil of Caesarea attempts to distinguish between what we hear in faith and what we believe on the basis of faith—in Polanyi's terms, how we attend from particulars in order to attend to their

---

[37] Polanyi (1966), 22–3.   [38] Polanyi (1966), 67.
[39] Polanyi (1966), 44.   [40] Polanyi (1966), 35–6.
[41] Polanyi (1966), 61.   [42] Polanyi (1966), 61–2.
[43] Polanyi (1966), 75–9.   [44] Polanyi (1966), 91.
[45] In the closing paragraph of *The Tacit Dimension* Polanyi comments, 'Perhaps this problem cannot be resolved on secular grounds alone. But its religious solution should become more feasible once religious faith is released from pressure by an absurd vision of the universe, and so there will open up instead a meaningful world which could resound to religion' (Polanyi (1966), 92).

joint whole—he does so by contrasting the publically proclaimed good news, or *kerygma*, of the Church's preaching, with the hidden, unarticulated beliefs, or *dogma*, which arise from this preaching and which inform the believer's subsequent reception and practice of the faith in the liturgy. For example, the Holy Spirit's divinity is tacitly believed on the basis of the Church's public teaching, but it is never openly proclaimed or explained (because it transcends human knowing); the practices of facing east, of crossing oneself...are likewise actions informed by faith in God, the Trinity, and His inexpressible transcendence and holiness. The faith and actions of the Church are therefore essentially matters of tacit understanding, based upon 'literate listening'— being able to hear and 'attend from' what is heard (*kerygma*) to 'attend to' what they signify (*dogma*).[46] Of course, this movement is not simply dependent on the words of the evangelist, but rather on all the tacit presuppositions which make it possible for their listeners not only to hear them but believe them: it rests on everything that has gone before, which binds speaker and hearer together in the present: it rests explicitly upon a shared language, history, and society, and, implicitly, upon shared customs, habits, ritual, and symbolism. Crucially, it rests on trust in the authority of the Church's teaching, its Scriptures, rules, and creeds. But, above all, the movement of attending from what is heard to attending to what it signifies depends upon an openness to its still unknowable, transcendent object. It is this characteristic openness of faith—what we have identified as a culture of tacit, literate listening in time— which I would like to reflect on a little further below, for it is this, I would argue, that offers the key to the movement of 'listening from' to 'listening to'— or from listening to hearing.

LISTENING FROM ECHOES

The fathers were well aware that when they attempted to voice Scripture for the ears of their congregations they were working with echoes and resonances, rather than rationally verifiable truth. They could presuppose the rule of the faith which had been impressed upon the congregation's minds at baptism, and the way in which this would reverberate for them with the images impressed by what they had heard from preaching on Scripture, but although both the rule and Scripture conveyed God's word to fallen human beings, impressed the Christian faith in a definitive manner, and were capable of

---

[46] Basil, *On the Holy Spirit*, 27.66–8 (Anderson, 98–103); De Mendieta (1965); see Louth (1983), 85–6, who examines this passage in a similar context, in a chapter on 'Tradition and the Tacit', all of which is relevant here; and Caseau (1999), 103–4, who refers to a 'grammar of acceptable gestures' in this context.

forming and reforming the minds and hearts of those who heard them, the fathers were acutely aware that what they impressed were images, not reality; signs, not ultimate truth; *faith*, not rational understanding and vision. I would therefore like to draw together what we discovered concerning the role of images and the work of catechesis and preaching in creating literate listeners, by reflecting further on how the fathers' teaching and preaching is based precisely on this basic insight: that the images impressed upon listeners by God's inward or outward revelation, by rules and creeds, or by preaching upon Scripture, are exactly that: images. They are copies and impressions, which correspond, reflect, and allude to what they image, but are not the thing itself: they are *imagines rerum* not *res*. As Augustine puts in *Confessions*, Book 11, 'When a true narrative of the past is related, the memory produces not the actual events, which have passed away, but words conceived from images of them, which they fixed in the mind like imprints as they passed through the senses.'[47] Although paradigmatic, these 'words conceived from images' are never as fixed or definitive as they might at first appear. As we have seen, the rules and creeds provide overarching images which function as a frame, grammar, or theory; they ensure that all subsequent hearing and images can be received in a meaningful context—one in which they will always relate harmoniously to each other, and complement and illumine each other. In other words, they ensure that the mental filing system of the devout Christian will function in a manner which always retains the fundamental outlines of the faith and enables him or her to relate everything else that comes to their mind to them in a constructive way. They are the first step, then, in 'literate listening'. But what I would like to investigate here is the way in which these paradigmatic images also embody what we described above as the essential 'openness' of the faith, in that they make possible, indeed invite, creative re-presentation, imaginative allusion, and improvisation in the way in which they are recalled and related to each other.

In order to do this we need to pursue our examination of memory in Chapter 3 just a little further, in order to take account, not only of how the memory records the images which are impressed upon it, but how it recollects them in relation to different needs and circumstances. How was this done? We saw in Chapter 4 that the authoritative, unified, concise, oral nature of the paradigmatic rules of faith were clearly believed to be the most effective means of impressing the images of the faith in such a manner that they could be remembered and stored for subsequent recollection and representation. In Chapter 5 we examined how early Christian preaching on Scripture did indeed deploy these rules or summaries, recollecting and representing them in order to interpret the equally authoritative, unified, and inspired words of Scripture,

---

[47] *Confessions*, 11.18.23.

thereby adding to the images of the faith already stored in the mind of the early Christian. But the process of recollection and re-presentation was not without its own effect, and I think that that it is in this context that we find individual Christians, as well as the Christian community, forming and transforming their identities as Christians, and effectively becoming literate listeners, by following the process of *anamnesis* and *mimesis* which we outlined above: in other words, by recalling and re-presenting the faith to themselves and each other in speaking and listening to it in many different contexts.

Let us first examine how the memory was understood to go about this process of *anamnesis* or recollection. It could not be an automatic, direct recall: what had been impressed upon it in the past, at a particular time and in specific circumstances, could not just be dragged into the present without some element of modification. It would need not only to be remembered (if it had been forgotten), and re-collected from where it had been stored, but also re-presented, re-imagined, and, presumably, in the process, undergo some sort of creative reapplication and interpretation, or *mimesis*, for it to be brought consciously and usefully into the present. Since what is retrieved is an image,[48] rather than the thing itself, the process by which it is retrieved can never be a straightforward one: it is not an objective account of a particular place, person, event, or experience, but a personal and subjective record, an incomplete and allusive sketch of a now distant time and place. The memory, like the Christian preacher and teacher, can therefore also be understood to operate in the manner of an artist: it works within a particular tradition, according to accepted rules and practices, and the necessary constraints they impose, but it must nevertheless find a means to record what it is given, to recollect and reflect upon it, convey and communicate it to others. It is here that the analogy of improvisation might, I think, help us to examine what is going on in the recollection and re-presentation of the memorial images created by listening.

All artists generally agree that before they can practise their art they need to master it by studying theory, and by constant practice and endless repetition, so that it becomes more a matter of habit and tacit ability than self-conscious, reasoned application. Only then, within the necessary constraints of theory, and the discipline of practice, can they rely upon habit and innate ability to develop their own personal creativity and be in a position in which they can 'let go', express themselves, and perhaps do something original with the material they have mastered and which has, unconsciously, become almost

---

[48] See Carruthers (1990), 23–5. She writes, 'This position is common to both Aristotelians and Platonists, those who believe the mind stores and makes use only of *phantasmata* derived from the sensory mediation of "objects", and those who believe the memory also has been stamped by divine ideas, which humans have "forgotten" because of original sin or simply in the act of birth' (25).

second nature.[49] There is an obvious analogy here with the rules of faith derived from authoritative Scripture and tradition already present within the memory of the believer, which, when observed, rehearsed, and practised, both structure the mind of the individual, inculcate good habits, lead to ethical lives, and simultaneously open up a freedom for the individual to reappropriate them, and reapply them creatively and imaginatively, in relation to their own personal experiences, and their social, cultural, and historical context.[50] Following Polanyi, we have already examined the helpful notion of a 'tacit dimension' in this respect. Two other, related notions, might also help us to investigate what this process of improvisation, or creative recollection (*anamnesis*) and representation (*mimesis*) involves: cogitation, drawn from the Latin *cogitatio* and imagination or *phantasia*.

Cogitatio

When the ancients discuss the notion of *cogitatio*, it is very much the idea of creative improvisation, the collecting together of the images already contained in the memory, that they seem to be describing. Carruthers helpfully suggests that *cogitatio* 'is a pre-rational process even though it involves making judgements, for these are emotionally and intuitively based . . . *cogitatio* translates, . . . not as our phrase "reasoning out" (with its emphasis on logical connections) but as "mulling over", a process that depends heavily on free association and one's "feeling for" a matter . . . reason alone cannot help that frantically murmuring student,' she comments, 'for he has not yet gathered his memorial images to the point where reason can process them. All that can help is recollected heuristic, a trained memory which proceeds by habit and emotion, pre-rationally.[51] . . . composition, is not an act of writing, it is rumination, cogitation, dictation, a listening and a dialogue, a "gathering" (*collectio*) of voices from their several places in memory.'[52] Note that trained memory (the rules, principles, and structures) comes before the emotional, intuitive activity of free association and meditative listening to the voices of the mind; they are the basis for composition, but composition itself is a much freer, more open, discursive matter of reflection, allusive relations, and listening to resonances. Whilst this is clearly the case for all composition, it is perhaps most

---

[49] See, for example, the comments of the jazz saxophonist, Joshua Redman—Saturday, 4 April 2009, 16.00 on BBC Radio 3, Jazz Library.

[50] Kolbet (2010), 54, quotes Pierre Hadot (1998), 51: 'dogmas are not mathematical rules, learned once and for all and then mechanically applied. Rather they must somehow [through exercises] become achievements of awareness, intuitions, emotions and moral experiences.'

[51] Carruthers (1990), 200–1.

[52] Carruthers (1990), 198.

evident in the work of jazz musicians, where the theory or formal structures (the fixed chords, modes, or riffs, used as the basis for a performance or composition) are simply the necessary presupposition for creative improvisation, free association, and allusion, based on habit, intuition, emotion, and the interplay between the different players and their audience, rather than rational thought or logical processes, or a performance based on an already complete, definitive, written-out score. What results is a performance which, when heard by both the performers and their audience, operates at a number of different levels: it resonates with what their memories already contain, with ways of hearing that have become habitual and intuitive, but also prompts them, through the daring and creative variations, transpositions, echoes, and allusions of improvisation, to recollect, or gather them together in a new, and perhaps transformative way, open to yet further transformations. What else is happening in the fathers' sermons but this?

Augustine's sermon on 1 John 4, which we encountered in the Third Impromptu, has already provided us with an excellent example of such a live performance. In the course of his reflections on memory in *Confessions*, Book 10, he provides a more formal description of what is actually going on when he discusses how we become aware of the truths of the liberal arts which are inherent in the memory. He suggests that this comes about through the process of *cogitatio* or thought: 'by thinking,' he comments, 'we as it were gather together ideas which the memory contains in a dispersed and disordered way, and by concentrating our attention we arrange them in order as if ready to hand, stored in the very memory where previously they lay hidden, scattered and neglected'. Augustine proceeds to make the point that unless these inherent truths are *continually* recollected they will, as he puts it, 'sink below the surface and slip away into the remote recesses, so that they have to be thought out as if they were quite new, drawn again from the same store'. Although the liberal arts have not come to the mind through the impression of external sense impressions, but are inherent in it, it still has to work at knowing them through continual, creative recollection; its awareness of even eternal and immutable truths is still a matter of continual practice and awareness. The same might presumably be said for what the mind originally knew, directly and intuitively, of divine truth, when it still had access to it, and it is certainly true of the rule of faith through which it is now communicated to sinful humanity: we need to be continually prompted to remember, retrieve, and bring these to conscious thought in order to form the mind according to the faith. This is precisely what the fathers' homilies sought to effect. As Chrysostom observes to his congregation, 'I wanted to say as much as you were able to retain in your memory and leave here having gained some benefit . . . I will believe that I have received sufficient compensation if I see your progress in paying attention carefully to what I say, and if you store these words in the recesses of your mind, continually turning them over and ruminating on them.'[53] When Augustine describes the manner in which he prepares a sermon he gives us a revealing insight into what this process involves. He observes that he first plans his sermon mentally, as a sort of 'inner word'; that, as he puts it, 'I speak with you before I come before you, I mentally compose (*cogitaui*) in advance what I will say to you. When I have composed what I will say to you, then the word is in my memory. Nor would I speak to you, unless I had previously composed in my mind.'[54] His sermons are therefore the fruit of his attempts to gather together and recollect what he has in his mind into an articulate 'word', which he can then communicate to his hearers. He has done the creative reflection, mulling over and thinking through—a silent dry run, so to speak, of speaking and listening—before he speaks to their listening ears.

Another way of expressing this is to say that when the mind seeks to know the images and truths it contains it does so by recollecting and gathering them together from their various places in the memory, but that this process is never simply a matter of rote memory—a straightforward retrieval by ordered reference—but always more a matter of reminiscence;[55] of suggestive echoes, resonances, and allusions which somehow inspire associations and connections between what it contains. These are not so much formal strategies for exact recall as tacit, intuitive habits of recall which need to be practised, repeated, and continually performed, so that what is brought to the surface of the mind does not fall back into what Augustine calls 'the abyss of forgetfulness' or into the unexplored depths of the filing cabinet! We have all had the experience of hearing one thing, which jogs our memory into remembering something else that we had forgotten; of hearing a single note or chord and being able to hear the whole piece; of suddenly feeling we have grasped something, understood it for the first time or seen it in a new light, which comes as a moment of insight; of things falling into place and making sense in a way they hadn't in their disparate, disorganized parts; of momentarily grasping something beyond what we were hearing, thinking, or seeing—a moment of awareness, perhaps even of transcendent awareness, which comes and, just as soon, is gone, leaving only a memory. What provokes these moments is almost never a rational, step-by-step, logical thought process, but rather an image, or a combination of images, which provoke all sorts of tacit resonances and associations in our minds, which, in turn, draw together what we already know in a new way. This is the process we must bear in mind in examining how early Christian listeners received and understood their faith: not as something to be rationally articulated and understood, but as a collection of images imprinted through listening to it being rehearsed

---

[53] *Homily on Genesis*, 28.1 (PG 53.252), cited by Maxwell (2006), 105.
[54] *Sermon*, 225.3 on John 1:1 (WSA III.6 248–9).
[55] A distinction made by Carruthers (1990), 19–20.

in many different contexts, stored according the rule of faith, and retrieved by continual recollection of these images, so that early Christian listeners built up tacit, habitual modes of thinking and acting. What prompted these recollections, and thereby gradually shaped what has been referred to rather felicitously as 'habits of the heart',[56] would, of course, vary according to need and circumstance, but each recollection, like improvisations on a chord, would be a new, creative addition to the memorial images that were already there, so that the faith was never allowed to 'sink below the surface and slip away to the remote recesses' but was always alive and relevant in the mind of the individual Christian. All the early Christian texts we now have were meant to serve this purpose and should be read (or better, heard) by us in this light. A few illustrations might be useful: one musical and the others patristic.

In an article on Bach, Jeremy Begbie refers to the *Goldberg Variations* as an example of how a complex web of resonances, echoes, references, and allusions can be created within the memory by a series of elaborations, or variations, on an original, deceptively simple, tune. He observes that, 'In the Goldberg Variations . . . we are given thirty variations on the bass line and chords of a lyrical and stately saraband. After an hour and a quarter of elaboration, Bach asks for the aria to be played at the end, *da capo*, note for note. Now we cannot hear it apart from the memory of all the variations in which it has now been imagined. In other words, we now hear the aria as varied, replete with diversity. It has acquired a richness, an untold profundity, of light and darkness, joy and melancholy, levity and gravity; it is all ornamentation and change.'[57] A piece of jazz improvisation, the extended allegories, or the juxtaposed intertexts of a patristic sermon, can have the same effect. What happens in each case is, in a real sense, an instance of *cogitatio*: the bringing together, or bringing to the surface, of the memorial images already imprinted upon the memory, by means of complex and varied repetition, variation, allusion, and interplay upon paradigmatic images and types. This enables the latter to be re-collected and re-represented in new, creative, informative—perhaps transformative—ways. Having heard the variations the memory will always subsequently recollect and hear the themes/images it already contains with new, multiple, and rich resonances. It will be changed and, hopefully, enriched by them.

What Augustine has to say about the role of the double commandment of love in *Instructing Beginners in the Faith* has the same process in mind: this simple summary of the faith is one which should always inspire, and be the means and goal of, all Christian teaching, so that whatever is done or said in any context, should be related to, and serve to expound, it. He writes, 'Keeping this love before you then as the goal to which you direct all that you say,

---

[56] Used by Cameron (1994), 28, in reference to Bellah (1985).
[57] Begbie (2007), 136.

recount every event in your historical exposition in such a way that your listener by hearing it may believe, by believing may hope, and by hoping may love.'[58] When Augustine famously comments 'love and do what you will' (*dilige et fac quod uis*) he has precisely this in mind. Love of God and love of neighbour, as enshrined in the double commandment, is the paradigm of the faith and the basis for all Christian teaching and action; as long as what we believe, do, or say resonates with it, then it is acceptable. The basic paradigm of the faith is open to infinite reapplication and variation.

Gregory of Nyssa seems to have had in mind this same process of *cogitatio* when he describes the effect of his sister Macrina's death as an 'ember for the memory'. He writes, 'For all, affection was mingled with anguish: some longed to hear something, as an ember for the memory; others wished to say something, but did not dare.'[59] It is as if the coals of the images of faith (its creeds and rules), which lie smouldering within the memory, need to be kindled and reignited by hearing the words of those who best embody it.[60]

In his homily on Saint Meletius, Chrysostom is aware that all that is needed to set off a whole series of resonating recollections and transformative re-presentations in the minds of his congregation is simply the mention of the martyr's name. By constantly repeating it and weaving it into his sermon he was persuaded that everything else that they knew about him and felt for him would be tacitly evoked, so that every aspect of their lives could be conformed to his example: 'For he has so inflamed your mind towards passion for him that you are heated through by just his name and are excited at the very mention of it.'[61] Indeed, Chrysostom urges that remembering and imitating the life of a saint was effectively to resurrect them: to make a dwelling place for them in one's mind, allow them to live within oneself, and to speak through one's deeds. Thus, he writes on the martyr Saint Eustathius, 'For saints' memorials are not urns or coffins or columns or inscriptions, but good works and a zeal for faith and a healthy conscience towards God. My point is that this church has risen up more brilliant than any column over the martyr, carrying inscriptions that are not voiceless but that through events themselves cry out his memory and brilliance louder than a trumpet, and each of you who are present is that saint's tomb, a tomb that has life and soul. For if

[58] *Instructing Beginners in Faith*, 4.8 (Canning, 72).
[59] *Oration* 8. 22 (Daley, 74). Daley (2006), 74 n. 69) notes that the expression 'an ember for the memory' (*mnemes empureuma*) seems to be original to Gregory, that he uses it again in *Oration* 24.3 and that it seems to have become proverbial among some later Christian writers—e.g. Leontius of Byzantium—Preface to *Against Nestorius and Eutyches* (*Contra Nestorianos et Eutychianos*, PG 86.1268B).
[60] Plutarch, *On Listening* (Moralia, 48C; Loeb, 197, 256–7): 'For the mind does not require filling like a bottle, but rather, like wood, it only requires kindling to create in it an impulse to think independently and an ardent desire for the truth.'
[61] Meyer and Neil, 42.

I were to open up the conscience of each of you who are present, I would find this saint dwelling in your mind.'[62]

Clearly, Gregory Nazianzen has precisely this process of creative and recreative *cogitatio* in mind when he uses the distinction between *anamnesis* and *mimesis* to refer to the great feasts of the Christian year as acts of recollection and representation: in the celebration of the feasts, God's past acts are called up from the memory and, by the act of recollection and repetition, and in the giving of praise and glory to God in worship, they are made present, and re-impressed on the minds and hearts of those who celebrate them in a manner which resonates with their past experiences, reforms their existing mental images, and purifies and transforms them towards the life to come.[63] As Gregory puts it, 'How many festivals there are, for each of the mysteries of Christ! Yet there is one conclusion to all of them: my perfection, my re-shaping, my return to the first Adam.'[64]

The process of hearing, like *cogitatio*, is therefore never less than creative, formative, and potentially transformative; it builds up a complex and rich world of tacit, intuitive understanding and practice, with which further hearing will resonate, and, perhaps, in turn, transform.

IMAGINED IMAGES

Heard melodies are sweet but those unheard are sweeter . . . [65]
And harmonies unheard in sound create the harmonies we hear and wake the soul to the consciousness of beauty . . . [66]

The other means we suggested that might help us to examine the process by which the memory recollects and gathers together the images which have been imprinted upon it by the senses, so that it is led to new insights and understanding, was imagination. The fathers were, of course, notoriously suspicious of imagination (*phantasia*). It created images (*phantasmata*) from images (*phantasia*), which were themselves merely copies of something else, and so

---

[62] Meyer and Neil, 54.
[63] Harrison (2006).
[64] *Oration* 38 On the Theophany, 16 (Daley, 126). As Verna Harrison comments, 'Anamnesis thus unites past, present and future in a single present event of worship' (V. Harrison (2008), 25).
[65] John Keats, *Ode on a Grecian Urn* (Stillinger, 1991). See Chretien (2003), 22–3, on listening to the 'silent music' of a work of art. Of Keats he writes, 'Although the ode is "on" a Grecian urn, and not "to" it, the poem begins with a familiar "thou", a word addressed to the work being contemplated; "Thou still unravish'd bride of quietness" . . . To address a visible work is to see while listening to, or to listen to while seeing, its silence. Only this listening can give the poet speech: he does not take speech, he receives it. He receives it as an act of listening to a silence that is worthy of obedience (*audire, obaudire*) . . .'
[66] Plotinus, *Ennead*, 1.6.3 (MacKenna, I.81).

it seemed to be a faculty of the mind which moved further and further away from truth, or *res*, and immersed it deeper and deeper into a realm of images (*imagines*) or phantasms (*phantasmata*) where it was difficult to distinguish truth from falsehood. But, as we have seen, images were the necessary way in which the memory received perceptions from outside itself; they played a positive role: first of all in the creation, recording, and storing of what came to mind from the senses; secondly, in the recollection and retrieval of what had formed the memory in the past, so that they conveyed and contained within themselves an identity which had been shaped by habit, custom, and tradition; finally, they were instrumental in ensuring that the memory never became fixed, or took anything as an end in itself, but was aware that what it knew it knew in and through images and signs—that the truth lay beyond it. In other words, images—precisely because they are images and not the reality itself—point beyond themselves, resist idolatry, maintain a sense of openness, and thus, as in the activity of *cogitatio*, invite not so much rational, logical reflection, as exploration, creative improvisation, and allusive, playful extemporization—in short, imagination—reaching towards their archetypes.

I think we might also argue that it is the images created by hearing that best lend themselves to this particular imaginative role, rather than those created by any of the other senses, and that in this context, as we saw earlier in relation to the contrast between speaking and writing, auditory images have a certain priority over visual images. There are a number of reasons for this.

Firstly, the act of listening is itself inherently open-ended. As we saw at the beginning of this chapter, unlike the other senses, hearing can only take place in time, across space, in an ordered sequence which recollects the past, is conscious of the present, and which must anticipate—imaginatively (for it has not yet happened)—what is to come. It is this imaginative aspect of hearing which also, I think, leaves it open to the transcendent: to that which lies not just in the future, but beyond the images contained within the memory; beyond the conventions and tacit understandings that have been built up; beyond the standard types and figures in which these understandings are articulated. Rather, these provoke the hearer to look beyond their temporal manifestation as signs, and to search out and discover their eternal inspiration and truth. In other words, precisely because hearing is a matter of signs rather than ultimate truths, and is forever shifting and nudging the attention from one thing to the next, it is open to variations and anticipated—or unanticipated—developments. The very experience of hearing can prompt in the hearer a search for the immutable—either in attempting to make sense of what has gone before, or in imaginatively anticipating what cannot yet be grasped.

The characteristic open-endedness of listening could therefore have the positive effect of inculcating a sense of intellectual humility, based on the fact that the listener does not yet have the answers but is, as it were, 'living the questions',[67] reaching after imponderables, and wondering 'what next'? The sense of restless exploration and uncomprehending doubt—or sheer longing—which faith in a transcendent God occasioned in the listener, was therefore given direction and expression in the imaginative exploration of these experiences and the search for their resolution—for what indeed does come next[68]—and this proved, in turn, to be both formative of Christian hope and transformative of Christian identity. Early Christian typology and figurative exegesis,[69] as well as its guiding images of pilgrimage and ascent, were all inspired by this context (we will examine Gregory's treatment of Abraham and Moses' ascents below).[70]

Secondly—and thinking back to Plato's contrast between speaking and writing in the discussion between Theuth and Thamos in the *Phaedrus*—unlike visual images, which are immobile and voiceless, auditory images are, as it were, alive, spontaneous and able to engage and address the listener directly. As we noted in Chapter 6, in relation to prayer, they therefore, much more immediately, invite participation and response, not least because hearing only takes place when there is someone else to hear and respond to in a direct and immediate way. Again, there is much more potential for imaginative, transformative interplay between speaker and hearer (whether the speaker or hearer is God, the preacher, or one's neighbour) than there is between author and reader. The contrast between a live performance in which the player is

---

[67] Rilke, *Letters to a Young Poet* (C. Louth (2011), 23–4): 'be patient towards all that is unresolved in your heart and try to love *the questions themselves* like locked rooms, like books written in a foreign tongue. Do not now strive to uncover answers: they cannot be given you because you have not been able to live them. And what matters is to live everything. *Live* the questions for now. Perhaps then you will gradually, without noticing it, live your way into the answer, one distant day in the future.' This is rather like Keats' negative capability, 'the capacity to be in uncertainties, mysteries, doubts without any irritable reaching after fact and reason', Letter to George and Thomas Keats, 21 December 1817 (Rollins (1958), vol. 1, 193–4).

[68] Williams (2002), 30–1, identifies this sense of uncertainty as a distinctive feature of some Christian poetry (e.g. George Herbert, Geoffrey Hill, R. S. Thomas), which he describes as 'the licensed experimentation with the "dangerous edge of things" . . . that will in some way show what cannot be said "straight" in a context in which the direct utterance of the faith has become embarrassed or stale, when it no longer . . . makes a difference'. The whole volume in which his essay appears is of interest for reflections on the importance, and the creative role, of imagination. As the playwright, Nigel Forde, puts it, 'the imagination . . . can reveal truths that no other discipline has found a way to countenance. It is not a vestigial organ like the tonsils or the appendix that may be removed without harm. True understanding, as opposed to mere knowledge, is a work of the imagination and we neglect it at our peril' (2002), 69.

[69] See Dawson (1999).

[70] Cox Miller (2009), 80, gives an apposite quotation from the French philosopher Gaston Bachelard which I cannot resist recalling in this context: 'We always think of the imagination as the faculty that *forms* images. On the contrary, it *deforms* what we perceive; it is, above all, the faculty that frees us from immediate images and *changes* them. If there is no change, or unexpected fusion of images, there is no imagination; there is no *imaginative act*. If the image that is *present* does not make us think of the one that is *absent*, if an image does not determine an abundance—an explosion—of unusual images, then there is no imagination. There is only perception . . . an habitual way of viewing form and color' (Bachelard (1988), 1).

able to freely extemporize and respond to the occasion, to 'inspiration', to their own mood, and to the audience's response, leaves much more room for personal interaction (in throwing and catching the ball of live speech) than the reading of a fixed, written text, or even the performance of a completely written out piece of music from a score, can ever allow. It is not without reason that the words for hearing in French and German—*entendre* and *horen* are directly related to words signifying relation—*s'entendre* (to get on with) and *gehoren* (to belong to—to be someone's friend). Live performance is always much more engaging than a recording or a book; live performance which is unscripted, and in which anything can happen, is even more so. In this context, words do not so much impart information as inform the relation between speaker and hearer, so that they are able to align themselves with each other and learn something from and about each other.

Thirdly, whereas we can close our eyes in order not to see, we cannot close our ears: ears do not have lids. This means that hearing unavoidably provokes a response; it cannot be ignored, even though our responses can differ: we can be attentive or inattentive; receptive or unreceptive; obedient or disobedient hearers. Hearing can therefore be potentially formative or de-formative but it cannot be neutral: it is an always an ethical act; an act of will, which demands a response, even if the response is an unwillingness to hear. Christ's words, 'He who has ears to hear let him hear' (Mt. 11:15, 25:30), were generally interpreted by the fathers in this manner, as indicating that those who had ears to hear, that is, those who believed in him, would be able to hear, whereas those who were hostile, that is, those who did not believe in him, did not have ears to hear, and would remain deaf to his words.

Finally, there is nothing material or tangible about hearing which fixes it in some way for the hearer; there are no images which already exist, as there are in writing, sculpture, painting, or poetry, for the hearer to either contemplate or to use. Rather (unless the speaker has done the imagining for them, as we will see in the case of rhetoric below, or the musician has transcribed sound into notation), the listener has to find some means of capturing what their senses perceive through hearing—in other words, of inventing images by which what they hear can be inscribed upon the memory. Unlike visual images, then, which are already either an inscribed or pictorial image that can be readily transferred to the mind, auditory images require the hearer to imaginatively participate in their inscription. How can sound be transcribed or described?[71] How *are* words impressed upon the mind? (As written words? As visual images?[72] As synaesthetic images? As words heard by the inner ear?). As

[71] This is, of course, one of the perennial issues in music. See R. Barthes (1977), 179: 'How then does language manage when it has to interpret music? Alas, it seems very badly.'

[72] As Conybeare notes, Augustine refers to the 'image of the apprehended voice' (*perceptae uocis imago*) in *Literal Commentary on Genesis*, 12.16.33. She adds, 'so the mapping of hearing

we saw in Chapter 3, the answer is far from straightforward, but I would argue that, whatever the answer, as in the other cases we have just examined, auditory images, far more than visual images, invite, and leave the way open for, imaginative, creative engagement; for participation and open-ended improvisation, and thus for reaching towards, and perhaps even attaining, the reality of which they are an image, sign, or pointer.

FROM THE BOTTOM TO THE BOTTOMLESS

Let me try to give some examples of this process: one is classical, one contemporary, and the last two are patristic. All of them are based on the idea which we saw McGilchrist suggest in our First Impromptu: that one must, to some extent, be prepared to *pass through* temporal, corporeal images; *pass through* the accepted and the customary, in order to reach out towards the transcendent and 'listen to the voice of Being'. One must be prepared, in other words, to imaginatively gather together and improvise upon what one has heard; to rely on habit, intuition, and emotion; to use metaphor and symbols—perhaps in new, unexpected, but (because unexpected) ultimately revealing and transformative ways, which leave open the possibility of touching, or even attaining, their transcendent subject.

For the classical illustration I have been unable to resist the seductive allure of Longinus' wonderful treatise *On Sublimity*. As we saw in some detail in Chapter 2, in the course of this work Longinus discusses the particular effect which the hearing of various rhetorical figures has upon the mind or memory of the hearer; how specific techniques are used in order to impress certain images upon the mind of the hearer which will provoke in them the desired reaction and response. The rhetor did not attempt to convey rational, logical proofs but rather to persuade through the effect that his spoken images had upon the memory and emotions of his hearers. That this was transformative is quite clear, but that it could enable the hearer to glimpse the transcendent, or what he calls 'genius', is also something that Longinus wants to demonstrate. He is convinced that the effect of verbal imagery does not just depend upon the careful and close observance of the rules, techniques, and figures of rhetoric, or on creating lifelike verbal imitations. Rather, it is when a speaker, possessed of what he calls 'greatness' (by which he seems to mean inspiration) dares to move beyond customary, expected practice to do something new and unexpected, perhaps in contravention of the accepted rules, that what he does

onto an imaginary connected with visual patterning, while not richly substantiated [this is the only example she gives/can find], is not far-fetched'. Conybeare (2012a), 145.

is not just effective but communicates the sublime, and embodies not merely polished accomplishment but genius.[73]

My second example is taken from comments made by the director Phyllida Lloyd in relation to her production of Schiller's play, *Mary Stuart*. In a newspaper article which appeared in the *Telegraph* in 2006,[74] she reflects on the challenges the director faces in creating an ensemble of actors who will eventually be able play in concert; to, as she puts it, 'make each of the actors feel safe to be as dangerous as they must be on stage'. Like Longinus, she realizes that a great performance comes not just from minute and meticulous attention to the text, but from letting go, giving inspiration freedom to express itself, allowing an actor to improvise and take risks. These two approaches she found embodied in the two actresses who played the two queens of the play, Elizabeth I and Mary Stuart. She observes, 'One thinks that improvisation will release the scene, the other that she is so old she can barely learn the lines she has, let alone improvise them. And this is a play set in two worlds, the court of Elizabeth I and the prison of Mary Stuart, a Catholic world and a protestant world, and it soon became apparent . . . that each of the actresses, each of the queens, was building her own court—the court of the mind, and the court of the heart. The court of the mind rehearsed with forensic attention to detail. Meanwhile in the court of the heart there was improvisation, rawness, chaos. The difficulty came when we rehearsed the great and fictitious scene in which the two queens meet. The court of the mind needed to analyse and steady the process, the court of the heart was impeded by the cold scrutiny, aching to "just try something". Now all great acting is a synthesis of mind and heart, but each of the actresses was moving towards their goals from different poles. As the work went on, the court of the mind allowed passion and chaos into its borders, while the court of the heart began to focus, edit and balance.' What Lloyd is describing resonates with Longinus' description of genius—it is not just correct, flawless, controlled speaking, but allows for improvisation; for the passion, rawness, chaos, and flaws of genius. Demosthenes spoke not only with the mind, but with the heart. It is the heart, of course, that controls the imagination, and, without it, we would remain at the level of the mundane, rather than glimpsing the transcendent.

My third, patristic example is drawn from the fathers' reflections on the music of the Psalms. I hope to pursue the subject of early Christian singing and music in more detail in my next book, but it would be helpful to observe here that the fathers were generally as suspicious of music as they were of rhetoric, and tended to reject it in a Christian context as too tainted by paganism, and too likely to tempt, seduce, and lead astray the attention of the hearer from a proper focus on *what* is being said, to *how* it was being

---

[73] *On Sublimity*, 32.8–36.4 (Winterbottom, 175–9).
[74] *Telegraph*, Saturday, 29 July 2006, Arts, 8–9.

said; to aesthetic rather than ethical or philosophical concerns. But their suspicion of music, like their suspicion of rhetoric—and, indeed, of the imagination—is grounded in their tacit acknowledgement of its sheer power to move the hearer, to shape their mind, thoughts, and feelings through the impression it makes upon their memory, or—as they more often put it—their soul. The combination of words and music or words and rhetorical figures, was like setting fire to a touchpaper. The words would no longer simply inform or teach, but would be given an emotively seductive power to shape the soul by impressing an auditory image which could not simply be allocated to an appropriate place to be filed and stored, but which captured its attention and provoked a response—in other words, which sparked off the recollection and re-presentation of existing memorial images in ways which led to new, transforming insights—and perhaps even to a glimpse of the transcendent. The one type of music which the fathers did—albeit reluctantly and ambivalently—allow, was the chanting of the psalms, and it is in this context that we see them articulating their awareness of the power of such auditory images to inform (and transform) not only the memory, but the heart and soul, through the ears. One of the common themes which most of the fathers revert to at some point when commenting upon the Psalms is that of the calming, pacifying effect which David's playing had upon Saul. As Athanasius comments in his *Letter to Marcellinus* on the Psalms, 'Blessed David, then... drove away from Saul the troubled and frenzied disposition, making his soul calm. The priests who sang thus summoned the souls of the people into tranquillity, and called them into unanimity with those who form the heavenly chorus. Therefore the Psalms are not recited with melodies because of a desire for pleasant sounds. Rather this is a sure sign of the harmony of the soul's reflections. Indeed, the melodic reading is a symbol of the mind's well-ordered and undisturbed condition.'[75] The chanting or playing of the psalms therefore has a reciprocal effect: it both gives expression to the soul's 'inner spiritual harmony' and creates this 'harmony' in the disordered and discordant soul of the listener. Athanasius attributes the unique power which chant possesses to two things: first, the fact that it is poetry, rather than prose, which is being sung, means that what he describes as the 'freer, less restricted' form of verse allows people to 'express their love to God with all the strength and power they possess'. Secondly, the fact that chanting demands the whole of one's concentration also means that the speaker remains wholly undistracted and completely focused in mind and body upon what they are singing.[76] This is a discipline which gradually reforms and frees the soul to anticipate what is to come: 'for thus beautifully singing praises'', Athanasius observes, ' he brings rhythm to his soul and leads it, so to speak, from disproportion to proportion,

[75] 29 (Gregg, 125).
[76] Athanasius *Letter to Marcellinus* 28-29 (Gregg, 124–5).

with the result that, due to its steadfast nature, it is not frightened by something, but rather imagines positive things, even possessing a full desire for future goods'.[77] Thus, through singing and listening to the freer, less restricted form of verse in the psalms, the soul is harmonized both within itself and with others. There is, at once, both openness here—in the 'freer, less restricted form of verse'—but also discipline, concentration, order, and unity. As with Longinus' contrast between correctness and greatness, or the two different courts of the heart and the mind of the two actresses rehearsing Shaffer's play, it is the interaction of the two in the freedom (and inevitable improvisation) of live performance, that makes possible the unique effect of the psalms upon the souls of both singer and listener.

And what of the early Christian preacher? As we have seen, he, more than anyone, knew the potential of live performance: the power of rhetoric to stir the emotions; the importance of rules and authoritative text; the need to take risks, and of breaking– or at least transcending—rules to attain the sublime; about extemporizing and tacit reference and resonance; about the importance of participation, and of conversation, which only speaking and hearing could involve. The freedom with which Christian preachers abandoned themselves to their preaching, innovating with classical forms in creating the new genre of the Christian homily and a new Christian style, is indeed striking, and allowed them to provoke, challenge, and shock their listeners, whilst retaining their attention and leading them into uncharted territory—faith in, and perhaps even momentary glimpses of, the transcendent God.[78]

ECHOES AND RESONANCES

Listening, then, is something that emphatically resists the idea that what we know we know through reason; that what we experience through the senses should either be discounted as worthless or else rationally assimilated by the mind. Rather, as we have seen, it is characterized by what cannot be captured and pinned down for rational analysis—by faith or openness to the presence of the ineffable and the transcendent.

The work of the Italian philosopher, Gemma Corradi Fiumara (*The Other Side of Language: A Philosophy of Listening*),[79] whilst rigorously secular, is one of the few studies which articulate this insight specifically in relation to listening. Her argument is that, when philosophers discuss language they generally do so only from the side of the speaker, not that of the listener:

---

[77] Athanasius *Letter to Marcellinus* 29 (Gregg 126).
[78] For the new freedom of the homiletic form, see Auksi (1995), 10–11.
[79] Corradi Fiumara (1990).

they work, as she puts it, with 'only a partial sense of logos understood as a capacity for ordering and explaining, detached from any propensity to receive and listen' (10). She observes that their rigorously objective, scientific approach, based purely upon reason and the desire to systematize and attain certainty, ignores the other half of the meaning of *logos*; the other side of language, and is the antithesis of what is actually needed to listen to and receive what is said. Reflecting on the latter, she confirms what we have found to be case throughout this book, and what we saw McGilchrist identify as characteristic of the brain's right hemisphere: that listening requires an openness to what lies beyond reason, 'an attitude of individual attention and holding, an attitude also capable of letting anything be in its entireness' (15). She further describes this approach as one of 'heeding' and 'hearkening . . . anchored to humility and faithfulness, an approach,' she observes, 'which is unheard of in our current thinking, revolving around grasping, mastering, using. This perspective is characterized by the requirement that we dwell with, abide by, whatever we try to know, that we aim at co-existence—with, rather than knowledge-of' (15).

Whilst Corradi Fiumara does not refer to Polanyi, her work certainly confirms his insistence on the essentially participatory nature of knowing, and of the necessity to 'dwell with' and to 'attend from' someone or something, in order to 'attend to' them. Both philosophers also work with the sense that 'we know more than we can tell': that what we know does not lend itself to clear, consistent, ordered analysis but rather requires an ability to 'live the questions', and to work with what Tanner described above as 'polyvalent ambiguities' rather than 'totalising theories'.[80] As Corradi Fiumara puts it, 'Whereas a logocentric tradition tends to scoff benevolently at, or study in an objective fashion, the "magical", "absurd" or "banal" attitudes stemming from other *Weltanschauungen*, listening opens up the possibility of a philosophical activity that is no less rigorous, but which neither opposes the tradition of western logos nor excommunicates anything that "normal" rationality is unable to grasp or systematise' (19). She makes the important point that when we ask questions of someone or something, the answer we receive will always be in the frame of the theoretical language in which we addressed them (25, 35). An approach based on scientific certainty will therefore never be able to hear anything other than rational answers and will remain deaf to the ambivalences which only an approach based on listening is able to hear: in short, it is based on the presupposition that 'one can speak to others without being able to listen' (29). Listening, on the other hand, is able to pay heed to what is ambiguous or anomalous; to what cannot be explained away. In this context she reaffirms the traditional hierarchy of sight and hearing: that 'the

---

[80] Corradi Fiumara (1990), 86.

eyes are more exact witnesses than the ears',[81] but interestingly notes that 'the lesser reliability of the ears as objective witnesses is, however, an index of the vast cognitive and hermeneutic potential that can be explained only by listening' (41).

Listening is therefore a much riskier, complex, and uncertain business than either looking, or an approach based on scientific/philosophical reason, but only listening is able to hear what eludes scientific explanation or philosophical certainty. Corradi Fiumara observes that the attempt to listen therefore often presents us with a disquieting situation 'in which we have to take provisional, impossible steps in order to continue to listen and thus consent that something may come across' (47); to 'co-exist . . . with the incomprehensible . . . opaque, open, perplexing' (51). This is, of course, what we saw McGilchrist describe as characteristic of the right hemisphere of the brain, and what we have described as an attitude of literate listening based upon faith.[82]

'Human kind/cannot bear very much reality'[83]

The arguments that philosophers such as Polanyi and Corradi Fiumara rehearse for tacit, personal knowing in the face of scientific rationalism, were not unfamiliar to the fathers, who similarly sought to counter those, such as Eunomius, who argued that the nature of the Godhead could be known by human reason.[84] What they have to say in this context should, I think, enable us to reflect further on the nature of literate listening based upon faith.

In his *Five Theological Orations* against Eunomius, Gregory Nazianzen tells his hearers that the point of his sermon is 'the incomprehensibility of deity to the human mind and its totally unimaginable grandeur'.[85] What he has to say is based on his faith in the eternal, immutable, and incorporeal God who can

---

[81] Heraclitus fragment 101a (in Corradi Fiumara (1990), 203 n. 31).

[82] Corradi Fiumara attempts to further describe it as 'based on modes of thinking that can be qualified as "mild", "moderate", "modest", "available", "vulnerable", "welcoming", "patient", "contained", "tolerant", "conciliatory", "receptive", "pitiful" (with reference to *pietas*), "humble" (with reference to *humus*), "poor" (with reference to parsimony), "disciplined" (with reference to *discere*), "vital" (with reference to life): all those qualities that are not based on weakness but on a devoutly exercised strength' (69). In making her case against scientific rationalism she is rehearsing an argument which has been made in many different forms, by scholars in different disciplines, all concerned to challenge the post-Enlightenment tradition. We have mentioned her specifically simply because she makes the case in relation to listening. If we had time and space it would no doubt be fruitful to also examine the work of H. G. Gadamer in philosophy, H. Urs von Balthasar and Andrew Louth in theology, Jeremy Begbie in music, Geoffrey Hill in literary criticism.

[83] T. S Eliot, 'Burnt Norton', *Four Quartets* (1944), 14.

[84] See Young (1993) for an interesting take on this.

[85] *Theological Orations* 2 (28).11 (Williams and Wickham, 45).

never be fully known or even described by His temporal, mutable, corporeal creation:[86] just as 'fish cannot swim out of water . . . no more can embodied beings keep incorporeal company with things ideal'.[87] For Gregory, as for all fourth-century theologians, there exists a dizzying ontological chasm between creation and Creator which cannot be bridged by either the senses or the intellect: when confronted by the 'naked reality' of the truth our senses simply become perplexed and lead us astray, whilst our intellect cannot receive direct and sure impressions.[88] Gazing upon the precipitous abyss which separates divine and human we must cling to what is within our grasp. In other words, we can only meaningfully talk about God in terms of what we are and He is not, that is, in terms of negation or apophasis: God is without body, without limits, without form, impalpable, invisible, ingenerate, unoriginate, immortal, incomprehensible.[89] Whereas Eunomius taught that God's glory and majesty could be captured by human reason, Gregory is insistent that it forever eludes us: 'the superiority of the stars to the grasp of our fingers is nothing in comparison with that of the nature which exceeds every mind to our earthly reasoning'.[90] We can never talk about God as He is in Himself, but must rather rely on indirect, vague correspondences and sketchy outlines to create what Gregory describes as a 'faint and feeble mental image'.[91]

What we do know with certainty, however, is that God exists. As we have already seen in relation to the image of God in humankind, His inspiration of Scripture and His revelation in creation, history, and the incarnation, God is made known to human beings through his works and actions—what Gregory of Nyssa calls his characteristics (*idiomata*) and activities (*energeai*)[92]—just as an artist is made known through his art: we perceive not the artist himself, but a reflection of his character and proof of his artistry or creativity. As Gregory Nazianzen puts it, using both visual and auditory analogies, 'No one seeing a beautifully elaborated lyre with its harmonious, orderly arrangement, and hearing the lyre's music, will fail to form a notion of its craftsman–player, or to recur to him in thought though ignorant of him in sight.'[93] The

---

[86] *Theological Orations* 2 (28). 4 (Williams and Wickham, 39–40).
[87] *Theological Orations* 2 (28). 12 (Williams and Wickham, 46).
[88] *Theological Orations* 2 (28). 21 (Williams and Wickham, 52–3); cf. Gregory of Nyssa, *Homily* 6 On the Beatitudes (Meredith, 94), which we examined in Chapter 3. He writes, 'The divine nature in and of itself, whatever its essential character, lies beyond our human apprehension . . . There has never been found among men anyone to grasp the ungraspable with the human intelligence, nor has there ever been found a method of comprehending the incomprehensible.'
[89] *Theological Orations*, 2 (28) 7, 9 (Williams and Wickham, 41–2, 43–4).
[90] *Against Eunomius*, 95–6 (Meredith, 91).
[91] *Theological Orations*, 2 (28) 17 (Williams and Wickham, 49–50); cf. *Oration 38 on the Theophany*, 7 (Daley, 170).
[92] *Homily* 6 On the Beatitudes (Meredith, 94–5).
[93] *Theological Orations*, 2 (28) 6 (Williams and Wickham, 41).

craftsman–player therefore exists, even if we only know him indirectly, through seeing his beautiful workmanship and listening to his resonant playing. Many of the fathers likewise understood the beauty of God's creation,[94] or the wondrous microcosm of the human body, to be a wordless paean of praise and glory which points towards its Creator.[95]

The fathers and their listeners were well aware, however, of the dramatic Scriptural accounts of heroic individuals such as Elijah, Abraham, Moses, and Paul, who essayed the heights of divine incomprehensibility, and who looked upon things which are not to be seen, and heard words human lips may not utter.[96] How did these pioneers fit into the argument that God transcended human reason? They presented an interesting challenge, but it proved to be a creative one for the fathers, and one that prompted them to reflect further on the fact that we do indeed (in Polanyi's words) 'know more than we can tell'; to reiterate their conviction that God is ultimately unknowable to human reason and inexpressible in human language; and to elucidate in greater detail the all-important role of faith (or what we have described as an attitude characterized by listening) in apprehending anything of the divine nature. Thus, Gregory Nazianzen observes that Paul, who had ascended into the third heaven, talks of 'the wealth and depth of God' (Rom. 11:33), in acknowledgement of the incomprehensibility of God's judgements; that David, who had similarly approached God, calls God's judgement a 'great abyss' fathomless by sense (Ps. 36 (35):6 (7)) . . . 'too wonderful' . . . 'too excellent' for him 'to be able to grasp' (Ps. 139 (138):6). But it is the lives of Abraham and Moses who best exemplify these insights. Gregory of Nyssa's *Life of Moses* structures Moses' ascent of Mount Sinai by examining the three theophanies in which Moses encounters the unknowable God: first, at the Burning Bush, where God is revealed as 'the really real', *to ontos on* (Greek) or *Idipsum* (Latin), 'I am who I am' (or in the LXX 'I am He who is') (Exod. 3:1–14); secondly, in the 'thick darkness [*gnophos*/cloud] where God was' (Exod. 20:21); thirdly, in his request to see God's face (Exod. 33:23). All three prove to be theophanies in the sense that they reveal a God who is above anything that human senses or intellect can grasp: the nearer Moses comes to God the more he is made aware of his ultimate transcendence. As Gregory puts it, 'the further the mind advances and the greater and more perfect its attention to, and knowledge of, the realm of reality becomes, the nearer, in fact, that it draws close to contemplation (*theoria*), so much the more is it aware of the unavailability of the divine nature to human knowledge . . . it is precisely in this that true knowledge of what is sought consists, and precisely in this that seeing consists, that is in not

---

[94] E.g. *Confessions*, 10.
[95] *Theological Orations*, 2 (28) 22 (Williams and Wickham, 53–4); *Oration* 44.11 (Daley, 155–6).
[96] *Theological Orations*, 1 (28) 9 (Williams and Wickham, 43–4).

seeing, because we seek what lies beyond all knowledge, shrouded in incomprehensibility in all directions, as it were by some cloud'.[97] As we shall see below, this meant for Gregory that human life here, as well as hereafter, was characterized by an endless, insatiable desire for, and stretching out towards, the infinite and eternally unknowable God: we can never see his face, but only his back (Exod. 33:23).[98]

Gregory of Nyssa's account of Abraham's journey in *Against Eunomius*—his physical journey from his homeland and people into a foreign land, and his spiritual journey from the sensible perception of God's beauty in His creation to the intellectual perception of God's eternal power and goodness, to his attempt to contemplate God, the primal beauty, Himself—is one that similarly concludes that the journey not only progresses in faith, but ends in faith. Even though Abraham 'grasped as much of God as it was possible for our limited and frail power at its most exalted to comprehend',[99] Gregory comments that, 'He came out, not knowing where he was going (Hebrews 11:8), incapable of grasping the name of the one he loved.'[100] Abraham therefore concludes, like Moses, that what we know of God is what we do not and cannot know: 'This he laid down as an infallible and clear sign that we know God—the conviction that God is superior to, and higher than, every semantic marker'[101] . . . 'that there is no other way of drawing close to God except through the medium of faith, that of itself knits together into one the searching mind and the incomprehensible nature'.[102] Abraham, too, then, is described as never achieving his goal, but as using every stage of his journey as a stepping stone in order to 'stretch out to what lay ahead' (Phil. 3:13);[103] he walks forever by faith, not by sight. The lesson for Eunomius is that we need to be 'believers instead of logicians'.[104]

'At the still point of the turning world'[105]

The idea of faith 'knitting together into one the searching mind and the incomprehensible nature' is one that bears further reflection: it describes the way in which human beings bridge the ontological divide between themselves

---

[97] *Life of Moses*, 2. 162–3 (Meredith, 105).

[98] *Life of Moses*, 2.233 (Meredith, 106). God replies to Moses' request to see his face in Exod. 33:23: 'My back parts you will see, but my face you will not see.'

[99] *Against Eunomius*, 2. 86 (Meredith, 89). See Frances Young's (1993), 271–2, discussion of this passage, to which I am indebted here.

[100] *Against Eunomius*, 2.87 (Meredith, 89).

[101] *Against Eunomius*, 2. 88 (Meredith, 89–90).

[102] *Against Eunomius*, 2.91 (Meredith, 90).

[103] *Against Eunomius*.

[104] Gregory Nazianzen, *Theological Oration*, 3 (29) 8 (Williams and Wickham, l).

[105] T. S. Eliot, 'Burnt Norton', *Four Quartets* (1944), 15 and 17.

and their Creator, not by attempting to capture Him by reason, but, rather, by attending to what He reveals of Himself, and then by constantly stretching out towards what remains ultimately unknowable. These are the two aspects of faith: attending to God and then stretching out towards Him. I would like to argue that attention is characterized by a momentary stillness; stretching out by endless movement. Both are held together in the tension created by God's infinite incomprehensibility, for the stillness, insofar as it can exist, is always poised above His unfathomable transcendence, which will inexorably draw it away from remaining fixed, into an endless search.

These two aspects of faith are also the two characteristic aspects of listening: we must first attend to (or, as Polanyi puts it, 'attend from') what addresses us, and then be aware that what we hear is but an image or sign which invites further exploration. Another way of putting this is that listening, like faith, is always a matter of relation and participation: neither are ever fixed or static, but both are characterized by their openness to the other, and allow for change, or even transformation.

We encountered all of these ideas most sharply when we reflected on the nature of Christian prayer in Chapter 6, for here, the one who is attended to, or listened to, is God. We discovered that the very process of listening to God is in itself transformative, for in order to listen to God—or, indeed, to anyone else—we need to align ourselves with, and as it were, 'dwell with', or accommodate ourselves to, them. As Gregory insists in his *Theological Orations*, in order to do theology, or attend to the divine, the theologian must attempt to purify themselves, be free from distraction, and achieve stillness.[106] In other words, temporal, bodily temptations should be put aside—'our undisciplined eyes, our greedy ears, our immoderate talk, our wandering thoughts'[107]—and the mind prepared to listen to the divine and receive its impress or image unobscured. The Eunomians, in contrast, with their idle 'chatter on theology and clever deployment of arguments'[108] are wholly unprepared: they think they can speak without having first listened, and therefore simply hear their own voices and make an idol of their own dialectic, rather than hearing God.

In this sense, theology, or talk about God, is first and foremost an attending to, or listening to, God: 'If you are a theologian, you will pray truly; if you pray truly, you will be a theologian' as Evagrius has it.[109] Theology is possible for fallen human beings and created human reason, because God first addresses us, reveals Himself to us, and graciously descends to speak to us, both outwardly and inwardly: the theologian is one who needs to practise listening. As we saw at the very end of Chapter 6, in relation to the practice of silent prayer, or prayer of

---

[106] *Theological Orations*, 1 (27) 3 (Williams and Wickham, 27).
[107] *Theological Orations*, 1 (27) 7 (Williams and Wickham, 30).
[108] *Theological Orations*, 1 (27) 3 (Williams and Wickham, 27).
[109] Evagrius, *On Prayer*, 61 (Tugwell, 18).

the heart, the highest form of listening consists in attending from, or dwelling in, God—in silent receptiveness to God's presence in the mind or heart.

It is this which I think best describes what Gregory calls 'stillness'. When Moses entered the dark cloud God commanded him to 'be still and know that I am God'. This episode represents a moment of true listening, in which Moses is able to be receptive to the one who is present and who addresses him, and to hear what human ears cannot—the transcendent God. As we have seen, Augustine and Monnica's 'audition' of God at Ostia is a similar episode, in which, having ascended, like Moses, to leave behind the tumult and noise of the senses, they enter silence and are able to hear God Himself.[110]

There are some pieces of music which have this effect—I am thinking most especially of such works as Arvo Pärt's *Spiegel im Spiegel* or Bill Evans' *Peace Piece*, in which a very simple, pared-down melody, played in constant repetition,[111] resonates in the mind of the listener to build up a sense of immanence, of being in the moment, in stillness, in suspended animation, as it were, and thereby opens up a sense of the timeless, the infinite, the unmoving, and the transcendent.[112] Mystical ascents and journeys often end in the same way.

As we saw in Chapter 5 in relation to the preacher, having listened to God, the theologian, or, more precisely, the one who prays, can then mediate and communicate what continues to resonate within their minds and hearts to the minds of others, so that they, in turn, can, as it were, listen to their listening; hear the echoes of their encounter with God; attend to the music of the divine composer resonating in his arranger, or of the divine musician resonating in his instrument. Like Plato's poets, their divine inspiration or possession makes what they say not a matter of art (*techne*), but of divine power (*Theia dunamei*); they are like a magnetic field attracting whoever hears them to the source of their words.[113]

> **We shall not cease from exploration**
> **And the end of all our exploring**
> **Will be to arrive where we started**
> **And know the place for the first time.**[114]

However, what Elijah, Abraham, Moses, and Paul, or, for that matter, Gregory of Nyssa, Augustine, and Monnica, heard or saw at the height of their ascents

---

[110] *Confessions*, 9. 10.25.
[111] This is usually referred to as Pärt's 'tintinnabuli style'. Bareza (2011), 3, describes it thus: 'two voices moving homophonically in a predetermined relationship. The melodic first voice moves mostly step-wise within a diatonic scale; the second voice generally alternates among the three pitches of the triad. Thus, the diatonic scale and a broken triad form the basis of this style.'
[112] Bareza (2011) refers to the idea of *nepsis* or watchfulness, in the Orthodox tradition, as characteristic of this stillness in the present. She cites Ware (1979), 153.
[113] Plato, *Ion*, 533–4 (Winterbottom (1972), 4–5).
[114] T. S. Eliot, 'Little Gidding', *Four Quartets* (1944), 48.

toward God, is never something they can clearly articulate in words, or fix, so as to make it a matter of permanent contemplation. Rather, as they descend and fall back to an even more acute sense of their own temporal, mutable, fallen humanity, what they take with them is an overwhelming conviction of God's majesty, a dizzying glimpse of his transcendence, an awed sense of his unfathomable depths, and a yearning for his infinite greatness. In short, what they encountered was not something that they could encompass by either their senses or their reason, but was rather something that could only be expressed in terms of images or analogies which remained open to their ineffable archetype.[115] If the first aspect of faith or listening is attention, the second is an endless stretching out or exploration. In the last chapter of *The Tacit Dimension* Polanyi uses the metaphor of exploration when he attempts to summarize the nature of tacit knowing: the limitless and inexplicable profundity of both other people and the world around us means that knowledge of them is always open to further exploration and deeper discovery. He urges that, in our search for knowledge, we should become 'a society of explorers'.[116]

Confronted by God's 'deep but dazzling darkness',[117] and with God's words to Moses resonating in his ears: 'My face thou shalt not see', Gregory of Nyssa similarly observes that there is no end to our stretching out, or *epektasis*; that the infinite God can never be comprehended by finite creatures, but that our perfection consists in endlessly seeking and desiring Him.[118] Towards the end of the *Life of Moses* he expresses this in Platonic terms—in terms of beauty: 'the true vision of God consists in this, in never reaching satiety of the desire. We ought always to look through the things that we can see and still be on fire with the desire to see more. So let there be no limit to curtail our growth in our journey upward to God. This is because no limit to the beautiful has been found nor can any satiety cut short the progress of the soul in its desire for the beautiful.'[119]

The word *epektasis* is borrowed from Paul, from Philippians 3:13, 'stretching out (Greek) to the things that are before . . .'. We may remember that the same text was used by Augustine in *Confessions*, Book 11 in a similar manner—to describe the way in which temporal, mutable human beings resist fragmentation and distraction by comprehending time, and God's words and actions in time, within the mind—remembering the past, attending to the present, and '"extended" towards "those things which are before" (Phil. 3:13)'.[120] For Augustine, as for Gregory, stretching out (*epektasis/extensio*) is characteristic of the creature distended in time, in contrast to the 'unchangeably eternal'[121]

---

[115] Cf. *Life of Moses*, 2.231 (Meredith, 106).   [116] The title of ch. 3.
[117] Henry Vaughan, 'The Night' (Rudrum, 1976).
[118] *Life of Moses*, 2.162–5 (Meredith, 105–6).
[119] *Life of Moses*, 2. 239 (Meredith, 107–8).
[120] *Confessions*, 11.30.40.   [121] *Confessions*, 11.31.41.

God, for whom past, present, and future are one, and who suffers, as Augustine puts it, no 'tension between past and future in your activity'.

We must be still and still moving
Into another intensity
For a further union, a deeper communion[122]

The state of tension in which all temporal, mutable creatures are held, between the past, the present, and the future; memory, attention, and expectation, can, as we have observed earlier in this chapter, be both a negative and a positive one. If the creature fails to remember, attend to, and stretch out towards the 'unchangeably eternal' God (or, as Gregory puts it, to be purified, disciplined, and still), their attention will simply be fragmented and distracted by His mutable, temporal creation. If, however, they hold God's words and actions within their memory, attend to them in the present, and stretch out towards his limitless majesty, they can be formed, reformed, and transformed in his image. The latter, as we have seen, is a matter of faith, open to infinite developments—because God forever transcends human reason and can only be grasped indirectly, through images, echoes, and resonances. We have argued that early Christian listening was understood and practised in precisely this context: remembering God's words and works in the past, attending to them in the present, and stretching out towards their inexpressible archetype and signification. Voices, images, echoes, and resonances were attended to and their signification endlessly explored.

We have identified two aspects of listening: stillness (or attention) and movement (or stretching out). But, as we have seen, even in the case of those who have ascended the heights of contemplation, stillness or attention is never more than momentary: it is as fleeting as the present moment; a transitory glimpse of what far transcends human knowing, and thus almost immediately gives way to stretching out. Listening happens within the tension created by these two movements. In his work entitled, simply, *Listening* (*À l'écoute*),[123] the French philosopher, Jean Luc Nancy, captures this necessary tension well by reverting to another distinction which we have frequently had occasion to mention but have, as yet, not elucidated: the distinction between listening (*écouter*) and hearing (*entendre*). Hearing (*entendre*), for Nancy, is characteristic of the philosopher, who claims to possess understanding (*entente*), but, in making this claim, he suggests that the philosopher has failed to listen (*écouter*), or 'neutralizes' listening (*écoute*) (1). Thus, whereas the work of the philosopher is usually described in such terms as, to 'make

---

[122] T. S. Eliot, 'East Coker', *Four Quartets* (1944), 27.
[123] Nancy (2007) (original French edition, 2002).

overtly evident' (3) or to 'make sense' (6), the one who listens is concerned with what is more internal, less straightforwardly evident, and with what does not 'make sense' but which rather resounds and resonates for the senses. This prompts Nancy to ask, 'Why, in the case of the ear, is there withdrawal and turning inward, a making *resonant*, but, in the case of the eye, there is manifestation and display, a making *evident*?' (3).Whereas the verb 'to hear' (*entendre*) can also mean 'to understand' (*comprendre*), the verb 'to listen' (*écouter*), he observes, is less fixed and more uncertain. It has to do with 'a tension, an intention, and an attention . . . a concern, a curiosity or an anxiety (5), a straining forward to a possible meaning . . . one that is not immediately accessible' (5–6). Thus, for Nancy, 'to be listening is always to be on the edge of meaning' (7).

Nancy dwells on the temporality of sound and its resonance: unlike the philosophic–scientific understanding of chronological time, in which time is measured in an ordered succession, like a point on a line, what he calls 'sonorous time', or 'space time', 'is hollowed out . . . envelops or separates. stretches out or contracts . . . it opens up a space that is its own, the very spreading out of its resonance, its expansion and its reverberation (13) . . . here time becomes space (14)'.[124] Whereas visual presence, like chronological time, is already there, immediate and graspable, listening takes place only through this 'sonorous event', in the opening up of time and space and the resonances it creates (15–16). It is the difference, he further explains, between 'manifest-ation' and 'evocation'; between bringing the presence of something to light, and summoning, evoking, invoking, or calling presence to itself. The latter is a matter of memory and anticipation, the one who evokes remaining 'suspended and straining between the two' (20).

What we have called attention, or stillness, then, is, in Nancy's words, 'a question of going back to, or opening oneself up to, the resonance of being, or to being as resonance' (21); and what we have called stretching out, or movement, is the opening up and hollowing out, expansion and contraction of sonorous time—creating its own space in which to endlessly resonate in infinite shaping and reshaping. For the listener, there is none of the rational certainty or resolution of the philosopher, but rather an attention to sound, and an endless tension, or stretching out, which evokes and call forth its echoes and resonances, but can never fix or capture them.

In more familiar language: listening is a way for temporal, mutable human beings to recollect together their temporal experience of hearing sound (which involves memory, attention, and anticipation) into an atten-tive present, which forever stretches out towards the eternity of what

---

[124] He is quoting Wagner's *Parsifal*.

transcends human knowing. In more theological language: in the tension created between attending to God's words and works and stretching out towards his eternal being, listening both forms and transforms the mind and heart of the listener by enabling them first to encounter God—not just as truth, but also as the beautiful and the good (*anamnesis*),—and then to desire to discover their archetype through imitating Him (*mimesis*), through discipline and purification (*askesis*), and, above all, through stretching out towards Him in longing love.

In his *Inscriptions on the Psalms* Gregory of Nyssa makes a similar distinction between chronological time, which has to do with history and the narrative of salvation, and the spiritual, inward meaning of a passage whereby the heart is reformed by the eternal Word. The order of the Psalms, he observes, clearly does not follow the sequence of history, but is rather an order intended to form and reform human beings in God's image. Like a piece of rock being carved by a sculptor, there is indeed a necessary order whereby the rock gradually takes the form which the sculptor desires: by methodically hewing, hollowing, polishing, and smoothing he eventually achieves a finished work. It is precisely in this way that the Word of God works through Scripture to form and reform our nature into the divine likeness, separating it from evil, stripping off excesses, scraping and polishing the understanding, in order to recover the form of Christ in us.[125] It is this order which the Psalter follows, since the aim of the Spirit 'is not to teach us mere history, but to form our souls in accordance with God through virtue'. In the process, the Spirit operates like the ultimate arranger or improviser, choosing whatever tools are necessary and appropriate, not in order to follow a historical sequence, but rather to hallow out the soul in virtue and form the divine image in it. This is very much the process we saw early Christian preachers adopting in their approach to Scripture; following the prompt of its author, they clearly felt free to engage in imaginative transpositions, variations, and improvisations on its images and types in order to form the minds of their listeners according to the eternal Word. Ultimately, it is not the form of words, or their ordered sequence that matter, but the way in which they function to bring about the formation of the image of God in the soul through the formation of an ordered will.

---

[125] *Inscriptions on the Psalms*, 2.9.131–7 (Heine, 163–5). Cf. 2. 13.178 (Heine, 177–8); 2.13.194 (Heine, 184); 2.14.223 (Heine, 193). Gregory no doubt has Plotinus, *Ennead*, 1.6.4–5 (MacKenna I.82–3) in mind here, where the same image is used for the moral and intellectual purification of the soul.

'YOU ARE GREAT, LORD, AND HIGHLY TO BE PRAISED'
(PS. 47:2; *CONFESSIONS*, 1.1.1)

The preacher first prayed (or listened to God) before he spoke; he was an *orator* before he became a *dictor*. In the same way, the early Christian listener first listened to God before they praised Him; they were an *auditor* before they became a *laudator*. It seems that the natural outcome of listening to God—of attending to and stretching out towards Him—was an expression, or better, a confession, of praise. As Augustine puts it in *On Christian Doctrine*, 'while nothing really worthy of God can be said about him, he has accepted the homage of human voices, and has wished us to rejoice in praising him with our words'.[126] Why praise? Because it was the instinctive response of the creature to the benevolence of the Creator; because it best gave expression to an overwhelming sense of God's greatness and majesty; because it naturally gave voice to the hearer's stretching out towards the incomprehensible, infinite God? It was all of these—and more. Praise wells up from the heart and soul, rather than the mind or reason; it attempts to express the inexpressible in sound; it gives free reign to the imagination; allows for—indeed invites—repetition; expresses and prompts imitation or *mimesis*; inspires improvisation and extemporization in breaking through set forms in order to evoke its transcendent object. Repeated 'allelujahs', sinuous melismas, rending ululations all nudged the worshipper beyond the conventions of language in order to find a means to express the inexpressible.[127] Indeed, wordless or non-verbal sounds often proved the only way of expressing what welled up within the heart—in cries of jubilation, groans of sadness, sighs of longing, the wailing of confession, weeping of grief, or laughter of joy. Such sounds come directly from the heart and soul and, being heard, directly affected the heart and soul.[128] To 'sing with jubilation' is, Augustine observes, to 'sing ineffably';[129] it is to give voice to otherwise inexpressible rejoicing, 'What does "shout with joy" (Ps. 65.1) suggest? Burst out into a joyful noise, if you cannot find words to express what you feel. Shouting does not necessarily imply words. We hear people rejoicing simply by making a noise, like the sound of a heart labouring to bring forth into its voice its happiness over what it has conceived,

---

[126] *On Christian Doctrine*, 1.6.6 (Robertson, 10–11).

[127] *Inscriptions on the Psalms*, 2.7.69 (Heine, 141–2): 'There is, therefore, the use of *alleluia* as a mystical exhortation which awakens our hearing to the praise of God, so that "praise the Lord" would be the meaning of this word. For in those parts of holy scripture in which this term which means "praise the Lord" is added, such is the meaning signified in the Hebrew scriptures by the word *alleluia*.'

[128] In one sense, polyphony has this effect: there are so many separate voices in counterpoint that it often simply becomes a wave of non-verbal sound. Of course, this is why it had its critics, but this very aspect proves most effective in enabling it to reach towards the transcendent God.

[129] *Expositions on the Psalms*, 32.ii.2 (WSA III.15 392).

something that cannot be put into words.'[130] Indeed, Augustine seems to suggest that after the resurrection we will say 'amen' and 'allelujah', not in the transient sounds of words, but with the affection of the soul—*non sonis transeuntibus sed affectu animi.*[131]

When the fathers tentatively turn their attention to the life to come, and began to imagine what it might be like—on the basis of Scripture, but, above all, from their experience of the liturgy, where heaven was believed to come to earth in the sacraments of baptism and the Eucharist—they are unanimous that, whereas faith and hope will no longer be necessary in the life to come, love will remain. For Gregory of Nyssa this is the endless stretching out of *epektasis*: 'At this time the understanding which proceeds by guesswork concerning knowledge is idle, and our activity which is concerned with hope is also idle. Both are replaced by that condition which is inexpressible, inconceivable, and better than all understanding, which eye has not seen, nor ear heard, nor has the human heart received.'[132] For Augustine it is the endless praise with which heaven will resonate, when the elect, joining the eternal chorus of the angelic host, will be still, and express their love for God whom they now know and see: 'There we shall be still and see; we shall see and we shall love; we shall love and we shall praise. Behold what will be, in the end, without end! For what is our end but to reach that kingdom which has no end?'[133] Even though Gregory thinks that God will never be fully seen, he, like Augustine, also teaches that what will remain in the life to come is love expressed in praise: 'all things,' he writes, 'will praise God in harmony when they have equally acquired immutability in respect to evil ... and have lifted up together the sound of praise to his greatness, as if with the loud blast of a trumpet. Whenever the whole creation, consisting of all things superior and all things inferior, has been united in one choir, both the spiritual creation and that which has been separated and has been at a distance on account of sin will produce the good sound, like a cymbal, from our concord. Whenever humanity unites with the angels ... then the praise of every breathing creature occurs, which continues the gratitude forever and causes the blessedness to abound, through increase, to perpetuity ...'[134]

---

[130] *Expositions on the Psalms*, 65. 2 (WSA III.17 286).
[131] Cited by Conybeare (2012a).
[132] *Inscriptions on the Psalms*, 1.9.123. Cf. 2.24.221 (Heine, 123, 192): 'The whole successive sequence of the psalm describes the recalling of human nature. The summation of this victory against the rival is indelible, like the memorial of a stela of God's love for mankind, which is set forth to all creation as the basis of praise. Wherefore he says in the last lines of the psalm, looking to this stela, "In God will I praise the word, in the Lord will I praise speech, in God I have hoped."'
[133] *City of God*, 22.30 (Bettenson, 1091).
[134] *Inscriptions on the Psalms*, 1.9.121-2 (Heine, 122-3). Gregory maintains that the first humans used to sing in chorus with the angelic powers before the Fall put an end to this (*Inscriptions on the Psalms* 2.6.60).

Early Christian literature was written by theologians; by those who first prayed, or listened to God, and only then spoke or wrote. As readers of their work, we become privileged listeners to their listening, and are invited to share their response. This response rarely takes the form of rational reflection or argument (though it can, if necessary, be articulated in this way against heretics and detractors) but is most often expressed in confession—a confession of the author's unworthiness as a fallen human being and a confession of praise before the awe-inspiring mystery of the transcendent, ineffable God— followed by an attempt to share their faith in teaching and preaching. On overhearing their prayer and listening to their teaching and preaching, their audiences were effectively drawn into their conversations with God and impelled to make their confessions their own; to imitate their abject sense of unworthiness as well as their desire to find a means to extol the ineffable majesty of God. They were also initiated into the faith through the preacher's exposition of its rules and creeds, stories and narratives, as well as his infinite variations and improvisations on it in preaching and teaching upon Scripture. In the process, early Christian listeners were first of all purified, disciplined, and sealed with the faith, so that they were able to attend to (from) its transcendent object by being reformed in His image; but they were also caught up and stretched out in the praise which has no end, to listen and to respond to the eternal, transcendent God who can never be fully captured by human language and images, but who can only be encountered in imaginative explor- ation and exploitation of these images, in the silence of wordless prayer, or in ecstatic, melismatic, wordless praise. This is what early Christian writers, teachers, and preachers made possible for their congregations, make possible for their future readers—if we are prepared to listen to them, rather than simply read and analyse them—and will continue in the voices of the host of heaven. If one follows Augustine, God will be seen in the life to come; if one follows Gregory of Nyssa, the infinite God can never be seen, but whatever may be the case, He will certainly be heard to resonate in an endless response of praise. Listening, like love, will endure.

Bibliography

Texts

Abbreviations

ACW	Ancient Christian Writers (New York: Paulist)
ANCL	Ante-Nicene Christian Library
BA	Bibliothèque Augustinienne
CCL	Corpus Christianorum, Series Latina (Turnhout: Brepols)
CPG	Clavis Patrum Graecorum, ed. M. Geerard, 5 vols (Turnhout: Brepols)
CSEL	Corpus Scriptorum Ecclesiasticorum Latinorum (Vienna: Tempsky)
CWS	Classics of Western Spirituality (New York: Paulist)
Daley	Brian Daley, *Gregory of Nazianzus* (London: Routledge, 2006)
FC	The Fathers of the Church (Washington, DC: Catholic University of America)
GCS	Griechischen Christlichen Schriftsteller (Berlin: J.C. Hinrich'sche Buchhandlung)
LCC	Library of Christian Classics (London: SCM)
Loeb	Loeb Classical Library (Cambridge, MA: Harvard University Press and London: Heinemann)
Mayer and Allen	Wendy Mayer and Pauline Allen, *John Chrysostom* (London: Routledge, 2000)
Mayer and Neil	Wendy Mayer and Bronwen Neil, *The Cult of the Saints: Select Homilies and Letters* (Crestwood, NY: St Vladimir's Seminary, 2006)
NPNF	Nicene and Post-Nicene Fathers, Series 1–2
PG	*Patrologia Graeca*, ed. J. P. Migne
PL	*Patrologia Latina*, Cursus Completus, ed. J. P. Migne
SC	Sources Chrétiennes (Paris: Cerf)
Sykes	Stuart Sykes (ed.), *Tertullian, Cyprian and Origen: On the Lord's Prayer* (Crestwood, NY: St Vladimir's Seminary, 2004)
WSA	*The Works of Saint Augustine: A Translation for the 21st Century*, ed. John E. Rotelle (Hyde Park, NY: New City Press)

The Revised Standard Version of the Bible has been used for quotations.

Anonymous

Rhetorica ad Herrenium, tr. H. Caplan, Loeb Classical Library (London: Heinemann, 1954).

Ambrose

On the Duties of the Clergy
Ambrose: De Officiis, vol. 1: *Introduction, Text and Translation*, ed. Ivor J. Davidson (Oxford: Oxford University Press, 2001).
De officiis ministrorum, CCL 15.

Explanation of the Creed for Those about to be Baptised
Explanation of the Creed for Those about to be Baptised, ed. R. H. Connolly, Text and Studies X (Cambridge: Cambridge University Press, 1952).
Explanatio Symboli ad Initiandos, CSEL 73: 1–12.

On the Sacraments
'On the Sacraments', in Edward Yarnold, *Awe-Inspiring Rites of Initiation* (2nd edn, Collegeville, MN: Liturgical Press, 1994), 99–127.
De Sacramentis: St Ambrose on the Sacraments, ed. Henry Chadwick, Studies in Eucharistic Faith and Practice (London: Mowbray, 1960).
De Sacramentis, SC 25.

On Virgins
Ramsey, Boniface, *Ambrose* (London: Routledge, 1997).
De Uirginibus, PL 16. 197–244.

Andrew of Crete

'Oration on the Annunciation of the Supremely Holy Lady, our Theotokos', in Mary Cunningham (ed. and tr.), *Wider Than Heaven: Eighth-century Homilies on the Mother of God* (New York: St Vladimir's Seminary, 2008), pp. 197–219.
CPG 8174.

Aristotle

De Anima, tr. and intro. W. D. Ross (Oxford: Oxford University Pres, 1961).
Rhetoric, tr. J. H. Freese, Loeb Classical Library (London: Heinemann, 1959).

Athanasius

Letter to Marcellinus
Athanasius: The Life of Antony and the Letter to Marcellinus, tr. R. C. Gregg, Classics of Western Spirituality (Mahwah, NJ: Paulist, 1980).
PG 27.11–46.

Augustine

Against the Academics
ACW 12; FC 1.
Contra Academicos, CCL 29.

On the Greatness of the Soul
FC 4.
De animae quantitate, CSEL 89.

City of God
City of God, tr. Henry Bettenson (Harmondsworth: Penguin, 1972).
De ciuitate Dei, CCL 47–8.

On Christian Doctrine
Augustine: On Christian Doctrine, tr. D. W. Robertson, Library of Liberal Arts 80
   (Indianapolis: Bobbs-Merrill, 1958).
De doctrina Christiana, CCL 32.

Confessions
Chadwick, Henry, *Augustine: Confessions* (Oxford: Oxford University Press, 1991).
Solignac, A. *Bibliothèque Augustinienne*, vols 13–14 (Paris: Études Augustiniennes, 1962).

On the Creed, to Catechumens (Sermon, 398)
WSA III.10.
De symbolo ad catechumenos, CCL 46.

Expositions of the Psalms
WSA III.14–17.
Enarrationes in Psalmos, CCL 38–40.

Enchiridion
LCC 8.
CCL 46.

Epistles
WSA II.1–3.
Letter 130, FC 18.
Letter 160, FC 18.
Epistulae, PL 33.

On Faith and Works
WSA I.10.
De fide et operibus, CSEL 41.

On Faith and the Creed
WSA I.8.
De fide et symbolo, CSEL 41.

Literal Commentary on Genesis
ACW 41–2.
De Genesi ad Litteram, CSEL 28.1.

On Genesis against the Manichees
FC 84.
De Genesi aduersus Manicheos, CSEL 91.

On Music
FC 4.
De musica, PL 32.

On the Sermon on the Mount
FC 11.
De sermone Domini in monte, CCL 35.

De catechizandis rudibus, CCL 46.
Instructing Beginners in the Faith
Instructing Beginners in the Faith, tr. R. Canning, WSA I.10 (Hyde Park, NY: New City Press, 2006).

On Order (Divine Providence and the Problem of Evil)
FC 5.
De Ordine, CCL 29.

Sermons
WSA III.1–11.
Sermons, 212–65, FC 38.
Sermones, CCL 41.

Soliloquies
FC 5.
Soliloquia, CSEL 89.

Tractates on the Gospel of John
WSA III.12 (for Homilies 1–40); FC 78, 79, 88, 90, 92.
In Johannis euangelium tractatus, CCL 36.

Homilies on the First Epistle of John
WSA III.14.
In epistulam Joannis ad Parthos tractatus, SC 75.

The Teacher
LCC 6.
De Magistro, CCL 29.

The Trinity
WSA I.5.
De Trinitate, CCL 50/50A.

Basil of Caesarea

On the Holy Spirit
On the Holy Spirit, tr. David Anderson (New York: St Vladimir's Seminary, 1980).
PG 32.

Letters
Letter, 207.
FC 28.
tr. Roy J. Deferrari, Loeb Classical Library, 4 vols (London Heinemann 1970–).

Cassian

Conferences
Ramsey, Boniface, *John Cassian: The Conferences*, ACW 47 (New York: Paulist, 1997).
CSEL 13.

Chrysostom

On Lazarus
PG 48.991.

On Saint Barlaam
Mayer and Neil, 177–89.
PG 50.675–82.

On Saint Eustathius
Mayer and Neil, 49–62.
PG 50.597–606.

On Eutropius
Meyer and Allen, 132–9.
PG 52.391–6.

On Saint Meletius
Meyer and Allen, 39–48.
PG 50.515–20.

Homily on the Holy Martyrs
Mayer and Neil, 217–26.
PG 50.705–12.

New Homily 1 Homily Delivered after the Remains of the Martyrs
Mayer and Allen, 85–92.
PG 63. 467–72.

New Homily 7 Against the Games and the Theatres
Mayer and Allen, 118–25.
PG 56. 263–70.

New Homily 10 On: 'My Father's Working Still' (John 5:17)
Mayer and Allen, 143–7.
PG 63. 511–16.

Homily 7 On Colossians
Mayer and Allen, 73–84.
Tou en hagiois patros hemon Ioannou archiepiskopou Konstantinoupoleos tou chrysos-tomou hypomnemata eis tas pros Philippesious kai Kolossaeis kai Thessalonikeis epistolas, ed. F. Field (Oxford: Oxford University Press, 1855), pp. 241–52.

Homily 3 On Acts 1:12
Mayer and Allen, 177–83.
PG 60.33–42.

Homily 11 On Ephesians 4:4–7
Mayer and Allen, 59–72.
PG 62.79–86.

Homily 21 On 1 Corinthians 9:1–12
Mayer and Allen, 168–76.
PG 61.169–80.

On: I Opposed Him to His Face (Gal. 2:11)
Mayer and Allen, 140–2.
PG 51. 371–88.

Oration 1 Against the Jews
Mayer and Allen, 148–67.
PG 48.843–56.

On His Return
Mayer and Allen, 98–103.
Wenger, A. 'L'homélie de saint Jean Chrysostome "à son retour d'Asie"', *Revue des études byzantines*, 1961, pp. 110–23.

Baptismal Instructions
ACW 31.
SC 50.

Homily on Eleazer and the Seven Boys
Mayer and Neil, 119–34.
For a reconstruction of the Greek text see note in Meyer and Neil (2006), 119–20.

On the Holy Martyr Ignatius
Meyer and Neil, 101–17.
PG 50.587–96.

On the Priesthood
On the Priesthood tr. Graham Neville (New York: St Vladimir's Seminary, 1996).
PL 48.

Cicero

De Oratore, tr. E. W. Sutton and H. Rackham, Loeb Classical Library, 2 vols (London: Heinemann, 1942; 1948).
Brutus, tr. G. L. Hendrickson, Loeb Classical Library (London: Heinemann, 1939; rev. edn, 1962).
De Inventione, tr. H. M. Hubbell, Loeb Classical Library (London: Heinemann, 1949; 1960).

Cyril of Jerusalem

Procatechesis
Edward Yarnold, *Cyril of Jerusalem* (London: Routledge, 2000), pp. 79–86.
Cyrilli Hierosolymorum Opera Omnia, ed. W. K. Reischl and J. Rupp (Munich, 1848–60).

Catecheses
Edward Yarnold, *Cyril of Jerusalem* (London: Routledge, 2000), pp. 87–168.
Cyrilli Hierosolymorum Opera Omnia, ed. W. K. Reischl and J. Rupp (Munich, 1848–60).

Mystagogic Catecheses
Edward Yarnold, *Cyril of Jerusalem* (London: Routledge, 2000), pp. 169–82.
Frank Leslie Cross (ed.) *Lectures on the Christian Sacraments: The Procatechesis and The Five Mystagogical Catecheses*, Texts for Students 51 (London: SPCK, 1951).
SC 126.

Cyprian

To Quirinus
FC 3.
Ad Quirinum, CCL 3.

On the Unity of the Catholic Church
FC 36.
De Unitate Catholicae Ecclesiae, CSEL 3.

On the Lord's Prayer
Sykes, 65–93.
De Dominica Oratione, CCL 3A.

Eusebius

The History of the Church, tr. G. A. Williamson; rev. and ed. A. Louth (London: Penguin, 1989).
Eusebius, tr. Kirsopp Lake and J. E. L. Oulton, Loeb Classical Library, 2 vols (Cambridge MA: Harvard University Press;, and London: Heinemann, 1926–32).

Evagrius

On Prayer
Simon Tugwell, *Evagrius Ponticus: Praktikos and On Prayer* (Oxford: Faculty of Theology, 1987).
Simon Tugwell, *Evagrius Ponticus: De oratione* (Oxford: Faculty of Theology, 1981).

Germanos of Constantinople

Oration on the Annunciation of the Supremely Holy Theotokos
Mary Cunningham (ed. and tr.), *Wider Than Heaven: Eighth-century Homilies on the Mother of God*, SVS (New York: St Vladimir's Seminary, 2008).
PG 98.

Gregory of Nyssa

Homily 6 On the Beatitudes
Antony Meredith (tr. and commentary), *Gregory of Nyssa* (London: Routledge, 1999), pp. 91–9.

De Beatitudinibus, ed. Johannes F. Callahan, Gregorii Nysseni Opera VII (Leiden: Brill, 1992).

On the Lord's Prayer
The Lord's Prayer, tr. Hilda Graef, ACW 18 (New York: Paulist, 1954), pp. 21–71.
De Oratione Dominica, ed. Johannes F. Callahan, Gregorii Nysseni Opera VII (Leiden: Brill, 1992).

Inscriptions on the Psalms
Ronald E. *Heine, Gregory of Nyssa's Treastise on the Inscriptions of the Psalms* (Oxford: Oxford University Press, 1995).
In inscriptiones Psalmorum, ed. J. McDonough, Gregorii Nysseni Opera V (Leiden: Brill, 1962).

Against Eunomius
Antony Meredith (tr. and commentary), *Gregory of Nyssa* (London: Routledge, 1999).
Contra Eunomium, ed. W. Jaeger, Gregorii Nysseni Opera I and II (Leiden: Brill, 1960).

Life of Moses
Life of Moses, tr., intro. and notes Abraham J. Malherbe and Everett Ferguson, CWS (New York: Paulist, 1978).
Extracts in Antony Meredith, *Gregory of Nyssa* (London: Routledge, 1999), 99–128.
SC 1.

Gregory Nazianzen

Letter 51 To Nicoboulos
Daley, 177–8.
Paul Gallay (ed.), *Gregor Von Nazianz: Briefe*, GCS 53, I. 66–8.

Oration 2
Daley, 56.
SC 247.

Oration 8 Funeral Oration for His Sister Gorgonia
Daley, 64–75.
SC 405, 246–99.

Oration 14 On love of the poor
Daley, 76–98.
PG 35.857–909.

Oration 20 On Theology, and the Appointment of Bishops
Daley, 98–105.
SC 270.

Oration 24
FC 107.
SC 284.

Oration 38 On the Theophany
Daley, 117–27.
SC 358.

Oration 39 On the Holy Lights
Daley, 128–38.
SC 358.

Carmina II.1, 39
'On His Own Verses', Daley 163–5,
Poemata de seipso, PG 37.1329–36.

Carmina II.1, 24–6
'On His Own Verses', Daley, 170–1.
Poemata de seipso, PG 37.1284–6.

Carmina I. 1 (Poemata dogmatica) 35
Daley, 168–9.
PG 37.517.

Carmina I, 1 (Poemata dogmatica) 30
Daley, 166.
PG 37.508–10.

Concerning His Own life
Gregory of Nazianzus: Autobiographical Poems, tr. and ed. Carolinne White
(Cambridge: Cambridge University Press, 1996), pp. 10–153.

Five Theological Orations
Frederick J. Williams, Lionel R. Wickham (trs and eds), *On God and Christ: The Five
    Theological Orations and Two Letters to Cledonius*, SVS (New York: St Vladimir's
    Seminary, 2002).
A. T. Mason (ed.), *Cambridge Patristic Texts* (Cambridge: Cambridge University Press,
    1899).

Irenaeus

Against Heresies
Book 1, ACW 55; Book 3, ACW 64; Books 2, 4, and 5, ANCL 9.
SC 263–4, 293–4, 210–11, 100, 152–3.

Demonstration of the Apostolic Preaching
Iain M. MacKenzie (tr. and commentary), *Irenaeus's Demonstration of the Apostolic
    Preaching: A Theological Commentary and Translation* (Aldershot: Ashgate, 2002).
SC 406 (Greek version of Armenian).

John Damascene

Andrew Louth (ed. and tr.), *On the Divine Images*, SVS (New York: St Vladimir's
    Seminary, 2003).

Die Schriften des Johannes von Damaskos ed. B Kotter, Patristische Texte und Studien 17 (Berlin and New York: De Gruyter, 1969–88).

Lactantius

On the Workmanship of God
FC 54.
De opificio Dei, CCSL 27.

Longinus

On Sublimity
D. A. Russell and Michael Winterbottom (eds), *Classical Literary Criticism* (Oxford: Oxford University Press, 1972), pp. 143–87.
D. A. Russell (ed.) (Oxford: Oxford University Press, 1964).

Martyrdom of Polycarp

Maxwell Staniforth (tr.) and Andrew Louth (rev.), *Early Christian Writings* (London: Penguin, 1987), pp. 125–35.
J. B. Lightfoot (ed.), *The Apostolic Fathers* (Peabody, MA: Hendrickson, 1989).
Michael W. Holmes (text and tr.), *The Apostolic Fathers* (Grand Rapids, MI: Baker, 2007).

Nicetas of Remesiana

Liturgical Singing
FC 7, 65–76.
De utilitate hymnorum: C. H. Turner '*De uigiliis* and *De utilitate hymnorum* based on Cod. Vatic. Reg. lat. 131, saec 3–10', *Journal of Theological Studies*, 24, 233–52.

The Vigils of the Saints
FC 7, 55–64.
De uigiliis seruorum Dei: C. H. Turner '*De uigiliis* and *De utilitate hymnorum* based on Cod. Vatic. Reg. lat. 131, saec 3–10', *Journal of Theological Studies*, 24, 233–52.

Origen

On First Principles
G. W. Butterworth, *Origen on First Principles* (London: SPCK, 1936).
PG 11.

On Prayer
Skyes, 111–14.
De Oratione, ed. Paul Koetschau, Origenes Werke II, GCS 3.

Letter to Gregory
J. W. Trigg, *Origen* (London: Routledge, 1998), pp. 210–13.
SC 148.

Palladius

Lausiac History
ACW 34.
C. Butler, *The Lausiac History of Palladius*, Texts and Studies: Contributions to Biblical and Patristic Literature 6 (Cambridge: Cambridge University Press, 1898; repr. 1904).

Plato

Euthyphro
Euthyphro, tr. H. N. Fowler, Loeb Classical Library (London: Heinemann, 1914; repr. 1971).

Gorgias
tr. Terence Irwin, *Gorgias* (Oxford: Oxford University Press, 1979).
Plato: Gorgias rev., intro., and commentary E. R. Dodds (Oxford: Clarendon Press, 1990).

Ion
D. A. Russell and Michael Winterbottom (eds), *Classical Literary Criticism* (Oxford: Oxford University Press, 1972), pp. 1–13.

Phaedo
tr. David Gallop *Phaedo*, Oxford World Classics (Oxford: Oxford University Press, 2009).
Platonis Opera, ed. E. A. Duke et al., Oxford Classical Texts 1 (Oxford: Clarendon Press, 1995).

Phaedrus
tr. Robin Waterfield, *Phaedrus* Oxford World Classics (Oxford: Oxford University Press, 2009).
Platonis Opera, ed. J. Burnet, Oxford Classical Texts 2 (Oxford: Clarendon Press, 1963).

Republic
tr. Robin Waterfield, *The Republic* Oxford World Classics (Oxford: Oxford University Press, 1993).
Platonis Respublicam, ed. S. R. Slings, Oxford Classical Texts (Oxford: Oxford University Press, 2003).
Plato on Poetry, ed. Penelope Murray, Cambridge Greek and Latin Classics (Cambridge: Cambridge University Press, 1996).

Plotinus

Enneads
Enneads tr. Stephen MacKenna, 5 vols (London and Boston: Medici Society, 1926–30).
Plotini Opera: Enneades, ed. Paul Henry and Hans-Rudolph Schwyzer, Oxford Classical Texts, 3 vols (Oxford: Oxford University Press, 1964, 1977, 1983).

Plutarch

On Listening to Lectures
Plutarch's Moralia, vol. 1, tr. Frank Cole Babbitt, Loeb Classical Library, 197 (London: Heinemann, 1969).
Hillyard, Brian P., *Plutarch, De Audiendo: Text and Commentary* (Salem, NH: Ayer, 1988).

Quintilian

Institutio Oratoria, tr. D. A. Russell, Loeb Classical Library, 5 vols (London: Heinemann, 2001).

Tertullian

On the Lord's Prayer
Sykes, 41–64.
Ernest Evans (text, tr. and notes), *Tertullian's Treatise on the Prayer* (Cambridge: Cambridge University Press, 2011).

Theodore of Mopsuestia

On the Lord's Prayer
A. Mingana (ed. and tr.), *Commentary of Theodore of Mopsuestia on the Lord's Prayer and on the Sacraments of Baptism and the Eucharist*, Woodbrooke Studies 6 (Cambridge: Heffers, 1933).

Bibliography

Secondary Literature
Allen, Pauline (1998), 'The Sixth-Century Greek Homily: A Re-assessment', in Cunningham and Allen (eds), pp. 201–26.
Allen, Pauline and Meyer, Wendy (eds) (2000), *Chrysostom, Carer of Souls* (London: Routledge).
Allen, Pauline, Meyer, Wendy, and Cross, Lawrence (eds) (1999), *Prayer and Spirituality in the Early Church*, 2 vols (Brisbane: Watson Ferguson).
Anderson, George (1993), *The Second Sophistic: A Cultural Phenomenon in the Roman Empire* (London: Routledge).
Ashbrook Harvey, Susan (2006), *Scenting Salvation: Ancient Christianity and the Olfactory Imagination* (Berkeley and Los Angeles: University of California Press).
Auksi, Peter (1995), *Christian Plain Style: The Evolution of a Spiritual Ideal* (Montreal and Kingston: McGill-Queen's University Press).
Ayres, Lewis (2005), 'Augustine on the Rule of Faith: Rhetoric, Christology and the Foundation of Christian Thinking', *Augustinian Studies*, 36/1, pp. 33–49.
A Religious of CSMV (tr. and ed.) (1963), *On the Incarnation and To Marcellinus on the Interpretation of the Psalms* (London: SPCK).
Bachelard, Gaston (1988), *Air and Dreams*, tr. Edith R. Farrell and C. Frederick Farrell (Dallas: Dallas Institute).

Back, Les (2007), *The Art of Listening* (Oxford: Berg).

Balough, J. (1927), 'Voces Paginarum: Beiträge zur Geschichte des lauten Lesens und Schreibens', *Philologus*, 82, pp. 84–109.

Barkhuizen, J. H. (1998), 'Proclus of Constantinople: A Popular Preacher in Fifth-Century Constantinople', in Cunningham and Allen (eds), pp. 179–99.

Barthes, R. (1977), 'The Grain of the Voice', in *Image, Music, Text* (London: Fontana).

Beare, J. I. (1906), *Greek Theories of Elementary Cognition from Alcmaeon to Aristotle* (Oxford: Oxford University Press).

Begbie, Jeremy (ed.) (2002), *Sounding the Depths: Theology Through the Arts* (London: SCM).

——(2007a), 'Created Beauty: The Witness of J. S. Bach', in D. J. Treier, M. Husbands, and R. Lundin (eds) *The Beauty of God: Theology and the Arts* (Westmont IL: IVP Academic), pp. 19–44.

——(2007b), 'Wise Beyond Words', in Begbie (ed.), *Resounding Truth: Christian Wisdom in the World of Music* (Grand Rapids, MI: Baker Academic), pp. 118–39.

Bellah, R., William M. Sullivan, Ann Swidler, Steven M. Tipton et al. (1992), *Habits of the Heart. Individualism and Commitment in American Life* (Berkeley and Los Angeles: University of California Press).

Bereza, Sarah (2011), 'Listening in the Moment: Arvo Pärt's Tintinnabuli Music and the Divine Liturgy of the Orthodox Church', paper presented at the Forum for Music and Christian Scholarship, Wheaton, IL, 19 March.

Berger, P. L. and Luckmann, T. (1967), *The Social Construction of Reality* (Harmondsworth: Penguin).

Bradshaw, Paul F. (1981), *Daily Prayer in the Early Church* (London: SPCK).

Brock, Sebastian (ed.) (1987), *The Syriac Fathers on Prayer and the Spiritual Life* (Kalamazoo, MI: Cistercian).

Brown, Peter (1987), 'The Saint as Exemplar in Late Antiquity', in J. S. Hawley (ed.), *Saints and Virtues* (Berkeley, CA: University of California Press), pp. 2–14.

——(1992), *Power and Persuasion in Late Antiquity: Towards a Christian Empire* (Wisconsin: University of Wisconsin Press).

Bull, Michael and Back, Les (eds) (2003), *The Auditory Culture Reader* (Oxford and New York: Berg).

Bulloch, Anthony, Erich S. Gruen, A. A. Long, and Andrew Stewart (eds) (1993), *Images and Ideologies: Self-Definition in the Hellenistic World* (Berkeley and London: University of California Press).

Bunge, J. G. (1987), *Geistgebet, Studien zum Traktat 'De Oratione' des Evagrios Pontikos* (Cologne: Luthe-Verlag).

——(2002), *Earthen Vessels: The Practice of Personal Prayer according to the Patristic Tradition* (San Francisco: Ignatius).

Burton Christie, Douglas (1992), *The Word in the Desert: Scripture and the Quest for Holiness in Early Christian Monasticism* (Oxford: Oxford University Press).

——(2001), 'Listening, Reading, Praying: Orality, Literacy and Early Christian Monastic Spirituality', *Anglican Theological Review*, 83/2, pp. 197–221.

Cameron, Averil (1994), *Christianity and the Rhetoric of Empire* (Berkeley, Los Angeles and Oxford: University of California Press).

Carpenter, H. J. (1993), 'Creeds and Baptismal Rites in the First Four Centuries', in E. Ferguson (ed.).

Carruthers, Mary (1990), *The Book of Memory: A Study of Memory in Medieval Culture* (Cambridge: Cambridge University Press).

Caseau, Béatrice (1999), 'Christian Bodies: The Senses and Early Byzantine Christianity', in Liz James, pp. 101–9.

Cherry, Deborah (ed.), *Art: History: Visual: Culture* (Oxford: Blackwell).

Chesnut, G. F. (1986), *The First Christian Histories: Eusebius, Socrates, Sozomen, Theodoret and Evagrius* (Macon, GA: Mercer University Press).

Chidester, David (1992), *Word and Light: Seeing, Hearing and Religious Discourse* (Urbana, IL: University of Illinois Press).

Chrétien, Jean-Louis (2003), *Hand to Hand: Listening to the Work of Art*, tr. Stephen E. Lewis (New York: Fordham University Press).

Classen, Constance (1993), *Worlds of Sense: Exploring the Senses in History and Across Cultures* (London and New York: Routledge).

——(1995), 'The Witch's Senses: Sensory Idelogies and Transgressive Femininities from the Renaissance to Modernity', in Howes, pp. 70–84.

——(1998), *The Color of Angels: Cosmology, Gender and the Aesthetic Imagination* (London and New York: Routledge).

Conybeare, Catherine (2012a), 'Beyond Word and Image: Aural Patterning in Augustine's Confessions', in G. De Nie and T. F. X. Noble (eds), *Envisioning Experience in Late Antiquity and the Middle Ages: Dynamic Patterns in Texts and Images* (Farnham and Burlington, VT: Ashgate), pp. 143–64.

——(2012) 'Reading the Confessions', in M. Vessey (ed.), *The Blackwell Companion to Augustine* (Oxford: Blackwell), pp. 99–110.

Corbin, Alain (1995), *Time, Desire and Horror: Towards a History of the Senses*, tr. Jean Birrell (Cambridge: Polity).

——(1998), *Village Bells: Sound and Meaning in the 19th-Century French Countryside*, tr. Martin Thom (New York: Columbia University Press).

Corradi Fiumara, Gemma (1990), *The Other Side of Language: A Philosophy of Listening*, tr. Charles Lambert (London: Routledge).

Cox Miller, Patricia (2001), *The Poetry of Thought in Late Antiquity: Essays in Imagination and Religion* (Aldershot: Ashgate).

——(2009), *The Corporeal Imagination: Signifying the Holy in Late Antique Christianity* (Pennsylvania: University of Pennsylvania Press).

Coyle, Kevin J. (1999), 'What Was "Prayer" for Early Christians?', in Allen, Meyer, and Cross (eds), pp. 25–42.

Cullmann, Oscar (1949), *The Earliest Christian Confessions*, tr. J. K. S Reid (London: Lutterworth).

Cunningham, Mary (1990), 'Preaching and the Community', in R. Morris (ed.), *Church and People in Byzantium* (Birmingham: University of Birmingham Press), pp. 29–47.

——(1997), 'Andreas of Crete's Homilies on Lazarus and Palm Sunday: The Preacher and his Audience', *Studia Patristica*, 31, pp. 22–41.

——(1998), 'Andrew of Crete: A High Style Preacher of the Eighth Century', in Cunningham and Allen (eds), pp. 267–194.

——(ed.) (2008), *Wider than Heaven: Eighth-century Homilies on the Mother of God* (Crestwood, NY: St Vladimir's Seminary).

——and Allen, Pauline (eds) (1998), *Preacher and Audience: Studies in Early Christian and Byzantine Homiletics* (Leiden, Boston, and Cologne: Brill).

Daley, Brian (2006), *Gregory of Nazianzus* (London: Routledge).

Davies, Douglas (2006), 'Inner Speech and Religious Traditions', in James A. Beckford and John Walliss (eds), *Theorising Religion* (Aldershot: Ashgate), pp. 211–23.

Dawson, David (1992) *Allegorical Readers and Cultural Revision in Ancient Alexandria* (Berkeley CA: University of California).

——(1999), 'Figure, Allegory', in Fitzgerald (ed.), pp. 365–8.

Deffarari, R. J. (1922), 'Saint Augustine's Method of Composing and Delivering Sermons', *American Journal of Philology*, 43, pp. 97–123, 193–219.

De Mendieta, Emanuel Amand (1965), 'The Pair "Kerygma" and "Dogma" in the Theological Thought of St Basil of Caesarea', *Journal of Theological Studies*, NS 16/1 (April), pp. 129–42.

Dillon, John M. (1986), 'Aisthêsis Noêtê: A Doctrine of Spiritual Senses in Origen and Plotinus', in A. Caquot, Aa Caquot, and Am Hadas-Lebel (eds), *Hellenica et Judaica: Hommage à Valentin Nickiprowetzky* (Leuven: Peeters), pp. 443–55.

Dowler, Robert Edward (2006), 'Songs of Love: A Pastoral Reading of St Augustine of Hippo's Enarrationes in Psalmos', PhD thesis, Durham University.

Dunn, Geoffrey D. (2004), *Tertullian* (London: Routledge).

Dysinger, L. (2005), *Psalmody and Prayer in the Writings of Evagrius Ponticus* (Oxford: Oxford University Press).

Eliot, T. S. (1944), *Four Quartets* (London: Faber).

——(1950), 'Tradition and the Individual Talent', in *The Sacred Wood: Essays on Poetry and Criticism* (London: Methuen).

Ellspermann, Gerard Leo (1949), *The Attitude of the Early Christian Latin Writers toward Pagan Literature and Learning* (Washington: Catholic University of America).

Elsner, Jas (1995), *Art and the Roman Viewer* (Cambridge: Cambridge University Press).

Esler, Philip F. (ed.) (2000), *The Early Christian World*, vols 1 and 2 (London: Routledge).

Ferguson, Everett (ed.) (1993), *Conversion, Catechumenate, and Baptism in the Early Church* (New York and London: Garland).

Fitzgerald, Allan (ed.) (1999), *Augustine through the Ages: An Encyclopedia* (Grand Rapids, MI: Eerdmans).

Fontaine, Jacques (1992), *Ambroise de Milan: Hymnes* (Paris: Cerf).

——and Pietri, Charles (eds) (1985), *Le monde latin antique et la Bible*, Bible de Tous les Temps (Paris: Beauchesne).

Forde, Nigel (2002), 'The Playwright's Tale', in Begbie (ed.), pp. 60–73.

Francis, James A. (2003), 'Living Icons: Tracing a Motif in Verbal and Visual Representation from the Second to Fourth Centuries C.E.', *American Journal of Philology*, 124, pp. 575–600.

Frank, Georgia (2000), *The Memory of the Eyes: Pilgrims to Living Saints in Christian Late Antiquity* (Berkeley, Los Angeles, and London: University of California Press).

Fredouille, J. C. (1985), 'Les lettrés chrétiens face à la Bible', in Fontaine and Pietri (eds), pp. 25–42.

Gamble, H. Y. (1995), *Books and Readers in the Early Church: A History of Early Christian Texts* (New Haven, CT, and London: Yale University Press).

Geertz, C. (1966), 'Religion as a Cultural System', in M. Barton (ed.), *Anthropological Approaches to the Study of Religion* (New York: Praeger), pp. 1–45.

Goldhill, Simon and Osborne, Robin (eds) (1994), *Art and Text in Ancient Greek Culture* (Cambridge: Cambridge University Press).

Graumann, Thomas (1997), 'Saint Ambrose on the Art of Preaching', *XXV incontro di studiosi dell'antichità christiana* (Rome), pp. 587–600.

Hadot, Pierre (1998), *The Inner Citadel: The Meditations of Marcus Aurelius*, tr. Michael Chase (Cambridge, MA: Harvard University Press).

Haines-Eitzen, Kim (2000), *Guardians of Letters: Literacy, Power and the Transmitters of Early Christian Literature* (Oxford: Oxford University Press).

Hall, Stuart G. (1991), *Doctrine and Practice in the Early Church* (London: SPCK).

——(1991a), 'Ministry, Worship and Christian Life', in Iain Hazlett (ed.), *Early Christianity: Origins and Evolution to AD 600* (London: SPCK).

Hamman, A. (ed.) (1961), *Early Christian Prayers* (London: Longmans, Green).

Hand, Thomas A. (1963), *Saint Augustine on Prayer* (Dublin: Gill).

Harl, Marguerite (1975), 'La bouche et le coeur de l'apôtre: Deux images bibliques du "sens divin" de l'homme (Proverbes 2,5) chez Origene', in *Forma Futuri: Studi in onore del Cardinale Michele Pelligrino* (Turin: Erasmo), pp. 17–42.

Harmless, William (1995), *Augustine and the Catechumenate* (Collegeville, MN: Liturgical Press).

Harries, Jill (1991), 'Patristic Historiography', in Iain Hazlett (ed.), *Early Christianity: Origins and Evolution to AD 600* (London: SPCK), pp. 269–79.

Harris, William V. (1991), *Ancient Literacy* (Harvard, MA: Harvard University Press).

Harrison, Carol (2000), 'The Rhetoric of Scripture and Preaching: Classical Decadence or Christian Aesthetic?', in Robert Dodaro and George Lawless (eds), *Augustine and His Critics* (London: Routledge), pp. 214–30.

——(2004), *Augustine: Christian Truth and Fractured Humanity* (Oxford: Oxford University Press).

——(2011), 'Enchanting the Soul: The Music of the Psalms', in A. Andreopoulos, A. Casiday, and Carol Harrison (eds), *Meditations of the Heart: The Psalms in Early Christian Thought and Practice* (Turnhout: Brepols), pp. 205–23.

Harrison, Nonna Verna (2006), 'Gregory of Nazianzus' Festal Orations: Anamnesis and Mimesis', *Journal of Philosophy and Theology*, 18, pp. 27–51.

——(2008), *Festal Orations: Saint Gregory of Nazianzus* (New York: St Vladimir's Seminary).

Hart, Trevor (2000), 'Creeds, Councils and Doctrinal Development', in Esler, pp. 636–59.

Hauck, Robert J. (1988), '"They Saw What They Said They Saw": Sense Knowledge in Early Christian Polemic', *Harvard Theological Review*, 81/3, pp. 239–49.

Hazlett, Ian (ed.) (1991), *Early Christianity: Origins and Evolution to AD 600* (London: SPCK).

Heine, Ronald E. (1995), *Gregory of Nyssa's Treatise on the Inscriptions of the Psalms* (Oxford: Oxford University Press).

Hendrickson, G. L. (1929), 'Ancient Reading', *The Classical Journal*, 25/3, pp. 182–96.

Hopkins, Gerard Manley (1930), *Poems*, ed. Robert Bridges (2nd edn, Oxford: Oxford University Press).

Horsley, Richard (2003), 'Oral Tradition in the New Testament', *Oral Tradition*, 18/1, pp. 34–6.

Houghton, Hugh (2008), *Augustine's Text of John: Patristic Citations and Latin Gospel Manuscripts* (Oxford: Oxford University Press).

Howes, David (1995), *Empire of the Senses: The Sensual Culture Reader* (Oxford and New York: Berg).

——(2003), *Sensual Relations: Engaging the Senses in Culture and History* (Ann Arbor, MI: University of Michigan Press).

Hunter, David (ed.) (1989), *Preaching in the Patristic Age: Studies in Honour of Walter J. Burghardt SJ* (New York and Mahwah: Paulist).

Ihde, Don (2003), 'Auditory Imagination', in Michael Bull and Les Back (eds), *The Auditory Culture Reader* (Oxford and New York: Berg), 61–6.

James, Liz (ed.) (1999), *Desire and Denial in Byzantium* (Aldershot: Ashgate).

——(2005), 'Senses and Sensibility in Byzantium', in Deborah Cherry (ed.), pp. 44–59.

Jonas, Hans (1966), *The Phenomenon of Life: Towards a Philosophical Biology* (New York: Dell).

Jousse, Marcel (1925), *Le Style Oral rythmique et mnémotechnique chez les Verbomoteurs* (Paris: Beauchesne).

Jütte, Robert (2005), *A History of the Senses: From Antiquity to Cyberspace* (Cambridge: Polity).

Kalleres, D. (2002), 'Exorcising the Devil to Silence Christ's Enemies: Ritualized Speech Practices in Late Antique Christianity', PhD dissertation, Brown University, Providence, RI.

Kannengiesser, C. and Petersen, W. L. (eds) (1988), *Origen of Alexandria: His World and Legacy* (Notre Dame, IN: University of Notre Dame).

Kaster, Robert (1988), *Guardians of Language: The Grammarian and Society in Late Antiquity* (Berkeley, Los Angeles, and London: University of California Press).

Kecskemeti, Judit (1993), 'Doctrine et Drame dans la Prédication Grecque', *Euphrosyne*, 21, pp. 29–67.

Kelly, J. N. D. (1972), *Early Christian Creeds* (London: Longman).

Kennedy, G. A. (1980), *Classical Rhetoric and its Christian and Secular Tradition from Ancient to Modern Times* (Croom Helm: London).

Kiley, Mark et al. (eds) (1997), *Prayer from Alexander to Constantine: A Critical Anthology* (London and New York: Routledge).

Kolbet, Paul R. (2006), 'Athanasius, the Psalms, and the Reformation of the Self', *Harvard Theological Review*, 99/1, pp. 85–101.

——(2010), *Augustine and the Cure of Souls: Revising a Classical Ideal* (Notre Dame IN: University of Notre Dame Press).

Kreider, Alan (1999), *The Change of Conversion and the Origin of Christendom* (Harrisburg, PA: Trinity Press).

La Bonnardière, Anne-Marie (ed) (1986), *Saint Augustin et la Bible*, Bible de Tous les Temps 3 (Paris: Beauchesne).

Lai, Pak Wah (2010), 'John Chrysostom and the Hermeneutics of Exemplar Portraits', PhD thesis, Durham University.

Lamberton, Robert (1986), *Homer the Theologian: Neoplatonist Allegorical Reading and the Growth of the Epic Tradition* (Berkeley: University of California).

Lane Fox, Robin (1986), *Pagans and Christians* (London: Penguin).

——(1994), 'Literacy and Power in Early Christianity', in A. K. Bowman and G. Woolf (eds), *Literacy and Power in the Ancient World* (Cambridge: Cambridge University Press), pp. 126–148.

Leclerq, Jean (1977), *The Love of Learning and the Desire for God* (New York: Fordham University Press).

Leemans, Johan, Meyer, Wendy, Allen, Pauline, and Dehandschutter, Boudewijn (eds) (1983), *'Let us Die that we May Live': Greek Homilies on Christian Martyrs from Asia Minor, Palestine and Syria (c.AD 350–AD 450)* (London: Routledge).

Leyerle, Blake (2001), *Theatrical Shows and Ascetic Lives: John Chrysostom's Attack on Spiritual Marriage* (Berkeley: University of California Press).

Lienhard, Joseph (1989), 'Origen as Homilist', in David Hunter (ed.), *Preaching in the Patristic Age: Studies in Honour of Walter J. Burghardt SJ* (New York and Mahwah: Paulist), pp. 36–52.

Louth, Andrew (1983), *Discerning the Mystery: An Essay in the Nature of Theology* (Oxford: Oxford University Press).

Louth, Charlie (ed. and tr.) (2011), *Rainer Maria Rilke: Letters to a Young Poet* (London: Penguin).

Love, Andrew (2008), 'Process and Product in Theology and Musical Aesthetics: Improvisation as Interdisciplinary Topos' *Nineteenth-Century Music Review*, 5/1, pp. 47–65.

McClary, Susan (2003), 'Bessie Smith: "Thinking Blues" ', in Michael Bull and Les Back (eds), *The Auditory Culture Reader* (Oxford and New York: Berg), 427–34.

McGilchrist, Iain (2010), *The Master and His Emissary: The Divided Brain and the Making of the Western World* (New Haven and London: Yale University Press).

McGuckin, John (1986), *Saint Gregory Nazianzen: Selected Poems* (Oxford: Sisters of the Love of God).

——(1999), 'The Prayer of the Heart in Patristic and Early Byzantine Tradition', in Pauline Allen, Wendy Meyer, and Lawrence Cross (eds), *Prayer and Spirituality in the Early Church*, 2 vols (Brisbane: Watson Ferguson), vol. 2 pp. 69–108.

MacKenzie, Iain M. (2002), *Irenaeus's Demonstration of the Apostolic Preaching: A Theological Commentary and Translation* (Aldershot: Ashgate).

McKinnon, J. (1989), *Music in Early Christian Literature* (Cambridge: Cambridge University Press).

McLuhan, Marshall (1964), *Understanding Media: The Extensions of Man* (New York: McGraw-Hill).

——(1969), *The Gutenberg Galaxy: The Making of Typographic Man* (New York: Signet).

MacMullen, R. (1989), 'The Preacher's Audience (AD 350–400)', *Journal of Theological Studies*, NS 40, pp. 503–11.

Madec, Goulven (1994) *Petites Études Augustiniennes* (Paris: Études Augustiennes).

Malherbe, Abraham, J. (1987), *Paul and the Thessalonians: The Philosophic Tradition of Pastoral Care* (Philadelphia: Fortress).

Markus, R. A. (ed.) (1972), *Augustine: A Collection of Critical Essays* (Garden City, NY: Anchor Books).

——(1975), 'Church History and the Early Church Historians', in D. Baker (ed.), *The Materials, Sources and Methods of Ecclesiastical History: Studies in Church History*, vol. 11 (Oxford: Blackwell), pp. 1–17.

——(1990), *The End of Ancient Christianity* (Cambridge: Cambridge University Press).

Marrou, H. I. (1948), *Histoire de l'éducation dans l'Antiquité* (Paris: Seuil).

——(1968), *Théologie de l'Histoire* (Paris: Seuil).

Martin, Dale B. and Cox Miller, Patricia (eds) (2005), *The Cultural Turn in Late Ancient Studies: Gender, Asceticism, and Historiography* (Durham, NC: Duke University Press).

Martin, Elena (2006), 'Iconic Women: Martyrdom and the Female Body in Early Christianity', MA thesis, Durham University.

Matthews, G. B. (1972), 'The Inner Man', in R. A. Markus (ed.), *A Collection of Critical Essays* (Garden City, NY: Anchor Books), pp. 176–90.

Maxwell, Jaclyn L. (2006), *Christianisation and Communication in Late Antiquity: John Chrysostom and His Congregation in Antioch* (Cambridge: Cambridge University Press).

Mayer, Wendy (1998), 'John Chrysostom: Extraordinary Preacher, Ordinary Audience', in Mary Cunningham and Pauline Allen (eds), *Preacher and Audience: Studies in Early Christian and Byzantine Homiletics* (Leiden, Boston, and Cologne: Brill), pp. 105–37.

——(2000), 'Who Came to Hear John Chrysostom Preach? Recovering a Late Fourth-Century Preacher's Audience', *Ephemerides Theologicae Lovanienses*, 76, pp. 73–87.

——and Neil, Bronwen (2006), *St John Chrysostom: The Cult of the Saints*, Popular Patristics Series (New York: St Vladimir's Seminary).

Meredith, Antony (1999), *Gregory of Nyssa* (London: Routledge).

Merleau-Ponty, Maurice (1945), *Phénoménologie de la Perception* (Paris: Gallimard).

Milburn, R. L. P. (1954), *Early Christian Interpretations of History* (London: Adam and Charles Black).

Miller, J. Hillis (1976), 'Stevens' Rock and Criticism as Cure, II', *Georgia Review*, 30, pp. 333–48.

Mingana, A. (ed.) (1933), *Commentary of Theodore of Mopsuestia on the Lord's Prayer*, Woodbrooke Studies 6 (Cambridge: Heffers).

Mitchell, W. J. T. (1995), 'The Pictorial Turn', in *Picture Theory: Essays in Verbal and Visual Representation* (Chicago: Chicago University Press), pp. 11–34.

Mohrmann, Christine (1958), *Études sur le latin des chrétiens* (Rome: Edizioni di Storia e Letteratura).

Monaci Castagno, Adele (1998), 'Origen the Scholar and Pastor', in Mary Cunningham and Pauline Allen (eds), *Preacher and Audience: Studies in Early Christian and Byzantine Homiletics* (Leiden, Boston, and Cologne: Brill), pp. 65–88.

Morrison, Ken (1987), 'Stabilizing the Text: The Institutionalization of Knowledge in Historical and Philosophic Forms of Argument', *Canadian Journal of Sociology*, 12, pp. 242–74.

Moss, Candida R. (2010), 'On the Dating of Polycarp: Rethinking the Place of the *Martyrdom of Polycarp* in the History of Christianity', *Early Christianity*, 4, pp. 539–74.

Murphy, Francis X. (1989), 'The Sermons of Pope Leo the Great: Content and Style', in David Hunter (ed.), *Preaching in the Patristic Age: Studies in Honour of Walter J. Burghardt SJ* (New York and Mahwah: Paulist). pp. 183–97.

Nancy, Jean Luc (2007), *Listening*, tr. Charlotte Mandell (New York: Fordham University Press); *À l'écoute* (Paris: Éditions Galilée, 2002).

Nauroy, Gérard (1985), 'L'ecriture dans la pastorale D'Ambroise de Milan', in Jaques Fontaine and Charles Pietri (eds), *Le monde latin antique et la Bible*, Bible de Tous les Temps (Paris: Beauchesne), pp. 371–408.

Niditch, Susan (2003), 'Oral Tradition and Biblical Scholarship', *Oral Tradition* 18/1, pp. 43–4.

Notopoulos, James A. (1938), 'Mnemosyne in Oral Literature', *Transactions and Proceedings of the American Philological Association*, 69, pp. 465–93.

Oberhelman, Steven M. (1991), *Rhetoric and Homiletics in Fourth-Century Christian Literature* (Atlanta: Scholars Press).

O'Daly, Gerard (1987), *Saint Augustine's Philosophy of Mind* (London: Duckworth).

O'Donnell, J. J. (1992), *Augustine: Confessions*, 3 vols (Oxford: Oxford University Press).

Olivar, A. (1991), *La predicación Cristiana antigua* (Freiburg: Herder).

Ong, Walter (1982), *Orality and Literacy: The Technologizing of the Word* (London: Routledge).

Paoli-Lafaye, Elisabeth (1986), 'Les lecteurs des texts liturgiques', in Anne-Marie La Bonnardière (ed.), *Saint Augustin et la Bible*, Bible de Tous les Temps 3 (Paris: Beauchesne), pp. 59–74.

Penny Small, Jocelyn (1997), *Wax Tablets of the Mind: Cognitive Studies of Memory and Literacy in Classical Antiquity* (London: Routledge).

Polanyi, Michael (1958), *Personal Knowledge: Towards a Post-Critical Philosophy* (London: Routledge).

——(1966), *The Tacit Dimension* (London: Routledge).

Polanyi, Michael and Prosch, Harry (1977), *Meaning* (Chicago: University of Chicago Press).

Quasten, J. (1983), *Music and Worship in Pagan and Christian Antiquity*, tr. B. Ramsey, NPM Studies in Church Music and Liturgy (Washington, DC: National Association of Pastoral Musicians).

Radcliffe Reuther, Rosemary (1969), *Gregory of Nazianzus: Rhetor and Philosopher* (Oxford: Oxford University Press).

Rahner, Karl (1932), 'Le début d'une doctrine des cinq sens spirituels chez Origène', *Revue d'ascétique et de mystique*, 14, pp. 113–45.

Ramsey, Boniface (1985), *Beginning to Read the Fathers* (London: Darton, Longman and Todd).

Raven, J. E. (1965), *Plato's Thought in the Making* (Cambridge: Cambridge University Press).

Ricoeur, Paul (1990), *Soi-même comme un autre* (Paris: Seuil).

Rist, John M. (1994), *Augustine: Ancient Thought Baptised* (Cambridge: Cambridge University Press).

Roberts, C. H. (1979), *Manuscript, Society and Belief in Early Christian Egypt* (London: Oxford University Press for the British Academy).

Roberts, Michael (1989), *The Jeweled Style: Poetry and Poetics in Late Antiquity* (Ithaca, NY: Cornell University Press).

Rollins, H. E. (1958), *Letters of John Keats 1814–1821*, 2 vols (Cambridge, MA: Harvard University Press).

Roueché, Charlotte (1984), 'Acclamations in the Later Roman Empire: New Evidence from Aphrodisias', *Journal of Roman Studies*, 74, pp. 181–99.

Rousseau, Philip (1998), '"The Preacher's Audience": A More Optimistic View', in T. W. Hilliard, R. A. Kearsley, C. E. V. Nixon, and A. M. Nobbs (eds), *Ancient History in a Modern University*, vol. 2 (Grand Rapids, MI: Eerdmans).

Rudrum, A. (ed.) (1976), *Henry Vaughan: The Complete Poems* (London: Penguin).

Russell, D. A. and Winterbottom, Michael (eds) (1972), *Classical Literary Criticism* (Oxford: Oxford University Press).

Saenger, Paul (2003), 'Silent Reading: Its Impact on Late Medieval Script and Society', *Viator*, 13, pp. 367–414.

Schmidt, Leigh Eric (2000), *Hearing Things: Religion, Illusion and the American Enlightenment* (Cambridge, MA: Harvard University Press).

——(2003), 'Hearing Loss', in Michael Bull and Les Back (eds), *The Auditory Culture Reader* (Oxford and New York: Berg), pp. 41–59.

Sears, Elizabeth (1991), 'The Iconography of Auditory Perception in the Early Middle Ages: On Psalm Illustration and Psalm Exegesis', in Charles Burnett, Michael Fend, and Penelope Gouk (eds), *The Second Sense: Studies in Hearing and Musical Judgement from Antiquity to the Seventeenth Century* (London: Warburg Institute), pp. 19–42.

Shaw, Brent (1996) "Body/Power/Identity: Passions of the Martyrs" *Journal of Early Christian Studies*, vol. 4, pp. 269–312.

Sheerin, Daniel (1988), 'The Role of Prayer in Origen's Homilies', in C. Kannengiesser and W. L. Petersen (eds), *Origen of Alexandria: His World and Legacy* (Notre Dame, IN: University of Notre Dame), pp. 200–14.

Simpson, Robert L. (1965), *The Interpretation of Prayer in the Early Church* (Philadelphia: Westminster Press).

Smith, Mark M. (2007), *Sensing the Past: Seeing, Hearing, Smelling, Tasting and Touching in History* (Berkeley and Los Angeles: University of California Press).

Snyder, H. Gregory (2000), *Teachers and Texts in the Ancient World: Philosophers, Jews and Christians* (London and New York: Routledge).

Sorabji, Richard (1977), 'Aristotle on Demarcating the Five Senses', in Jonathan Barnes, Malcolm Schofield, and Richard Sorabji (eds), *Articles on Aristotle*, vol. 4 (London: Duckworth), pp. 134–65.

Soskice, Janet (1985), *Metaphor and Religious Language* (Oxford: Oxford University Press).

Stevenson, J. and Frend, W. H. C. (eds) (1987), *A New Eusebius: Documents Illustrating the History of the Church to* AD *337* (London: SPCK).

Stewart, Columba (2001), 'Imageless Prayer and the Theological Vision of Evagrius Ponticus', *Journal of Early Christian Studies*, 9/2, pp. 173–204.

Stillinger, Jack (ed.) (1991), *John Keats. Complete Poems* (Harvard, MA: Harvard University Press).

Sutherland, C. M. (1990), 'Love as Rhetorical Principle: The Relationship between Content and Style in the Rhetoric of Saint Augustine', in H. Meynell (ed.), *Grace, Politics and Desire* (Calgary: University of Calgary Press).

Sykes, Stuart (2001), *Melito of Sardis: On Pascha* (New York: St Vladimir's Seminary).

——(ed.) (2004), *Tertullian, Cyprian and Origen: On the Lord's Prayer*, Popular Patristics Series (Crestwood, NY: St Vladimir's Seminary).

Szendy, Peter (2008), *Listen: A History of Our Ears* (New York: Fordham University Press).

Tanner, Kathryn (1987), 'Theology and the Plain Sense', in G. Green (ed.), *Scriptural Authority and Narrative Interpretation* (Philadelphia: Fortress).

——(1997), *Theories of Culture: A New Agenda for Theology* (Minneapolis: Augsburg Fortress).

Treier, D. J., Husbands, M. and Lundin, Roger (eds) (2007), *The Beauty of God: Theology and the Arts* (Westmont, IL: InterVarsity Press).

Trevett, Christine (2006), *Christian Women and the Time of the Apostolic Fathers (*AD *80–160)* (Cardiff: University of Wales Press).

Tsironis, Niki (1998), 'Historicity and Poetry in Ninth-Century Homiletics: The Homilies of Patriarch Photios and George of Nicomedia', in Mary Cunningham and Pauline Allen (eds), *Preacher and Audience: Studies in Early Christian and Byzantine Homiletics* (Leiden, Boston, and Cologne: Brill), pp. 295–316.

Uthemann, Karl-Heinz (1998), 'Forms of Communication in the Homilies of Severian of Gabala: A Contribution to the Reception of the Diatribe as a Method of Exposition', in Mary Cunningham and Pauline Allen (eds), *Preacher and Audience: Studies in Early Christian and Byzantine Homiletics* (Leiden, Boston, and Cologne: Brill), pp. 139–78.

Valantasis, Richard (ed.) (2000), *Religions of Late Antiquity in Practice* (Princeton, NJ: Princeton University Press).

Van Dam, R. (2003), *Becoming Christian: The Conversion of Roman Cappadocia* (Philadelphia, PN: University of Pennsylvania).

Van der Meer, F. (1961), *Augustine the Bishop* (London and New York: Sheed & Ward).

Vasaly, Ann (1993), *Representations: Images in the World of Ciceronian Oratory* (Berkeley and Los Angeles: University of California Press).

Vickers, Brian (1989), *In Defence of Rhetoric* (Oxford: Oxford University Press).

Viladesau, Richard (1999), *Theological Aesthetics: God in Imagination, Beauty and Art* (New York: Oxford University Press).

——(2000), *Theology and the Arts: Encountering God through Music, Art and Rhetoric* (New York: Paulist).

Bibliography 293

——(2006), *The Beauty of the Cross: The Passion of Christ in Theology and the Arts—from the Catacombs to the Eve of the Reformation* (Oxford: Oxford University Press).

Walker, J. (2000), *Rhetoric and Poetics in Antiquity* (Oxford: Oxford University Press).

Wannenwetsch, Bernd (2006), ' "Take heed what ye hear": Listening as a Moral, Transcendental and Transformative act', paper presented 'Listening: Interdisciplinary Perspectives' conference at the Centre for Research in the Arts, Social Sciences and Humanities, Cambridge, 24–5 November.

Ware, Kallistos (1979), *The Orthodox Way* (New York: St Vladimir's Seminary).

Webb, Ruth (1991), ' "To Understand Ultimate Things and Enter Secret Places": Ekphrasis and Art in Byzantium', *Art History*, 14, pp. 1–17.

——(1999), 'The Aesthetics of Sacred Space: Narrative, Metaphor, and Motion in "Ekphraseis" of Church Buildings', *Dumbarton Oaks Papers*, 53, pp. 59–74.

Weidmann, Frederick W. (1997), 'Polycarp's Final Prayer', in Mark Kiley et al. (eds), *Prayer from Alexander to Constantine:A Critical Anthology* (London and New York: Routledge), pp. 285–90.

White, Carolinne (1996), *Gregory of Nazianzus: Autobiographical Poems* (Cambridge: Cambridge University Press).

——(ed.) (2000), *Early Christian Latin Poets* (London: Routledge).

Wickham, Lionel (2002), *On God and Christ: The Five Theological Orations and Two Letters to Cledonius* (New York: St Vladimir's Seminary).

Wilder, Amos N. (1964), *The Language of the Gospel: Early Christian Rhetoric* (New York: Harper & Row).

Wilken, Robert (1983), *John Chrysostom and the Jews: Rhetoric and Reality in the Late Fourth Century* (Berkeley, Los Angeles, and London: University of California Press).

Willis, G. G. (1962), *St Augustine's Lectionary* (London: SPCK).

Williams, Rowan (2002), 'Parthenogenesis: Making it Strange: Theology in Other(s) Words', in Jeremy Begbie (ed.), *Sounding the Depths: Theology Through the Arts* (London: SCM), pp. 19–32.

Wolfson, Henry Austyn (1935), 'The Internal Senses in Latin, Arabic and Hebrew Philosophic Texts', *Harvard Theological Review*, 28, pp. 69–133.

Yates, Frances (1966), *The Art of Memory* (London: Routledge and Kegan Paul).

Young, Frances (1980), 'The God of the Greeks and the Nature of Religious Language', in W. R. Schoedel and R. Wilken (eds), *Early Christian Thought and the Classical Tradition: Festschrift for R.M. Grant*, Theologie Historique 53 (Paris: Beauchesne), pp. 45–74.

——(1986), 'John Chrysostom on I and II Corinthians', *Studia Patristica*, 18/1, pp. 349–5.

——(1990), *The Art of Performance: Towards a Theology of Holy Scripture* (London: Darton, Longman and Todd).

——(1993), 'Paideia and the Myth of Static Dogma', in S. Coakley and D. Palin (eds), *The Making and Remaking of Christian Doctrine: Essays in Honour of Maurice Wiles* (Oxford: Clarendon Press), pp. 265–83.

——(2007), *Biblical Exegesis and the Formation of Christian Culture* (Cambridge: Cambridge University Press).

Index

Printed and bound by CPI Group (UK) Ltd, Croydon, CR0 4YY